Programming perl

Programming perl

Larry Wall and Randal L. Schwartz

O'Reilly & Associates, Inc.
103 Morris Street, Suite A
Sebastopol, CA 95472

Programming perl
by Larry Wall and Randal L. Schwartz

Editor: Tim O'Reilly

Printing History:

January 1991:	First Edition.
August 1991:	Minor corrections.
March 1992:	Minor corrections.

ISBN: 0-937175-64-1

Table of Contents

Preface

Perl in a Nutshell
The Rest of This Book and Other Books
How To Get Perl
Conventions Used in This Book
Acknowledgements
We'd Like to Hear From You

Perl in a Nutshell

Perl is a language for easily manipulating text, files, and processes. Perl provides a more concise and readable way to do many jobs that were formerly accomplished (with difficulty) by programming in the C language or one of the shells. While this book is primarily intended for users of the UNIX operating system, Perl runs on several other operating systems, and provides a portable model of computing across diverse architectures.

Perl is quite popular, and getting more so, not just because it is good for what it was intended, but also because it is a Perl of Very Little Price—it is, in fact, freely available (and available for free). Unlike many proprietary products, Perl is likely to be available wherever you choose to work. And if it isn't, you can get it and install it easily.

In the beginning, Perl was intended to be a data reduction language: a language for navigating among various files in an arbitrary fashion, scanning large amounts of text efficiently, invoking commands to obtain dynamic data, and printing easily-formatted reports based on the information gleaned. And it does these things quite well—the pattern matching and textual manipulation capabilities of Perl often outperform dedicated C programs. But as Perl developed, it also became a convenient file manipulation language—that is, a language in which you can deal with the files themselves apart from their contents, moving them, renaming them, changing their permissions, and so on. And it also became a convenient process manipulation language, allowing you to create and destroy processes, to control the flow of data between them, to preprocess their input and postprocess their output, and to clean up after them when they blow up. And it became a networking language, with the ability to communicate to other processes on other machines via sockets.

These things can be done in other languages, such as C or one of the shells. But the solutions are difficult and ugly, because C can't easily do many of the things that a shell can do, and a shell can't do many of the things that C lets you do. Perl fills a rather large niche between them—providing you with those things that are easy to do in both languages (all in one convenient place), thus bridging the gap between shell programming and C programming.

On the other hand, knowledge of Perl can actually help you in learning the C language, if that is your goal. And if you already know C, then learning Perl will be easy, since the languages are structured quite similarly. Perl also shares features with many of the UNIX utilities that a shell would invoke, and this can ease your learning of both Perl and UNIX.

It has been stated that a language is not worth knowing unless it teaches you to think differently. Perl is the exception to that rule (for those who know UNIX), because much of Perl is derived in spirit from other portions of UNIX. To those who merely like Perl, it is the Practical Extraction and Report Language. To those who love it, it's the Pathologically Eclectic Rubbish Lister. And to the minimalists in the crowd who think there should only be one way to do something, Perl looks hopelessly redundant and derivative. But somehow, by a grave violation of the minimalistic UNIX toolbox philosophy, Perl has become the UNIX tool of choice for many tasks of small-to-medium complexity, and ends up fitting quite happily back into the toolbox. Perl can be said to be the toolsmith's workbench from which new tools are derived.

Perl is in many ways a simple language. The types and structures used by Perl are easy to use and understand, and you can often tell what a well-written piece of Perl code is doing just by glancing at it. You don't have to know any special incantations to compile a Perl program—you can just execute it like a shell script. You don't have to know everything there is to know about Perl before you can write useful programs. Throughout this book we strive to provide useful examples that everyone from applications programmers to system administrators will find beneficial. We've indexed these examples so that you can use this handbook as a kind of cookbook to whip up something quickly to get the job done.

Though simple in many ways, Perl is also a rich language, and there is much to be learned about it. Although it will take some time for you to absorb all that Perl can do, you will be glad that you have access to the extensive capabilities of Perl when the time comes that you need them. We noted above that Perl borrows many capabilities from the shells and C, but Perl also possesses a strict superset of *sed* and *awk* capabilities. There are, in fact, translators supplied with Perl to turn your old *sed* and *awk* (and *nawk*, and *gawk*) scripts into Perl scripts, so you can see how the features you may already be familiar with correspond to those of Perl.

There are other more mundane reasons why people like Perl. Many UNIX utilities have undocumented limitations: they don't like lines longer than n, where n is some mysterious power of two, or they blow up if you feed them binary data. These limitations are to some extent encouraged by the C language in which they are written. Perl, however, does not have these limitations. Your lines (and arrays) may grow as long as you like. Your subroutine recursion may go as deep as you like. Variable names can be as long as you like. Binary data will not cause problems. The hashed tables used by associative arrays expand as necessary to avoid degradation of performance. And if you don't know what associative arrays are, that's okay; we'll explain them. You can emulate all kinds of fancy data structures with them. And you can keep them in database files called DBM files. More later.

You might also like to learn Perl because it will allow you to write programs more securely. Through a dataflow tracing mechanism, Perl can determine which data is derived from insecure sources, and prevent dangerous operations before they happen. System administrators will particularly love this feature.

You might like Perl because it lets you develop programs quickly. As an interpreted script language, you get instant feedback when something isn't right. And there's a symbolic debugger built in that understands any Perl expression because it's written in Perl (and because a running Perl script is itself good at executing random bits of Perl code).

People have been calling Perl a "system administration language" primarily because system administrators have been talking about it, but we think it has a much broader appeal. In this book, we're not writing just to high-powered system administrators; after all, they're the ones who have been learning Perl already from the bare-bones manual page, and they'll be able to cope with a book that is oriented more towards the general programmer.

We start with a small tutorial designed to present Perl "small end first," so that people can get going without having to know every gritty detail. This is followed by a series of more extended examples demonstrating Perl's full range of capabilities. Later chapters present Perl in a more straightforward reference fashion. There are lots of examples, and lots of indexing and cross-referencing, so that people can easily find out how to do a particular thing without necessarily knowing the "official" name for it.

Whether you are learning Perl because you are curious, or because your boss told you to, this handbook will lead you through both the basics and the intricacies. And although we don't intend to teach you how to program, the perceptive reader will be able to absorb some of the art, and a little of the science, of programming. You will also learn much about UNIX, and how to balance the benefits of the integrated-tool approach with the benefits of the toolbox approach. We will encourage you to develop the three great virtues of a programmer: laziness, impatience, and hubris. Along the way, we hope you find the book mildly amusing in some spots (and wildly amusing in others). And while we're at it, we firmly believe that learning Perl will increase the value of your resume. So keep reading.

The Rest of This Book and Other Books

Here's how the book is laid out:

Chapter 1, *An Overview of Perl*. Getting started is always the hardest part. This chapter presents the fundamental ideas of Perl in an informal, curl-up-in-your-favorite-chair fashion.

Chapter 2, *Practical Programming*. Once you have a feeling for what Perl is all about, we'll begin to show you how to apply Perl to the kinds of problems you meet in real life. After reading this chapter, you'll know when it's appropriate to say, "This looks like a job for Perl."

Chapter 3, *The Gory Details*. The meat of Perl, except for the function descriptions. Here you will find the syntax and semantics of the language described in excruciating detail.

Chapter 4, *Functions*. Anything in Perl that looks like **foo(bar,bletch)** is talked about in here (and then some). Together with the previous chapter, you'll get a complete description of Perl. The functions are listed in alphabetical order to make it easy to find them by name.

Chapter 5, *Common Tasks with Perl*. Got a task? Don't know how to do it in Perl? This is the chapter for you. Many common tasks are described here, along with a Perl template with drop-in parameters. This chapter is good for learning how to "think Perl."

Chapter 6, *Real Perl Programs*. Many example programs stolen from actual use (usually). Varying applications and styles to demonstrate how to use Perl to get from the beginning to the end (or should that be from **#!/usr/bin/perl** to **exit**?).

Chapter 7, *Other Oddments*. Things about Perl that didn't quite fit under syntax or functions, like command-line invocations, the debugger, and some hints on efficiency. This chapter also explains how to write secure Perl scripts. OK, so we could have called this the "kitchen-sink" chapter.

Appendix A, *Semi-Formal Description*. Perl described using a hacked BNF, for you people who want to know just what is and isn't allowed, syntactically.

Appendix B, *The Perl Library*. Nothing is worse in programming than having to reinvent the wheel. And the Perl distribution comes with a whole bunch of little (and big) wheels to help you along your way. Here's where they're described.

Glossary. Words and definitions. What'd you expect? But, if you get a fuzzy moment, and your Perl code isn't working quite right, you might want to check out some of these definitions. They aren't exactly what you'd expect in a *normal* glossary, but Perl is not really a normal language (nor are the authors of this book really normal authors, or normally real authors).

Index. Words, and page numbers. OK, so this is pretty standard. Hopefully, everything that you might want to look up, we've put.

Perl Reference Guide. We've included Johan Vromans' popular quick reference (which is also available in PostScript form over the net) as a separate booklet. This guide provides a quick summary of Perl syntax, and may be useful for an overview of Perl as well as for later reference.

Additional resources:

- *perl*(1). Besides this book, you can (and should) still refer to the manpage. For one thing, the manpage is (probably) online, so you can get answers without going back to your cubicle to dig up your dog-eared marked-up copy of *Programming Perl*. But more importantly, although nearly everything from the manpage at the time of this writing is in this book somewhere, there's no doubt Larry will add three new features between the time we ship the book to the publisher and the time the book first hits the bookstands. So check the manpage (or maybe the distribution if it's *too* large) for an errata sheet of newly introduced features after the publication of this book, which purports to document version 4.0 patchlevel 10 (or so) of the Perl language (even though we know that Perl is at patchlevel 19 at the time we are sending this book off to the printer. Sigh.)

- *comp.lang.perl*. An additional source of information is the Usenet newsgroup about Perl. Since it was established at the end of 1989, it has carried over 250 articles per month (many of them by one or the other of us). Like Perl itself, the newsgroup is meant to be useful, and no question is too silly to ask.[1]

- *The Perl distribution*. Perl is distributed under the GNU "Copyleft," meaning briefly that if you can execute Perl on your system, you should have access to the source of Perl for no additional charge (or perhaps a small copying charge). Alternately, Perl may be distributed under the "Artistic License," which some people find less threatening than the Copyleft. Within the Perl distribution, you will find some example programs in the *eg/* directory. You may also find other tidbits. Poke around in there on some rainy afternoon. Study the source for Perl (if you're a C hacker with a masochistic streak). Look at the test suite. See how *Configure* determines if you have the *mkdir* system call. Or whatever else suits your fancy.

  See the section below entitled *How to Get Perl* if you don't already have it, or if you need an updated copy.

- *The AWK Programming Language*, by Aho, Kernighan, and Weinberger (published by Addison-Wesley), and *Sed and Awk*, by Dale Dougherty (published by O'Reilly & Associates). These fine books contain many examples that can be translated into Perl by the awk-to-perl translator *a2p* or by the sed-to-perl translator *s2p*. These translators won't produce idiomatic Perl, of course, but if you want to do something like one of those examples but can't figure out how to do it entirely in awk or sed, the translated Perl script will give you a good place to start.

How To Get Perl

The Perl distribution is available from a number of sites, including any *comp.sources.unix* archive. However, these machines definitely have it available for anonymous FTP:

---

[1] Of course, some questions are too silly to answer...

ftp.uu.net	137.39.1.9
archive.cis.ohio-state.edu	128.146.8.52
jpl-devvax.jpl.nasa.gov	128.149.1.143

For those not on the Internet, it is available via anonymous uucp from both *uunet* and *osu-cis*.

Because Larry is always tinkering with Perl, it is difficult to give precise and unchanging directions on which files to get. The location of the source is also a bit different on each of these machines. However, we hope to give you enough information here to keep you from calling customer service at O'Reilly & Associates.

Where the Files Are

On *ftp.uu.net*, the Perl distribution is in the single archive file called *gnu/perl-4.0.19.tar.Z*. On *jpl-devvax.jpl.nasa.gov*, it is in the directory *pub/perl.4.0*; on *archive.cis.ohio-state.edu*, it is in *perl/4.0*.[2]

Within this directory, you should see at least the following subdirectories:

patches   A directory containing numbered patches, which can be applied to update any existing copy of the Perl sources to the latest patch level. For example, if you'd retrieved the contents of *kits@10*, you'd need only the file *patch11* to update your sources to patchlevel 11.

kits@<number>   The actual Perl distribution. The kit *<number>* indicates the patch level. If the *patches* directory contains any patches with a higher number than the kit you have, you need to get and apply those patches (with *patch*(1)) in order to have the latest version.

                 There may be more than one *kits* directory. You need only get the contents of the latest one.

                 The *kits* directories contain the distribution in up to 40 parts (in *kit@19*), in both compressed and uncompressed format. The file names, respectively, look like *perl.kit.**nn*** and *perl.kit.**nn**.Z*, where ***nn*** is a number from 1 to 40 (as of this publication — as the distribution grows in size, so will the number of parts).

---

[2] These directory names are relative to the attach point for anonymous ftp (˜*ftp*); for uucp, they are relative to UUCP's public directory (˜*uucp*).

The files you retrieve are shell archives. If you took the compressed versions, uncompress them. Then run the files through *sh*. When all 40 kits have been run, read the README file for more instructions.

scripts   A variety of Perl scripts, mostly taken from the net. The subdirectory *scripts/nutshell* contains the examples from this book. (You can also find the examples on *ftp.uu.net* in the file *nutshell/perl/perl.tar.Z.*)

Current information on Perl distributions appears periodically in the Frequently Asked Questions posting in *comp.lang.perl*.

Using Anonymous FTP

In the event you've never used anonymous ftp, here is a quick primer, in the form of a sample session, with comments. Text in boldface is what you should type; comments are in italics.

```
% ftp jpl-devvax.jpl.nasa.gov
Connected to jpl-devvax.jpl.nasa.gov.
220 devvax FTP server (Version 4.171 Thu Dec 1 01:36:06 EST 1988) ready.
Name (jpl-devvax.jpl.nasa.gov:tim): anonymous
331 Guest login ok, send ident as password.
Password: tim@ora.com (use your user name and host here)
230 Guest login ok, access restrictions apply.
ftp> cd pub/perl.4.0/kits@10
250 CWD command successful.
ftp> binary (you must specify binary transfer for compressed files)
200 Type set to I.
ftp> get perl.kit01.z
200 PORT command successful.
150 Opening ASCII mode data connection for FILE.
226 Transfer complete.
        .
        .    (repeat this step for each file you want)
        .
ftp> quit
221 Goodbye.
%
```

Using UUCP

You can get Perl via anonymous uucp from the site osu-cis, thanks to J. Greely <jgreely@cis.ohio-state.edu> or <osu-cis!jgreely>.

You should use the following lines in your *L.sys* or *Systems* file:

```
#
# Direct Trailblazer
# The modem is occasionally unavailable.
#
osu-cis Any ACU 19200 1-614-292-5112 in:--in:--in: Uanon
#
# Direct V.32 (MNP 4)
# dead, dead, dead...sigh.
#
#osu-cis Any ACU 9600 1-614-292-1153 in:--in:--in: Uanon
#
# Micom port selector, at 1200, 2400, or 9600 bps.
# Replace ##'s below with 12, 24, or 96 (both speed and phone number).
#
# The following line is really one line.  Just don't type the
# backslash-return that we've added to make it fit this book.
osu-cis Any ACU ##00 1-614-292-31## "" \r\c Name? osu-cis nected \
\c GO \d\r\d\r\d\r\d\r\d\r\d\r in:--in:--in: Uanon
```

Of course, you may need to modify this information, as appropriate for your site, to deal with your local telephone system. There are no limitations concerning the hours of the day you may call, and the only charge is your long distance call.

You should probably get these two files first:

```
osu-cis!~/GNU.how-to-get.
osu-cis!~/ls-lR.Z
```

This will give you a listing of all the sources available at that site. However, the current Perl distribution is in the files:

```
osu-cis!~/perl/4.0/kits@19/perl.kitXX.Z (XX=01-40)
```

As noted above, this information is subject to change, and may be out-of-date by the time you read this book.

At any rate, if you have trouble, you can send e-mail to *osu-cis!uucp*.

To obtain sources from *uunet*, call 1-900-468-7727 and use the login "uucp" with no password. The Perl distribution is in the file `~uucp/gnu/perl-4.0.10.tar.Z`. The examples from this book are in `~uucp/nutshell/perl/perl.tar.Z`. As of this writing, the cost is 40 cents per minute. The charges will appear on your next telephone bill. The Perl distribution is about 700,000 bytes, compressed, so don't do this unless you have a Telebit Trailblazer or other very high speed modem.

Once you have the files, uncompress and un-tar them as follows:

```
% cat *.tar.Z | uncompress | tar xvf -
```

Conventions Used in This Book

Since we pretty much made them up as we went along, to fit different circumstances, we describe them as we go along, too. In general, though, the names of files and UNIX utilities are printed in *italics*, while names of Perl functions, statements, and variables (and any other snippets of Perl code that are mentioned in the text) are printed in **bold**. Examples and syntax lines are set off in:

```
Courier (constant width)
```

In syntax lines, items for which you're expected to supply your own values are printed in ALL CAPS.[3] In syntax lines, square brackets are sometimes used to show optional arguments, but more often, we just show several alternate forms for the syntax of the function.

At any rate, you should rely on the context, or on local explanations, to help you make sense of any deviations from this general picture.

Acknowledgements

We would like to thank Tom Christiansen, Steven Grady, Steve Jenkins, Brian Mathess, Brett McCoy, Chip Salzenberg, and Johan Vromans for contributing some of the examples in this book. Johan also graciously offered to let us include his Perl Reference Guide. We would like to thank Tom Christiansen, Rob Kolstad, Mike Loukides, Ted Stefanik, and Johan Vromans for reviewing this book on short notice, and for their many helpful criticisms and suggestions.

Randal says: I would like to thank Connie Woodworth & Intel iWarp (for time off to write this book), Seth Bradley, Mike Smith, Jim Sutton, Lori Eshelman (reviewers), The "Net" (without which I wouldn't have known about Perl), Tim O' & ambar & the crew (for taking a chance with the two of us), Lyle & Jack (for teaching me nearly everything I know about writing).

---

[3] The difference between these syntax items and the dummy parameters in the procedures in Chapter 5, which are printed in italics, is that the dummy parameters can represent almost any piece of text you might want to type in, while the syntax items are generally non-terminals, such as LIST or EXPR, which have a complex but constrained set of possible forms best learned by example, or, if you're fond of precision, by studying the semi-formal grammar in Appendix A.

Larry says: I would like to thank John Diehl, Bob Collinge, John Gainsborough, the Jet Propulsion Laboratory, and the Telos Corporation (for time off to write this book, and for pardoning occasional bleary eyes), Mark Biggar, Daniel Faigin, Jesse Wright (reviewers and co-conspirators), Sharon Hopkins and all the other Rusty Mechanicals (who told me when I was being *too* incoherent), and particularly my sweetie Gloria, who knew what she was getting into and married me anyway so that she could be my favorite Literary Critic. Thanks also to everyone on the "Net" for spec'ing and testing most of Perl for me. And I would like to express special gratitude to Tim O'Reilly for encouraging authors to write the sort of books people might enjoy reading.

We would also like to thank the friendly, competent, and generally fantastic Associates of O'Reilly, especially Donna Woonteiler, the production manager, Lenny Muellner, who worked on the scripts to convert the book to the Nutshell format, Mike Sierra and Eileen Kramer for producing the book, Ellie Cutler who worked on the index, and Edie Freeman, who designed the cover. (But blame Larry for wanting a camel.)

We'd Like to Hear From You

We have tested and verified all of the information in this book to the best of our ability, but you may find that features have changed (or even that we have made mistakes!). Please let us know about any errors you find, as well as your suggestions for future editions, by writing:

```
O'Reilly & Associates, Inc.
103 Morris Street, Suite A
Sebastopol, CA 95472
1-800-998-9938 (in the US or Canada)
1-707-829-0515 (international/local)
1-707-829-0104 (FAX)
```

You can also send us messages electronically. To be put on the mailing list or request a catalog, send email to:

```
info@ora.com      (via the Internet)
uunet!ora!info    (via UUCP)
```

To ask technical questions or comment on the book, send email to:

```
bookquestions@ora.com   (via the Internet)
```

An Overview of Perl

Getting Started
Lists
Variable Interpolation
Pattern Matching
Associative Arrays

Getting Started

We think that Perl is an easy language to learn and use, and we hope to convince you that we're right. One of the things that makes Perl easy is that you don't have to say much before you say what you want to say. In many programming languages, you have to declare the types, variables, and subroutines you are going to use before you can write the first statement of executable code. And for complex problems demanding complex data structures, this is very good idea. But for many simple, everyday problems, you would like a programming language in which you can simply say:

```
print "Howdy, world!\n";
```

and have the program do just that.

Perl is such a language. In fact, the example above is a complete Perl program. If you feed it to the Perl interpreter, it will print **Howdy, world!** on your screen, followed by a newline, represented in the code by **\n**. Nothing mysterious or magical there.

Filehandles

Here is a slightly longer example. (Perl uses **#** to introduce comments.)

```
print "Enter Hexadecimal Number: ";   # Ask for a number.
$answer = <STDIN>;                     # Input the number.
print hex($answer),"\n";               # Print out new number.
```

This program prompts for a number, takes the line you type in, and puts it into a variable called **$answer**. On the last line the program then converts **$answer** from hexadecimal to decimal using the **hex( )** function and prints that out, followed by a newline. The **<STDIN>** symbol just says to read in a line from the standard input, ordinarily your keyboard. You might think of it as an exotic variable that has a different value each time you look at it. This example isn't very magical either, except for the **hex**.

If **STDIN** is the name of the input, then you'd expect **STDOUT** to be the name of the output. And you'd be right. The **print** statement (such as the one above) has an optional argument that tells it where to put the output, and **STDOUT** just happens to be the default. Thus, you could have written the final line above as:

```
print STDOUT hex($answer),"\n";
```

STDIN and **STDOUT** are called filehandles. A filehandle is just a name that you give to a file, device, pipe, or socket so that you can do input or output easily. You can create filehandles and attach them to files using the **open** statement, but Perl gives you **STDIN** and **STDOUT** for free. It also gives you the **STDERR** filehandle so that your program can make snide comments off to the side while it transforms (or attempts to transform) your input into your output.[4]

In addition, there's a filehandle called **ARGV** which can be used to work your way through all the files the user mentioned on the command line. As you plow through each file, the special variable **$ARGV** holds the name of the current file. Plowing through the files is done by reading the filenames from the special array

---

[4] The reason Perl can give you these filehandles for free is that UNIX provides them for free. UNIX processes inherit standard input, standard output, and standard error from their parent process, typically a shell. One of the duties of a shell is to set up these I/O streams so that the child process doesn't need to worry about them.

variable **@ARGV**, which contains the list of the filenames from the command line.[5]

To create your own filehandles and attach them to files, you can use the **open( )** function, like this:

```
open(FIZZLE,"myfilename");
```

To open files for writing, or to open pipes, you can add the characters to the filename that you would ordinarily use to redirect I/O for the corresponding operation within one of the UNIX shells:

```
open(FIZZLE,"> myfilename");           # Create file.
open(FIZZLE,">> myfilename");          # Append to file.
open(FIZZLE,"| output-pipe-command");  # Set up output filter.
open(FIZZLE,"input-pipe-command |");   # Set up input filter.
```

After the open statement, the FIZZLE filehandle may be used to access the file or pipe until the filehandle is closed, or the filehandle is attached to some other file by a subsequent **open( )**. You're also allowed to close and reopen the **STDIN**, **STDOUT**, and **STDERR** filehandles.

Variables

You'll note that we didn't have to tell Perl what kind of variable **$answer** is. That's because the **$** character itself tells Perl that **$answer** can hold a single value, which can be either a string or a number. We call this a scalar variable. There are other kinds of variables that start with other funny characters like **@** and **%**.[6] (We just mentioned that **@ARGV** holds a list, so you know what the **@** means too.) Here are all of Perl's funny characters, just so you know how little you'll have to learn:

FIZZLE   A filehandle or directory handle.

$FIZZLE   A scalar variable.

---

[5] **@ARGV** might also contain switches and other arguments to your program. Your program will presumably remove such elements from **@ARGV** before using the remaining arguments as filenames.

[6] Some consider that having the variables all start with funny characters makes Perl an ugly language. Perhaps so. But this has two major benefits: first, it's very easy to read Perl scripts because you can easily distinguish variables from keywords, and second, it means that a new keyword could be added to the language without breaking old scripts, because Perl can easily distinguish variables from keywords, too.

`@FIZZLE`	An array indexed by number.
`%FIZZLE`	An array indexed by string.
`&FIZZLE`	A subroutine.
`*FIZZLE`	Everything named FIZZLE.

You can modify scalar variables by supplying scalar values, here expressed as scalar literals on the right side of the assignment statement:

```
$answer = 42;              # integer
$pi = 3.14159265;          # numeric
$avocados = 6.02e23;       # scientific notation
$pet = ´dog´;              # string
$sign = "Beware of $pet\n"; # string with interpolation
$curdir = `pwd`;           # command
```

As in the shell, double quotes allow variable interpolation and single quotes don't. (We'll explain variable interpolation later in the chapter.) That last line with the backticks is not really a literal, since it executes a system command and returns the results, but we'll let it slide . . .

If you don't initialize your variables in Perl, they automatically spring into existence with a null value that means either ´´ or 0 as necessary. Arrays spring into existence without any elements. Depending on where you use them, variables will be interpreted automatically as strings, as numbers, as "true" and "false" values (commonly called Boolean values), or as array values. Various operators expect certain kinds of values, so we will talk about these operators as supplying a scalar context, a numeric context, a string context, a Boolean context, or an array context. Perl will automatically convert the data into the form required by the current context. For example, if you say:

```
$camels = "123";
print $camels + 1, "\n";
```

the original value of **$camels** is a string, but it is converted to a number to add **1** to it, and then converted back to a string to be printed out as **"124"**.

How to Do It

You're probably wondering by now how to run a Perl program. There's More Than One Way To Do It.[7]

---

[7] That's the Perl Slogan, and you'll get tired of hearing it, unless you're a consultant, in which case you'll get tired of saying it.

Assuming you are running Perl on a machine running some version or other of the UNIX operating system, you could enter our first example as an argument right on the command line, using the **–e** switch:

```
% perl —e 'print "Howdy, world!\n";'
```

Or, you can put the program in a file with your favorite text editor (or any other text editor) and then say, presuming you named the file **howdy**:

```
% perl howdy
```

On systems that support the **#!** syntax for specifying the name of an interpreter, you can put a magical line at the front of the file so that the operating system knows what program to interpret your file with, like this:

```
#!/usr/bin/perl
print "Howdy, world!\n";
```

(putting the proper path in place of */usr/bin/perl* if that isn't the path on your system to the Perl interpreter[8]) and then all you have to say is:

```
% howdy
```

(presuming that the file has the execute bit set; see the manpage for *chmod*(1)[9]). If your system doesn't support the **#!** syntax, all hope is not lost. You can replace the **#!** line in the previous example with this:

```
eval 'exec /usr/bin/perl —S $0 ${1+"$@"}'
    if 0;
```

and your shell will be fooled into executing the script for you.

Enough of that. We will use *#!/usr/bin/perl* as a shorthand for one of the above invocation methods, and you'll know what we mean.

---

[8] And if it isn't, shame on your system administrator. Note that many versions of UNIX will not allow an interpreter name to be longer than 32 characters. If your Perl pathname is longer than that (as it is in some instances of the Andrew File System), and if for some reason you can't get around that fact administratively, say this (including the comment):

```
#!/bin/sh — # A comment mentioning perl, to prevent looping.
eval 'exec /your/long/path/name/leading/to/perl —S $0 ${1+"$@"}'
    if 0;
```

[9] That odd notation simply means that if you want to find out about the *chmod* command, say "**man 1 chmod**", and your system may say something interesting about it, if it's a UNIX system.

A Very Special Variable

Back to the subject of scalar variables, there's one scalar variable, called $_, that is particularly important because a number of operations magically affect it (or are affected by it). This is not without precedent. Pattern matches do their searching on $_ by default, so it acts like the default pattern space in the *sed* editor. It is often used to hold the current line, like the $0 field of *awk*. We would like to underscore the fact that in Perl, $_ is customarily (though not necessarily) used for these purposes.

There are other special variables in Perl that are used for various purposes. We'll introduce the most important ones as we go along, but you can find them all listed in the section "Special Variables" in Chapter Three. Included in those listings are mnemonics to help you remember which variable is which, if you have any trouble that way. You can also look up the special variables (and many other things) in the *Quick Reference Guide* that comes with this book.

Conditional Constructs

As do many languages, Perl has a while loop that can do the loop body as long as a condition is true:

```
#!/usr/bin/perl
$countdown = 10;
while ($countdown != 0) {    # While $countdown doesn't equal 0
    print "$countdown...\n"; # Print time left.
    sleep 1;                 # Wait one second.
    —$countdown;             # Decrement $countdown.
}
print "BOOM!\n";
```

The conditional **$countdown != 0** is true until **$countdown** is decremented to 0. The != (not equal) operator compares two numeric values and returns a value of true if the first is unequal to the second, and a value of false otherwise. In Perl, the rule is very simple: a value is true if it isn't the null string (´´) or 0 or "0". So relational operators like == and != return a 1 if they are true, and a 0 if they are false. Other operators might return other numbers or strings for true, and might return a null string (´´) for false. Note that a space or a newline character is true, and so is a string like "00" even though it would convert itself to 0 if used in a numeric context. But the string "0" is always false because that's what a numeric 0 converts to when used in a string context, and because we want you to be able to pretend that numeric values are always stored as strings.

When we say true or false, we're just talking about Perl's rule for evaluating the truth of conditional expressions—Perl doesn't actually recognize the words true and false, nor is there any need for a special Boolean type in Perl, since any type can be interpreted as a Boolean type.

So then, anything that has a value may be used as the conditional of a while loop. You could even use an assignment statement, since assignment statements return the final value of the variable you changed:

```
#!/usr/bin/perl
while ($_ = <ARGV>) {
    print $_;
}
```

This is actually a useful program, and if you've been paying attention, you can probably guess what it does. You see that we are reading input from that funny filehandle **ARGV**, which yields, one-by-one, each of the lines from all the files mentioned on the command line. If you called the above script **meow**, then you might invoke it as:

```
% meow Abel Baker Charlie
```

The first time through the while loop, the first line from file **Abel** is assigned to our friend, the special variable $_. The **print** statement inside the loop writes the value of $_ back out to **STDOUT**. Then the next line from **Abel** is read in and printed out. After **Abel** is exhausted, **Baker** will be read, and then **Charlie**. The output will be the concatenation of the three input files. This behavior may or may not remind you of the UNIX program *cat*.

The program above may seem quite simple already, but for convenience it can be shortened in three ways. First, the input symbol **<ARGV>** can be written with a null filehandle as **<>**. Second, when an input symbol is used by itself in the conditional of a while loop, it will automatically assign its value to $_ for you, so you don't have to put in the assignment explicitly. Third, a **print** statement that has nothing else to print out will print $_. So you can type this:

```
#!/usr/bin/perl
while (<>) {
    print;
}
```

You didn't type $_ at all, but it's lurking there just the same. We mentioned earlier that $_ is also what pattern matches look at. The following little script is a barebones *grep* program, and introduces a simple form of the "if" conditional:

```
#!/usr/bin/perl
$pattern = shift(@ARGV); # Extract first argument into $pattern.
while (<>) {             # Treat the rest of @ARGV as filenames.
    if (/$pattern/) {    # If the pattern matches...
        print;           # Print the line.
    }
}
```

It just prints out the lines that match the pattern you passed in as the first argument on the command line. The pattern match operator /**$pattern**/ will test **$_** on each line input to it, but returns a true value only if line matches the regular expression contained in **$pattern**. (Regular expressions are explained later in this chapter.) If you call it **baregrep**, you could invoke it as:

```
baregrep ´hump.*hump´  dromedary
```

and it would print out all the lines from the file named *dromedary* that happened to contain two occurrences of the word hump (or chump, or thump). The .* characters match the arbitrary sequence of characters between the two occurrences, because the . matches an arbitrary character, and the * says to match as many as possible (0 or more) of the previous item.

What Is Truth?

Now some of you clever folks might look at the conditional of that while loop, and wonder about blank lines. "Aha," you say, "a blank line contains no characters, and Perl treats the null string as false. Therefore, the while loop will exit prematurely when it hits the first blank line in the input."

Not so. You're assuming that the newline at the end of a blank line is automatically discarded. It isn't. Perl keeps the newline, so a blank line has the value "**\n**", which works out to a true value. You may explicitly chop the newline off the current input line if you desire. There's a special operator called **chop** to do just that. You can say:

```
chop $_;
```

or just:

```
chop;
```

(Remember that for many operations, **$_** is the default operand.)

By the same token, the **print** statement doesn't automatically add a newline back on. You have to add it on yourself if you want one. Suppose you wanted to change the **meow** program above to print out only lines that are not blank. You could write it like this:

```
#!/usr/bin/perl
while (<>) {
    chop;                        # Remove newline.
    print $_,"\n" if $_ ne "";   # Print non-null lines.
}
```

The **chop** operator removes the newline from **$_**, and the **print** statement adds one back on if the line is to be printed. Earlier, we saw that the **!=** operator does numeric comparison and returns true if the two operands are not numerically the same. The **ne** (not equal) operator above does a string comparison instead of a numeric comparison, and returns true if the strings don't contain the same sequence of characters. Similarly, == tests for numeric equality, while **eq** tests for string equality. The > operator tests for numeric ordering, while **gt** tests for string ordering (according to ASCII collating sequence), and so on:

Numeric test	String test	Meaning
==	eq	Equal to
!=	ne	Not equal to
>	gt	Greater than
>=	ge	Greater than or equal to
<	lt	Less than
<=	le	Less than or equal to
<=>	cmp	Not equal to, with signed return

You have to be careful to specify which kind of test you want. If **$a** has the value "5" and **$b** has the value "10", then **$a < $b** is true, because 5 is less than 10, but **$a lt $b** is false, because the character **1** sorts before the character **5**.

That last example printed lines that weren't blank. It probably wasn't the best way to write that program. Some language purists will prefer to avoid using the statement modifier form of **if**, and instead use the standard **if** syntax that C programmers are familiar with:

```
while (<>) {
    chop;
    if ($_ ne "") {
        print $_,"\n";
    }
}
```

If you write the program like this, the parentheses around the conditional are required, as in C. Unlike C, the curly braces are also required—Perl doesn't let you have dangling statements. Of course, the entire example is contrived, since you'd probably write:

```
while (<>) {
    print unless $_ eq "\n";
}
```

or maybe:

```
while (<>) {
    print unless /^$/;
}
```

or even:

```
while (<>) {
    s/^\n$//;
    print;
}
```

But you can write it however you want. If you're coming to Perl from a C background, you'll probably prefer a different set of constructs than someone coming from a shell background, or BASIC, or RPG II. That's okay—just don't expect everyone else to write it the same way. There's no *correct* way to write Perl. Perl doesn't mind a little pluralism—a Perl script is correct if it's halfway readable and gets the job done before your boss fires you.

Scalar Operators

Perl has many operators, a good share of which are derived from the C language. In fact, the only C operators that Perl doesn't have are the type casting operator, the address operators (unary **&** and *****), and the structure member operators (**.** and **->**). Some operators are borrowed from *sed*, *awk*, and various UNIX utilities that are commonly invoked from shells, such as the file tests. If you want an operator to do something in particular, there's probably one there already to do it—look for it in the index. We won't list all the operators yet, but here are some of the more important ones:

Pattern matching		Result
`$a =~ /pat/`	Match	True if $a contains pattern
`$a =~ s/p/r/`	Substitution	Replace occurrences of p with r in $a
`$a =~ tr/a-z/A-Z/`	Translation	Translate to corresponding characters
Logical operators		**Result**
`$a && $b`	And	True if $a is true and $b is true
`$a || $b`	Or	$a if $a is true, otherwise $b
`! $a`	Not	True if $a is not true
Arithmetic operators		**Result**
`$a + $b`	Add	Sum of $a and $b
`$a — $b`	Subtract	Difference of $a and $b
`$a * $b`	Multiply	Product of $a times $b
`$a / $b`	Divide	Quotient of $a divided by $b
`$a % $b`	Modulus	Remainder of $a divided by $b
`$a ** $b`	Exponentiate	$a to the power of $b
`++$a,$a++`	Autoincrement	Add 1 to $a
`—$a,$a—`	Autodecrement	Subtract 1 from $a
`rand($a)`	Random	A random number in range 0 .. $a

String operations		Result
`$a . $b`	Concatenation	Values of $a and $b as one long string
`$a x $b`	Repeat	Value of $a strung together $b times
`substr($a,$o,$l)`	Substring	Substring at offset $o of length $l
`index($a,$b)`	Index	Offset of string $b in string $a

Assignment operators		Result
`$a = $b`	Assign	$a gets the value of $b
`$a += $b`	Add to	Increase $a by $b
`$a -= $b`	Subtract from	Decrease $a by $b
`$a .= $b`	Append	Append string $b to $a (see . above)

File operations		Result
`-r $a`	Readable	True if file named in $a is readable
`-w $a`	Writable	True if file named in $a is writable
`-d $a`	Directory	True if file named in $a is a directory
`-f $a`	Regular file	True if file named in $a is regular file
`-T $a`	Text file	True if file named in $a is a text file

You'll notice that some of the "operators" in the table are elsewhere described as functions. You'll find that sometimes we distinguish between operators and functions, and sometimes we don't. Historically, the term "operator" has been applied to those operations that are written with an infix or unary prefix notation, while the term "function" has been applied to those operations that are written with their arguments in parentheses. (This is a syntactic distinction, not a semantic one, since all of them take some number of inputs and produce an output.) Here we're using the terms in the historical sense, because we're describing the syntax of Perl. However, in most of this book, we often use the term "operator" to refer to both classic operators and functions. And we use the term "function" to refer not only to those operators that *must* have parentheses around their arguments, but also to those operators that *may* have parentheses around their arguments (the named unary operators and the list operators). Thus, sometimes we'll talk about the **print** operator, and sometimes the **print( )** function. Humor us.

At any rate, most of these operators are straightforward, but **substr** is a little tricky. First, it normally counts offsets from 0, so the beginning of the string is at offset 0. Second, you can assign to **substr**, and it will replace that chunk of string with whatever you assign to it, shifting the rest of string left or right as necessary.

The autoincrement and autodecrement operators (**++** and **--**) may be placed either before or after the variable to be modified, depending on whether you want the variable incremented before or after it is referenced.

The logical operators **&&** and **||** are called "short-circuit" operators because they never evaluate the right operand if the left operand is sufficient to tell what the overall value should be. Because of this behavior, these two operators can be used to evaluate their right operand conditionally. A frequently seen idiom is:

```
open(FILE, $filename) || die "Can't open $filename: $!\n";
```

which translates to "Open this file or die!" Use of the short-circuit operator preserves the visual flow of important actions down the left side of your screen by hiding secondary actions on the right side of your screen. (The $! variable contains the error message returned by the operating system when there has been a system error.)

There are many more scalar operators, but those we've listed are enough to get started with. C, shell, *sed*, and *awk* programmers will have an advantage, but the rest of you should catch on quickly.

A Brief Diversion

Here for your viewing pleasure (and to remind you of what you've learned so far) is a program that opens an input pipe to find all the files in the current directory and its subdirectories. It then prints the names of any text files which contain any of the words mentioned on the command line. There are several new things in this example—see if you can figure out how some of them work.

```
#!/usr/bin/perl

open(FIND, "find . -print |") || die "Couldn't run find: $!\n";

FILE:
while ($filename = <FIND>) {
    chop $filename;
    next FILE unless -T $filename;
    if (!open(TEXTFILE, $filename)) {
        print STDERR "Can't open $filename—continuing...\n";
        next FILE;
    }
    while (<TEXTFILE>) {
        foreach $word (@ARGV) {
            if (index($_, $word) >= 0) {
                print $filename, "\n";
                next FILE;
            }
        }
    }
}
```

The open statement opens a pipe from the UNIX *find* program, which will traverse this directory (and all its subdirectories and print out all the filenames it finds. The next nonblank line is a loop label (**FILE:**), which just gives the following **while** loop a name so that the **next** operator can talk about it. The **next** operator is a flow control operator that starts the next iteration of a loop similarly to the **continue** statement in C. The **next** operator, however, can specify the label of the loop that is to be continued.

Each time through the **FILE** loop, another filename is read from the *find* program via the **FIND** filehandle. The **chop** operator removes the newline from the filename. The line after that skips the filename unless the file is a text file, using the **–T** file test operator to make the determination. If it is a text file, we try to open it, and complain if unsuccessful. If we can open it, we read each line from the **TEXTFILE** filehandle into the **$_** variable.

At this point we want to search the line for all the words that were specified on the command line (and thus reside in the **@ARGV** array). The **foreach** construct is a looping construct that causes **$word** to take on the value of each element of the array, one after the other. Within that loop, we search for the current word in the current line using the **index()** function, which attempts to locate one string in another. If it succeeds, we report that fact and skip back out to the next iteration of the outer loop.[10]

Lists

In addition to scalar operators, Perl has many operators that do things with lists. Much of the power of Perl comes from the ability to process multiple items with a single command. Many of the problems you run into in the real world are most naturally solved with a list.

What's a List?

A list is simply an ordered set of scalars, and you already know what scalars are. Your list can be a list of numbers, or a list of strings, or a mixture of both. Some lists are named, and we'll call these lists "arrays." Other lists are merely values that are passed from one operation to another, and we'll call those "array values" or "lists" interchangeably.

---

[10] Nit pickers will point out that there's a potential problem with false positives here—it is difficult to check for word boundaries using **index()**. And you'll get false negatives when capital letters don't match lowercase letters. The solution is to use regular expressions, which we'll cover later in this chapter.

Since the values in a list are ordered, it makes sense to talk about the "first" one, the "second" one, on through the "last" one. You can select an individual scalar out of an array by "subscripting" into the array. The first item in the list is number 0, the second item is number 1, and so on. For instance, when you start up a Perl program, the command line arguments are copied into the @ARGV array so that:

```
$ARGV[0]
```

is the first argument, and:

```
$ARGV[$#ARGV]
```

is the last. **$#ARGV** is the subscript of the last element of array **@ARGV**.[11]

Since **$#ARGV** is the final subscript, you'll often find it on the right side of the .. operator, also called the **range** operator. (The range operator produces the list of values you'd get by counting from the value of its left operand up to the value of its right operand.) For example, the following script prints out all the arguments from the command line, just like the UNIX *echo* command:

```perl
#!/usr/bin/perl
foreach $i (0 .. $#ARGV) {
    print $ARGV[$i];
    if ($i == $#ARGV) {
        print "\n";
    }
    else {
        print " ";
    }
}
```

We'll talk about list values and arrays, but when we shout LIST in capitals, we're referring to the syntactic structure for constructing a list value out of its components. The LIST construction operator in Perl is simply a comma, used between each element of the list. (There are other uses for comma, which means you can only use the comma as a LIST builder when the surrounding context is looking for a LIST.)

---

[11] We use the $ in **$ARRAY[SCALAR]** to indicate that we are selecting a scalar value even though it's coming from an array that is named **@ARRAY**. That will be confusing to you until you discover that you can use @ in **@ARRAY[LIST]** as the notation for array slices, and you figure out that the $ or @ is controlling the context of the subscript. But you don't know that yet, so take our word for it that **$fiddle[15]** is related to **@fiddle**, but *not* related to **$fiddle**.

A LIST looks like this:

```
'first', 'second', 'third', 'fourth'
```

or:

```
1,1,2,3,5,8,13
```

One of the places that Perl looks for a LIST is inside a set of parentheses. (Parentheses are also used for other things, like specifying a function's arguments. But we are talking about bare parentheses here.) So you can use a LIST to initialize an entire array like this:

```
@growing_things = ('oats','peas','beans','barley');
@count = (1,2,3,4,5,6,7,8,9,10);      # Same as (1 .. 10).
@colors = ($red, $green, $blue);
```

(Note that the parentheses are necessary because the precedence of the comma operator is lower than that of the assignment operator.)

We saw a real-life example of a LIST when we said:

```
print $_, "\n";
```

because the **print** statement takes a LIST as an argument. This example shows two things. First, an item in a LIST doesn't have to be a literal—the initial element of this list is the variable $_, and in fact you can have any arbitrary expression as an item in a LIST. Second, parentheses are not always necessary around a LIST.

A parenthesized LIST that is composed entirely of named or subscripted scalars can be assigned the value of anything that returns a list value:

```
($red, $green, $blue) = (0..2);
($name,$pw,$uid,$gid,$gcos,$home,$shell) = split(/:/, <PASSWD>);
($a[2], $a[0], $a[3], $a[1]) = @growing_things;
```

The **..** operator returns a list of numbers counting up from **0** to **2**; that is, **(0,1,2)**; these values are assigned to each of the corresponding variables in the list. The **split( )** operator returns the list of strings that result from taking the next line of the password file and breaking it apart at each colon character; again, the resulting values are assigned to the variables in the list. The third example adds a new dimension. Various elements of the **@a** array are loaded with values from **@growing_things**. (This is called an array slice.) Note that if **@growing_things** was larger than the list on the left side of the assignment, the unused values would be discarded. If it was smaller, some of the variables would have undefined values. And, naturally enough, an array like **@growing_things** can return an array value.

Speaking of @**growing_things**, arrays can grow and shrink. Items can be inserted into or deleted from the front of the list, the middle of the list, or the end of the list. You saw us shrink the @**ARGV** array earlier by using the **shift** operator to pull the first argument from the front of the list. There is one special list function called **splice( )** that can do any of these things. It looks like this:

```
@growing_things = ('oats', 'peas', 'beans', 'barley');
@legumes = splice(@growing_things, 1, 2, 'wheat', 'rice', 'corn');
```

After you do this, @**growing_things** will contain oats, wheat, rice, corn, and barley, in that order. And @**legumes** will contain peas and beans. How did that happen? (See Figure 1-1.) It is now necessary to introduce one of those horrible syntax summaries, but we'll try to make the best of it. The words in ALL CAPS represent syntactic items, and the [square brackets] enclose optional material:

```
splice(ARRAY, OFFSET, LENGTH [, LIST])
```

What **splice** does is to count over OFFSET scalars from the beginning of the list in ARRAY (or from the end, if OFFSET is negative), and substitute LIST for the next LENGTH scalars.[12] Note that the first element in the array is at an OFFSET of 0 (just like the first character of a string is at offset 0 when you use **substr**). If no LIST is given, **splice** inserts a null list (that is, the **splice( )** reduces to a deletion operation). It then returns the list of scalars it removed from ARRAY.

Now that you've waded through this lengthy explanation of **splice( )**, we should tell you that you'll almost never use it, because there are other operators such as **shift** to do the most common operations. But now we can explain those array operations in terms of **splice**:

Operator	Equivalent
$a = shift(@abz)	$a = splice(@abz,0,1)
$z = pop(@abz)	$z = splice(@abz,$#abz,1)
unshift(@abz,$a)	splice(@abz,0,0,$a)
push(@abz,$z)	splice(@abz,$#abz+1,0,$z)

---

[12] You might have thought that the 1 and 2 in the example were part of a LIST, but they aren't. The first three commas are separating function arguments. Since the last argument is a LIST, however, any commas found there are taken to be LIST commas. You'll discover that whenever LIST occurs in the syntax for a function, it's always last, so that it can gobble up all the rest of the commas it finds.

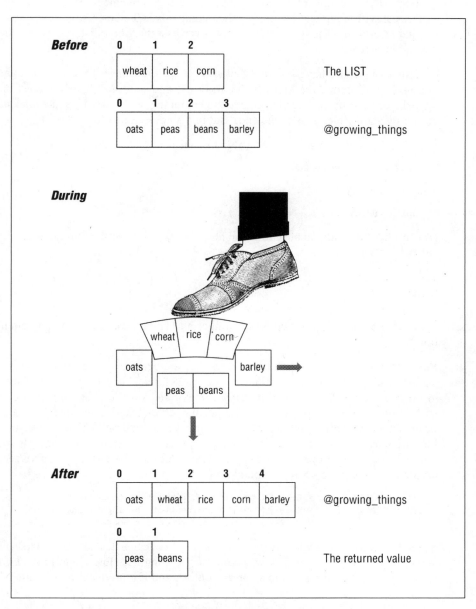

Figure 1-1. splice(@growing_things,1,2,"wheat","rice","corn")

The first splice counts over 0 elements, removes 1 element and replaces it with nothing. The second splice counts over to the last element, removes it and replaces it with nothing. The third splice counts over 0 elements, removes nothing and inserts $a. The final splice counts over past the whole list, removes nothing and inserts $z.

Of course, we could have just said that **shift** chops the front off the array list and returns it, **pop** chops the end off the array list and returns it, **unshift** does the opposite of **shift** by adding elements to the beginning, and **push** does the opposite of **pop** by adding elements to the end. But that's not as much fun.

Additionally, setting a subscripted value like this:

```
$ARGV[$i] = ´new value´;
```

has the same effect as:

```
splice(@ARGV, $i, 1, ´new value´);
```

(except that the assignment returns the new value, and the **splice( )** returns the old value.)

Wake Up!!!

Now we are about to say two Really Important Things about lists, so pay attention.

First, certain operators care about whether they are being evaluated as one item of a LIST, and return different values inside a LIST than they do in other places. We'll call the inside of a LIST an array context, and we'll call any other place a scalar context. If an operator cares about its context, it will return a list value inside an array context, and a scalar value in a scalar context, which makes some kind of sense. Most of the operators you've seen so far don't care, and always return a scalar value even in an array context. But one operator that you've seen *does* care, namely the **< >** input operator:

```
$a = <STDIN>;      # Sets $a to the next line of standard input.
@a = <STDIN>;      # Sets @a to all the rest of the input lines!
                   #   (BEWARE: this may produce a HUGE array!!!)
```

Second, a LIST (the syntactic structure) always concatenates all its scalars and array values together as if they were one, single, long list. Each item in the LIST is evaluated as an expression in an array context, and if it produces a list value, all the values of that list value are added to the value of the LIST at that point, as if they'd all been individually specified. Thus:

```
@a = (1..3);        # Same as @a = (1, 2, 3);
@b = (0, @a, 4);    # Same as @b = (0, 1, 2, 3, 4);

@a = (2);           # Same as @a = 2;
@b = (0, @a, 4);    # Same as @b = (0, 2, 4);

@a = ();            # Same as $#a = -1;   i.e. make null list.
@b = (0, @a, 4);    # Same as @b = (0, 4);
```

Because that @a in the LIST is evaluated in an array context, it returns an array value, namely the list of its elements. Now it so happens that in a *scalar* context an array simply returns the number of elements in the array, which is normally one more than the offset of the last element. This has a couple of nice benefits. First, it's traditional to use the array name in a simple conditional, like this:

```
while (@ARGV) {
    $next_element = shift;
    # Your code here.
}
```

Second, we could have written that **push**-equivalent **splice** as:

Operator	Equivalent
push(@abz,$z)	splice(@abz,@abz,0,$z)

The second **@abz** is in a scalar context, so it returns the number of elements, which is the correct offset to the end of the array. That **$z** there is a scalar, but since the last argument is really a LIST, it's interpreted as part of a list value containing a single item. The following four statements do the same thing, namely append an array to itself:

```
@abz = (@abz,@abz);
splice(@abz,0,0,@abz);
splice(@abz,@abz,0,@abz);
push(@abz,@abz);
```

That first **@abz** argument in **splice()** or **push()** is considered to be in *neither* an array context nor a scalar context, because it's not an expression—the first argument of such array operations must be an explicit array name.

Just so you don't think the **splice()** function is totally useless, here's an actual use for it: a program that shuffles its input lines into a random order. We repeatedly use the **rand** operator to pick a line number in the range of **0..$#lines** and then snip that line out of the array and print it, like this:

```
#!/usr/bin/perl
srand;                       # Randomize the rand function.
@lines = <>;                 # Read in all the lines.
while (@lines) {             # While more than 0 elements.
    print splice(@lines, rand @lines, 1);
}
```

Just as there are a number of scalar operators, so too there are quite a few list operators. Here are some of the most commonly used. These examples assume that @**growing_things** already has the value:

```
('oats', 'peas', 'beans', 'barley')
```

Subscripting	**Result**
`$growing_things[2]`	'beans' -- a scalar value
Slicing	**Result**
`@growing_things[1,3]`	('peas', 'barley') -- a list value
Sorting	**Result**
`sort @growing_things`	('barley', 'beans', 'oats', 'peas')
Reversing	**Result**
`reverse @growing_things`	('barley', 'beans', 'peas', 'oats')
Sorting, then reversing	**Result**
`reverse sort @growing_things`	('peas', 'oats', 'beans', 'barley')
Selecting by pattern	**Result**
`grep(/ea/, @growing_things)`	('peas', 'beans')
Generating ranges	**Result**
`3 .. 7`	(3, 4, 5, 6, 7)
Generating reversed ranges	**Result**
`reverse 3 .. 7`	(7, 6, 5, 4, 3)
Slice using range	**Result**
`@growing_things[0 .. 2]`	('oats', 'peas', 'beans')

How to Do Things With Lists

With all that out of the way, we can get back to more practical matters. Suppose that your login directory is as cluttered as mine, and it's difficult to find the text files among all the binary files and directories. Here's a little script that may help. Invoke it as:

```
tlist *
```

and it will print out all your text file names on a line.

```perl
#!/usr/bin/perl
while (@ARGV) {
    $file = shift @ARGV;
    push(@textfiles, $file) if -T $file;
}
print join(´ ´,@textfiles), "\n";
```

The **while** conditional provides a scalar context for **@ARGV**, so it returns the number of values in **@ARGV**. So the **while** loop runs until the **shift** operator has drained **@ARGV**. The next line pulls the next filename out of **@ARGV** using **shift**. Then we add the file to the **@textfiles** array, but only if it is a text file. After we've done this for all the filenames, **@textfiles** contains the text files that we found. We print those out after joining all the array items together into a single string with spaces between. The following program does exactly the same thing, but relies on the **grep** function to select the text files for us:

```perl
#!/usr/bin/perl
print join(´ ´, grep(-T, @ARGV)), "\n";
```

The **grep** function, just like its UNIX counterpart, will select certain elements of an array according to some criterion, returning just those elements selected. However, Perl's **grep** function is far more powerful, since it can use not just a regular expression as its criterion, but any Perl expression. It works a bit like the "apply" operator supplied by certain other languages—it sets **$_** to each value of the list you give it, and then evaluates its first argument, the **–T** file test operator in this case, for each value of the array in turn. (It so happens that **–T** will evaluate **$_** if you don't give it anything else to evaluate.) The **grep** in our example returns a list of text files to the **join** function, which is of course expecting a LIST as its second argument. The **join** function then glues the list together into a scalar string value (even though called in the array context of the **print**—**join** is one of the functions that *doesn't* care about its context), and returns it as part of the **print** operator's LIST. The **print** operator is expecting a list, and prints out the string containing the filenames, followed by the newline. If you did a **join** with "**\n**" instead of ´ ´, you would get the filenames on separate lines.

This all sounds complicated, but it mostly does exactly what you expect. It's just hard for us to explain what you expect . . .

If you wanted the filenames sorted alphabetically, you could say:

```
#!/usr/bin/perl
print join(´ ´, sort grep(-T, @ARGV)), "\n";
```

The **sort** takes the array value returned by **grep** and sorts it before passing it on to the **join**. If you wanted it sorted in reverse, you could pass the output of the **sort** operator on to the **reverse** operator:

```
#!/usr/bin/perl
print join(´ ´, reverse sort grep(-T, @ARGV)), "\n";
```

Although many operators such as **reverse** and **sort** let you omit the parentheses, it behooves you to insert them whenever it would improve the readability or help you be sure what's going on. Saying:

```
print(join(´ ´, reverse(sort(grep(-T, @ARGV)))), "\n");
```

is probably overkill on the parentheses, but it may make some Lisp programmers happier. Any time you make a Perl operator look like a function this way, it really *is* a function, and only examines the arguments in parentheses. (See the discussion of "operators" versus "functions" earlier in this chapter if you are confused.)

Anyway, the following *function* prints the value 4:

```
print (1 + 3) * 20;
```

The value of the **print** function is then multiplied by **20** and discarded. This really is rather dreadful, but that's the penalty you pay for having all your favorite languages rolled into one. To get the "right" answer, say any of these:

```
print ((1 + 3) * 20);
print +(1 + 3) * 20;
print STDOUT (1 + 3) * 20;
```

The first way uses **print** as a function correctly, while the other two ways use **print** as a list operator (albeit with only one argument).

Some of our examples have used the **foreach** loop, which iterates over the values of an array somewhat like the **grep** function. We could have written our echo program like this:

```
#!/usr/bin/perl
foreach $arg (@ARGV) {
    print $space, $arg;
    $space = ´ ´;
}
print "\n";
```

The **foreach** command actually makes the scalar you mention represent each element of the array, so you can modify the elements by modifying the scalar, as in this version of *echo*:

```
#!/usr/bin/perl
foreach $arg (@ARGV) {
    $arg .= ' ';              # Add a space to each argument.
}
$ARGV[$#ARGV] =~ s/ $/\n/;  # Change last space to a newline.
print @ARGV;
```

Of course, that's a bit silly when you can simply say:

```
#!/usr/bin/perl
print join(' ', @ARGV),"\n";
```

Variable Interpolation

There's an even more concise way to write *echo* (though it's not actually any faster). Earlier we used the command:

```
print "$countdown...\n";
```

As you might realize, this command interpolates[13] the scalar **$countdown** into the string. Similarly, you can interpolate an entire array into a string, and it will (by default) be inserted with spaces between the elements. So our *echo* program is most simply written as:

```
#!/usr/bin/perl
print "@ARGV\n";
```

Note that in the prior version of this we printed **@ARGV** without double quotes, so it didn't automatically add spaces for us. Note also that variable interpolation doesn't happen in single quotes. If we named the script **myecho**, and said:

```
myecho a b c d
```

---

[13] Note that we use this word with the original literary meaning of Subsequent Textual Insertion, not the derived mathematical meaning of Guessing an Intermediate Point. Variable interpolation is also called variable substitution, but we don't want you to confuse interpolation with the substitution operator, which is introduced in the next section.

the following statements in **myecho** (on the left) would produce the output on the right:

Statement	Output	
print "@ARGV\n";	a b c d	(followed by a newline)
print @ARGV;	abcd	(no newline)
print ´@ARGV\n´;	@ARGV\n	(literally!)

In a shell, you can interpolate variables just about anywhere, except within single quotes. In Perl, variables (and \n-ish things) are interpolated only in certain locations, double quotes being the prototypical place. A string enclosed by backticks does variable and backslash interpolation just like double quotes. The difference between that and double quotes is the extra step of executing the string as a command and then using the output of that command as the value:

```
$lines = `wc -l $filename`;
```

(Note: if you simply want to run a system command without redirecting any of its input or output, use the **system( )** function—see Chapter Four, *Functions*.)

Interpolations can also happen inside pattern matches, as we'll see in the next section.

If the characters following the variable reference look like they could be part of the variable name, you must enclose the variable name in curly braces, as in:

```
/the merry ${mo}nth of May/;    # Interpolates $mo,
                       # followed by "nth".
```

Without the braces, the variable **$month** would be interpolated instead.

Pattern Matching

Perl has two pattern matching operators, known as **m//** and **s///**—the match operator and the substitution operator. (Any non-alphanumeric character may be used in place of the slashes.) The **m//** operator is also known as the // operator because the **m** is optional if slashes are used for the delimiter. (And also because in many other UNIX programs, slashes are the *only* available delimiter.) The **m//** operator searches through a string for a pattern (specified between the delimiters) and returns either true or false depending on whether the string matches (contains the pattern). The **s///** operator does the same thing, but in addition replaces that portion of the string matched with something else, specified between the second and third delimiters.

The patterns themselves are specified using **regular expressions**. You are probably already familiar with regular expressions through your use of other UNIX tools such as *sed* or *vi*, but you should look carefully at this list in any case, since Perl recognizes a superset of nearly every other regular expression anyway):

.	Matches any character except newline
[a–z0–9]	Matches any single character of set
[^a–z0–9]	Matches any single character *not* in set
\d	Matches a digit, same as [0–9]
\D	Matches a non-digit, same as [^0–9]
\w	Matches an alphanumeric (word) character [a–zA–Z0–9_]
\W	Matches a non-word character [^a–zA–Z0–9_]
\s	Matches a whitespace char (space, tab, newline...)
\S	Matches a non-whitespace character
\n	Matches a newline
\r	Matches a return
\t	Matches a tab
\f	Matches a formfeed
\b	Matches a backspace (inside [ ] only)
\0	Matches a null character
\000	Also matches a null character because...
\nnn	Matches an ASCII character of that octal value
\xnn	Matches an ASCII character of that hexadecimal value
\cX	Matches an ASCII control character
\metachar	Matches the character itself (\\|, \\., *...)
(abc)	Remembers the match for later backreferences
\1	Matches whatever first of parens matched
\2	Matches whatever second set of parens matched
\3	and so on...
x?	Matches 0 or 1 x's, where *x* is any of above
x*	Matches 0 or more x's
x+	Matches 1 or more x's
x{m,n}	Matches at least *m* x's but no more than *n*
abc	Matches all of a, b, and c in order
fee|fie|foe	Matches one of fee, fie, or foe
\b	Matches a word boundary (outside [ ] only)
\B	Matches a non-word boundary
^	Anchors match to the beginning of a line or string
$	Anchors match to the end of a line or string

Unlike some implementations of regular expressions, Perl does not want you to put a backslash in front of the parentheses, the brackets, or the vertical bar to get their special meanings. Quite the contrary—you put a backslash in front of them to get their ordinary meanings. (This makes a great deal of sense, because you'll use the special meanings much more often, and it helps prevent that dreaded disease, *backslashitis*. It also makes it fairly easy to quote metacharacters, as we'll see in a moment.) Perl also has special abbreviations for digits, alphanumerics, and whitespace characters.

Like other implementations of regular expressions, when you match a pattern with parentheses, you can then use any of \1, \2, \3, ... later in the pattern to refer to a previously matched set of parentheses (where the digit counts left parentheses starting from the left of the pattern). For this reason, \1 and so on are called backreferences. Note that a backreference refers to what the parentheses actually matched, not just to the pattern contained by the parentheses. The backreference must match exactly the same sequence of characters. If you'll recall the **baregrep** program earlier in this chapter, we could invoke it like this:

```
baregrep ´(\w+)\s*=\s*\1´ *.c
```

and it would print out all the lines of all your C files that assign a variable to itself, like **hump = hump**. (It would also match **hum = ump**. Can you guess why? Hint: \b can be used to match word boundaries.)

The part of the matched string that those parentheses enclose is called a substring. Many languages allow you to have backreferences to substrings in your patterns or replacements, but Perl goes one step further. After a pattern has been successfully matched, any substrings live on in the special Perl variables $1, $2, $3, etc. These are numbered just like the corresponding backreferences. Using these variables is preferable to using the corresponding backreferences (except in the pattern match itself, since they haven't been created yet). So, for example, expect to see $1, $2, etc. in place of \1 or \2 in the replacement string of a substitution.

We mentioned in the previous section that patterns are subject to variable interpolation just like double-quoted strings.
Within a pattern, variable interpolation happens as long as the $ doesn't look like an end-of-string anchor:

```
/the merry month of $mo/;   # This interpolates $mo.
/the merry month of May$/;  # But this matches at end of line.
```

Likewise, in substitutions, you can do variable interpolation in both the pattern and in the replacement:

```
s/$monthname/$monthnum/;    # Turn April into 4, or some such.
s/\r\n$/\n/;                # Turn CRLF into LF at end of line.
s/(\S+)\s+(\S+)/$2 $1/;     # Swap first two words.
```

Within a pattern, a variable is interpolated *before* the pattern is compiled, so the regular expression parser doesn't see the variable reference, but only the string after all interpolations have taken place. Thus, any metacharacters in the variable's value will be interpreted as metacharacters in the resulting pattern. To protect any metacharacters in the variable from interpretation, it suffices to insert a backslash before any non-alphanumeric characters in the string, like this:

```
$string =~ s/(\W)/\\$1/g;
/a pattern containing a $string to be interpreted literally/;
```

The backslash is itself backslashed to prevent its interpretation as a metacharacter. The **g** modifier on the substitution causes it to match "globally"—that is, as many times as possible within the string. You'll note that variable interpolation in the replacement section happens each time the pattern matches within a string. If it didn't, the **$1** in this construct wouldn't work right.

Let's talk a bit more about the use of parentheses in matching, because they are near and dear to the heart of Perl. Suppose you are parsing a news article or mail message, and want to find the subject line, which looks like this:

```
Subject: You're Fired for Gross Laziness!!!
```

If that line is in **$_**, and you say:

```
if (/^Subject: (.*)/) {
    $subject = $1;
}
```

then **$subject** will end up with:

```
"You're Fired for Gross Laziness!!!"
```

Making use of the "logical AND" operator **&&**, this pattern match can be written more succinctly (and lazily) as:

```
/^Subject: (.*)/ && ($subject = $1);
```

Since it's a short-circuit operator, the **&&** operator is exactly equivalent to an **if**. (If this use of **&&** bothers you greatly, just think of the way it is in English when you say, "Feed me artichokes **and** I'll love you forever!" It means the same thing as "**If** you feed me artichokes, I'll love you forever!" Likewise, the "logical OR" operator **||** corresponds to "Feed me artichokes **or** I'll walk out on you!" That means the same thing as "**Unless** you feed me artichokes, I'll walk out on you!")

Let's continue parsing the same message we were parsing before. Suppose you want to find the date on which the message was sent. The line in **$_** currently contains:

```
Date: 1 Apr 91 12:34:56 GMT
```

so you might make use of **\d** (match a digit) and **\w** (match an alphanumeric) to parse out the line in this manner:

```
/^Date: (\d+) (\w+) (\d+) (\d+):(\d+):(\d+) (.*)$/;
$mday     = $1;         # gets "1"
$month    = $2;         # gets "Apr"
$year     = $3;         # gets "91"
$hour     = $4;         # gets "12"
$minute   = $5;         # gets "34"
$second   = $6;         # gets "56"
$timezone = $7;         # gets "GMT"
```

The ^ at the front says that the **Date:** must match at the beginning of the string—any occurrence of **Date:** in the middle of the string doesn't count. The **$** at the end says that the previous field must match all the way up to the end of the string, or to a newline, if there is one. (In this case, the **$** is actually unnecessary because the **.*** will match all the characters it can find up to the end of the string or to a newline, so the **$** is redundant, and superfluous, and unneeded. But it doesn't hurt to put it.)

Suppose you nested your parentheses thus:

```
/^Date: ((\d+) (\w+) (\d+)) ((\d+):(\d+):(\d+)) (.*)$/;
$date     = $1;         # gets "1 Apr 91"
$mday     = $2;         # gets "1"
$month    = $3;         # gets "Apr"
$year     = $4;         # gets "91"
$time     = $5;         # gets "12:34:56"
$hour     = $6;         # gets "12"
$minute   = $7;         # gets "34"
$second   = $8;         # gets "56"
$timezone = $9;         # gets "GMT"
```

Remember that the paren pairs are numbered by counting left parens from the left end of the pattern, so a particular stretch of string can end up as part of more than one substring. In many implementations of regular expressions (and in some older versions of Perl), you're limited to 9 pairs of parentheses. In recent versions of Perl you may have as many as you like. The variable **$10** refers to the 10th substring, **$11** to the 11th, and so on. A backreference like **\10** can be used within the pattern as long as there actually are that many paren pairs before it—otherwise it will be interpreted like **\010**, a backspace. If you have many fields, it may be more efficient to use the **split** or **unpack** functions.

There are several other magical variables that are set when you do a pattern match. The **$&** variable ends up containing the text of what you matched, as if you put a single set of parens around the whole pattern and then said **$1**. The $` variable holds everything before the match, and $´ holds everything after the matched string. The values can of course be null if the match occurs at the front or end of the string, such as when you anchor the search with ^ or $.

We mentioned that some operators act differently if you use them in an array context instead of a scalar context. The pattern matching operator is one of these. If you say:

```
@fields = /^Date: (\d+) (\w+) (\d+) (\d+):(\d+):(\d+) (.*)$/;
```

then the **@fields** array gets the substrings that would ordinarily go to **$1** through **$7**, and **$1** through **$7** aren't set (nor are **$&** et al). It can actually be quite readable (and is considered Good Perl Style) to assign the substrings to a list of named variables like this:

```
($mday, $month, $year, $hour, $minute, $second, $timezone) =
    /^Date: (\d+) (\w+) (\d+) (\d+):(\d+):(\d+) (.*)$/;
```

Note that the pattern match is examining the default variable **$_**. To tie the pattern match to some other variable, use the =~ operator, which binds more tightly (is higher precedence) than assignment:

```
($mday, $month, $year, $hour, $minute, $second, $timezone) =
    $date =~ /^Date: (\d+) (\w+) (\d+) (\d+):(\d+):(\d+) (.*)$/;
```

Associative Arrays

The final topic we'll cover in this chapter is in some ways the most important, because until you learn to think in terms of associative arrays, you aren't thinking in Perl. With associative arrays you can construct many of the recursive data types that seem to be missing from Perl, such as trees.

A normal array lets you look up entries using small numbers as the subscript. An associative array is just the same except that you can look up entries using arbitrary strings. Since the entries you're looking up can also be strings, you can associate any pair of arbitrary strings this way—which is why they're called associative arrays.

An associative array value is a list value like a normal array, except that instead of single values that are indexed by position, you have pairs of values that are indexed by the first element of each pair, which is called the key. Internally, the keys are stored in a hash table, so lookups are always very fast regardless of how many entries are in the array.

The entire array is denoted by prefixing the identifier with a %, like this:

```
%longday = (
    ´Mon´,  ´Monday´,
    ´Tue´,  ´Tuesday´,
    ´Wed´,  ´Wednesday´,
    ´Thu´,  ´Thursday´,
    ´Fri´,  ´Friday´,
    ´Sat´,  ´Saturday´,
    ´Sun´,  ´Sunday´,
);
```

Notice that an associative array value can be represented as pairs of values, using the normal list notation. If you evaluate %longday in an array context, you'll get the same pairs back out, but probably in a different order, because they're returned in the (fairly random) order that the hash table stores them.

Subscripting an associative array is just like subscripting a normal array, except that you use curly braces instead of square brackets, since you're doing something fancier:

```
$longday = $longday{ substr($date,0,3) };
$home = $ENV{´HOME´};
$SIG{´HUP´} = ´IGNORE´;
```

In the first line, note that the $longday scalar variable is unrelated to the $long-day{} array reference, although both are used in that first line. The last two lines refer to two associative arrays that are built into Perl: %ENV lets you read and set environment variables, and %SIG lets you set signal handlers for named signals.

Associative arrays can be used to map any set of strings to any other set of strings (or numbers, or Boolean values). Thus, they tend to fill the role that pointers fill in other languages. Since a string can be broken up into substrings, a string might contain symbolic pointers to many other items.

Suppose you wanted to keep track of a tree of file dependencies, such as which files in a directory include which other files. You could use the following Perl script:

```
#!/usr/bin/perl

# First extract the include lines from each file.

foreach $file (@ARGV) {
    open(FILE, $file) || warn "Can´t open $file: $!\n";
    while (<FILE>) {
        if (/^#include\s+[´"<]([^´">]*)[´">]/) {
```

```
            $included = $1;
            $includes{$file} .= $included . ´ ´;
        }
    }
}

# Now print them out in sorted order.

foreach $target (sort keys(%includes)) {
    $dependencies = $includes{$target};
    foreach $dependency (split(/ /, $dependencies)) {
        print "$target: $dependency\n";
    }
}
```

This program doesn't really do anything fancy, once you look at it a bit. The first loop looks at each file, and finds all the lines that look like one or the other of these lines:

```
#include "filename"
#include <filename>
```

The regular expression uses \s+ to skip the whitespace between the "include" and the following delimiter. It then uses the character class, ["<], to skip the opening delimiter itself. After that, all we have to do is use parentheses to remember all the non-delimiters, represented by the complemented character class, [^">]. The final character class matching the final delimiter is actually unnecessary, since the * matches as many items as possible.

Once we've extracted the filename from the line, we merely append it (using the string concatenation assignment operator, .=) to the associative array element whose key is the filename. We also append a space as a delimiter.

In the second loop, we use the **keys()** function to produce a list of the keys of the associative array, so that we can process the array elements in the order desired. The idiom:

```
foreach $key (sort keys(%arrayname)) { ...
```

is frequently seen in Perl scripts that wish to iterate over all the elements of an associative array, since the **keys()** function returns the keys in a haphazard order. Note that once you have the key as the loop variable, you can always get back to the associated value by subscripting back into the associative array.

This particular problem could have been solved by merely appending to a normal array and sorting that, but suppose you had wanted the inverse relationship, namely, which files are included by a particular file? To solve that problem, all you need to do is swap the meanings of the keys and the values. Instead of:

```
$includes{$file} .= $included . ´ ´;
```

you would have said:

```
$includes{$included} .= $file . ´ ´;
```

(and you also would have changed the final loop to print out that array instead.)

Another thing to note about this example is that there is no reason why the same filename might not have been both an includer and an includee. If so, the filename can be thought of as a symbolic pointer in a tree structure, where each array entry is a node in the tree, and the value of the node may refer to the key of another node. This example did not process the array as a tree, but Chapter Two, *Practical Programming*, will provide examples of this and other uses of associative arrays.

Whenever you find yourself writing a loop to scan a normal array for some value, you can usually replace it with an associative array lookup. It'll be more concise, and it will run faster. And it's the Perl Way. Learn to make frequent use of this powerful feature.

2

Practical Programming

Lines and Paragraphs
Tabular Data
Fixed-length Records and Fields
Abstraction
Summing Up

In this chapter, we will show you how Perl can be used on some practical, every-day problems. Many of these problems—especially those early in the chapter—can also be solved with *sed* or *awk*, but many of the solutions benefit from unique features of Perl. If you already know *sed* or *awk*, you will see how to do some of the same things more easily in Perl.

Lines and Paragraphs

Perl is mostly about text processing, so let's process some text. Imagine for a moment that you are a publisher, and have received the following text, which contains some spelling errors. The text is actually from the end of the book of Job (pronounced to rhyme with robe).

```
After Job had prayed for his freinds, the Lord made him pros-
perous again and gave him twice as much as he had before.  All
his brothers and sisters and everyone who had known him before
came and ate with him in his house.  They comforted and consoled
```

> him over all the trouble teh Lord had brought upon him, and each
> one gave him a peice of silver and a gold ring.
>
> The Lord blessed the latter part of Job´s life more than the
> first. He had fourteen thousand sheep, six thousand camels,
> a thousand yoke of oxen, and a thousand donkeys. And he also
> had seven sons and three daughters. The first daughter was
> named Dove, the second Cinnamon and the third Eyeshadow Kit.
> Nowhere in all the land were there found women as beautiful as
> Job´s daughters, and their father granted them an inheritance
> along with their brothers.
>
> After this, Job lived a hundred and forty years; he saw his
> children and their children to teh fourth generation. And so
> he died, old and full of years.[14]

You could, of course, just go in with an editor and fix the errors, but you might miss some of them. If there are some words that are misspelled consistently, it might be better to write a program to find them all, like this program does:

```
#!/usr/bin/perl
while (<>) {
    print if /peice/;
    print if /freind/;
    print if /teh/;
}
```

This program loops over all the lines of the input files, and puts each line into the $_ variable. Then each pattern match within the loop examines $_ to see if the current line should be printed. If you call this program *check*, and if the file containing the text is called **job**, you could say:

    check job

and it would print out these lines:

> After Job had prayed for his freinds, the Lord made him pros—
> him over all the trouble teh Lord had brought upon him, and each
> one gave him a peice of silver and a gold ring.
> children and their children to teh fourth generation. And so

That's all well and good, but sometimes you need to get fancier with your patterns. You have the full power of regular expressions at your disposal (see the section "Regular Expressions" in Chapter 3, *The Gory Details*). For example,

---

[14] Scripture taken from the HOLY BIBLE, NEW INTERNATIONAL VERSION, Copyright © 1973, 1978, 1984 International Bible Society. Used by permission of Zondervan Bible Publishers. Errors have been introduced only for didactic purposes and are not in the original text. Some names have been rendered into English.

you could combine the searches above into one search using the | character to express **alternation** and parentheses to express **grouping**:

```
print if /(p|fr)ei(ce|nd)|teh/;
```

This will also match "peind" and "freice," but that shouldn't be much of a problem. (However, we don't recommend that you combine patterns unnecessarily—it may be more concise but it's generally less readable and may run more slowly.) Another more useful regular expression might be **/friends?/**, which uses the **?** metacharacter to indicate that the **s** is optional—that is, the word may be either singular or plural.

Now, suppose you searched for the word "came," as in this program:

```
#!/usr/bin/perl
while (<>) {
    print if /came/;
}
```

You would find the following lines:

```
before came and ate with him in his house.  They comforted and
first.  He had fourteen thousand sheep, six thousand camels,
```

As you can see, some camels have wandered in where they don't belong. You wanted "came" to match a whole word, and it matched a partial word. To get around this, you can use the character sequence \b any place you want to match a word boundary. So your program should have said:

```
#!/usr/bin/perl
while (<>) {
    print if /\bcame\b/;
}
```

Similarly, you can use the ˆ character to force a match only at the beginning of the line, and the $ character to force a match only at the end of the line.

Command-line Switches

At this point, we would like to introduce some labor-saving devices. The **check** program above can also be written like this:

```
#!/usr/bin/perl -n
print if /\bcame\b/;
```

The **−n** makes Perl supply the while loop implicitly, much like the *awk* and *sed* programs automatically iterate over their lines of input. Written as a UNIX command, the program above then becomes:

```
perl −n −e 'print if /\bcame\b/' job
```

or, bundling the switches together:

```
perl −ne 'print if /\bcame\b/' job
```

This method of invocation is desirable within a shell script because you don't have to store the program off in some other file that might get lost. It's still a *check* program at heart, but you haven't even given it a name—it's an anonymous program. We'll be using this notation off and on throughout the book, so whenever you see an example starting with the word "perl," you'll know that it's just a way of writing an anonymous program.

The **−n** switch is useful when you want to scan large amounts of input and throw most of it away. Sometimes, however, you want to scan large amounts of input and keep most of it. For this purpose, there is a **−p** switch, which works just like **−n**, but also prints out each line at the end of the loop. Since our **meow** program of Chapter 1 did nothing but print out its lines, we could have written it simply as:

```
perl −pe '' Abel Baker Charlie
```

The **−n** and **−p** switches are called "command-line switches" because they are typically used on the command line, as in the examples above. You'll note that we also used a switch on the **#!** line above, though that's not strictly a command line. If your machine supports the **#!** notation, you are allowed to put a single switch or bundle of switches there, but no more than one.

The **−p** switch is useful in combination with the **−i** switch, which allows you to easily edit files in place. It just takes any output that would be sent to the **STDOUT** filehandle and redirects it back to the filename that the **<>** symbol is currently inputting from. If there is anything after the **−i** switch, it is used as an extension in renaming the original file to make a backup file. See the examples in the next section.

Substitution

Back to our publishing job, the truly lazy programmer will not just wish to find the spelling errors, but also to correct them automatically. The substitution command will do the trick; it works just like the equivalent command in *sed*, except that it recognizes Perl's fuller set of regular expressions:

```
#!/usr/bin/perl -p
s/\bfreind\b/friend/g;
s/\bpeice\b/piece/g;
s/\bteh\b/the/g;
```

If you called this program **fix**, you would invoke it like this:

```
fix job >job.new
```

Note that we use the **-p** switch here because we want to print out all the lines instead of just some of them. The lines are printed to **STDOUT**, so it would be up to the person who invokes the program to redirect the output to the desired location. In this case, the old file keeps the name **job**, and the fixed file is called **job.new**. If you want, you can use the **-i** switch we mentioned earlier to let someone edit files in place, like this:

```
#!/usr/bin/perl -pi.old
s/\bfreind\b/friend/g;
s/\bpeice\b/piece/g;
s/\bteh\b/the/g;
```

Then the command would be:

```
fix job
```

which puts the fixed version back under the name **job**, renaming the original file from **job** to **job.old**. This switch avoids the "shell wrapper" required with *sed* or *awk*.

The **g** modifier on each substitution above causes a "global" substitution. That is, it will replace all the occurrences on the line instead of just the first one. On our sample input it didn't matter, because there was only one occurrence of each word per line, but it's best to write bulletproof code *before* the shooting starts.

Now, you may have noticed that whoever typed in our sample text tended to confuse the order of "e" and "i"—a common failing. In large measure, learning to program consists of learning to generalize, so it would be nice if there was a way to correct the spelling via a general rule. This is what regular expressions are for. You can easily write rules that say things such as "i before e, except after c." Expressed as a substitution, it would look like this statement:

```
s/([^c])ei/$1ie/g;
```

This switches "ei" to "ie" but only if the whole pattern matches. Since the first thing it wants to match is [^c], which matches any character *except* c, it will fix both "freind" and "peice." Your English teacher would be proud of you. Note, however, that the substitution replaces *everything* that matched, so you have to be careful to plug the first character, whatever it was, back into the replacement side of the substitution. The pattern remembers the character by using parentheses, and recalls the character on the replacement side using **$1**. Don't forget to do this, or you'll turn "freind" into "fiend"!

Now, as with most generalizations, this one has some exceptions. To use our new rule on our sample text, we'd actually have to say:

```
#!/usr/bin/perl -p
s/([^c])ei/$1ie/g;
s/\bthier\b/their/g;
```

The second substitution undoes some of what the first substitution does. In this case, it comes out to the same number of rules as explicitly searching for /**freind**/ and /**peice**/, but often it's faster to do the most general transformations first, and then clean up the exceptions.

Words versus Lines versus Paragraphs

You'll note a minor problem with the way we've been doing things. The first line of our sample text was hyphenated, so that it was split over two lines. Had we been searching for "prosperous," we would not have found it, because our searches were searching each line separately. For this and other reasons, you may prefer to process your file one paragraph at a time rather than one line at a time. This is easily done when paragraphs are separated by a blank line, simply by setting the input record separator to the null string.[15] The input record separator is stored in the special variable $/ (which is easy to remember because the / character is used to separate lines when you're quoting poetry).

```
#!/usr/bin/perl
$/ = "";                      # Enable paragraph mode.
$* = 1;                       # Enable multi-line patterns.
while (<>) {
    s/-\n//g;                 # Dehyphenate hyphenations.
    print if /\bprosperous\b/;
}
```

This program prints out any *paragraph* that contains the word "prosperous." Each time through the loop, $_ contains an entire paragraph, including all embedded newlines. The substitution merely deletes any line-ending hyphen and its associated newline. $* is a special variable that, if set to a non-zero value,

---

[15] The input record separator normally is a newline, so you get lines that are terminated with newlines. You can set it to some other character than newline to get lines terminated with that character instead. Setting the input record separator to the null string is a special case, and (as in *awk*) enables paragraph mode on input.

enables pattern matches to work on strings with embedded newlines. Otherwise, Perl will assume that pattern matches are being done on strings that contain a single line, and optimize away certain matches involving the ˆ and $ characters. We didn't use those particular characters here, but it's a good idea to get in the habit of setting $* whenever you're matching a multi-line string.

Sometimes you want to process individual words. You can easily accomplish this by reading a paragraph at a time, massaging the $_ string a bit, and then splitting the string into a list of separate words. The program below prints a count of how many times each word occurs in the text:

```
#!/usr/bin/perl
$/ = "";                        # Enable paragraph mode.
$* = 1;                         # Enable multi-line patterns.

# Now read each paragraph and split into words.  Record each
# instance of a word in the %wordcount associative array.

while (<>) {
    s/-\n//g;                   # Dehyphenate hyphenations.
    tr/A-Z/a-z/;                # Canonicalize to lowercase.
    @words = split(/\W*\s+\W*/, $_);
    foreach $word (@words) {
        $wordcount{$word}++;    # Increment the entry.
    }
}

# Now print out all the entries in the %wordcount array.

foreach $word (sort keys(%wordcount)) {
    printf "%20s %d\n", $word, $wordcount{$word};
}
```

When run using our sample text for input, this produces a listing of 104 words:

```
       a 5
   after 2
   again 1
     all 3
   along 1
    also 1
      an 1
     and 16
      . . .
     who 1
    with 2
   women 1
   years 2
    yoke 1
```

There are a couple of tricky things in the program. The **tr///** function changes every letter to lowercase so that we don't end up with separate entries for "And"

and "and." The **split()** function searches for each sequence of characters separating words. Each sequence is required to have at least one whitespace character (\s+), surrounded by zero or more non-word characters (\W*). This prevents the program from breaking up words like "Job's" while deleting those single quotes not used as apostrophes. This is a fairly complicated **split()** pattern—most of the time you'll be splitting on a single character or on simple whitespace. To split on a comma, for instance, the pattern would merely be /,/. To split on whitespace, you can use the form:

```
@result = split(´ ´, $_);
```

which is special-cased to split on contiguous whitespace characters. It's equivalent to:

```
@result = split(/\s+/, $_);
```

except that it also ignores any leading whitespace.

Back to our program, when we autoincrement **$wordcount{$word}**, we're taking advantage of the fact that array values spring into existence as necessary with a 0 value. New keys are added to the **%wordcount** array only when a word is seen for the first time. Subsequent instances of the word merely increment the already existing entry. In the final loop, we use the **keys()** function to recall all the words we saw from the **%wordcount** array. By the nature of associative arrays, any list returned by the **keys()** function contains only unique keys. The only remaining task is to sort the words into the right order and print the information for each word. The **sort()** function takes a list as an argument and sorts it alphabetically, returning the sorted list, so we can just shove it in as the LIST argument of the **foreach** loop.

The **printf()** function works much like the corresponding function in C or *awk*. The first argument is a format string that says how to print out the rest of the arguments. In this case, the format string says that we want to print a string 20 characters long (right-justified), followed by a space, followed by a decimal number, followed by a newline. (To avoid boring the C and *awk* hackers, we won't list all the possible format specifiers here, but if you want to refer to them now, see the discussion of the **sprintf()** function in Chapter 4, *Functions*.)

Now it's a little known fact that Job's economic recovery was due in part to his use of Perl to manage his database. The following data was found recently on a laser-etched clay tablet:

```
Sheep:14023:Lightning:0.29:256
Camels:5972:Chaldeans:3.79:1279
Oxen:2016:Sabeans:4.95:1008
Donkeys:1001:Sabeans:0.99:1001
Sons:7:Tornadoes:22.00:13
Daughters:3:Tornadoes:19.95:37
```

Each line of a tabular file contains a set of fields that are separated by a delimiter, a colon in this case. A well-formed table will generally have a field (or combination of fields) that can be considered to be the key field, and each entry should be uniquely identified by its key. In this table, the key field is the first field. By archeological reconstruction it has been determined that the fields in this table represented, respectively, the name of the asset, the current head count, the kind of insurance policy for the asset, the annual premium for the insurance (per beastie), and the number of servants allocated to manage the asset.

Formatting a Report

As should be obvious, Job's first problem was that his database was a bit too compact to read easily. So his first program was to print out a nicely formatted report. The report also derives a couple of fields from the raw data. This program makes use of the formatting capabilities of Perl, which you haven't seen yet.

```perl
#!/usr/bin/perl

    # Set configuration parameters.

$ANNUAL_PAY_RATE = 52 * 5;       # That's 5 shekels per week.

    # First open my database.  Complain if unable.

open(STUFF, "stuff") || die "Can't open stuff: $!\n";

    # Now process each line.

while (<STUFF>) {

    # Split the record into its fields.

    ($beastie, $noses, $hazard, $premium, $servants)
```

```
      = split(/:/, $_);

   # Derive some fields.

   $totprem = $premium * $noses;
   $cost = $totprem + $servants * $ANNUAL_PAY_RATE;

   # Write a formatted record to STDOUT.

   write;
}
exit;


##############################################################

   # Here is the top of form format, with column headings.

format STDOUT_TOP =
                        Job´s Stuff, Inc.
Beastie      Nose Insured       Premium    Servants  Total Est.
Name         Count Against    Each    Total          Yearly Cost
_____      _____ _____    ____   _____   _____  _____

.

   # Here is the format for each record.

format STDOUT =
@<<<<<<<< @#### @<<<<<<<<<@#.## @####.##  @>>>>>>  @#######.##
$beastie, $noses,$hazard,$premium,$totprem,$servants,$cost

.
```

When run, the program produces the following report:

```
                        Job´s Stuff, Inc.
Beastie      Nose Insured       Premium    Servants  Total Est.
Name         Count Against    Each    Total          Yearly Cost
_____      _____ _____    ____   _____   _____  _____

Sheep       14023 Lightning  0.29  4066.67     256    70626.67
Camels       5972 Chaldeans  3.79 22633.88    1279   355173.88
Oxen         2016 Sabeans    4.95  9979.20    1008   272059.20
Donkeys      1001 Sabeans    0.99   990.99    1001   261250.99
Sons            7 Tornadoes 22.00   154.00      13     3534.00
Daughters       3 Tornadoes 19.95    59.85      37     9679.85
```

There are two formats specified for the write function in this program. The **STDOUT** format is printed every time the write function is called. The **STDOUT_TOP** format is printed only when a new page is needed. (It is possible to bind other format names to an output filehandle—see $^ and $˜ in the section "Special Variables" in Chapter 3.)

The formats specify "picture" lines containing fields that are to be filled in with the values of the corresponding variables on the next line. There must be the same number of list elements as there were fields. (If a picture line contains no fields, it is printed as is, and the line listing the variables should be omitted.) Fields start with the @ character, and then use the < character to specify left justification, the > character to specify right justification, and the # and . characters to specify a numeric format. (See the section "Formats" in Chapter 3 for ways to do centered fields, filled text, page numbering, and so forth.)

Loading a Table into an Associative Array

Sometimes it's handy to load a table into an associative array so that it's available for doing lookups. System administrators often do this with the *letc/passwd* file to avoid scanning the file repeatedly when listing the owners of processes or files. Job had an interactive program that would print out letters to his insurance companies. It's natural that the key field of a table should load right into the key of an associative array.

```
#!/usr/bin/perl

    # First open my database.  Complain if unable.

open(STUFF, "stuff") || die "Can't open stuff: $!\n";

    # Open the clay tablet printer.

open(CTP, ">/dev/ctp") || die "Can't open /dev/ctp: $!\n";

    # Now load stuff into associative array.

while (<STUFF>) {
    ($beastie,$remainder) = split(/:/, $_, 2);
    $beastie =~ tr/A-Z/a-z/;
    $stuff{$beastie} = $remainder;
}

close STUFF;

    # Now loop forever, printing out letters on demand.

while (1) {

    # Find out what to do next.

    print "Letter for which beastie: ";
    chop($beastie = <STDIN>);
    last unless $beastie;
```

```
    # Get the information handy for selected beastie.

    ($noses, $hazard, $premium) = split(/:/, $stuff{$beastie});
    $payment = $premium * $noses;

    # Now print out the letter.

    print CTP <<"EndOfLetter";
Dear Shekelgrubbers:

    Please find enclosed $payment shekels in payment of the
annual premium for insuring $noses of my $beastie against
$hazard.

                         Sincerely,
                           Job

Quote of the day:
    "You can lead a camel to water, but you can't make
    it stink (any worse than it already does)."
EndOfLetter

    print CTP "\f";            # Eject the clay tablet.
}
```

There are several things you haven't seen before. The first **split()** function has a third argument that says how many fields to split into. If it were not supplied, **$remainder** would receive only the second field, instead of all the rest of the fields.

The final loop would be an infinite loop except that there is a **last** statement in the middle that allows the operator to bomb out of the program when desired. One often finds loops that exit from the middle when there is some overhead associated with getting the next value to test. In this case, the program has to prompt for the next answer and input it.

The line that inputs the answer makes use of a common idiom in Perl. A **chop** around an assignment statement is equivalent to doing the assignment and then chopping the variable assigned to.

The second **split()** produces 4 values, but only 3 are assigned in the list of variables. The final value is simply discarded by Perl.

Finally, there is a fancy quoting mechanism you haven't seen yet, unless you're a shell programmer. The construct beginning with **<<"EndOfLetter"** and ending with the line containing the string **EndOfLetter** is nothing more nor less than an ordinary double-quoted string. Variable interpolation happens just as in an ordinary double-quoted string. The only difference is that a line-oriented delimiter has been substituted for the double quotes. Thus, such a string can contain both single and double quotes. All you have to do is select a delimiting string that doesn't appear by itself on a line within the text. The final delimiter must be flush against the left margin.

There is a corresponding line-oriented single-quoting mechanism. Merely put single quotes around the initial identifier instead of double quotes.

Inverting on a Secondary Key

Job's database was nicely arranged for answering questions like "What do you know about camels?" But occasionally someone would ask an inside-out question like, "Which beasties are insured against Sabeans?" To answer this, Job needed to invert his database on the hazard field. Now the hazard of doing this is that there is more than one record with the same hazard, so there isn't a unique key any more. Job solved the problem by clever use of the string concatenation operator.

```
#!/usr/bin/perl

    # First open my database.  Complain if unable.

open(STUFF, "stuff") || die "Can't open stuff: $!\n";

    # Load inverted array.

while (<STUFF>) {

    # Split the record into its fields.

    ($beastie, $noses, $hazard, $premium, $servants)
        = split(/:/, $_);

    # Append to current list.  (Note .= assignment operator.)

    $beastie_list{$hazard} .= $beastie . ",";
}

    # Now print the inverted entries out.

foreach $hazard (sort keys(%beastie_list)) {
    chop($beastie_list{$hazard});        # Delete final comma.
    print $hazard;
    print " " x (16 - length($hazard));  # "tab" to column 16.
    print $beastie_list{$hazard}, "\n";
}
```

This program prints out the following report:

```
Chaldeans      Camels
Lightning      Sheep
Sabeans        Oxen,Donkeys
Tornadoes      Sons,Daughters
```

There is one programming trick in this script that we should point out. The items in each beastie list need to be separated by commas. The ordinary way to do that would be to test **$beastie_list{$hazard}** to see if it's already defined, and insert a comma only if one is needed (see the **defined( )** function in Chapter 4, *Functions*). Job has chosen instead to always append a comma, as if it were a field terminator rather than a separator. Then, when all the lists are finished, he just chops the extra commas off each list before printing it.

Fixed-length Records and Fields

Up till now, we've been using nothing but variable-length records and fields, even when dealing with tabular data. Variable-length items are exceedingly handy to deal with because you don't have to worry (very much) about something getting too large and overflowing the storage allocated for it. You just move the delimiters over to make room. Occasionally, however, you'll need to deal with fixed-length data, for any of several reasons. Delimited data has the disadvantage that the delimiters must be scanned for. And for very long files, it can become rather expensive to simply "move the delimiters over." When data is being stored into or sent through a very expensive medium, it may be considered too costly to even store the delimiters that are necessary to separate variable-length data. Numeric fields are often stored compactly as **binary** data, which can mimic delimiters and delude your program into splitting one real field into two or more bogus fields. Finally, fixed-length records in a file can be located easily by multiplying the record number by the record length, and seeking directly to the location of the record before reading it, like this:

```
$byteoffset = $recordwanted * $recordsize;
seek(REL, $byteoffset, 0)        || die "Can't find rec: $!\n";
read(REL, $record, $recordsize)  || die "Can't read rec: $!\n";
```

This can be handy when you have a table that is naturally keyed by small consecutive integers. (These are variously called "relative," "direct-access," or "random-access" files.) Every filehandle keeps track of where in the file the next input or output is supposed to happen. The **seek( )** function positions the filehandle to the desired location (**$byteoffset** in this case), so that the front of the file doesn't need to be read or written to get to the record desired. Once the filehandle has been positioned at the beginning of the record desired, a **read( )** function fetches the record by getting the next **$recordsize** bytes into the variable **$record**.

(Fixed-length records can be written in the same way, but there's no special function to do it, since our old friend the **print** operator is perfectly capable of writing either fixed-length or variable-length data.)

The **read( )** function returns false at the end of the file, so a file of fixed-length records can be stepped through like this:

```
$recnum = 0;
while (read(REL, $record, $recordsize)) {
    ...                     # Process the record.
    $recnum++;
}
```

The **$recnum** variable is incremented at the end of the loop so that the first record is considered to be at offset 0 in the file. Using C's handy three-part **for** loop, which Perl also supports, this could be written as:

```
for ($recnum = 0; read(REL, $record, $recordsize); $recnum++) {
    ...                     # Process the record.
}
```

The three parts are separated by semicolons. The first part is the initialization. The second part is the conditional for the implied **while** loop, and the third part is the code to be executed at the end of the loop.

After Job's great calamity, he became a little less patient than he had been (which is partly why he became a better programmer, of course.) He wanted to find out the status of his beasties without waiting for a messenger to run back and forth. So he hired a carrier pigeon service to carry digital clay tablets back and forth to his beastie keepers. Each tablet would say how many of a particular kind of beastie were gained or lost.

Now it's well known that the bandwidth of CTBCPP[16] is rather limited, but it's the best Job could do at the time. He was restricted to exactly 8 bytes per clay tablet. As each pigeon came in, it would drop its record into a tiny clay tablet reader, which the program would read. (The last pigeon was specially trained to feed an end-of-file tablet into the reader.) Each pigeon would then hop over to the clay tablet writer to take an acknowledgement back to the beastie keepers.

The first thing you'll note is that there isn't room in an 8-byte record for the full name of the beastie, since "daughters" is 9 bytes long and there needs to be room to store the count of new beasties. Job chose to abbreviate the name of the beastie down to two characters. (His consultant recommended that he abbreviate

---

[16] Clay Tablet By Carrier Pigeon Protocol, defined in RFC –39127.

down to one character, since there was little difference between daughters and donkeys. His consultant got fired.) So each record has 2 bytes for the beastie type and 6 remaining bytes to store a number.[17] The records are broken out into fields using the **unpack()** function, and put back together using **pack()**.

```perl
#!/usr/bin/perl

# We put any configuration constants here in front.  It helps
# to capitalize them for visibility later in the program.

$RECLEN = 8;

# Note how we can assign a list of pairs to an entire
# associative array in order to initialize it.

%fullname = (
    'sh', 'sheep',
    'ca', 'camels',
    'ox', 'oxen',
    'do', 'donkeys',
    'so', 'sons',
    'da', 'daughters',
);

# Open the files (devices, in this case).

open(PCTR, "</dev/pctr")
    || die "Couldn't open pigeon's clay tablet reader: $!\n";
open(PCTW, ">/dev/pctw")
    || die "Couldn't open pigeon's clay tablet writer: $!\n";

# Main loop.  This loop runs till last pigeon brings EOF tablet.

for ($recnum = 0; read(PCTR, $record, $RECLEN); $recnum++) {

    # Break apart the record into its fields.

    ($beastie, $count) = unpack("A2 A6", $record);

    # Add the count into the proper associative array entry.
    # Note that $count may be negative, in which case the
    # entry is decreased by the += operator.

    $count{$beastie} += $count;
```

---

[17] Job figured 6 bytes were sufficient, since that was enough to store a minus sign followed by a 5 digit number, and none of his beasties were numbered in more than 5 figures, so he couldn't lose more than that many at once. He also considered it unlikely for him to gain more than 999,999 beasties in a day. And if he did, they could always record it as two or more transactions. (This is how you have to think when you use fixed-length records.)

```
# Print out the acknowledgement for the return pigeon.
# Instead of sending a count back, we send back the record
# number, for the beastie keepers to check off as received.
# $newrec is guaranteed to be exactly 8 bytes long.

$newrec = pack("A2 A6", $beastie, $recnum);
print PCTW $newrec;
}

# End-of-Day processing.  We translate the abbreviated beastie
# name back to the full name to print it out, along with the
# accumulated count for the day.

foreach $key (sort keys(%count)) {
    printf "%-20s %d\n", $fullname{$key}, $count{$key};
}
```

The **pack( )** and **unpack( )** functions are how Perl deals with fixed-length fields. They correspond to the use of **join( )** and **split( )** for variable-length fields—**pack( )** takes a LIST and turns it into a string, while **unpack( )** takes a string and turns it into a list value. Instead of a delimiter, however, **pack( )** and **unpack( )** take as their first argument a template of how the record is structured. The template "A2 A6" indicates a record of 2 ASCII characters followed by 6 ASCII characters, for an implied total of 8 characters.

Now it came about one day that Job saw a lightning storm coming, and wanted to warn his shepherds that they should gather the flocks into the fold. But his communications scheme had no mechanism for doing this. When the reports came back after the storm that he had gained a negative number of sheep because of the lightning, he decided to revise his scheme. Unfortunately there was no room for growth in the 8-byte record, which was fixed by the protocol he was using. He hit upon the idea of packing the numeric data into a binary form. By using all the bits in the second half of the record, he could store a signed 32-bit number. Of the two remaining bytes, he used one as an unsigned 8-bit function code and reserved one for future use. His **unpack( )** and **pack( )** functions now looked like this (he turned the template into a configuration constant):

```
$TEMPLATE = "A2 C x l";
...
($beastie, $function, $count) = unpack($TEMPLATE, $record);
...
$newrec = pack($TEMPLATE, $beastie, $function, $recnum);
```

The template defines a record of 2 ASCII characters, followed by a 1-byte unsigned character integer, followed by a null byte, followed by a 4-byte signed long integer. (For a complete list of valid template fields, see the **pack( )** function in Chapter 4, *Functions*.)

Now all Job needed to do was to agree on function codes with his beastie keepers.
He put them into a normal array that he indexed by function code:

```
# Initialize @fun2text, a normal array.
# (Use $fun2text[$function] to find the text.)

@fun2text = (
    "Update",
    "Acknowledgement",
    "Lightning",
    "Sabeans",
    "Chaldeans",
    "Page Servant",
);

# Initialize %text2fun, an associative array, by inversion.
# (Use $text2fun{$text} to find the function code.)

$index = 0;
foreach $text (@fun2text) { $text2fun{$text} = $index++; }
```

The **%text2fun** array is derived from the **@fun2text** array, so that new entries
need only be entered in one place. With these two arrays, Job could translate in
either direction.

Abstraction

As Job grew older (and richer), he had more and more fun programming. Eventually he decided to pass the business on to his children, so he could have more time
to hack. When he did, he took some courses in computer science and discovered
that he'd been doing some things the hard way. His Comp Sci instructors told
him all about "abstraction," which he eventually figured out was just a fancy term
for making things simpler. This appealed to the Laziness in him.

Subroutines

Job had already figured out that he could pull certain Configuration Constants out
of his code and put them at the front of his program, so that he'd only have to
change them in one place. Using subroutines, he could do a similar thing with
commonly used chunks of code. Instead of:

```
if (!/camels (\d+)/) {
    print STDERR "Incorrect format—please try again!\n";
    $errors++;
}
```

```
if ($1 <= 0) {
    print STDERR "Incorrect format—please try again!\n";
    $errors++;
}
if (/pigs/) {
    print STDERR "Incorrect format—please try again!\n";
    $errors++;
}
```

he could simply say:

```
&reproach if !/camels (\d+)/;
&reproach if $1 <= 0;
&reproach if /pigs/;

sub reproach {
    print STDERR "Incorrect format—please try again!\n";
    $errors++;
}
```

The code has been factored out into a subroutine called **reproach**. The definition of a subroutine in Perl consists of the keyword **sub**, followed by the name of the subroutine, followed by the block of code in curly braces. A subroutine definition can be put anywhere in the program—it doesn't matter where. The subroutine is called by using the **&** character in front of the name of the subroutine. You see that by giving the chunk of code a descriptive name, Job has simplified his life as a programmer. He no longer needs to think of all the code in the subroutine; he can just think of the name of the subroutine. That's a form of abstraction.

There are also many cases in which you would like to factor out code that is similar but not identical. This can be done by passing *arguments* (also called *parameters*) to the subroutine. The arguments to be passed to the subroutine (known as *actual arguments*) are placed in a LIST after the name of the subroutine, in parentheses, like this:

```
&rebuke('daughter', 'danglesocket');
&rebuke('son', 'flea-infested, dunghill-rat-licking twerp');
```

The corresponding subroutine definition receives these arguments through the special @_ array:

```
sub rebuke {
    print "O my $_[0], you have become a $_[1]!\n";
}
```

In many computer languages you are forced as part of the subroutine definition to name your *formal arguments*—the names by which your subroutine refers to the actual arguments. Since Perl already provides the arguments as elements of the @_ array, there is no need to name formal arguments in Perl. It is customary, however, to copy the arguments immediately into a named list, which has the effect of naming the arguments:

```
sub rebuke {
    ($beastie,$epithet) = @_;
    print "O my $beastie, you have become a $epithet!\n";
}
```

This example, however, has the problem of clobbering any variables named **$beastie** or **$epithet**. We'll fix that problem in the next section.

Local Variables·

It's all very well to abstract out a piece of code and give it a name, but if that code has unnecessary effects on your main program, you can't properly forget about what the internals of the routine are. Thus your abstraction would be defeated.

A case in point is the list assignment in the last example. The variables **$beastie** or **$epithet** might well have some value already, and calling this subroutine shouldn't influence any existing variables. Perl provides a special function called **local( )** to solve this problem. A **local( )** function acts just like a LIST of variables in parentheses, except that each variable you mention is "localized" for the rest of the current block of statements. A localized variable can be modified, but the modification is temporary. After the block of statements is done, the localized variable will be restored back to its original value. Since **local( )** acts like a LIST in parentheses, you can assign to it. Thus, the correct way to write the **rebuke** subroutine is:

```
sub rebuke {
    local($beastie,$epithet) = @_;
    print "O my $beastie, you have become a $epithet!\n";
}
```

In this way, the rest of the program can ignore what **&rebuke** does with its variables.

The **local( )** function works in any block of statements, so you could use it within the block of an **if** statement, for instance:

```
if ($first >= $last) {
    local($tmp);

    $tmp = $first;
    $first = $last;
    $last = $tmp;
}
```

Normal and associative arrays may also be localized. Note that **local( )** is considered a list, even if there is only one variable name. Assignment to a **local( )** will therefore evaluate the right side of the assignment in an array context. This means that:

```
local($input) = <STDIN>;
```

will read all the lines available from standard input, then assign the first line to the variable. This is probably not what you want. You can force a scalar context by using the **scalar( )** function, like this:

```
local($input) = scalar(<STDIN>);
```

Using Subroutines as Functions

You can use any subroutine as a function merely by invoking it as part of an expression. The subroutine returns the value of the last expression evaluated within the subroutine. (There's also an explicit **return** operator for returning a value from deep within a subroutine—see Chapter 4, _Functions_.) A subroutine can return either a scalar or list value, depending on the context in which the subroutine was invoked.

Here's a handy function that prompts with a yes-or-no question and returns true or false depending on how the question was answered:

```
sub y_or_n {
    local($prompt) = @_;
    print STDOUT $prompt;
    local($answer) = scalar(<STDIN>);
    $answer =~ /^y/i;
}

&walk if &y_or_n("I'd walk a camel for a mile.  Would you? ");
```

Recursion

When you name a subroutine, you then have the ability to refer to that subroutine from many places within your program. This includes places within the subroutine itself! A subroutine that calls itself is known as a "recursive" subroutine. (The word is also used of subroutines that call themselves indirectly, via one or more other subroutines.) Not so oddly, recursive subroutines are useful for processing recursive data structures—data structures that are similar to themselves at different hierarchical levels—that is, tree structures.

Tree structures often arise in real life, because many problems are of a hierarchical or fractal nature. After Job turned his business over to his children, he discovered he had a problem keeping track of his descendants. Each of his 10 children decided to have 10 children too, so Job had 100 grandchildren. By the same process, he ended up with 1000 great-grandchildren, and 10,000 great-great-grandchildren. He really needed a database to keep track of who belonged to whom. So he fired up his editor, and started typing. First he made a little nested structure that listed his kids, like this:

```
Job {
    Dove
    Cinnamon
    Eyeshadow Kit
    Heth
    Teth
    Yodh
    Kaph
    Lamedh
    Mem
    Nun
}
```

Then he started adding in his grandchildren:

```
Job {
    Dove {
        Robin
        Martin
        Peregrine
        Jay
        Coot
        Finch
        Condor
        Budgie
        Curlew
        Kiwi
    }
    Cinnamon {
        Parsley
        Sage
        Rosemary
        Thyme
        . . .
    }
    Eyeshadow Kit {
        Maybelline®
        . . .
    }
    . . .
}
```

Then he added in the great-grandchildren:

```
Job {
    Dove {
        Robin {
            Marian
            John
            Will
            ...
```

And so on, unto the fourth generation.

Now Job wrote a program called **begat**, which would list out the lineage of any of his descendants. He began by loading the tree structure into an associative array, in which each entry of the array indicated a parent-child relationship. Then he used another recursive routine to print out the relationships. Note that a recursive subroutine must have some means of distinguishing when it has reached a so-called "leaf node." Otherwise it would go on recursing forever. In the case of **&load_kids()**, it knows to quit when there's no opening curly brace following the name. By the way, the structure of Job's file may or may not remind you of the structure of certain programming languages...

```perl
#!/usr/bin/perl

open(DESC, "descendants") || die "without issue\n";

# Load the kids of Job.

&load_kids('');

sub load_kids {
    local($parent) = @_;
    local($name);

    # Process all the current parent's children.

    while (<DESC>) {
        last if /}/;

        # Extract name from line with a regular expression.

        next unless /(\w.*\w)/;
        $name = $1;

        # Use associative array to store a tree.

        $parent{$name} = $parent;

        # See if this kid has kids.

        if (/{/) {
            &load_kids($name);
```

```
            }
        }
    }

    # Now we ask which name to print the lineage of, and print it.

    while (1) {
        print "Who: ";
        chop($who = <STDIN>);
        last unless $who;
        &do_a_begat($who);
    }

    # Recursively follow the tree of parents up to Job, printing
    # "begat" lines on the way back down.  (We're really just
    # showing off, since we could just as easily have done this
    # linear traverse of the tree using an ordinary loop.)

    sub do_a_begat {
        local($name) = @_;

        if ($parent{$name}) {
            &do_a_begat($parent{$name});
            print "$parent{$name} begat $name\n";
        }
    }
```

Note that each level of a recursive routine gets its own local variables, even though they have the same names as in the calling routine.

You might not have Job's particular problem, but you have related problems. Suppose you want to list out all the files in the current directory and all of its subdirectories. Here's a recursive solution that is very fast, because it doesn't need to "stat" any of the leaf node filenames to see if they are actually subdirectories. (This depends on the semantics of the UNIX filesystem, which links each directory into any of its subdirectories as the filename "..". If the current directory has a link count of only two, it has no subdirectories! Note, however, that if you have to stat all the files anyway for some other purpose, there's no point in using this trick.)

```
    #!/usr/bin/perl

    # Start at the top.

    &dodir('.');

    sub dodir {
        local($dir,$nlink) = @_;
        local($dev,$ino,$mode,$subcount);

        # At the top level, we need to find nlink ourselves.
```

```
($dev,$ino,$mode,$nlink) = stat(´.´) unless $nlink;

# Get the list of files in the current directory.

opendir(DIR,´.´) || die "Can´t open $dir";
local(@filenames) = readdir(DIR);
closedir(DIR);

if ($nlink == 2) {          # This dir has no subdirectories.
    for (@filenames) {
        next if $_ eq ´.´;
        next if $_ eq ´..´;
        print "$dir/$_\n";
    }
}
else {                      # This dir has subdirectories.
    $subcount = $nlink - 2;
    for (@filenames) {
        next if $_ eq ´.´;
        next if $_ eq ´..´;
        $name = "$dir/$_";
        print $name,"\n";
      next if $subcount == 0;   # Seen all the subdirs?

        # Get link count and check for directoriness.

        ($dev,$ino,$mode,$nlink) = lstat($_);
        next unless -d _;

        # It really is a directory, so do it recursively.

        chdir $_ || die "Can´t cd to $name";
        &dodir($name,$nlink);
        chdir ´..´;
        --$subcount;
    }
}
}
```

This routine makes use of several functions you haven't seen yet. The **opendir**(),
readdir(), and **closedir**() functions provide direct access to the list of filenames
in a directory. The **readdir**() function, when used in an array context as it is
here, returns all the filenames as a list. Note the use of **local**() on the array variable to hold the filenames.

The **for** loop over **@filenames** is really a form of the **foreach** loop, not the 3-part C **for** loop. You can tell the difference because there aren't any semicolons. The loop in the program is exactly equivalent to:

```
foreach $_ (@filenames) { ...
```

The file test **–d** tests a file to see if it's a directory. In this case, we perform the test on the special filehandle consisting of an underline, which merely retests the file we last did a file test or **stat()** on. This avoids the overhead of calling the operating system a second time to find out what Perl already knows about the file.

This routine also uses the **chdir()** function to descend into the directories it is going to scan. This is why the **opendir()** function always opens the current directory ".". It's faster to stat files in the current directory than to make the operating system parse long pathnames each time. After finishing with a directory, **chdir()** is again used to return to the parent directory "..".

Recursive Descent Parsing

Using the principles we've covered, Job decided to build himself a little calculator, using a simple language that has the following rules:

```
EXPR    ::=  TERM { ADDOP TERM }
ADDOP   ::=  + | −
TERM    ::=  FACTOR { MULOP FACTOR }
MULOP   ::=  * | /
FACTOR  ::=  NUMBER | `(´ EXPR `)´
```

The ::= symbol means "may be composed of," the curly braces mean "0 or more occurrences of," and the vertical bar means "either/or." The program below implements these rules as a **recursive descent parser**. It's really quite simple once you get the hang of it. Note how the syntax rules translate almost directly into subroutine calls, and the rules that are looking for actual tokens simply substitute the tokens from the front of the string as they find them.

```
#!/usr/bin/perl

&driver;

# First, the driver loop.

sub driver {
    while (<>) {            # For each line.
        s/\s+//g;          # Remove all white space, \n included.
        $val = &expr;      # Evaluate the expression.
        die "Expected an operator: $_\n" unless $_ eq "";
        print "$val\n";
    }
}
```

```perl
    exit;
}

# Parse an expression.

sub expr {
    local($left, $op, $right);

    $left = &term;
    while ($op = &addop) {
        $right = &term;
        if ($op eq '+')
            { $left += $right; }
        else
            { $left -= $right; }
    }
    $left;
}

sub addop {
    s/^([+-])// && $1;
}

# Parse a term.

sub term {
    local($left, $op, $right);

    $left = &factor;
    while ($op = &mulop) {
        $right = &factor;
        if ($op eq '*')
            { $left *= $right; }
        else
            { $left /= $right; }
    }
    $left;
}

sub mulop {
    s#^([*/])## && $1;
}

# Parse a factor.

sub factor {
    local($val);
    if (s/^([\d.]+)//) {          # Found a number.
        $val = $1;
    }
    elsif (s/^\(//) {             # Found a parenthesized expr.
        $val = &expr;
        s/^\)// || die "Missing right paren: $_\n";
```

```
    }
    else {
        die "Expected a factor: $_";
    }
    $val;
}
```

This is lots of fun, but the next section will explain a way to get a much more powerful calculator in much less space.

When Subroutines Aren't Enough

An ordinary Perl script is first compiled, and then executed. Subroutines are defined at compile time, so their behavior can only be modified by passing parameters. Occasionally you'd like your Perl script to have the flexibility to write Perl code itself. Of course, it's easy enough to build up a string that looks like a Perl program:

```
$little_program = ´print "Howdy, world\n";´;
```

or, equivalently:

```
$little_program = <<´End_Of_Program´;
print "Howdy, world\n";
End_Of_Program
```

The trick, of course, is to get it executed. This is the purpose of the **eval** function:

```
eval $little_program;
```

Upon executing this statement, "Howdy, world" will be printed out. The little program runs in the context of the current program very much like an ordinary subroutine call, in that all the variables of the program are visible to it, and you can make local variables that last just as long as the **eval()** does. Unlike subroutines, there's no argument passing mechanism at all, because you generally include the arguments you want as you build up the program string. But the value of the last expression is returned just like a subroutine.

The **eval()** function has a higher overhead than a subroutine call, since it has to parse the code before it executes it. However, there are several situations in which this is worthwhile. First of all, you can use it to express algorithms that would be difficult to express otherwise, such as assigning a variable to a dynamically selectable array:

```
$arrayname = $arrayname[rand(50)];       # Pick a random array.
eval ´$´ . $arrayname . ´{$beastie} = 1´; # Set a value in it.
```

The **eval** function is also useful for executing code that is input from the user at runtime. Recall Job's recursive descent calculator. Job scrapped his calculator and replaced it with the following:

```
#!/usr/bin/perl
while (<>) {
    print eval $_;
    die $@ if $@;
}
```

Not only is this much shorter than his previous calculator, but recognizes all the operators that Perl does, not just the basic arithmetic operators. The **eval** returns whatever the expression in **$_** returns, which is then printed out. If there was a syntax error within **$_**, nothing is returned, and so nothing is printed by the **print** operator. However, the **eval** operator always sets the special $@ variable to be the error message (if any) returned by the **eval**. Thus, ordinarily fatal errors within an **eval** are trapped, and don't cause the program to fail. The conditional **die** statement you see in this program is the idiom you can use when you wish to propagate outward any error message originating from within the **eval**.

This brings us to a third major use for **eval**, namely, trapping errors. Consider the recursive descent parser in the last section. As it presented there, any error within the parser is fatal to the entire program. But suppose, instead of saying:

```
&driver;
```

at the beginning, we had said:

```
while (1) {
    eval "&driver";
    warn $@;
}
```

The **eval** would trap any errors within the parser, and the **warn** operator would print out the error message. (The **warn** operator is just like **die**, except that it doesn't. Both operators print messages to STDERR though.) The program then restarts the driver. In another program, this feature could be used to guarantee that your program cleans up after itself, even if it dies in the middle for some reason.

The fourth reason for using **eval** is, paradoxically, efficiency. There are certain constructs that the Perl compiler is very good at optimizing, provided it can determine what it's supposed to be doing at compile time. In particular, if you're searching for multiple patterns that aren't known until run time, it's much more efficient to build up a loop containing multiple pattern match commands, and then **eval** that, than it is to try to search using variable interpolations in the pattern, which force recompilation of the pattern each time the pattern is used. (After all, variables are called that for a reason!) For a good example of this technique, see the **study** function in Chapter 4. The "grep" programs in Chapter 6 also use this trick for maximum speed.

More About Localizing Variables

The subroutine, **eval**, and **local( )** mechanisms allow you to make abstractions of particular operations, but they are limited in letting you abstract sets of related operations, because the related operations can't share variables via the **local( )** mechanism. And yet, you don't want to use global variables for the inner workings of these related functions, because the functions should be able to hide their inner workings from the rest of the program.

Perl's answer to this is to let you have sets of variables that act like globals as far as your related routines are concerned, but are not actually global variables. Instead, they are local to a particular *package*, which your related routines know how to access. Typically, your routines are related by the fact that they all manipulate a particular kind of object. You might name the package after the object that the routines manipulate. Computer Scientists like to call this an "abstract type." Your program only needs to know about the operations that affect the object in question, but nothing about the inner workings of it. The packaging mechanism in Perl lets you "encapsulate" the private parts of your package so that they don't interfere with the rest of the program, and vice versa.

That's a bunch of highfalutin talk that you don't have to understand. Here's how you can actually use Perl packages to implement a pair of routines that share a prioritized queue:

```
sub add_entry {
    package Priority_Queue;
    ($priority,$message) = @_;
    for ($i = 0; $i <= $#queue; $i++) {
        last if $queue[$i] < $priority;
    }
    splice(@queue, $i, 0, "$priority;$message");
}

sub next_entry {
    package Priority_Queue;
    if (@queue) {
        $message = shift(@queue);
        split(/;/, $message, 2);    # return (priority, message)
    }
    else {
        ();                         # return null list
    }
}
```

These routines implement a priority queue—one in which you can stuff entries by priority, and then draw out the highest priority item. Job would use them something like this:

```
&add_entry(23,"Shear the sheep");
&add_entry(86,"Bathe the camels");
&add_entry(51,"Write my memoirs");
&add_entry(77,"Hack on begat s´more");

print "Your jobs:\n";
while (($priority, $message) = &next_entry) {
    print ++$i, ´. ´, $message, "\n";
}
```

Note that **&next_entry** returns a list containing the priority and the message, but the **print** statement ignores the priority. This program prints out:

```
Your jobs:
1. Bathe the camels
2. Hack on begat s´more
3. Write my memoirs
4. Shear the sheep
```

The two routines actually implement an insertion sort based on the priority. The nice thing about a priority queue, of course, is that you can intermix the queueing and the dequeueing (though Job's program doesn't).

Look back at the two subroutine definitions. Even though **package Priority_Queue** is declared in more than one place, both declarations refer to the same package. A package declaration makes all the variable names in the rest of the block refer to the variables in the package, by default. (It's possible to refer to variables in another package, but you must do so explicitly by prefixing the variable name with the package name and a single quote, as in **$fiddle´sticks**.)

Since the names of the subroutines are not in the scope of a package declaration, the subroutines themselves aren't in **Priority_Queue**. Only their variables are. (It is possible to have subroutines that are local to a package.) In particular, the variable **@queue** is shared by the two routines, but if the main part of the program talks about **@queue**, it will be referring to a different array. In fact, the main part of the program is in a package called **main**, so a reference to **@queue** in the main program is talking about **@main´queue**, while the references in package **Priority_Queue** are talking about **@Priority_Queue´queue**, a different array entirely. Note that there is no need to use **local( )** at all, except as necessitated by the semantics of the package itself, such as if it had a routine that called itself recursively.

Many of the files in the Perl library (see Appendix B) make use of **package** declarations. These files are read in and executed using the **require** operator, which is just a fancy **eval** operator that works on files instead of strings. Since the files are executed using an **eval( )**-equivalent operator, the statements of the file are treated as a block, and any **package** declaration at the top of the file puts the rest of the file into the specified package. Often the subroutines are then placed explicitly back into the main package, by declaring them like this one:

```
sub main´doit { ... }
```

Note that this places only the subroutine name back into the main package. Variables in the body of the subroutine are still package local variables, because only a **package** declaration can influence the interpretation of subsequent symbols.

Summing Up

You now know enough about Perl to begin using it productively. There are still many details to be mastered, of course, but how you master them is up to you. If you like cramming all sorts of reference material into your head, Chapters 3 and 4 will delight you. If, on the other hand, you prefer to learn by example, you'll probably skim Chapters 3 and 4 with mild distaste and spend more time studying Chapters 5 and 6. (Remember, There's More Than One Way To Do It!)

Regardless of which way you prefer to learn, Chapter 7, *Other Oddments*, contains some interesting tidbits to help you debug your scripts, avoid common novice errors, and make your scripts more efficient. Good luck!

3

The Gory Details

Data Types and Objects
Operators
Statements
Subroutines
Regular Expressions
Formats
Special Variables
Packages

This chapter describes in detail the syntax and semantics of a Perl program. Individual Perl functions are described in Chapter 4.

Data Types and Objects

The most basic piece of data in Perl is called a **scalar.** A scalar is either a number[18] or a string; Perl converts between them as needed, so you can treat a number as a string or a string as a number, and Perl will do the Right Thing.[19] Apart from this mushy distinction between numbers and strings, Perl has three very distinct data types: scalars, arrays of scalars, and associative arrays of scalars. Normal arrays are indexed by number, and associative arrays by string. Variables are always one of these three types. (Other than variables, Perl also has some

---

[18] Perl stores numbers as double-precision floating-point values in the machine's native format.

[19] To convert from string to number, Perl uses C's **atof()** function. To convert from number to string, it does an **sprintf()** with a format of "*%.20g*" (on most machines).

partially hidden objects called filehandles, directory handles, subroutines, and formats, which you can think of as data types if you like.)

Expressions are of only two types: scalar and list. Both normal arrays and associative arrays evaluate to lists, and can be initialized with list values.

Expression Context

Every operation that you use in a Perl script is evaluated in a specific **context**, and how that operation behaves may depend on the requirements of that context. There are two major contexts: scalar and array. You will be miserable until you learn the difference, because certain operations know which context they are in, and return array values (lists) in contexts wanting an array, and scalar values in contexts wanting a scalar. (If this is true of an operation, it will be mentioned in the documentation for that operation.) Other operations *supply* the array contexts to their operands, and you can tell which ones those are because they all have LIST in their syntactic description.

Note however that the array context of a LIST can propagate down through subroutine calls, so it's not always obvious by inspection whether a given simple statement is going to be evaluated in a scalar or array context. The program can find out its context within a subroutine by using the **wantarray**( ) function. Note also that you can force a scalar context in the middle of a LIST by using the **scalar**( ) function.

Scalar context can be further classified into string context, numeric context, and don't-care context. Unlike the scalar versus array context distinction we just made, operations never know *which* scalar context they're in. They simply return whatever kind of scalar value they want to, and let Perl translate numbers to strings in string context, and strings to numbers in numeric context. Some scalar contexts don't care whether a string or number is returned, so no conversion will happen. (This happens, for example, when you are assigning the value to another variable.) Another don't-care context is the Boolean context, when we'll be checking the returned value to see if it's true or false. A number is "true" if it's not 0. A string is "true" if it's not the null string or "0". Boolean values returned by operators are typically 1 for true and 0 or ˝ (the null string) for false, but since every operation in Perl has a valid interpretation in scalar context, you can use any expression you like in a Boolean context.

There are actually scalars that have neither a numeric nor a string value, and these we call "undefined." An undefined scalar evaluates to 0 in a numeric context and to the null string in a string context. A defined null string evaluates exactly the same way, so ordinarily you can't distinguish an undefined null string from a defined null string. (The undefined scalar is always false, just like a normal null string.) Undefined scalars are returned when there is no real value for something, such as when there was an error, or at end of file, or when you refer to an uninitialized variable or element of an array. An undefined scalar will become defined the first time you access it in either a string or a numeric context, but prior to that you can use the **defined**( ) operator to determine whether the value is defined or not. In practice this is seldom necessary.

Variables

All variables are global unless localized within a block by the **local** function. (Actually, variables aren't really global, since variables are local to the package in which they are used. But within a particular package they appear to be global, much like **static** variables in C. See the section "Packages" later in this chapter.)

References to scalar variables always begin with **$**, even when referring to a scalar that is part of an array. Thus:

$days	A simple scalar variable.
$days[28]	29th element of array @days.
$days{´Feb´}	One value from an associative array.
$#days	Last index of array @days.

but entire arrays or array slices are denoted by @:

@days	($days[0], $days[1], ... $days[$#days])
@days[3,4,5]	Same as ($days[3],$days[4],$days[5])
@days{´a´,´c´}	Same as ($days{'a'},$days{'c'})

and entire associative arrays are denoted by %:

%days	(key1, val1, key2, val2 ...)

Any of these eight constructs may serve as an lvalue. That is, they may be assigned to. (It also turns out that an assignment is itself an lvalue in certain contexts—see examples under **s**, **tr** and **chop** in Chapter 4, *Functions*.) Assignment to a scalar variable evaluates the right-hand side in a scalar context, while assignment to an array or array slice evaluates the right-hand side in an array context.

You may find the length of array **@days** by evaluating **@days** in a scalar context:

```
$number_of_elements = @days;
```

Closely related is the special scalar value **$#**arrayname, which returns not the number of elements, but the subscript of the last element. This subscript is ordinarily one less than the number of elements because Perl, like C, uses arrays containing a 0th element. Assigning to **$#whatever** changes the length of the array. Shortening an array by this method does not actually destroy any values. Lengthening an array that was previously shortened recovers the values that were in those elements. You can also gain some measure of efficiency by pre-extending an array that is going to get big. (You can also extend an array by assigning to an element that is off the end of the array. This differs from assigning to **$#whatever** in that intervening values are set to undefined rather than recovered.) You can truncate an array down to nothing by assigning the null list () to it. The following assignments are exactly equivalent:

```
@whatever = ();
$#whatever = $[ - 1;
```

The special variable $[is the current array base, ordinarily 0, as we mentioned. You can change it to 1 if you prefer the FORTRAN approach, and then **$#whatever** will be equal to **@whatever**. Most Perl programmers prefer to leave $[at 0. Regardless, the following is always true:

```
@whatever == $#whatever - $[ + 1;
```

Multi-dimensional arrays are not directly supported, but you can say:

```
$stooges = $num_movies{$larry, $moe, $curly}
```

as a shorthand for:

```
$stooges = $num_movies{ join($;, $larry, $moe, $curly) }
```

See the discussion of the $; variable later for more on this subject. You could also write a subroutine or C preprocessor macro to turn multiple subscripts into a single subscript.

Names

Every data type has its own namespace—which means you can (without fear of conflict) use the same name for a scalar variable, a normal array, an associative array, a filehandle, a directory handle, a subroutine name, a format name, a statement label, and/or your new goldfish. Since variable references always start with $, @, or %, the "reserved" words aren't in fact reserved with respect to variable names. They *are* reserved, however, with respect to labels, filehandles, and directory handles, which don't have an initial special character. Since the reserved words are all lowercase, we recommend that you pick labels and handles that aren't all lowercase. For example, rather than saying something regrettable like **open(log,´>>logfile´)** you could say **open(LOG,´>>logfile´)**. The first open would use for its filehandle the base *e* logarithm of the current value of $_ (probably not what you want). Uppercase filehandles also improve readability and protect you from conflict with future reserved words, which are likely to be lower-case.

Case in names *is* significant—**FOO**, **Foo**, and **foo** are all different names. Names that start with a letter may contain any number of letters and digits, all of which are significant. Perl considers underscore to be a letter. Names that do not start with a letter are limited to one character; for example, $% or $$. (Most of these one-character names have a predefined significance to Perl. See the section "Special Variables" later in this chapter.)

Literals and Interpreted Literals

Numeric literals are specified in any of the usual floating-point or integer formats:

```
12345
12345.67
.23E—10
Oxffff  # hexadecimal
0377    # octal
```

Note that the leading **0x** for hex and **0** for octal work *only* for literals. The automatic conversion of a string to a number does not recognize these prefixes—you must do an explicit conversion with **hex( )** or **oct( )**.[20]

String literals are delimited by either single or double quotes. They work much like shell quotes: double-quoted string literals are subject to backslash and variable substitution; single-quoted strings are not (except for \´ and \\). You can embed newlines directly in your strings; that is, they can end on a different line than they begin. This is nice, but if you forget your trailing quote, the error will not be reported until Perl runs into the end of the file or finds another line containing the quote character, which may be much further on in the script. Fortunately, this usually causes an immediate syntax error on the same line, and Perl then warns you that you might have a runaway string.

---

[20] Some people think Perl should convert all incoming data for them. But there are far too many decimal numbers with leading zeroes in the world to make Perl do this automatically. You may have seen reports with "Page 009," or account numbers starting with zero. The zip code for O'Reilly & Associates' office in Cambridge, MA is **02140**. The postmaster would get upset if your mailing label program turned **02140** into **1120** decimal.

In double-quote interpretation, the usual backslash rules apply for making characters such as newline, tab, and so on. You may specify characters in octal, hexadecimal, or as control characters. In addition, there are sequences to modify the case of subsequent characters, as with the substitution operator in the _vi_ editor.

\n	Newline or line feed.
\r	Return.
\t	Tab.
\f	Form feed.
\b	Backspace.
\033	ESC in octal.
\x7f	DEL in hexadecimal.
\cC	Control-C.
\u	Force next character to upper case.
\l	Force next character to lower case.
\U	Force following characters to upper case.
\L	Force following characters to lower case.
\E	End \U or \L.

Double-quoted strings are also subject to variable substitution (also known as variable interpolation, to avoid confusion with the substitution operator s///). Variable substitution inside strings is limited to scalar variables, normal array values, and array slices. In other words, Perl searches your string for identifiers beginning with $ or @, followed by an optional bracketed ([] or {}) expression to be used as a subscript or list of subscripts. Whenever it finds one of these identifiers, it incorporates the value of that scalar or array variable at that point in the string. The following code segment prints out **"The price is $100.":**

```
$Price = '$100';            # not interpreted
print "The price is $Price.\n";     # interpreted
```

Note that you can put curly braces around the identifier to delimit it from following alphanumerics (which means there's no such thing as a ${ variable). Also note that a single-quoted string must be separated from a preceding word by a space, since single quote is a valid character in an identifier (see Packages later in this chapter).

You may use an alternate delimiter for a single- or double-quoted string using the **q/STRING/** and **qq/STRING/** syntax. These are syntactic sugar to let you avoid putting too many backslashes into quoted strings. The **q** construct is a generalized single quote, and the **qq** construct a generalized double quote. Any non-alphanumeric delimiter can be used in place of /, including newline and the null character (although the null character is unacceptable to some text editors). If the delimiter is an opening bracket or parenthesis, the final delimiter will be the corresponding closing bracket or parenthesis. (Embedded occurrences of the closing bracket need to be backslashed as usual.) Examples:

```
$foo = q!I said, "You said, 'She said it.'"!;
$bar = q('This is it.');
$_ .= qq
*** The previous line contains the naughty word "$&".\n
    if /(ibm|apple|awk)/;      # :-)
```

The construct $_ .= qq is a bit of cleverness that might not be immediately apparent. qq takes the next character as the delimiter. Here, it's followed by a newline, which has the effect of quoting the succeeding line.

Two special literals are __LINE__ and __FILE__, which represent the current line number and filename at that point in your program. They may be used only as separate tokens; they cannot be interpolated into strings. In addition, the special token __END__ may be used to indicate the logical end of the script before the actual end of file. Any following text is ignored (but is accessible by reading the special filehandle DATA, or by reading STDIN if the script was supplied to Perl that way). The two control characters ^D and ^Z are synonyms for __END__.

A word that doesn't have any other interpretation in the grammar will be treated as if it had single quotes around it. For this purpose, a word consists only of alphanumeric characters, and must start with a letter (underline is a letter, you'll recall).[21] For example:

```
print STDOUT hello,' ',world,"\n";
```

prints **hello world** followed by a newline on **STDOUT**. Note that leaving the filehandle out makes Perl try to interpret **hello** as a filehandle. The primary motivation for this feature is that you can pass unquoted words representing filehandle names as strings in function calls, as in:

```
sub say_hi {
        local($filehandle,$times) = @_;
        $times = 1 if $times if "";
        print $filehandle "hi to $filehandle!\n" x $times;
}

&say_hi(STDOUT);
&say_hi(STDERR,3);
```

---

[21] As with filehandles and labels, a bare word that consists entirely of lowercase letters risks conflict with future reserved words. If you use the **-w** switch, Perl will warn you about any such words.

But it also lets you say things like:

```
@days = (Mon,Tue,Wed,Thu,Fri);
```

Array values are interpolated into double-quoted strings by joining all the elements of the array with the delimiter specified in the $" variable, space by default. (Since in versions of Perl prior to 3.0 the @ character was not a meta-character in double-quoted strings, the interpolation of **@array**, **$array[EXPR]**, **@array[LIST]**, **$array{EXPR}**, or **@array{LIST}** happens only if **array** is referenced elsewhere in the program or is a predefined array like **@ARGV**.) The following two scripts are equivalent:

```
$temp = join($",@ARGV);
system "echo $temp";

system "echo @ARGV";
```

although the second is better written as:

```
system `echo`, @ARGV;
```

Within search patterns (which also undergo double-quotish substitution) there is a bad ambiguity: Is **/$foo[bar]/** to be interpreted as **/${foo}[bar]/** (where **[bar]** is a character class for the regular expression) or as **/${foo[bar]}/** (where **[bar]** is the subscript to array **@foo**)? If **@foo** doesn't otherwise exist, then it's obviously a character class. If **@foo** exists, Perl takes a good guess about **[bar]**, and is almost always right.[22] If it does guess wrong, or if you believe in paranoid programming, you can force the correct interpretation with curly braces as above.

A line-oriented form of quoting is based on the shell "here document" syntax. Following a **<<** you specify a string to terminate the quoted material, and all lines following the current line down to the terminating string are the value of the item. (The rest of the current line is parsed as normal, however.) The terminating string may be either an identifier (a word) or some quoted text. If quoted, the type of quotes you use determines the treatment of the text, just as in regular quoting. An unquoted identifier works like double quotes. There must be no space between the **<<** and the identifier or string. (If you put a space it will be treated as a null identifier, which is valid, and matches the first blank line—see the "Hurrah!" example below.) The terminating string must appear by itself (unquoted and with no surrounding whitespace) on the terminating line.

---

[22] The guesser is too complicated to describe in full, but basically takes a weighted average of all the things that look like character classes (**a–z**, **\w**, initial ^) versus things that look like expressions (variable references or reserved words).

```
        print <<EOF;             # Same as earlier example.
The price is $Price.
EOF


        print <<"EOF";           # The same with explicit quotes
The price is $Price.
EOF


        print <<'EOF';           # A single-quoted quote.
All things (e.g. a camel's journey through
A needle's eye) are possible, it's true.
But picture how the camel feels, squeezed out
In one long bloody thread, from tail to snout.
                        — C.S. Lewis
EOF


        print << x 10;           # Print next line 10 times;
The camels are coming!  Hurrah!  Hurrah!


        print <<`EOC`;  # Execute commands!
echo `Your .vacation.msg file says:`
cat .vacation.msg
EOC


        print <<foo, <<bar;      # You can stack them.
He said bactrian.
foo
She said dromedary.
bar
```

This last example merely prints out:

```
He said bactrian.
She said dromedary.
```

Array Values

Array values (lists) are constructed by separating individual values by commas, and enclosing the list in parentheses:

```
(LIST)
```

In a context not requiring an array value, the value of a list is the value of the final element, as with the C comma operator. For example:

```
@foo = ('cc', '-E', $bar);
```

assigns the entire array value to array **foo**, but:

```
$foo = (´cc´, ´-E´, $bar);
```

assigns the value of variable **bar** to variable **foo**. The last-value rule only applies to comma-separated lists—the value of an actual array in a scalar context is the length of the array; the following statements assign to **$foo** the value 3:

```
@foo = (´cc´, ´-E´, $bar);
$foo = @foo;                # $foo gets 3
```

You may have an optional comma before the closing parenthesis of an array literal, so that you can say:

```
@foo = (
         1,
         2,
         3,
);
```

Supplying the extra comma lets you maintain lists more easily with an editor.

A syntactic list is called a LIST, and if it has two or more elements, they are separated with commas. Many operators specify a LIST in their syntactic description—these are the very operators that supply an array context. When a LIST is evaluated, each element of the list is evaluated in an array context, and the resulting array value is interpolated into LIST just as if each individual element were a member of LIST. Thus arrays lose their identity in a LIST—the list:

```
(@fiddle,@faddle,&SomeSub)
```

contains all the elements of **@fiddle** followed by all the elements of **@faddle**, followed by all the elements returned by the subroutine named **SomeSub** (evaluated in an array context, so the **wantarray** function is true within the subroutine).

A list value may also be subscripted like a normal array. Examples:

```
$time = (stat($file))[8];        # stat returns array value
$hexdigit = (´a´ .. ´f´)[$digit-10];
return (pop(@foo),pop(@foo))[0];
```

This feature can be used to implement the comma operator's opposite: an operator that evaluates both expressions but returns the *first* value instead of the second. Moreover, the subscript is actually a LIST of its own, so:

```
(´a´ .. ´z´)[7,8,19,7,4,17,4]
```

returns the value:

```
("h","i","t","h","e","r","e")
```

but that's neither here nor there.

Array lists may be assigned to, if and only if, each element of the list is an lvalue:

```
($a, $b, $c) = (1, 2, 3);
($map{"red"}, $map{"blue"}, $map{"green"}) =
      (0x00f, 0x0f0, 0xf00);
```

The final element may be an array or an associative array:

```
($a, $b, @rest) = split;
local($a, $b, %rest) = @_;
```

You can actually put an array anywhere in the list, but the first array in the list will soak up all the values, and anything after it will get an undefined value. This may be useful in a **local( )**.

An associative array value contains pairs of values to be interpreted as a key and a value:

```
# same as map assignment above
%map = ("red",0x00f,"blue",0x0f0,"green",0xf00);

%wday = (Sun,0,Mon,1,Tue,2,Wed,3,Thu,4,Fri,5,Sat,6);
```

Array assignment in a scalar context returns the number of elements produced by the expression on the right side of the assignment:

```
$x = (($adam,$eve) = (3,2,1));  # set $x to 3, not 2
```

Input Operators

There are several other pseudo-literals that you should know about. All of them are associated with getting input from somewhere. If a string is enclosed by backticks (grave accents), the string first undergoes variable substitution just like a double-quoted string. It is then interpreted as a command, and the output of that command is the value of the pseudo-literal, as in a shell. (You may use the **qx//** form of the operator to specify alternate delimiters.) In a scalar context, a single string consisting of all the output of the command is returned. In an array context, an array of values is returned, one for each line of output. (You can set $/ to use a different line terminator.) The command is executed each time the pseudo-literal is evaluated. The status value of the command is returned in $? (see Special Variables later in this chapter for the interpretation of $?). Unlike *csh*, no translation is done on the return data—newlines remain newlines. Unlike in any of the shells, single quotes within the backticks do not hide variable names in the command from interpretation. To pass a $ through to the shell you need to hide it with a backslash.

Evaluating a filehandle in angle brackets yields the next line from that file. We'll call the angle-bracketed filehandle an **input symbol**. The value returned includes the newline, so the value is never false until EOF, at which time an undefined value is returned by the input symbol. Ordinarily you must assign that value of the input symbol to a variable, but there is one situation where an automatic assignment happens. If (and only if) the input symbol is the only thing inside the conditional of a **while** loop, the value is automatically assigned to the variable $_. (This may seem like an odd thing to you, but you'll use the construct in almost every Perl script you write.) Anyway, the following lines are equivalent to each other:

```
while ($_ = <STDIN>) { print; }
while (<STDIN>) { print; }              # Preferred.
for (;<STDIN>;) { print; }
print while $_ = <STDIN>;
print while <STDIN>;
```

The filehandles **STDIN**, **STDOUT**, and **STDERR** are predefined. (The filehandles **stdin**, **stdout**, and **stderr** are partially supported for compatibility with old versions of Perl, but we recommend you always use uppercase filehandles.) Additional filehandles may be created with the **open** function. Note that filehandle arguments do **not** have angle brackets around them. The angle brackets are part of the input operator, not part of the filehandle. Do not put angle brackets on the output filehandle for a **print** statement! It will be misinterpreted as a request to read all the lines available from your output filehandle. When (if ever) it has read in all those lines, it will print them all to STDOUT.

If an input operator such as **<FILEHANDLE>** is used in a context that is looking for an array, an array consisting of all the rest of the input lines is returned, one line per array element. It's easy to use up gobs of memory this way, so be careful. Also remember an array context is an array context even if you only supply a single argument—the following constructs typically fool people:

```
local($nextline) = <STDIN>;
print OUT <IN>;
```

The first construct reads *all* the lines of standard input, and assigns just the first one to **$nextline**. This is because the **local( )** is a kind of list, so it's an array assignment. The second prints all the rest of **<IN>** to **OUT**. Which is fine if that's what you want.

The null filehandle **< >** is special and can be used to emulate the input behavior of *sed* and *awk*. Input from **< >** comes either from standard input, or from the concatenation of all files listed on the command line, in the order listed. Here's how it works: the first time **< >** is evaluated, the **ARGV** array is checked, and if it is null, **$ARGV[0]** is set to ´–´, which when opened gives you standard input. The **ARGV** array is then processed as a list of filenames. The loop:

```
while (<>) {
        ...                     # code for each line
}
```

is equivalent to:

```
unshift(@ARGV, ´–´) unless @ARGV;
while ($ARGV = shift) {
        open(ARGV, $ARGV) || warn "Couldn´t open $ARGV";
        while (<ARGV>) {
                ...             # code for each line
        }
}
```

except that it isn't as cumbersome to say. It really does shift array **ARGV** and put the current filename into variable **ARGV**. It also uses filehandle **ARGV** internally—the null filehandle is just an abbreviation for it. (For this reason, the code above won't really work because the inner loop will be interpreted as a **while (< >)**.) You can modify **@ARGV** before the first **< >** as long as you leave the first filename at the beginning of the array. Line numbers (**$.**) continue as if the input was one big happy file. If you need the line number to reset at the beginning of each file, use this construct:

```
while (<>) {
    ...
    close(ARGV) if eof;
}
```

If you want to set **@ARGV** to your own list of files, go right ahead. If you want to pass switches into your script, you can process and delete the switches by putting a loop on the front, like this:

```
while ($_ = $ARGV[0], /^–/) {
        shift;
    last if /^––$/;
        /^–D(.*)/ && ($debug = $1);
        /^–v/ && $verbose++;
        ...                 # other switches
}
while (<>) {
        ...                 # code for each line
}
```

The **< >** symbol will return false only once. If you call it again after this it will assume you are processing another **@ARGV** list, and if you haven't set **@ARGV**, will input from **STDIN**.

If the string inside the angle brackets is a reference to a scalar variable (e.g. **<$foo>**), then that variable contains the name of the filehandle to input from. This is an example of an indirect filehandle. Unlike a directly specified filehandle, an indirect filehandle need not be a valid identifier. Any string will work okay. (In fact, one clever trick is to use the filename as the indirect filehandle.)

If the string inside angle brackets is not a filehandle (direct or indirect), it is interpreted as a filename pattern to be globbed, and either an array of filenames or the next filename in the list is returned, depending on context. (For better control of directory reading, see the **readdir( )** operation.) One level of $ interpretation is done first, but you can't say **<$foo>** because that's an indirect filehandle as explained in the previous paragraph. You could insert curly braces to force interpretation as a filename glob: **<${foo}>**. This is the only case in Perl where **$foo** and **${foo}** don't mean the same thing. For example:

```
while (<*.c>) {
        chmod 0644, $_;
}
```

is equivalent to:

```
open(FOO, "echo *.c | " .
        "tr -s ´ \t\r\f´ ´\\012\\012\\012\\012´|");
while (<FOO>) {
        chop;
        chmod 0644, $_;
}
```

In fact, as of this writing, it's implemented that way. (Which means it will not work on filenames with spaces in them unless you have */bin/csh* on your machine. And also that you might get the error "Arguments Too Long" if your globs expand too much.) Of course, the shortest way to do the above is:

```
chmod 0644, <*.c>;
```

Until globbing is built into Perl, however, it will be faster[23] to use this approach:

```
opendir(DIR,´.´);
chmod 0644, grep(/\.c$/, readdir(DIR));
closedir(DIR);
```

---

[23] This assumes you have **readdir**, of course, otherwise it is infinitely slower.

Operators

Perl has many operators, most borrowed mainly from C, but some unique to Perl. Although a knowledge of C is not necessary, it'd be helpful in the following discussions.

Operator Precedence

Perl operators have the following associativity and precedence (from lowest (loosest) to highest (tightest)) (in the absense of parentheses (and such)):

Associativity	Operators
nonassoc	The list operators
left	,
right	= += −= *= etc.
right	?:
nonassoc	..
left	||
left	&&
left	| ^
left	&
nonassoc	== != <=> eq ne cmp
nonassoc	< > <= >= lt gt le ge
nonassoc	The named unary operators
nonassoc	−r −w −x etc.
left	<< >>
left	+ − .
left	* / % x
left	=~ !~
right	**
right	! ˜ and unary minus
nonassoc	++ −−
left	´(´

Now here is an important rule that simplifies things greatly, but produces occasional counterintuitive results for the unwary. If any list operator (such as **print**) or any named unary operator (such as **chdir**) is followed by a left parenthesis as the next token on the same line,[24] the operator and arguments within parentheses

---

[24] And we nearly had you convinced Perl was a free-form language...

are taken to be of highest precedence, just like a normal function call. The rule is: If it *looks* like a function call, it *is* a function call. You can make it look like a non-function call by prefixing with a unary plus, which does absolutely nothing—it doesn't even convert the argument to numeric. For example (recalling that || has lower precedence than **chdir**):

Statement	Equivalent
chdir $foo || die;	(chdir $foo) || die
chdir($foo) || die;	(chdir $foo) || die
chdir ($foo) || die;	(chdir $foo) || die
chdir +($foo) || die;	(chdir $foo) || die

but, because * has higher precedence than **chdir**:

Statement	Equivalent
chdir $foo * 20;	chdir ($foo * 20)
chdir($foo) * 20;	(chdir $foo) * 20
chdir ($foo) * 20;	(chdir $foo) * 20
chdir +($foo) * 20;	chdir ($foo * 20)

Likewise for numeric operators:

Statement	Equivalent
rand 10 * 20;	rand (10 * 20)
rand(10) * 20;	(rand 10) * 20
rand (10) * 20;	(rand 10) * 20
rand +(10) * 20;	rand (10 * 20)

In the absence of parentheses, the precedence of list operators such as **print, sort,** or **chmod** is either very high or very low depending on whether you look at the left side of the operator or the right side of it. For example, in:

```
@ary = (1, 3, sort 4, 2);
print @ary;              # prints 1324
```

the comma on the right of the **sort** is evaluated before the sort, but the commas on the left are evaluated after. In other words, a list operator tends to gobble up all the arguments that follow it, and then act like a simple term with regard to the preceding expression. Note that you have to be careful with parens:

```
# These evaluate exit before doing the print:
print($foo, exit);      # Obviously not what you want.
print $foo, exit;       # Nor is this.

# These do the print before evaluating exit:
(print $foo), exit;     # This is what you want.
```

```
print($foo), exit;       # Or this.
print ($foo), exit;      # Or even this.
```

Also note that:

```
print ($foo & 255) + 1, "\n";
```

probably doesn't do what you expect at first glance, because the **print** function call happens before the addition or comma operator.

Autoincrement and Autodecrement Operators

Like C, Perl has increment and decrement operators, in both prefix and postfix form. For example, **$a++** increments the value of scalar variable **$a**, returning the value *prior* to increment. And:

```
—$b{(/(\w+)/)[0]}
```

decrements the element of the associative array **%b** indexed by the first "word" in the default search variable **$_** (providing you haven't messed with **$[**) and returns the value *after* the decrement. (OK, so we threw in that last one just to see if you were paying attention. The point is that you can have a fairly complex expression leading to the simple scalar that actually gets incremented, or in this case, decremented).[25]

The autoincrement operator has a little extra built-in magic to it. If you increment a variable that is numeric, or that has ever been used in a numeric context, you get a normal increment. If, however, the variable has been used only in string contexts since it was set, and has a value that is not null and matches the pattern /^[a–zA–Z]*[0–9]*$/, the increment is done as a string, preserving each character within its range, with carry:

```
print ++($foo = ´99´);   # prints ´100´
print ++($foo = ´a0´);   # prints ´a1´
print ++($foo = ´Az´);   # prints ´Ba´
print ++($foo = ´zz´);   # prints ´aaa´
```

The autodecrement is not magical.

---

[25] Here's how that expression works. First, the pattern match finds the first word in **$_** using the regular expression \w+. The parentheses around that causes the word to be returned as a single-element array value, because the pattern match is in an array context. The array context is supplied by the slice operator, (...)[0], which returns the first (and only) element of the list. That value is then used as the subscript into the associative array, and the entry in the array is decremented and returned. In general, when confronted by a complex expression, analyze it from the inside out to see what order things happen.

Exponentiation Operator

Unlike C, Perl has a built-in exponentiation operator, expressed as **. So **2**3** is 8, and **–2**–3** (that is, **(–2)**(–3)**) is –1/8. Non-integral exponents require positive bases—Perl doesn't understand complex numbers (yet!).

Negating Operators

Perl provides three negating operators, similar to C. (For completeness, Perl also provides a unary plus operator, which does nothing except fill a syntactic niche.) All these operators are prefix operators, and have a precedence higher than the pattern binding operator, but lower than exponentiation.

Perl provides a unary minus, to change the arithmetic sign of a scalar value. For example, if **$x** has the value **123.45**, then **–$x** has the value **–123.45**.

Perl also provides a unary logical negation, in the form of **!**. The value is 1 if the operand is false (numeric 0, null string, undefined), and ´´ otherwise.

The bit negation operator is the prefix ˜. This operator provides the bitwise complement of the integer part of the numeric value of the operand. For example, on a 32-bit machine, the value of ˜**123** is 4294967172. If **vec( )** is present somewhere in the text of the program, the value of ˜**"123"** is determined by considering the string to be a bit vector. (See the description of the **vec( )** function discussed in Chapter 4, *Functions*, for details.) Otherwise, to preserve compatibility with older programs, the string is converted to an integer first.

Pattern Binding Operators

The operators **=˜** and **!˜** are used to bind a pattern match, substitution or translation to some other string than **$_**, the default. For **=˜**, the semantics and contextual behavior of the pattern match, substitution or translation are the same as the bare pattern operation. For **!˜**, a scalar context is forced, and the logical negation of the pattern operator's return value is returned. **$1**, **$2**, and so on, are still set, however. The following statements are thus equivalent:

```
$string !˜ /pattern/
!($string =˜ /pattern/)
```

Multiplicative Operators

Perl provides the C-like operators of * (multiply), / (divide), and % (modulus), as well as the string/list repetition operator **x**. The first three operators work like their C counterparts, converting strings to arithmetic values as necessary. The % operator converts to integers before finding the remainder.

The string repetition operator **x** returns a string consisting of the left operand repeated the number of times specified by the right operand. Examples:

```
print '-' x 80;          # print row of dashes
print '-' x80;           # illegal, x80 is identifier

print "\t" x ($tab/8), ' ' x ($tab%8);  # tab over

require "syscall.ph";
$buf = "\0" x 1024;      # extend string for ioctl or syscall
$read = syscall(&SYS_read, 0, $buf, 1024);
```

If **x** is used in an array context and its left operand is a LIST enclosed in parentheses, **x** works as a list replicator rather than a string replicator. This is useful for initializing all the elements of an array of indeterminate length to the same value:

```
@ones = (1) x @ones;
```

You can also generate array slices like this:

```
@keys = ("perls", "before", "swine");
@assoc{@keys} = ("") x @keys;
```

Note that the previous example creates defined values, unlike this:

```
@keys = ("perls", "before", "swine");
@assoc{@keys} = ();
```

Here's an example that uses a multi-valued list to create an array 256 elements long:

```
@hextrans = (0 .. 9, "a" .. "f") x 16;
```

Additive Operators

Like C, Perl has the + (addition) and – (subtraction) operators. Both operators convert their arguments from strings to numeric values if necessary, and return a numeric result. Additionally, Perl has the string concatenation operator **.**, as in **$str1.$str2**. The result is the concatenation of the two strings. (Numeric values are first converted to their string equivalent.) To concatenate a list, use the **join()** operator discussed in Chapter 4, *Functions*.

Shift Operators

Like C, Perl has the bitwise left-shift **<<** and right-shift **>>** operators. Bit-shifting is performed according to the underlying arithmetic properties of the machine, and may not be portable across all implementations, so beware.

File Test Operators

A file test operator is a unary operator that takes one argument, either a filename or a filehandle, and tests the associated file to see if something is true about it. If the argument is omitted, the operators test **$_**, except for **–t**, which tests **STDIN**. Most of the operators return **1** for true and ´´ for false, or the undefined value if the file does not exist. (**–s** returns the file size and **–M**, **–A**, and **–C** return file ages.) Precedence is higher than logical and relational operators, but lower than arithmetic operators. The operator may be any of the following:

–r	File is readable by effective uid.
–w	File is writable by effective uid.
–x	File is executable by effective uid.
–o	File is owned by effective uid.
–R	File is readable by real uid.
–W	File is writable by real uid.
–X	File is executable by real uid.
–O	File is owned by real uid.
–e	File exists.
–z	File has zero size.
–s	File has non-zero size (returns size in bytes).
–f	File is a plain file.
–d	File is a directory.
–l	File is a symbolic link.
–p	File is a named pipe (FIFO).
–S	File is a socket.
–b	File is a block special file.
–c	File is a character special file.
–u	File has setuid bit set.
–g	File has setgid bit set.
–k	File has sticky bit set.
–t	Filehandle is opened to a tty.
–T	File is a text file.
–B	File is a binary file (opposite of –T).
–M	Age of file (at startup) in days since modification.
–A	Age of file (at startup) in days since last access.
–C	Age of file (at startup) in days since inode change.

The interpretation of the file permission operators **–r**, **–R**, **–w**, **–W**, **–x**, and **–X** is based solely on the mode of the file and the uids and gids of the user. There may be other reasons you can't actually read, write, or execute the file. Also note that, for the superuser, **–r**, **–R**, **–w**, and **–W** always return 1, and **–x** and **–X** return 1 if any execute bit is set in the mode. Scripts run by the superuser may thus need to do a **stat( )** in order to determine the actual mode of the file, or temporarily set the uid to something else.

For example:

```
while (<>) {
        chop;
        next unless -f $_;      # ignore specials
        ...
}
```

Note that **–s/a/b/** does not do a negated substitution. Saying **–exp($foo)** still works as expected, however—only single letters following a minus are interpreted as file tests.

The **–T** and **–B** switches work as follows. The first block or so of the file is examined for odd characters such as strange control codes or metacharacters. If too many odd characters (>10%) are found, it's a **–B** file, otherwise it's a **–T** file. Also, any file containing a null in the first block is considered a binary file. If either **–T** or **–B** is used on a filehandle, the current stdio buffer is examined rather than the first block. Both **–T** and **–B** return true on a null file, or a file at EOF when testing a filehandle.

If any of the file tests (or either stat function) are given the special filehandle consisting of a solitary underline, then the stat structure of the previous file test (or stat operator) is used, saving a system call. (This doesn't work with **–t**, and you need to remember that **lstat** and **–l** will leave values in the stat structure for the symbolic link, not the real file. Likewise, **–l** _ will always be false after a normal **stat**.) For example:

```
print "Can do.\n" if -r $a || -w _ || -x _;

stat($filename);
print "Readable\n" if -r _;
print "Writable\n" if -w _;
print "Executable\n" if -x _;
print "Setuid\n" if -u _;
print "Setgid\n" if -g _;
print "Sticky\n" if -k _;
print "Text\n" if -T _;
print "Binary\n" if -B _;
```

File ages for **–M**, **–A**, and **–C** are returned in days (including fractional days) since the script started running. Thus, if the file changed after the script started, you would get a negative time.[26] Note that most times (86399 out of 86400, to be precise) are fractional, so testing for equality with an integer without using **int( )** is usually futile. For example:

```
next unless -M $file > .5;      # files older than 12 hours
&newfile if -M $file < 0;       # file is newer than process
&mailwarning if int(-A) == 90;  # file ($_) is 90 days old today
```

To reset the script's start time to the current time, incant this:

```
$^T = time;
```

Named Unary Operators

Some of the "functions" described in Chapter 4 are really unary operators, including:

alarm	getprotobyname	log	sin
chdir	gethostbyname	ord	sleep
cos	getnetbyname	oct	sqrt
chroot	gmtime	require	srand
exit	hex	reset	umask
eval	int	rand	
exp	length	rmdir	
getpgrp	localtime	readlink	

These are all unary operators, with a higher precedence than some of the other binary operators. For example:

```
sleep 4 | 3;
```

does not sleep for 7 seconds; it sleeps for 4 seconds, and then takes the return value of **sleep** (typically zero) and OR's that with 3, as if the expression were parenthesized as:

```
(sleep 4) | 3;
```

Compare this with:

```
print 4 | 3;
```

---

[26] Incredibly, this is believed by some to be a feature.

which *does* take the value of 4 or'ed with 3 before printing it (7 in this case), as if it were written:

```
print (4 | 3);
```

This is because **print** is a list operator, not a simple unary operator. Once you've learned which operators are list operators, you'll have no trouble telling them apart. When in doubt, you can always use parens to turn a named unary operator into a function. Remember, if it looks like a function, it is a function.

Another funny thing about named unary operators is that many of them default to $_ if you don't supply an argument. HOWEVER. If the thing following the named unary operator looks like it *might* be the start of an argument, Perl will get confused. When the next character in your program is one of the following characters, the Perl tokener returns different token types depending on whether a term or operator is expected:

Char	Operator	Term
+	addition	unary plus
—	subtraction	unary minus
*	multiplication	*name
/	division	/pattern/
<	less than, left shift	<filehandle>, <<EOF
.	concatenation	.3333
?	?:	?pattern?
%	modulo	%assoc
&	&, &&	&subroutine

So a typical boo-boo is:

```
next if length < 80;
```

in which the **<** looks to the parser like the beginning of the **< >** input symbol (a term) instead of the less than (an operator) you were thinking of. There's really no way to fix this, and still keep Perl pathologically eclectic. If you're so incredibly lazy that you cannot bring yourself to type the two characters $_, then say one of these instead:

```
next if length( ) < 80;
next if (length) < 80;
next if 80 > length;
next unless length >= 80;
```

Relational Operators

Perl has two classes of relational operators: one class operates on numeric values, and one class operates on string values. To repeat the table given in the overview:

Numeric test	String test	Meaning
==	eq	Equal to.
!=	ne	Not equal to.
>	gt	Greater than.
>=	ge	Greater than or equal to.
<	lt	Less than.
<=	le	Less than or equal to.
<=>	cmp	Not equal to, with signed result.

These operators return 1 for true, and ″ for false, except for the **<=>** and **cmp** operators, which return a –1 for less than, and a +1 for greater than. String comparisons are based on ASCII collating sequence, and unlike in some languages, trailing spaces count in the comparison. Note that relational operators are non-associating, so **$a < $b < $c** is a syntax error.

Bitwise Logical Operators

Like C, Perl has the bitwise AND, OR, and exclusive-OR operators (**&**, **|**, and **^**), with bitwise-AND having higher precedence. These operators work on numeric values that have first been converted to integer values. If the operands are strings (and the program doesn't contain a call to the **vec( )** function), the operands are first converted to numbers, and then to integers. So, for example:

```
"123.45" & "234.56"
```

is converted to:

```
123.45 & 234.56
```

which is converted to:

```
123 & 234
```

which evaluates to 106.

If a **vec( )** function is present in the program text somewhere, and both of the operands to one of these operators are strings, a bit-wise operation is performed directly on the bit-values of the strings, allowing binary data to be manipulated easily. See the description of **vec( )** in Chapter 4 for more information.

Short-circuit Logical Operators

Like C, Perl provides the **&&** (short-circuit AND) and **||** (short-circuit OR) operators. These operators examine the trueness or falseness of their operands, and return true or false after having evaluated as few operands as possible from left to right. For example, if the left operand of the **&&** operator is false, the right operand is not evaluated, because the result of the operator is false regardless of the value of the right operand.

Such shortcuts are not only timesavers, but are used frequently to control the flow of evaluation. For example, a frequently appearing idiom in Perl programs is something like:

```
open(FILE,"somefile") || die "Cannot open somefile: $!";
```

In this case, Perl first evaluates the **open** function. If the value is true (the open is successful), the execution of the **die** function is unnecessary, and is skipped. You can read this as "open some file or die!".

Note that the short-circuit operators are not commutative if the operands produce side effects. If you reverse the order of the operands, you would have completely changed the meaning of the expression. However, they can be cascaded, as in:

```
open(FILE,"file") && (@data=<FILE>) && close(FILE) ||
      die "Can´t process file";
```

which dies if any of the open, read, or close operations returns a false value.

The **||** and **&&** operators differ from C's in that, rather than returning 0 or 1, they return the last value evaluated. Thus, a portable way to find out the home directory might be:

```
$home = $ENV{´HOME´} || $ENV{´LOGDIR´} ||
    (getpwuid($<))[7] || die "You´re homeless!\n";
```

And a way of setting default arguments might be:

```
$arg = shift || ´a.out´;
```

This uses ´**a.out**´ as the default if there is nothing available to shift.

Range Operator

The range operator is really two entirely different operators depending on the context. In an array context, the operator returns an array of values counting (by ones) from the left value to the right value. This is useful for writing "**for (1..10)**" loops and for doing slice operations on arrays.

In a scalar context, .. returns a Boolean value. The operator is bi-stable, like a flip-flop. Each .. operator maintains its own Boolean state. It is false as long as its left operand is false. Once the left operand is true, the range operator stays true until the right operand is true, *after* which the range operator becomes false again. (It doesn't become false until the next time the range operator is evaluated. It can become false on the same evaluation it became true, but it still returns true once.) The right operand is not evaluated while the operator is in the "false" state, and the left operand is not evaluated while the operator is in the "true" state.

Confused? You may actually be quite familiar with this behavior. The scalar .. operator is primarily intended for doing line number ranges after the fashion of *sed*, *awk*, or *ed* clones like *vi*. The precedence is lower than || and &&. The value returned is either the null string for false, or a sequence number (beginning with 1) for true. The sequence number is reset for each range encountered. The final sequence number in a range has the string ´E0´ appended to it, which doesn't affect its numeric value, but gives you something to search for if you want to exclude the endpoint. You can exclude the beginning point by waiting for the sequence number to be greater than 1. If either operand of scalar .. is a static number (that is, either a number or a numeric expression that can be evaluated at compile time), that operand is implicitly compared to the $. variable, the current line number. See the first example below. If your line number is in a variable, however, you'll have to test it against $. as in the final example.

Here .. is used as a scalar operator:

```
if (101 .. 200) { print; }       # print 2nd hundred lines

next line if 1 .. /^$/;          # skip header lines

$beginend = /^begin/ .. /^end/;
$uudec .= $_ if $beginend && $beginend !~ /^1$|E/;

s/^/> / if /^$/ .. eof();        # quote body

print if $. == $first .. $. == $last;
```

Note that this last example is not the same as:

```
print if $first .. $last;
```

because the implicit comparison to $. only happens with static numbers.

Here are some examples of .. used as an array operator:

```
for (101 .. 200) { print; }      # prints 101102103104...199200

@foo = @foo[$[ .. $#foo];        # an expensive no-op
@foo = @foo[$#foo-4 .. $#foo];   # slice last 5 items
```

Try to avoid saying anything like **for (0..1000000)**, since Perl currently feels that it has to construct the entire array value before starting the loop. Someday this may be optimized.

The range operator (in an array context) makes use of the magical autoincrement algorithm if the first and last values are strings. (If the last value is not in the sequence that the magical increment would produce, the sequence goes until the next value would be longer than the last value.) You can say:

```
@alphabet = (´A´ .. ´Z´);
```

to get all the letters of the alphabet, or:

```
$hexdigit = (0 .. 9, ´a´ .. ´f´)[$somenumber & 15];
```

to get a hexadecimal digit, or:

```
@z2 = (´01´ .. ´31´);  print @z2[$mday];
```

to get dates with leading zeros. Saying (´aa´ .. ´zz´), will generate all combinations of two lowercase letters. Don't try (´aaaaaa´ .. ´zzzzzz´) unless you have *lots* of memory.

Conditional Operator

Like C, Perl has the three-operand conditional operator, as in:

```
TEST-EXPR ? IF-TRUE-EXPR : IF-FALSE-EXPR
```

If the **TEST-EXPR** is true, only the **IF-TRUE-EXPR** is evaluated, and the value of that expression becomes the value of the entire expression. Otherwise, only the **IF-FALSE-EXPR** is evaluated, with its value similarly becoming the value of the entire expression. This works for both scalar context and array context. Examples:

```
print $sex eq ´f´ ? ´pink´ : ´blue´;

@stat = $opt_L ? stat($name) : lstat($name);
```

Assignment Operators

Like C, Perl has assignment operators. There are quite a few of them:

```
=           **=         <<=
            *=          >>=
+=          /=          &=
-=          %=          |=
.=          x=          ^=
```

Each operator requires an lvalue (a variable or array element) on the left side, and some expression on the right side. For the plain assignment operator, =, the value of the expression is stored into the designated variable. (Array assignment is currently allowed only with the plain assignment operator.) For all the other operators, Perl pretends that the expression:

```
$var OP= $value
```

was written as:

```
$var = $var OP $value
```

except that the variable reference is not computed twice. For example:

```
$foo <<= 3;
```

shifts the value of **$foo** left by three places, and:

```
$bar{++$n} .= " smurf";
```

attaches the word **smurf** to the end of the string stored in associative array element **$bar{$n}** after **$n** has been incremented.

In all cases, the value of the assignment is the new value of the variable. Since assignment operators associate right-to-left, this can be used to assign many variables to the same value easily, as in:

```
$a = $b = $c = 0;
```

which assigns 0 to **$c**, and the result of that expression to **$b** (still 0), and the result of *that* expression (still 0) to **$a**.

Array assignment may be done only with the plain assignment operator, =. In an array context, array assignment returns the list of new values just as scalar assignment does. In a scalar context, array assignment returns the number of values that were available on the right side of the assignment. This makes it useful for testing functions that return a null list when they're false, as in:

```
while (($key,$val) = each %gloss) {...

next unless ($dev,$ino,$mode) = stat $file;
```

Comma Operator

Like C, Perl has a comma operator, which simply evaluates its left operand, discards the result, and then evaluates the right operand, returning that as the value of the expression. (This is useful when the left operand is to be evaluated only for its side effects, such as incrementing a variable, or calling a subroutine.) For example:

```
$a = (1, 3);
```

assigns 3 to **$a**. Do not confuse the comma operator with the list-constructor usage of comma, nor the argument separation usage of comma. Neither of these discard the first value. For example, if you change the above example to:

```
@a = (1, 3);
```

you are actually constructing a two-element list, because the array assignment supplies an array context to the right side. And if you change it to:

```
atan2(1, 3);
```

you are calling the function **atan2** with two arguments. Note, however, that **(1,3)[1]** is exactly equivalent to the comma operator (though slower), and **(1,3)[0]** does the reverse comma operator, returning the 1 instead of the 3. And **(1,3)[1,0]** is **(3,1)**.

Regardless of which kind of comma you're using, comma-separated expressions are always evaluated left-to-right in Perl.

Statements

The operators in the last section are used to glue together expressions, which in turn are used to construct statements. The executable part of a Perl program consists of a series of statements, which can be either simple or compound.

Simple Statements

A simple statement is an expression evaluated for its side effects, with a possible modifier. Every expression (simple statement) must be terminated with a semicolon. Note that this is like C, but unlike Pascal (and *awk*).

The expression of a simple statement may optionally be followed by a single modifier, just before the terminating semicolon. The possible modifiers are:

```
if EXPR
unless EXPR
while EXPR
until EXPR
```

The **if** and **unless** modifiers work pretty much as you'd expect if you speak English:

```
&take(´trash´,´out´) if $you_love_me;
&shutup unless $you_want_me_to_leave;
```

The **while** and **until** modifiers evaluate the expression repeatedly as long as the modifier allows it:

```
$extension++ while -e "$filename$extension";
&kiss(´me´) until $I_die;
```

The loop conditional is evaluated before the expression, except when applied to a **do–BLOCK** or a **do–SUBROUTINE** command, in which case the block executes once before the conditional is evaluated. This is so that you can write loops like:

```
do {
        $_ = <STDIN>;
        ...
} until $_ eq ".\n";
```

See the **do** operator later for more details. Note also that the loop control commands mentioned in the section "Compound Statements" will **not** work in this construct, since modifiers don't take loop labels. The solution to this will be shown in that section.

Compound Statements

A sequence of statements may grouped together by enclosing them in curly braces ({}). We will call this a BLOCK. Compound statements are built out of expressions and BLOCKs.

The following compound statements may be used to control flow:

```
if (EXPR) BLOCK
if (EXPR) BLOCK else BLOCK
if (EXPR) BLOCK elsif (EXPR) BLOCK ... else BLOCK
LABEL: while (EXPR) BLOCK
LABEL: while (EXPR) BLOCK continue BLOCK
LABEL: for (EXPR; EXPR; EXPR) BLOCK
```

```
LABEL: foreach VAR (ARRAY) BLOCK
LABEL: BLOCK continue BLOCK
```

Note that, unlike C and Pascal, these constructs are defined in terms of BLOCKs, not statements. This means that the curly braces are *required*—no dangling statements are allowed. If you want to write conditionals without curly braces there are several other ways to do it. The following statements all do the same thing:

```
if (!open(foo)) { die "Can't open $foo: $!"; }
die "Can't open $foo: $!" unless open(foo);
open(foo) || die "Can't open $foo: $!";     # i.e. foo or bust!
open(foo) ? 'hi mom' : die "Can't open $foo: $!";
        # a bit exotic to use the conditional operator for this
```

The **if** statement is straightforward. Since BLOCKs are always bounded by curly braces, there is never any ambiguity about which **if** an **else** goes with. If you use **unless** in place of **if**, the sense of the test is reversed. That is:

```
unless ($one_hump_or_two) ...
```

is equivalent to:

```
if (!$one_hump_or_two) ...
```

The **while** statement repeatedly executes the block as long as the expression is true. The LABEL is optional, and if present, consists of an identifier followed by a colon. The LABEL identifies the loop for the loop control statements **next**, **last**, and **redo**. If there is a **continue** BLOCK, it is always executed just before the conditional is about to be evaluated again. This behavior is similar to the third part of a **for** loop in C. Thus it can be used to increment a loop variable, even when the loop has been continued via a **next** statement.

If the word **while** is replaced by the word **until**, the sense of the test is reversed, but the conditional is still tested before the first iteration.

Within the BLOCK of any compound loop statement, you may use the following simple statements to control the flow:

```
next
next LABEL
last
last LABEL
redo
redo LABEL
```

If the **LABEL** is omitted, the loop control statement refers to the innermost enclosing loop. In many of the examples in this book, you'll note how the **LABEL** can be used, along with a modifier, to make such a statement nearly self-documenting. The **next** statement resumes control at the next interation of the loop, skipping the rest of the current iteration. It is similar to the **continue** statement of C. The **last** statement is like the **break** statement of C, and causes the loop to exit immediately. The **redo** statement is similar to the **next** statement, but restarts the current iteration without evaluating the loop conditional again.

In either the **if** or the **while** statement, you may replace the conditional **(EXPR)** with a BLOCK, and the conditional is true if the value of the last command in that block is true.

The **for** loop works exactly like the corresponding **while** loop:

```
for ($i = 1; $i < 10; $i++) {
        ...
}
```

is the same as:

```
$i = 1;
while ($i < 10) {
        ...
} continue {
        $i++;
}
```

(Note that defining the **for** loop in terms of a **continue** block allows us to preserve the correct semantics even when the loop is continued via Perl's **next** statement. This is unlike C, in which there is no way to write the exact equivalent of a continued **for** loop without chicanery.)

Recall our problem at the end of the previous section. We couldn't use loop control statements inside a:

```
do {
        $_ = <STDIN>;
        ...
} until $_ eq ".\n";
```

because the **do** BLOCK is really a simple expression. But suppose you wanted that loop to weed out comments—just change it to a compound statement like this:

```
for (;;) {
        $_ = <STDIN>;
        next if /^#/;
        ...
        last if $_ eq ".\n";
}
```

The "**for**(;;)" construct is the customary way to write an infinite loop in both C and Perl, and should lead you to expect that a loop exit is to be found somewhere within the loop. For consistency, you can also write an infinite loop as **while** ().

A **foreach** loop iterates over a normal array value and sets the variable VAR to be each element of the array in turn. The variable is implicitly local to the loop, and regains its former value upon exiting the loop. The **foreach** keyword is actually identical to the **for** keyword, so you can use **foreach** for readability or **for** for brevity. (The crucial difference between the normal **for** loop and the **foreach** loop is the presence or absence of semicolons.) If VAR is omitted, $_ is set to each value. If ARRAY is an actual array (as opposed to an expression returning an array value), you can modify each element of the array by modifying VAR inside the loop. Examples:

```
for (@ary) { s/foo/bar/; }

foreach $elem (@elements) {
        $elem *= 2;
}

for (10,9,8,7,6,5,4,3,2,1,'BOOM') {
        print $_, "\n"; sleep(1);
}

for (1..15) { print "Merry Christmas\n"; }

foreach $item (split(/:[\\\n:]*/, $ENV{'TERMCAP'})) {
        print "Item: $item\n";
}
```

Note that there is no way with **foreach** to tell where you are in the list. You can compare adjacent elements by remembering the previous one in a variable, but sometimes you just have to break down and write an ordinary **for** loop with subscripts. That's what **for** is there for, after all..

A BLOCK by itself (labeled or not) is equivalent to a loop that executes once. Thus you can use **last** to leave the block or **redo** to restart the block. For reasons that may or may not become clear upon reflection, a **next** also exits the block. The **continue** block is optional, and is executed by **next**, but not by **last**. This construct is particularly nice for doing case structures.

```
FOO: {
        if (/^abc/) { $abc = 1; last FOO; }
        if (/^def/) { $def = 1; last FOO; }
        if (/^xyz/) { $xyz = 1; last FOO; }
        $nothing = 1;
}
```

There is no official switch statement in Perl, because there are already several ways to write the equivalent. In addition to the example shown above, you could write:

```
FOO: {
        $abc = 1, last FOO  if /^abc/;
        $def = 1, last FOO  if /^def/;
        $xyz = 1, last FOO  if /^xyz/;
        $nothing = 1;
}
```

or:

```
FOO: {
        /^abc/ && do { $abc = 1; last FOO; };
        /^def/ && do { $def = 1; last FOO; };
        /^xyz/ && do { $xyz = 1; last FOO; };
        $nothing = 1;
}
```

or:

```
FOO: {
        /^abc/ && ($abc = 1, last FOO);
        /^def/ && ($def = 1, last FOO);
        /^xyz/ && ($xyz = 1, last FOO);
        $nothing = 1;
}
```

or even, horrors:

```
if (/^abc/)
        { $abc = 1; }
elsif (/^def/)
        { $def = 1; }
elsif (/^xyz/)
        { $xyz = 1; }
else
        {$nothing = 1;}
```

As it happens, these constructs are all optimized internally to a switch structure, so Perl jumps directly to the desired statement, and you needn't worry about Perl executing a lot of unnecessary statements when you have a string of 50 **elsif**'s, as long as you are testing the same simple scalar variable using **==**, **eq**, or pattern matching as above. (If you're curious as to whether the optimizer has done this for a particular case statement, you can compile Perl with **–DDEBUGGING** and use the **–D1024** switch to list the syntax tree.)

Subroutines

A subroutine is defined by a subroutine declaration, which is not an executable statement, so you can put it anywhere in your script. (A subroutine *contains* executable statements, but their meaning isn't related to the location of the subroutine definition.[27]) Subroutines are defined by order of compilation, so in the case of a duplicate name, the latest one compiled takes precedence over any earlier one. In particular, since all calls to the **eval** operator happen after the main program is compiled, any subroutine compiled within an **eval** will override any subroutine defined in the main program, even if the text of the **eval** is earlier in the script.

A subroutine may be declared as follows:

```
sub NAME BLOCK
```

Any arguments passed to the routine come in through the @_ array, that is ($_[0], $_[1], ...). The array @_ is a local array, but its values are references to the actual scalar parameters, which are modifiable. (Nonexistent array values must be created before being passed to a subroutine, if you want to modify them.) The return value of the subroutine is the value of the last expression evaluated, and can be either an array value or a scalar value. Alternately, a **return** statement may be used to specify the returned value and exit the subroutine (at the expense of a little more overhead). In either case, the expression furnishing the return value will be evaluated in a scalar context if the subroutine was called in a scalar context, and in an array context if called in an array context.[28] (You can test this with the **wantarray** function.)

A subroutine is called using the **do** operator or the **&** operator. The **&** operator is the preferred form.

For example:

```
sub MAX {
        local($max) = pop(@_);
        foreach $foo (@_) {
                $max = $foo if $max < $foo;
        }
```

---

[27] Actually, this is not quite true. If you declare a subroutine within the scope of a package definition, the variables within the subroutine will exist in the namespace of that package.

[28] Another fib. If the expression furnishing the return value is in a Boolean context, it's always evaluated in a scalar context even if the subroutine call wants an array value. Such a subroutine will return an array value consisting of a single true or false value.

```
        $max;
}

...
$bestday = &MAX($mon,$tue,$wed,$thu,$fri);
```

For example:

```
# get a line, combining continuation lines
#   that start with whitespace
sub get_line {
        $thisline = defined($lookahead) ? $lookahead : <STDIN>;
        line: while ($lookahead = <STDIN>) {
                if ($lookahead =~ /^[ \t]/) {
                        $thisline .= $lookahead;
                }
                else {
                        last line;
                }
        }
        $thisline;
}

while ($_ = &get_line()) {
        ...
}
```


Passing Arguments by Value

Since a subroutine is a BLOCK, you can create local variables using the **local**
function (see Chapter 4). Use array assignment to a local list to name your formal
arguments:

```
sub maybeset {
        local($key, $value) = @_;
        $foo{$key} = $value unless defined $foo{$key};
}
```

Assigning your parameters to a local list also has the effect of turning call-by-reference into call-by-value, since the assignment copies the values. **We recommend that you always do this except in exceptional cases.** While call-by-reference is efficient, it makes for some interesting aliasing problems that novices
could just as soon do without, especially in combination with the dynamic scoping provided by the **local** operator.[29]

---

[29] If you understood all that, then you're allowed to use call-by-reference any way you want.

Subroutines may be called recursively. If a subroutine is called using the **&** form, the argument list is optional. If omitted, no @_ array is set up for the subroutine; the @_ array at the time of the call is visible to subroutine instead.

```
do foo(1,2,3);       # Pass three arguments.
&foo(1,2,3);         # The same.

do foo();            # Pass a null list.
&foo();              # The same.
&foo;                # Pass no list at all—more efficient.
```

Passing Names

Sometimes you don't want to pass the value of an array to a subroutine but rather the name of it, so that the subroutine can modify the global copy of it rather than working with a local copy. In Perl, you can refer to all the objects of a particular name by prefixing the name with a star, as in ***foo**. This is called a "type glob," because the ***** represents all the funny characters that prefix variables. When evaluated as an rvalue, it produces a scalar value that represents all the objects of that name, including any filehandle, format, or subroutine. When used as an lvalue (typically by assigning a value within a **local( )** operation), it causes the name mentioned to refer to whatever ***** value was assigned to it. For example:

```
sub doubleary {
    local(*someary) = @_;
    foreach $elem (@someary) {
        $elem *= 2;
    }
}

&doubleary(*foo);
&doubleary(*bar);
```

calls the **doubleary** subroutine twice, once for array **@foo**, and once for array **@bar**. All the magic happens in the **local( )** function, where **@foo** or **@bar** is aliased to **@someary**. (Likewise, **$foo, $bar, %foo** and **%bar** are aliased to **$someary** and **%someary** at the same time, but are ignored by the subroutine.) As long as the aliasing is in effect, **@someary** can be used as a synonym for the array that was named by the subroutine call.

Assignment to ***name** is currently recommended only inside a **local( )**. You can actually assign to ***name** anywhere, but if you were previously using **name** as a real variable name elsewhere, the value of that old variable may be stranded forever, and the memory occupied by it may never be freed. If you do this, in other words, just make sure you dedicate that particular name to ***** operations only.

Another possible problem is that:

```
local(*x,*y) = (*y,*x);
```

isn't possible, since as soon as ***x** gets a new value, the symbol table entry that would have been assigned to ***y** is replaced.

Note that scalars are already passed by reference, so you can modify scalar arguments without using this mechanism by referring explicitly to the **$_[nnn]** in question. You can modify all the elements of an array by passing all the elements as scalars, but you have to use the ***** mechanism to push, pop, or change the size of an array. The ***** mechanism will probably be more efficient in any case.

A ***name** value contains unprintable binary data (a structure full of symbol table pointers, actually). Because of this, the **print, printf**, and **sprintf** statements will refuse to print out such a value, but will instead substitute a literal "***name**".

Even if you don't want to modify an array, this mechanism is useful for passing multiple arrays in a single LIST, since normally the LIST mechanism will merge all the array values so that you can't extract out the individual arrays. For example, to add the elements of two arrays, you might do this:

```
sub arrayadd {
        local(*a, *b) = @_;
        local($max) = $#a > $#b ? $#a : $#b;
        local(@sum);
        for (local($i) = 0; $i <= $max; $i++) {
                $sum[$i] = $a[$i] + $b[$i];
        }
        @sum;
}

@foo = (1,2,3);
@bar = (10,20,30);
@totals = &arrayadd(*foo, *bar);
```

You can assign other things to a ***** variable than just another ***** variable. If you assign a normal string to a ***** variable, it will look the string up as a symbol for you. (Note that it looks it up in the current package's symbol table, which might not be the same symbol table as the caller is expecting, if you're in a subroutine that was called from another package.) The following two lines have the same effect, though the first one is a hair more efficient because it does the symbol table lookup at compile time:

```
local(*foo) = *bar;
local(*foo) = 'bar';
```

Regular Expressions

The patterns used in the pattern matching and substitution operators are regular expressions similar to those used by the UNIX *egrep* program. They work like this:

- A regular expression matches a string if any of the alternatives of the regular expression match. Alternatives are separated by the | character (usually called a vertical bar), and are always evaluated left-to-right, stopping on the first complete match.

- An alternative matches if every item in the alternative matches in the order the items occur.

- An item consists of either an assertion or a quantified atom. Assertions are:

^	Matches the beginning of the string (or line, if $* set)
$	Matches the end of the string (or line, if $* set)
\b	Matches on word boundary (between \w and \W)
\B	Matches on non-word boundary

- A quantified atom consists of one of the atoms listed below followed by a quantifier, which indicates how many times the atom must or may occur. If there is no quantifier, the atom must occur exactly once. Quantifiers are:

{n,m}	Must occur at least n times but no more than m times
{n,}	Must occur at least n times
{n}	Must match exactly n times
*	0 or more times (same as {0,})
+	1 or more times (same as {1,})
?	0 or 1 time (same as {0,1})

Legal atoms are:

- A regular expression in parentheses matches whatever the regular expression matches.

- A . matches any character except \n.

- A list of characters in square brackets matches one of a class of characters. A caret at the front of the list negates the class. Character ranges may be indicated using the **a–z** notation. You may also use any of \d, \w, \s, \n, \r, \t, \f, or *nnn*, as listed below. A \b means a backspace in a character class. You may also use a backslash to protect a hyphen that would otherwise be interpreted as a range delimiter.

- A backslashed letter matches a special character or character class:

\n	Newline
\r	Carriage return
\t	Tab
\f	Formfeed
\d	A digit, same as [0–9]
\D	A non-digit
\w	A word character (alphanumeric), same as [0–9a–z_A–Z]
\W	A non-word character
\s	A whitespace character, same as [\t\n\r\f]
\S	A non-whitespace character

- A backslashed single digit number matches whatever the corresponding parentheses actually matched (except that \0 matches a null character). This is called a backreference to a substring. A backslashed multi-digit number such as \10 will be considered a backreference if the pattern contains at least that many substrings prior to it, and the number does not start with a 0.

- A backslashed 2 or 3 digit octal number such as \033 matches the character with the specified value, unless it would be interpreted as a backreference.

- A backslashed x followed by two hexadecimal digits, such as \x7f, matches the character having that hexadecimal value.

- A backslashed c followed by a single character, such as \cD, matches the corresponding control character.

- Any other backslashed character matches that character.

- Any character not mentioned above matches itself.

As mentioned above, \1, \2, \3 . . . are equivalent to whatever the corresponding set of parentheses matched, counting opening parentheses from left to right. (If the particular pair of parentheses had a quantifier such as * after it, such that it matched a series of strings, only the last match counts.) Outside of the pattern (in particular, in the replacement of a substitution operator) you can continue to refer to these strings by using $ instead of \ in front of the number. The variables $1, $2, $3 . . . are automatically localized, and their scope (and that of $`, $&, and $´ below) extends to the end of the enclosing BLOCK or **eval** string, or to the next pattern match with subexpressions. (The \1 notation sometimes works outside the current pattern, but should not be relied upon.) $+ returns whatever the last bracket match matched. **$&** returns the entire matched string. **$`** returns everything before the matched string.[30] **$´** returns everything after the matched string. Examples:

```
s/^([^ ]*) *([^ ]*)/$2 $1/;    # swap first two words

/(\w+)\s*=\s*\1/;              # match "foo = foo"

/.{80,}/;                      # match line of at least 80 chars

/^(\d+\.?\d*|\.\d+)$/;         # match valid Perl number

if (/Time: (..):(..):(..)/) { # pull fields out of a line
        $hours = $1;
        $minutes = $2;
        $seconds = $3;
}
```

Normally, the ^ character will match only at the beginning of a string, the $ character only at the end (or before the newline at the end). Perl does certain optimizations with the assumption that the string contains only one line. You may, however, wish to treat a string as a multi-line buffer, such that the ^ will also match after any newline within the string, and $ will match before any newline. At the cost of a little more overhead, you can do this by setting the variable $* to 1. This can be turned on or off at will—setting it back to 0 makes Perl revert to its normal behavior.

To facilitate multi-line substitutions, the . character never matches a newline (even when $* is 0). In particular, the following leaves a newline on the $_ string:

```
$_ = <STDIN>;
s/.*(some_string).*/$1/;
```

If the newline is unwanted, try one of these:

```
s/.*(some_string).*\n/$1/;
s/.*(some_string)[^\000]*/$1/;
s/.*(some_string)(.|\n)*/$1/;
```

---

[30] In the case of something like **s/pattern/length($`)/eg**, which does multiple replacements if the pattern occurs multiple times, the value of **$`** does not include any modifications done by previous replacement iterations. To get the other effect, say:

```
1 while s/pattern/length($`)/e;
```

For example, to change all tabs to the corresponding number of spaces, you could say:

```
1 while s/\t+/´ ´ x (length($&) * 8 — length($`) % 8)/e;
```

```
chop; s/.*(some_string).*/$1/;
/(some_string)/ && ($_ = $1);
```

You will note that all backslashed metacharacters in Perl are alphanumeric, such as \b, \w, and \n. Unlike some other regular expression languages, there are no backslashed symbols that aren't alphanumeric. So anything that looks like \\, \(, \), \<, \>, \{, or \} is always interpreted as a literal character, not a metacharacter. This makes it simple to quote a string that you want to use for a pattern but that you are afraid might contain metacharacters. Just quote all the non-alphanumeric characters:

```
$pattern =~ s/(\W)/\\\1/g;
```

Hint: instead of writing patterns like /(...)(..)(.....)/, use the **unpack** function.

Formats

Output record formats for use with the **write** operator are defined by the **format** declaration. The **format** declaration is not an executable statement, so it doesn't much matter where it goes in your script (apart from packaging considerations). Formats are defined by order of compilation, so in the case of a duplicate name, the latest one compiled takes precedence over any earlier one. Thus, you can redefine formats using **eval**.

Formats are bound to a filehandle by assigning the format name to the special variables $^ and $~, which respectively change the top-of-form format and the normal format for the currently selected filehandle. (A filehandle starts off using the format of the same name as itself. It will also use a top-of-form format of the same name with "_TOP" appended.) You can explicitly set the formats for the **BURBLE** filehandle like this:

```
local($oldhandle) = select(BURBLE);
$^ = "BURBLE_TOP";
$~ = "BURBLE";
select($oldhandle);
```

or, more succinctly:

```
select((select(BURBLE), $^ = "BURBLE_TOP", $~ = "BURBLE")[0]);
```

The syntax of a format declaration is:

```
format NAME =
FORMLIST
```

If **name** is omitted, format **STDOUT** is defined. FORMLIST consists of a sequence of lines, each of which may be of one of three types:

1. A comment line beginning with **#**.

2. A "picture" line giving the format for one output line.

3. An argument line supplying values to plug into the previous picture line.

Picture lines are printed exactly as they look, except for certain fields that substitute values into the line. Each picture field starts with either @ or ˆ. The @ field (not to be confused with the array marker @) is the normal case; ˆ fields are used to do rudimentary multi-line text block filling. The length of the field is supplied by padding out the field with zero or more **<**, **>**, or **|** characters to specify, respectively, left justification, right justification, or centering. If any of the values supplied for these fields contains a newline, only the text up to the newline is printed. Alternatively, the field may be padded with **#** characters and an optional decimal point. In this case it is formatted as a number with the decimal point in the specified location. The special field @* can be used for printing multi-line values. It should appear by itself on a line.

If a picture field contains any @ or ˆ fields, the corresponding values are specified on the following line, in the same order as the picture fields. The values should be separated by commas. Arbitrary expressions are allowed, but they must all fit on the line.

Picture fields that begin with ˆ rather than @ are treated specially. The value supplied must be a scalar variable or array element containing a text string. Perl puts as much text as it can into the field, and then chops off the front of the string so that the next time the variable is referenced, more of the text can be printed. (This munges your variable, so beware!) Normally you would use a sequence of fields in a vertical stack to print out a block of text. If you like, you can end the final field with **...**, which will appear in the output if the text was too long to appear in its entirety. You can change which characters are legal to break on by changing the variable **$:** to a list of the desired characters. The default value of **$:** allows breaks on space, newline, and hyphen.

Since use of ˆ fields can produce variable length records if the text to be formatted is short, you can suppress blank lines by putting the tilde (˜) character anywhere in the line. (Normally you should put it in the front if possible, for visibility.) The tilde will be translated to a space upon output. If you put a second tilde contiguous to the first, the line will be repeated until all the fields on the line are exhausted and the entire line evaluates to spaces. (If you use a field of the @ variety, the expression you supply had better not give the same value every time forever!) There is an example of this in the bug report format below.

The top-of-form format is printed whenever there is a transition to a new page. A transition happens before the first output record and before any subsequent record for which there is insufficient vertical space remaining on the current page. This is calculated by subtracting the size of the record in lines from the $- variable, which holds the lines remaining on the page. On each new page, the value of $- is reset to the number of lines on the page, stored in $=. Pages are delimited on output by a form feed character.

Examples:

```
#!/usr/bin/perl

# a report on the /etc/passwd file
format top =
                        Passwd File
Name                Login    Office   Uid    Gid Home
                                                            
         .
format STDOUT =
@<<<<<<<<<<<<<<<<<< @|||||||  @<<<<<<@>>>> @>>>> @<<<<<<<<<<<<<<<<
$name,              $login,   $office,$uid,$gid,  $home
         .

open(PASSWD, "/etc/passwd") || die "Can't open passwd: $!\n";
while (<PASSWD>) {
    chop;
    ($login,$passwd,$uid,$gid,$gcos,$home,$shell) = split(/:/);
    ($name,$office,$phone) = split(/,/,$gcos); # (BSD specific!)
    write;
}
```

These two formats would produce something resembling the following output:

		Passwd File			
Name	Login	Office	Uid	Gid	Home
Larry Wall	lwall	270Z	185	120	/u/staff/lwall
Randal Schwartz	merlyn	(none)	1	1	/u/smarty/merlyn
Murgatroyd McMurdo	mm	732AA	54	77	/u/guest/mm
Felice Snoozalot	snoozy	111ZZZ	321	123	/u/ghost/snoozy

. . .

Here is a pair of formats for a bug report. A more extensive example of this can be found under the name **flealist** in Chapter 6.

```
# a report from a bug report form
format top =
                        Bug Reports
@<<<<<<<<<<<<<<<<<<<<<<<<<     @|||       @>>>>>>>>>>>>>>>>>>>>>>
$system,                      $%,        $date
```

```
format STDOUT =
Subject: @<<<<<<<<<<<<<<<<<<<<<<<<<<<<<<<<<<<<<<<<<<<<<<<<<<<<
        $subject
Index: @<<<<<<<<<<<<<<<<<<<<<<<  ^<<<<<<<<<<<<<<<<<<<<<<<<<<
        $index,                  $description
Priority: @<<<<<<<<< Date: @<<<<<<<  ^<<<<<<<<<<<<<<<<<<<<<<<<<
        $priority,       $date,   $description
From: @<<<<<<<<<<<<<<<<<<<<<<<<<  ^<<<<<<<<<<<<<<<<<<<<<<<<<
        $from,                   $description
Assigned to: @<<<<<<<<<<<<<<<<<<<  ^<<<<<<<<<<<<<<<<<<<<<<<<<
            $programmer,          $description
--                                ^<<<<<<<<<<<<<<<<<<<<<<<<<
                                  $description
.
```

It is possible to intermix prints with writes on the same output filehandle, but you'll have to handle $- (lines left on the page) yourself.

If you are printing lots of fields that are usually blank, you should consider using the **reset** operator between records. Not only is it more efficient, but it can prevent the bug of adding another field and forgetting to zero it.

If you want to print footers as well as headers, you can do it by postprocessing the report, like this:

```
format TOP =
Camel Fight Digest                        @>>>>>>>>>>>>>>>>>
                                          $date


Who                                       Winner
FOOTER
@<<<<<<<<<<<<<<<<<           @|||          @>>>>>>>>>>>>>>>>>>>>>
$sponsor                     $%           $whose_pool
FOOTER
.

format OUT =
@<<<<<<<<<<<<<<<<<<<<<<<<<<<<<<<<<<<  @<<<<<<<<<<<<<<<<<<<<<<<<<
$who                                 $winner
.

# Open pipe to a child.

$pid = open(OUT,"|-");
if (!$pid) {                    # We're the child process.
    $/ = "\f";                  # Slurp entire page in.
    $* = 1;                     # Multi-line pattern match.
    while (<STDIN>) {
        ($head,$foot,$body) = split(/^FOOTER/);
        print $head,$body,$foot;    # Rearrange page's anatomy.
    }
}
```

```
else {                          # We´re the parent process.
    select OUT; $^ = ´TOP´; $~ = ´OUT´;
    while (<INPUT>) {
        ...
        write(OUT);             # Pretend footer is header.
    }
}
```

This script opens a pipe to a forked copy of itself by opening the special filename
|–. The parent process uses a top-of-form format that contains both the header
and the footer. The child process pulls in what the parent process writes, one
page at a time, and rearranges the page to put the footer at the bottom. A similar
trick could be used to alter the form feed character that **write** writes.

Special Variables

The following variables have special meaning to Perl. At first glance, they may
look a little like random line noise, but most of them have reasonable mnemonics,
or analogues in one of the shells. You can say one thing for them—they're certainly concise.

Per-filehandle Special Variables

These variables never need to be mentioned in a **local( )** because they always
refer to some value pertaining to the currently selected output filehandle—each
filehandle keeps its own set of values. When you select another filehandle, the
old filehandle keeps whatever values it had in effect, and the variables now reflect
the values of the new filehandle.

The most succinct way to set one or more of these variables for a particular
FILEHANDLE is like this:

```
select((select(FILEHANDLE), $| = 1, $^ = ´mytop´)[0])
```

$| If set to nonzero, forces a flush after every **write** or **print** on the currently
      selected output filehandle. Default is 0, meaning that Perl should rely on
      whatever buffering mechanism standard I/O defaults to. Note that
      STDOUT will typically be line buffered if output is to the terminal and
      block buffered otherwise. Setting this variable is useful primarily when
      you are outputting to a pipe, such as when you are running a Perl script
      under *rsh* and want to see the output as it's happening. It's also valuable

when forking, to prevent duplicate standard I/O buffers from lousing you up. (Mnemonic: when you want your pipes to be piping hot.)

$%   The current page number of the currently selected output filehandle. Incremented automatically by the **write** operator whenever it goes to top-of-form. (Mnemonic: % is page number in *nroff*.)

$=   The current page length (printable lines) of the currently selected output filehandle. Default is 60. (Mnemonic: = has horizontal lines.)

$−   The number of lines left on the page of the currently selected output filehandle. If the next invocation of the **write** operator would put more lines onto the current page than this, a form feed and the top-of-form format are output, followed by the lines that wouldn't fit on the previous page. You can force a top-of-form by saying **$− = 0**. (Mnemonic: **lines_on_page − lines_printed**. Or, if you prefer, T minus n lines and counting. . .)

$~   The name of the current report format for the currently selected output filehandle. You can bind any format to any filehandle by assigning to this when the filehandle is selected. (Mnemonic: closely related to $^.)

$^   The name of the current top-of-page format for the currently selected output filehandle. You can make any format be the top-of-form format for any filehandle by assigning to this when the filehandle is selected. (Mnemonic: points to top of page.)

Local Special Variables

There are several variables that are always local to the current block, so you never need to mention them in a **local( )**. All of them are associated with the last successful pattern match.

$1..$9
      Contains the subpattern from the corresponding set of parentheses in the last pattern matched, not counting patterns matched in nested blocks that have been exited already. If there were no corresponding parentheses that matched, the undefined value is returned. (Mnemonic: like \1..\9.)

$&   The string matched by the last pattern match, not counting patterns matched in nested blocks that have been exited already. (Mnemonic: like **&** in some editors.)

$` The string preceding whatever was matched by the last pattern match, not counting patterns matched in nested blocks that have been exited already. (Mnemonic: ` often precedes a quoted string in normal text.)

$´ The string following whatever was matched by the last pattern match, not counting patterns matched in nested blocks that have been exited already. (Mnemonic: ´ often follows a quoted string in normal text.) For example:

```
$_ = ´abcdefghi´;
/def/;
print "$`:$&:$´\n";      # prints abc:def:ghi
```

$+ The last bracket matched by the last search pattern. This is useful if you don't know which of a set of alternative patterns matched. For example:

```
/Version: (.*)|Revision: (.*)/ && ($rev = $+);
```

(Mnemonic: be positive and forward looking.)

Global Special Variables

There are quite a few variables that are global in the fullest sense—they mean the same thing in every package. If you want a private copy of one of them, you must localize it in the current block.

$_ The default input and pattern-searching space. The following pairs are equivalent:

```
while (<>) {...      # equivalent only in while!
while ($_ = <>) {...

/^Subject:/
$_ =~ /^Subject:/

y/a-z/A-Z/
$_ =~ y/a-z/A-Z/

chop
chop($_)
```

(Mnemonic: underline is understood to be underlying certain undertakings.)

$. The current input line number of the last filehandle that was read. Remember that only an explicit close on the filehandle resets the line number. Since **< >** never does an explicit close, line numbers increase across **ARGV** files. Note that, when you say **local($.)**, you're actually localizing Perl's memory of the last filehandle read, not the value of **$.** itself. (Mnemonic: many programs use **.** to mean the current line number.)

$/ The input record separator, newline by default. **$/** may be set to a value longer than one character in order to match a multi-character delimiter. Setting **$/** to a null string is the same as setting it to **"\n\n"**, causing Perl to read input a paragraph at a time, delimited by blank lines. If **$/** is undefined, no record separator is matched, and **<FILEHANDLE>** will read everything to the end of the current file. (Mnemonic: / is used to delimit line boundaries when quoting poetry. Or, if you prefer, think of mad slashers cutting things to ribbons.)

$\ The output record separator for the **print** operator. Ordinarily the **print** operator simply prints out the comma-separated fields you specify, with no trailing newline or record separator assumed. In order to get behavior more like *awk*, set this variable to a newline. (Mnemonic: you set **$** instead of adding **\n** at the end of the **print**. Also, it's just like /, but it's what you get "back" from Perl.)

$, The output field separator for the **print** operator. Ordinarily the **print** operator simply prints out the comma-separated fields you specify, with no intervening delimiter. You can set this variable to make it print out a delimiter such as a space between each element of the **print** operator's list. (Mnemonic: what is printed when there is a **,** in your **print** statement.)

$" This is similar to **$,** except that it applies to array values interpolated into a double-quoted string (or similar interpreted string). Default is a space. (Mnemonic: obvious, I think.)

$# The output format for numbers displayed via the **print** operator. (Does not apply to format declarations.) This variable is a half-hearted attempt to emulate *awk*'s **OFMT** variable. There are times, however, when *awk* and Perl have differing notions of what is in fact numeric. Also, the initial value is **%.20g** rather than **%.6g**, so you need to set **$#** explicitly to get *awk*'s value. In general, don't use this if you can. (Mnemonic: **#** is the number sign.)

$$ The process number of the Perl running this script. (Mnemonic: same as shells.)

$? The status returned by the last pipe close, backtick (``) command or **system** operator. Note that this is the status word returned by the **wait**() system call, so the exit value of the subprocess is actually (**$? >> 8**). **$? & 255** gives which signal, if any, the process died from, and whether there was a core dump. (Mnemonic: similar to *sh* and *ksh*.)

$* Set to 1 to do multi-line matching within a string, 0 to tell Perl that it can assume that strings contain a single line, for the purpose of optimizing pattern matches. Default is 0. (Mnemonic: * matches multiple things.)

$0 Contains the name of the file containing the Perl script being executed. Depending on your operating system, it may or may not include the full pathname. (Mnemonic: same as *sh* and *ksh*.) You may set **$0** to some other value to change what the *ps*(1) program sees as your command.

$[The index of the first element in an array, and of the first character in a substring. Default is 0, but you could set it to 1 to make Perl behave more like *awk* (or Fortran) when subscripting and when evaluating the **index**() and **substr**() functions. (Mnemonic: [begins subscripts.)

$] The first part of the string printed out when you say **perl –v**. It can be used to determine at the beginning of a script whether the Perl interpreter executing the script is in the right range of versions. If used in a numeric context, **$]** returns version + patchlevel / 1000.

(Mnemonic: Is this version of Perl in the "*right*bracket" ?)

$; The subscript separator for multi-dimensional array emulation. If you refer to an associative array element as:

    $foo{$a,$b,$c}

it really means:

    $foo{join($;, $a, $b, $c)}

But don't put:

    @foo{$a,$b,$c}   # a slice—note the @

which means:

    ($foo{$a},$foo{$b},$foo{$c})

Default is "\034", the same as **SUBSEP** in *awk*, but it would be reasonable to set it to the null character. Note that if your keys contain binary data there might not be any safe value for **$;**—building a key with **pack** would be your best bet in that case. (Mnemonic: comma (the syntactic subscript separator) is a semi-semicolon. Yeah, it's pretty lame, but **$,** is already taken for something more important.)

$! If used in a numeric context, yields the current value of **errno**, with all the usual caveats. (This means that you shouldn't depend on the value of **$!** to be anything in particular unless you've gotten a specific error return indicating a system error.) If used in a string context, yields the corresponding system error string. You can assign to **$!** in order to set **errno** if, for instance, you want **$!** to return the string for that value of **errno**, or you want to set the exit value for the **die** operator. All the usual warnings about using **errno** also apply here; for example, some stdio routines alter the value of **errno**, and will likewise mess up **$!** on some unspecified I/O operations. Sorry we can't be more specific, but it really depends on your library routines. If you don't invoke any system calls, you're probably safe. (But then *you* have to know which Perl operations invoke system calls and which don't. Sigh.) If you're wondering what **errno** is, it's the global variable through which UNIX returns error numbers to C programs. It's only for system errors. If you're interested in the Perl error message from the **eval**, **do–FILE**, or **require**, see **$@** instead. (Mnemonic: what just went *bang*?)

$@ The Perl syntax error or runtime error message from the last **eval**, **do–FILE**, or **require** command. If set, either the compilation failed, or the **die** function was executed within the code of the **eval**. If **$@** is null, then whatever you evaluated parsed and executed correctly (although the operations you invoked may have failed in the normal fashion, returning undefined values or **$!** values). (Mnemonic: where was the syntax error *at*?)

$<** The real uid (user ID) of this process. Probably not useful except on UNIX systems. Operations on **$< may be restricted on UNIX systems that support only the **setuid()** system call. (Mnemonic: it's the uid you came *from*, if you're running setuid.)

$> The effective uid (user ID) of this process. Probably not useful except on UNIX systems, where the real and effective uids can differ when you're running a setuid program. Examples:

```
$< = $>;        # set real uid to the effective uid
($<,$>) = ($>,$<);      # swap real and effective uid
```

Operations on **$>** may be restricted on UNIX systems that support only the **setuid()** system call. For instance, **$<** and **$>** can be swapped only on machines supporting **setreuid()**. (Mnemonic: it's the uid you went *to*, if you're running setuid.)

$(The real gid of this process. If you are on a machine that supports member-ship in multiple groups simultaneously, gives a space separated list of groups you are in. The first number is the one returned by **getgid( )**, and the subsequent ones by **getgroups( )**, one of which may be the same as the first number. (Mnemonic: parentheses are used to *group* things. The real gid is the group you *left*, if you're running setgid.)

$)   The effective gid of this process. If you are on a machine that supports membership in multiple groups simultaneously, gives a space separated list of groups you are in. The first number is the one returned by **getegid( )**, and the subsequent ones by **getgroups( )**, one of which may be the same as the first number. (Mnemonic: parentheses are used to *group* things. The effective gid is the group that's *right* for you, if you're running setgid.)

Note: **$(** and **$)** can be swapped only on machines supporting **setregid( )**.

$:   The current set of characters after which a string may be broken to fill continuation fields (starting with ˆ) in a format. Default is " \n–", to break on whitespace or hyphens. (Mnemonic: a colon in poetry is a part of a line.)

$ˆD   The current value of Perl's internal debugging flags—see the –D switch in Chapter 7. Setting this variable has no effect unless the –D switch was specified on the command line. (Perl must also have been compiled with the **–DDEBUGGING** flag.) Setting the **1024** bit has the side effect of causing an immediate printout of the syntax tree. (Mnemonic: "D" for debugging.)

$ˆF   The maximum system file descriptor, ordinarily 2. System file descriptors are passed to subprocesses, while higher file descriptors are not. During an open, system file descriptors are preserved even if the open fails. Ordinary file descriptors are closed before the open is attempted. (Mnemonic: "F" for file descriptor.)

$ˆI   The current value of the inplace-edit extension. Use **undef** to disable inplace editing. (Mnemonic: value of –i switch.)

$ˆP   The internal flag that the debugger clears so that it doesn't debug itself. You could conceivably disable debugging yourself by clearing it. (Mnemonic: "P" for *perldb.pl*.)

$ˆT   The time of day (in the same form that the **time** function returns) when the current script began execution. This time is used with the –A, –C, and –M, operators to compute how old a file is relative to the beginning of the script's execution. You may set this variable to any number (such as the value returned by **time** to perform file tests relative to the current time), or examine it to determine how long your program has been running. (Mnemonic: it's the time "T" at the beginning """ of your program.)

$^W   The current value of the warning switch. (Mnemonic: related to the **–w** switch.)

$^X   The name that *perl* itself was executed as, from argv[0]. (Mnemonic: "X" for executable.)

_   The special filehandle designator for file tests and the stat operators. This filehandle means to use the existing stat data, rather than performing a new stat on a file or filehandle. You can use this filehandle as a normal filehandle as long as you don't try to stat it!

ARGV
    The special filehandle that interates over command line filenames in **@ARGV.** Usually written as the null filehandle in **< >.**

$ARGV
    The variable containing the name of the current file when reading from **<ARGV>.**

@ARGV
    The array containing the command line arguments intended for the script. Note that **$#ARGV** is generally the number of arguments minus one, since **$ARGV[0]** is the first argument, NOT the command name. See **$0** for the command name.

DATA   The special filehandle that refers to anything following the **__END__** token in the file containing the script.

@F   The array into which the input lines are autosplit when the **–a** command line option is given; no special meaning otherwise.

@INC
    The array containing the list of places to look for Perl scripts to be evaluated by the **do EXPR** or **require** commands. It initially consists of the arguments to any **–I** command line switches, followed by the default Perl library, probably */usr/local/lib/perl*, followed by . to represent the current directory. When testing your own library routines you may wish to say **unshift(@INC, ´.´)** to give your file precedence over a library file.

%INC
    The associative array containing entries for each filename that has been included via **do** or **require**. The key is the filename you specified, and the value is the location of the file actually found. The **require** com-

mand uses this array to determine whether a given file has already been included.

%ENV

The associative array containing your current environment. Setting a value in **%ENV** changes the environment for child processes:

```
$ENV{´PATH´} = "/bin:/usr/bin";
```

Note that processes run as a *crontab* entry inherit a particularly impoverished set of environment variables. If you have a script that runs when invoked normally but won't run under *cron*, try setting your **PATH** explicitly to include all the directories you need.

%SIG

The associative array used to set signal handlers for various signals. Examples:

```
sub handler {   # 1st argument is signal name
        local($sig) = @_;
        print "Caught a SIG$sig—shutting down\n";
        close(LOG);
        exit(0);
}

$SIG{´INT´} = ´handler´;
$SIG{´QUIT´} = ´handler´;
...
$SIG{´INT´} = ´DEFAULT´;          # restore default action
$SIG{´QUIT´} = ´IGNORE´;          # ignore SIGQUIT
```

The **%SIG** array contains values only for the signals actually set within the Perl script. All signal handlers are assumed to be defined in **package main** unless you explicitly say something like:

```
$SIG{"INT"} = "foo´handler";
```

Don't forget that ignored signals will still be ignored across calls to **fork** and **exec**, including the implicit forking sometimes done by the **open()** function.

STDERR

The special filehandle for standard error in any package. (Also known as **main´stderr**.)

STDIN

The special filehandle for standard input in any package. (Also known as **main´stdin**.)

STDOUT
> The special filehandle for standard output in any package. (Also known as **main´stdout**.)

Packages

Sometimes a set of routines will want to have private data that other routines can't access. Perl provides a packaging mechanism to prevent routines from stomping on each other's variables. A package in Perl simply provides an alternate namespace for variables—you can have the same variable name in two different packages and they are two different variables. By default, a Perl script starts compiling into the package known as **main**. However, by use of the **package** declaration, you can switch namespaces. The scope of the package declaration (how long it lasts) is from the declaration itself to the end of the enclosing block (the same scope as the **local( )** operator). Typically the declaration would be the first thing in a block, or in a file to be included by the **require** operator, but the declaration can go anywhere, as in this bizarre example:

```
package pecan;
sub pie {
    $answer = <STDIN>;   # One variable.
    package canary;
    $answer = <STDIN>;   # A different variable.
}
```

You can declare the same package in more than one place; the declaration merely influences which symbol table (namespace) is used by the compiler for the rest of that block. You can refer to variables and filehandles in other packages by prefixing the identifier with the package name and a single quote. The previous example is equivalent to this one:

```
sub pecan´pie {
    $pecan´answer = <STDIN>;
    $canary´answer = <STDIN>;
}
```

Note that declaring the subroutine as **pecan´pie** does not automatically put the interior of the subroutine into package **pecan**. Only the **package** declaration itself can influence the packaging of subsequent statements.

If the package name is null, the **main** package as assumed, so **$´gadfly** and **$main´gadfly** are the same variable.

Only identifiers starting with letters are stored in the package's symbol table. All other symbols (all the special variables) are kept in the **main** package. In addition, the identifiers **STDIN, STDOUT, STDERR, ARGV, ARGVOUT, ENV, INC,** and **SIG** are forced to be in the **main** package, even when used for purposes other than their built-in one.

Strings passed to **eval** are compiled in the package in which the **eval** was compiled. (Assignments to $SIG{}, however, assume the signal handler specified is in the **main** package. Qualify the signal handler name if you wish to have a signal handler in a package.) For an example, examine **perldb.pl** in the Perl library.[31] It initially switches to the **DB** package so that the debugger doesn't interfere with variables in the script you are trying to debug. At various points, however, it temporarily switches back to the package the user is currently running in to evaluate various expressions in the context of that package.

The symbol table for each package happens to be stored in an associative array in the main symbol table. The name of the symbol table for package **blue** would be none other than **%_blue**.[32] When you use the ***name** notation, you are in fact referring to the value of the corresponding entry in the associative array for that symbol table. The following have the same effect (in package **main**, anyway):

```
local(*foo) = *bar;
local($_main{'foo'}) = $_main{'bar'};
```

Although these accomplish the same thing, the ***foo** is more efficient because it does the symbol table lookup once at compile time rather than each time the statement is executed.

You can use this knowledge to print out all the variables in a package, for instance. Here is an early version of **dumpvar.pl** from the Perl library:

```
package dumpvar;

sub main'dumpvar {
    ($package) = @_;

    # This next line gives us an alias for the associative array
    # containing the symbol table for the specified package.

    local(*stab) = eval("*_$package");

    # Now that we have defined %stab, look at all the symbol
    # table entries it contains.
```

---

[31] In fact, your best introduction to packages is simply to *cd* over to the Perl library and start looking at those **.pl** files containing the word "package."

[32] As you might expect, there's a **%_main** symbol table in the **main** package.

```
while (($key,$val) = each(%stab)) {

    # Alias the particular symbol table entry.

    local(*entry) = $val;

    # Now check for different objects of that name.
    # Is there a scalar?

    if (defined $entry) {
        print "\$$key = ´$entry´\n";
    }
    # Is there a normal array?
    if (defined @entry) {
        print "\@$key = (\n";
        foreach $num ($[ .. $#entry) {
            print "   $num\t´",$entry[$num],"´\n";
        }
        print ")\n";
    }
    # Is there an associative array that isn´t the one
    # we´re currently iterating through?
    if ($key ne "_$package" && defined %entry) {
        print "\%$key = (\n";
        foreach $key (sort keys(%entry)) {
            print "   $key\t´",$entry{$key},"´\n";
        }
        print ")\n";
    }
  }
 }
}
```

Note that, even though the subroutine is compiled in package **dumpvar**, the name of the subroutine is qualified so that its name is inserted into package **main**.

4

Functions

This chapter describes each of the Perl functions. They're presented one-by-one in alphabetical order. (Well, actually, some related functions are presented in pairs, or even threes or fours. This is usually the case when the perl functions simply make UNIX system calls or C library calls. In such cases, the description of the Perl function matches up with the corresponding UNIX "manpage" organization.)

Each function description begins with a brief presentation of the syntax for that function. Parameters in ALL CAPS represent placeholders for actual expressions, as described in the body of the function description. Some parameters are optional; the text describes the default values used when the parameter is not included.

Along with the literals and variables mentioned earlier, the operations in this chapter can serve as terms in an expression. Some of these operations take a LIST as an argument. Such a list can consist of any combination of scalar arguments or array values; the array values will be included in the list as if each individual element were interpolated at that point in the list, forming a longer single-dimensional array value. Elements of the LIST should be separated by commas. Each element of the LIST will be evaluated in an array context.

If the syntax for an operation is given both with and without parentheses around its arguments, it means you can either use it as a unary operator or as a function call. To use it as a function call, the next token on the same line must be a left parenthesis. (There may be intervening whitespace.) Such a function then has highest precedence, as you would expect from a function. (This means, in particular, that anything following the right parenthesis is **not** part of the arguments to the function!) If any token other than a left parenthesis follows, then it is a unary operator, with a precedence depending only on whether it is a LIST operator or not. LIST operators have lowest precedence. (This means that a LIST operator will gobble up all the arguments all the way to the semicolon or enclosing parenthesis.) All other named unary operators have a precedence greater than relational operators but less than arithmetic operators.

Some of the LIST operators impose special semantic significance on the first element or two of the list. For example, the **chmod** function requires that the first element of the list be the new permission to apply to the files listed in the remaining elements. Syntactically, however, the argument to **chmod** is really just a LIST, and you could say:

```
unshift(@array,0644);
chmod @array;
```

which is the same as:

```
chmod 0644, @array;
```

In these cases, the syntax summary at the top of the section mentions only the bare LIST, and any special initial arguments are documented in the description.

Many of these operations are based directly on the C library's functions. If so, we do not attempt to duplicate the UNIX system documentation for that function, but refer you directly to the manual page. Such references look like this: "See *getlogin*(3)." The number in parentheses tells you two things: first, that it's a manual page entry, and second, that the entry is customarily found in that particular section of the UNIX manual—typically section 2 for system calls and section 3 for the library routines built up on top of the system calls. (If you can't find a manual page for a particular C function on your system, it's likely that the corresponding Perl function is unimplemented. For example, not all systems implement socket calls.)

Occasionally you'll find that the documented C function has more arguments than the corresponding Perl function. These are almost always things that Perl already knows, such as the length of the previous argument, so you needn't supply them in Perl. Any remaining disparities are due to different ways Perl and C specify their filehandles and file descriptors.

/PATTERN/

```
/PATTERN/[g][i][o]
m/PATTERN/[g][i][o]
```

This construct searches a string for a pattern match, and in a scalar context returns true (1) or false (´´). PATTERN must be a regular expression—see the section "Regular Expressions" in Chapter 3. If no string is bound to the match operator via the =˜ or !˜ operator, the $_ string is searched. (The string specified with =˜ need not be an lvalue—it may be the result of an expression evaluation, but remember that =˜ binds rather tightly, so you may need parentheses around the expression.)

If / is the delimiter, then the initial **m** is optional. With **m,** you can use any pair of non-alphanumeric characters as delimiters.[33] This is particularly useful for matching UNIX pathnames that contain /. If the final delimiter is followed by the optional letter **i**, the matching is done in a case-insensitive manner. PATTERN may contain references to scalar variables, which will be interpolated (and the pattern recompiled) every time the pattern search is evaluated. (You can use single quotes as delimiters to suppress variable interpolation.) Note that $) and $| may not be interpolated, because they look like end-of-string tests. If you want an interpolated pattern to be compiled only once, add an **o** after the trailing delimiter. This avoids expensive runtime recompilations, and is useful when the value you are interpolating won't change over the life of the script.

If // is used in a context that requires an array value, a pattern match returns an array consisting of the subexpressions matched by the parentheses in the pattern (that is, "($1, $2, $3...)".) It does **not** actually set $1, $2, and so on in this case, nor does it set $+, $`, $&, or $´. If the match fails, a null array is returned. (Thus, if the match is on the right side of an array assignment, the array assignment itself will be false if the match fails.) If the match succeeds, but there were no parentheses, an array value of (1) is returned.

Here is a code fragment that gets input from the terminal and performs a subroutine only if the user said something beginning with **y** or **Y** (note the **i** modifier for case insensitivity):

```
open(TTY, ´/dev/tty´);
<TTY> =˜ /^y/i && &xyz( );      # do xyz if desired
```

The next pattern extracts the value of a header line containing a version number. Note that . is not a metacharacter inside square brackets.

---

[33] Well, not just *any* pair—the opening and closing delimiter have to be the same character.

```
if (/Version: *([0-9.]*)/) { $version = $1; }
```

The use of an alternate delimiter makes the next example much more readable than quoting the slashes with backslashes would.

```
next if m#^/usr/spool/uucp#;
```

Next we have a "grep" program, illustrating the use of the **o** modifier. Since **$arg** never changes over the life of the program, there's no reason to compile the pattern more than once.

```
# poor man's grep
$arg = shift;
while (<>) {
        print if /$arg/o;          # compile only once
}
```

This next one is worth studying a bit. It illustrates the use of a pattern in an array context to retrieve the substrings. It also illustrates the use of an array assignment in a scalar context.

```
if (($F1, $F2, $Etc) = ($foo =~ /^(\S+)\s+(\S+)\s*(.*)/))
```

The example splits **$foo** into the first two words and the remainder of the line, and assigns those three fields to **$F1**, **$F2**, and **$Etc**. The conditional is true if any variables were assigned, that is, if the pattern matched, since the scalar value of an array assignment is the number of values supplied by the right side of the assignment.

The **g** modifier allows you to do global matching on a string—that is, to match a given string as many times as possible. In a scalar context, it remembers where it left off searching the previous time, and starts searching again at that point. In computer science terms, it has an iterator built into it, so you might use it as the conditional of a **while** loop:

```
while (/\w+/g) { push(@words, $&); }
```

In an array context, the **g** modifier causes the pattern to return all the matches as a list. The following fragment does the same thing as the previous one:

```
push(@words, /\w+/g);
```

If the pattern contains parentheses, all the matched substrings from all the matched patterns are returned as a list. For instance, you could use such a pattern to pick out VARIABLE=VALUE pairs from a line and assign them all to an associative array, like this:

```
%userdefs = /(\b\w+)=(\S*)/g;
```

?PATTERN?

```
?PATTERN?[i][o]
```

This is just like the **/PATTERN/** search, except that it matches only once between calls to the **reset** operator, so it finds the first occurrence of something rather than the last. This is useful (and more efficient) when you want to see only the first occurrence of the pattern in each file of a set of files, for instance. Only those **??** patterns local to the current package are reset.

accept

```
accept(NEWSOCKET,GENERICSOCKET)
```

This function does the same thing as the **accept** system call—see *accept*(2). Used by server processes that wish to "accept" socket connections from clients. Execution is suspended until a connection is made, at which time it opens the NEWSOCKET filehandle and attaches it to newly made connection. The function returns the connected address if it succeeded, false otherwise (and puts the error code into $!). The GENERICSOCKET must be a filehandle already opened via the **socket**( ) operator and bound to the server's network address. For example:

```
unless ($peer = accept(NS, S)) {
    die "Can't accept a connection: $!\n";
}
```

See also the example in the section "Interprocess Communication" in Chapter 6.

alarm

```
alarm(EXPR)
alarm EXPR
```

This function causes the script to be signaled with a SIGALARM after EXPR seconds. On some systems, the systems sends alarms at the "top of the second," so, for instance, an **alarm 1** may go off anywhere between 0 to 1 second from now, depending on when in the current second it is. An **alarm 2** may go off anywhere from 1 to 2 seconds from now. And so on. For better resolution, you may be able to use **syscall**( ) to call the **itimer** routines that some UNIX systems support.

atan2

```
atan2(X,Y)
```

This function returns the arctangent of X/Y in the range $-\pi$ to π. A quick way to get the value of π is to say:

```
$pi = atan2(1,1) * 4;
```

bind

```
bind(SOCKET,NAME)
```

This function does the same thing as the **bind** system call—see *bind*(2). The function attaches an address (a name) to an already opened socket specified by the SOCKET filehandle. The function returns true if it succeeded, false otherwise (and puts the error code into **$!**). NAME should be a packed address of the proper type for the socket.

```
bind(S, $sockaddr) || die "Can´t bind address: $!\n";
```

See also the example in the section "Interprocess Communication" in Chapter 6.

binmode

```
binmode(FILEHANDLE)
binmode FILEHANDLE
```

This function arranges for the file to be read in "binary" mode in operating systems that distinguish between binary and text files. It should be called after the open but before any I/O is done on the filehandle. The only way to reset binary mode on a filehandle is to reopen the file.

On systems that distinguish binary mode from text mode, files that are read in text mode have \r\n sequences translated to \n on input and \n translated to \r\n on output. **binmode( )** has no effect under UNIX. If FILEHANDLE is an expression, the value is taken as the name of the filehandle. The following example shows how a Perl script might prepare to read a word processor file with embedded control codes:

```
open(WP, "$file.wp") || die "Can´t open $file.wp: $!\n";
binmode WP;
while (read(WP, $buf, 1024)) {...}
```

caller

```
caller(EXPR)
caller EXPR
caller
```

This function returns information about the subroutine call stack. Without an argument it returns the package name, filename, and line number that currently executing subroutine was called from:

```
($package, $filename, $line) = caller;
```

With an argument it evaluates EXPR as the number of stack frames to go back before the current one. It also reports some additional information, and magically sets **@DB´args** to the arguments passed in that stack frame. It's primarily used by the debugger to print out stack traces.

```
$i = 0;
while (($pack, $file, $line, $subname, $hasargs, $wantarray)
  = caller($i++)) {
    . . .
}
```

chdir

```
chdir(EXPR)
chdir EXPR
```

This function changes the working directory to EXPR, if possible. If EXPR is omitted, it changes to the home directory. The function returns 1 upon success, 0 otherwise (and puts the error code into **$!**). Since **chdir** is a named unary operator, it has a precedence higher than ||:

```
chdir "$prefix/lib" || die "Can´t cd to $prefix/lib: $!\n";
```

The following code can be used to move to the user's home directory, one way or another:

```
$ok = chdir($ENV{"HOME"} || $ENV{"LOGDIR"} || (getpwuid($<))[7]);
```

Alternately, taking advantage of the default, you could say this:

```
$ok = chdir() || chdir((getpwuid($<))[7]);
```

See also the **pwd.pl** library package, described in Appendix B, which lets you keep track of your current directory.

chmod

```
chmod(LIST)
chmod LIST
```

This function changes the permissions of a list of files. The first element of the list must be the numerical mode, as in *chmod*(2). (When using nonliteral mode data, you may need to convert an octal string to a decimal number using the **oct**() function.) The function returns the number of files successfully changed. For example:

```
$cnt = chmod 0755, ´foo´, ´bar´;
```

will set **$cnt** to **0**, **1**, or **2**, depending on how many files got changed (in the sense that the operation succeeded, not in the sense that the bits were different afterwards). Here's a more typical usage:

```
chmod 0755, @executables;
```

If you need to know which files didn't change, use something like this:

```
@cannot = grep(!(chmod 0755, $_), ´tom´, ´dick´, ´harry´);
die "$0: could not chmod @cannot\n" if @cannot;
```

This idiom makes use of the **grep** function to select only those elements of the list for which the **chmod** function failed.

chop

```
chop(LIST)
chop(VARIABLE)
chop VARIABLE
chop
```

This function chops off the last character of a string and returns the character chopped. The **chop** operator is used primarily to remove the newline from the end of an input record, but is more efficient than s/\n$//. If VARIABLE is omitted, the function chops the **$_** variable. For example:

```
while (<PASSWD>) {
        chop;   # avoid \n on last field
        @array = split(/:/);
        . . .
}
```

If you chop a LIST, each string in the list is chopped:

```
@lines = ´cat myfile´;
chop(@lines);
```

You can actually chop anything that is an lvalue, including an assignment:

```
chop($cwd = `pwd`);
chop($answer = <STDIN>);
```

Note that this is different from:

```
$answer = chop(<STDIN>);
```

which puts a newline into $answer, because **chop** returns the character chopped, not the remaining string.

To chop more than one character, use **substr** as an lvalue, assigning a null string. The following removes the last 5 characters of **$caravan**:

```
substr($caravan, -5) = ``;
```

The negative subscript causes **substr( )** to count from the end of the string instead of the beginning.

chown

```
chown(LIST)
chown LIST
```

This function changes the owner (and group) of a list of files. The first two elements of the list must be the *numerical* uid and gid, in that order. The function returns the number of files successfully changed. For example:

```
$cnt = chown $uid, $gid, `foo`, `bar`;
```

will set **$cnt** to **0, 1,** or **2,** depending on how many files got changed (in the sense that the operation succeeded, not in the sense that the owner was different afterwards). Here's a more typical usage:

```
chown $uid, $gid, @filenames;
```

Here's a subroutine that looks everything up for you, and then does the chown:

```
sub chown_by_name {
        local($user, $pattern) = @_;
        chown((getpwnam($user))[2,3], <${pattern}>);
}

&chown_by_name("fred", "*.c");
```

Notice that this forces the group of each file to be the gid fetched from the *passwd* file. An alternative would be to pass a -1 for the gid, which will leaves the group of the file unchanged.

chroot

```
chroot(FILENAME)
chroot FILENAME
```

This function does the same operation as the **chroot** system call—see *chroot*(2). If successful, FILENAME becomes the new root directory for the current process—the starting point for pathnames beginning with `/`. This directory is inherited across **exec** calls and by all subprocesses. There is no way to undo a **chroot**. Only the superuser can use this function. Here's some code that approximates what many FTP servers do:

```
chroot +(getpwnam('ftp'))[7] ||
        die "Can't do anonymous ftp: $!\n";
```

close

```
close(FILEHANDLE)
close FILEHANDLE
```

This function closes the file, socket, or pipe associated with the filehandle. You don't have to close FILEHANDLE if you are immediately going to do another **open** on it, since the next **open** will close it for you. (See **open**.) However, an explicit close on an input file resets the line counter (**$.**), while the implicit close done by **open** does not. Also, closing a pipe will wait for the process executing on the pipe to complete, in case you want to look at the output of the pipe afterwards, or prevent the script from exiting before the pipeline is finished.[34] Closing a pipe explicitly also puts the status value of the command into **$?**. For example:

```
open(OUTPUT, '|sort >foo');    # pipe to sort
...                            # print stuff to output
close OUTPUT;                  # wait for sort to finish
die "sort failed" if $?;       # check for sordid sort
open(INPUT, 'foo');            # get sort's results
```

FILEHANDLE may be an expression whose value gives the real filehandle name.

---

[34] Note, however, that a **dup**'ed pipe is treated as an ordinary filehandle, and close will not wait for the child on that filehandle. You have to wait for the child by closing the filehandle on which it was originally opened.

closedir

```
closedir(DIRHANDLE)
closedir DIRHANDLE
```

This function closes a directory opened by **opendir**. See the examples under **opendir**.

connect

```
connect(SOCKET,NAME)
```

This function does the same thing as the **connect** system call—see *connect*(2). The function initiates a connection with another process that is waiting at an **accept**. The function returns true if it succeeded, false otherwise (and puts the error code into $!). NAME should be a packed network address of the proper type for the socket. For example:

```
connect(S, $destaddr) ||
        die "Can´t connect to $hostname: $!\n";
```

To disconnect a socket, use the **shutdown** function. See also the example in the section "Interprocess Communication" in Chapter 6.

cos

```
cos(EXPR)
cos EXPR
```

This function returns the cosine of EXPR (expressed in radians). For example, the following script will print a cosine table of angles measured in degrees:

```
# Here´s the lazy way of getting degrees-to-radians.

$pi = atan2(1,1) * 4;
$piover180 = $pi/180;

# Print table.

for ($_ = 0; $_ <= 90; $_++) {
        printf "%3d %7.5f\n", $_, cos($_ * $piover180);
}
```

crypt

```
crypt(PLAINTEXT,SALT)
```

This function encrypts a string exactly like the **crypt()** function in the C library—see *crypt*(3). This is useful for checking the password file for lousy passwords.[35] Only the guys wearing white hats are allowed to do this.

To see if a typed-in password **$guess** matches the password **$pass** obtained from a file (such as */etc/passwd*), try something like the following:

```
if (crypt($guess, $pass) eq $pass) {
        # guess is correct
}
```

Note that there is no known way to decrypt an encrypted password apart from guessing. Also, truncating the salt to two characters is a waste of CPU time, although the manpage for *crypt*(3) would have you believe otherwise.

dbmclose

```
dbmclose(ASSOC_ARRAY)
dbmclose ASSOC_ARRAY
```

This function breaks the binding between a DBM file and an associative array. The values remaining in the associative array are useless unless you want to know what was in the cache for the DBM file. This function is useful only if you have NDBM, a version of DBM that can support multiple databases.

dbmopen

```
dbmopen(ASSOC,DBNAME,MODE)
```

This binds a DBM or NDBM file to an associative array. (DBM stands for Data Base Management, and consists of a set of C library routines that allow random access to records via a hashing algorithm. NDBM is a newer version that can support multiple databases.) ASSOC is the name of the associative array (with a %). DBNAME is the name of the database (without the **.dir** or **.pag** extension). If the database does not exist, and a valid MODE is specified, the database is created with the protection specified by MODE (as modified by the umask). To prevent creation of the database if it doesn't exist, you may specify a MODE of **undef**, and the function will return a false value if it can't find an existing database. If your system supports only the older DBM functions, you may have only one **dbmopen** in your program. If your system has neither DBM nor NDBM, calling

---

[35] What you really want to do is prevent people from adding the bad passwords in the first place. See the example *passwd* program in Chapter 6.

dbmopen produces a fatal error. (See the description of **eval** for a way to trap this error.)

Values assigned to the associative array prior to the **dbmopen** are lost. A certain number of values from the DBM file are cached in memory. By default this number is 64, but you can increase it by pre-allocating that number of garbage entries in the associative array before calling **dbmopen**. You can flush the cache if necessary with the **reset** command.

If you don't have write access to the DBM file, you can only read the associative array variables, not set them. If you want to test whether you can write, either use file tests or try setting a dummy array entry inside an **eval**, which will trap the error.

Note that functions such as **keys( )** and **values( )** may return huge array values when used on large DBM files. You may prefer to use the **each( )** function to iterate over large DBM files. This example prints out the history file pointers on a B-news system:

```
# print out history file offsets
dbmopen(%HIST, '/usr/lib/news/history', 0666);
while (($key,$val) = each %HIST) {
        print $key, ' = ', unpack('L', $val), "\n";
}
dbmclose(HIST);
```

Associative arrays bound to DBM files have the same limitations as DBM files, in particular the restrictions on how much you can put into a bucket. If you stick to short keys and values, it's rarely a problem. Another thing you should bear in mind is that many existing DBM databases contain null terminated keys and values because they were set up with C programs in mind. The B News and C News history file and the sendmail aliases file are examples. Just use "**$key\0**" instead of **$key**.

There is currently no built-in way to lock DBM files. This is probably a bug.

defined

```
defined(EXPR)
defined EXPR
```

This function returns a Boolean value saying whether the lvalue EXPR has a real value or not. A scalar that contains neither a valid string value nor a valid numeric value is known as the "undefined" value, or **undef** for short. Many operations return the undefined value under exceptional conditions, such as end of file, uninitialized variable, system error, and such. This function allows you to distinguish between an undefined null string and a defined null string when using operations that might return a real null string, such as referencing the elements of an array.

You may also check to see if arrays or subroutines exist. Arrays are "undefined" until you assign to them or otherwise add one or more elements. Using **defined** on the predefined special variables is not guaranteed to produce intuitive results.

Here is a fragment that tests a scalar value from an associative array. (Note that it's possible to have an undefined scalar value in an existing associative array entry.)

```
print if defined $switch{´D´};
```

In the next example we use the fact that some operations return the undefined value when you run out of data:

```
print "$val\n" while defined($val = pop(@ary));
```

The same thing goes for error returns from system calls:

```
die "Can´t readlink $sym: $!"
        unless defined($value = readlink $sym);
```

Here we use the **eval** function to hide the array assignment so that it allocates no storage unless the array already exists. By default, the parser would create the array the moment it sees the assignment.

```
eval ´@foo = ()´ if defined(@foo);
```

Since symbol tables for packages are stored as associative arrays, it's possible to check for the existence of a package like this:

```
die "No XYZ package defined" unless defined %_XYZ;
```

Finally, it's possible to avoid blowing up on nonexistent subroutines:

```
sub foo { defined &bar ? &bar(@_) : die "No bar"; }
```

See also **undef( )**.

delete

```
delete $ASSOC{KEY}
```

This function deletes the specified value from the specified associative array. If successful, the deleted value is returned; otherwise, the undefined value is returned. Deleting from $ENV{ } modifies the environment. Deleting from an array that is bound to a DBM file deletes the entry from the DBM file.

The following stupid example deletes all the values of an associative array:

```
foreach $key (keys %ARRAY) {
        delete $ARRAY{$key};
}
```

(But it would be faster to use the **reset** command. Saying **undef %ARRAY** is faster yet.)

die

```
die(LIST)
die LIST
die
```

Outside of an **eval**, this function prints the concatenated value of LIST to **STDERR** and exits with the current value of **$!** (*errno*). If **$!** is 0, it exits with the value of (**$? >> 8**) (`command` status). If (**$? >> 8**) is 0, it exits with 255. If LIST is unspecified, the string **"Died"** is used as the default. Equivalent examples:

```
die "Can´t cd to spool: $!\n" unless chdir ´/usr/spool/news´;

chdir ´/usr/spool/news´ || die "Can´t cd to spool: $!\n"
```

Within an **eval**, the function sets the **$@** variable equal to the error message that would have been produced otherwise, and aborts the **eval**, which then returns the undefined value. The **die** function can thus be used to raise named exceptions that can be caught at a higher level in the program. See the **eval** function later in this chapter.

If the final value of LIST does not end in a newline, the current script filename, line number, and input line number (if any) are appended to the message, as well as a newline. Hint: sometimes appending **", stopped"** to your message will cause it to make better sense when the string **"at scriptname line 123"** is appended. Suppose you are running script **canasta**:

```
die "/etc/games is no good";
die "/etc/games is no good, stopped";
```

which produces, respectively:

```
/etc/games is no good at canasta line 123.
/etc/games is no good, stopped at canasta line 123.
```

If you want your own error messages reporting the filename and linenumber, use the __FILE__ and __LINE__ special tokens:

```
die ´"´, __FILE__, ´"´, line ´, __LINE__, ", phooey on you!\n";
```

See also **exit** and **warn**.

do

```
do BLOCK
do SUBROUTINE(LIST)
do EXPR
```

The **do BLOCK,** form returns the value of the last command in the sequence of commands indicated by BLOCK. When modified by a loop modifier, Perl executes the BLOCK once before testing the loop condition. (On other statements the loop modifiers test the conditional first.)

The **do SUBROUTINE(LIST),** form executes a SUBROUTINE declared by a **sub** declaration, and returns the value of the last expression evaluated in SUBROUTINE. If there is no subroutine by that name, the function produces a fatal error. (You may use the **defined** operator to determine if a subroutine exists.) If you pass arrays as part of LIST you may wish to pass the length of the array in front of each array. (See the section "Subroutines" in Chapter 3.) SUBROUTINE may be a scalar variable (but not an array element), in which case the variable contains the name of the subroutine to execute. The parentheses are required to avoid confusion with **do EXPR**. In particular, if you say:

```
do fiddlefaddle;
```

it will not execute a subroutine, but will look for a library file called **fiddlefaddle** to include. Not finding the file, it will fail silently. Boo hiss.

Note that arguments to a subroutine are always evaluated in an array context, even if you only pass one argument. But see the **scalar** operator for a way to override this.

As an alternate (and preferred) form, you may call a subroutine by prefixing the name with an ampersand: **&foo(@args)**. If you aren't passing any arguments, you don't have to use parentheses. If you omit the parentheses, no @_ array is passed to the subroutine. The ampersand form is also used to specify subroutines to the **defined** and **undef** operators.

The **do EXPR,** form uses the value of EXPR as a filename and executes the contents of the file as a Perl script. Its primary use is (or rather was) to include subroutines from a Perl subroutine library, so that:

```
do ´stat.pl´;
```

is just like:

```
eval `cat stat.pl`;
```

except that it's more efficient, more concise, keeps track of the current filename for error messages, and searches all the **–I** libraries if the file isn't in the current directory (see also the **@INC** array in the section "Special Variables" in Chapter 3). It's the same, however, in that it does reparse the file every time you call it, so if you are going to use the file inside a loop you might prefer to use **–P** and **#include**, at the expense of a little more startup time. (The main problem with **#include** is that *cpp* doesn't grok **#** comments—a workaround is to use **;#** for standalone comments.) Note that the following are **not** equivalent:

```
do $foo;        # eval a file
do $foo();      # call a subroutine
```

This operator was the easiest way to include Perl library routines in version 3.0. As of version 4.0, the inclusion of library routines is better done with the **require** operator, which does everything the **do EXPR** operator does and more.

dump

```
dump LABEL
```

This function causes an immediate core dump. Primarily this is so that you can use the **undump** program to turn your core dump into an executable binary after having initialized all your variables at the beginning of the program. (The **undump** program is not supplied with the Perl distribution, and is not even possible on some architectures. There are hooks in the code for using the GNU **unexec**() routine as an alternative. Other methods may be supported in the future.) When the new binary is executed it will begin by executing a **goto LABEL** (with all the restrictions that **goto** suffers). Think of it as a **goto** with an intervening core dump and reincarnation. If LABEL is omitted, the function arranges for the program to restart from the top. Please note that any files opened at the time of the dump will **not** be open any more when the program is reincarnated, with possible confusion resulting on the part of Perl. See also the **–u** command-line switch. For example:

```
#!/usr/bin/perl
require `getopt.pl`;
require `stat.pl`;
%days = (
    `Sun`, 1,
    `Mon`, 2,
    `Tue`, 3,
    `Wed`, 4,
    `Thu`, 5,
    `Fri`, 6,
    `Sat`, 7);
```

```
dump QUICKSTART if $ARGV[0] eq '-d';

QUICKSTART:
&Getopt('f');
...
```

This startup code does some slow initialization code, and then calls the **dump** function to take a snapshot of the program's state. When the dumped version of the program is run, it bypasses all the startup code and goes directly to the **QUICKSTART** label. If the original script is invoked without the **-d** switch, it just falls through and runs normally.

each

```
each(ASSOC_ARRAY)
each ASSOC_ARRAY
```

This function returns a two-element array consisting of the key and value for the next value of an associative array, so that you can iterate over it. Entries are returned in an apparently random order. When the array is entirely read, a null array is returned (which when assigned to a list produces a false value). The next call to **each()** after that will start iterating again. The iterator can be reset only by reading all the elements from the array. You must not modify the array while iterating over it. There is a single iterator for each associative array, shared by all **each()**, **keys()**, and **values()** function calls in the program. The following example prints out your environment like the *printenv* program, only in a different order:

```
while (($key,$value) = each %ENV) {
        print "$key=$value\n";
}
```

See also **keys()** and **values()**.

eof

```
eof(FILEHANDLE)
eof()
eof
```

This function returns 1 if the next read on FILEHANDLE will return end of file, or if FILEHANDLE is not open. FILEHANDLE may be an expression whose value gives the real filehandle name. (Note that this function actually reads a character and then **ungetc**'s it, so it is not very useful in an interactive context.) An **eof** without an argument returns the eof status for the last file read. Empty parentheses () may be used to indicate the pseudo-file forms of the files listed on the command line. That is, **eof()** is reasonable to use inside a **while** (<>) loop to detect the end of only the last file. Use **eof(ARGV)** or **eof** (without the parentheses) to test EACH file in a **while** (**< >**) loop. For example, the following code inserts dashes just before the last line of *last* file:

```
while (<>) {
        if (eof()) {
                print "—" x 30, "\n";
        }
        print;
}
```

On the other hand, this script resets line numbering on *each* input file:

```
while (<>) {
        print "$.\t$_";
        if (eof) {        # Not eof().
                close(ARGV);
        }
}
```

Like $ in a *sed* program, **eof** tends to show up in line number ranges. Here's a script that prints lines from /pattern/ to end of each input file:

```
while (<>) {
        print if /pattern/..eof;
}
```

eval

```
eval(EXPR)
eval EXPR
```

The value returned by EXPR is parsed and executed as if it were a little Perl program. It is executed in the context of the current Perl program, so that any variable settings and subroutine or format definitions remain afterwards. The text of the eval is treated as a block, so local variables last until the eval is done. The value returned is the value of the last expression evaluated, just as with subroutines. If there is a syntax error or runtime error (including any produced by the **die** operator), the undefined value is returned by **eval**, and $@ is set to the error message. If there is no error, $@ is guaranteed to be set to the null string, so you can test it reliably afterwords for errors. If EXPR is omitted, the function evaluates $_. The final semicolon, if any, may be omitted from the expression. Here's a statement that assigns an element of some array that is chosen at runtime:

```
eval "\$$arrayname{\$key} = 1";
```

And here is a simple Perl shell:

```
while (<>) { eval; print $@; }
```

Note that, since **eval** traps otherwise-fatal errors, it is useful for determining whether a particular feature (such as **dbmopen** or **symlink**) is implemented. In fact, **eval** is the way to do all exception handling in Perl. A frequently asked question is how to set up an exit routine. In Perl, you can do this with an **eval**, like this:

```
#!/usr/bin/perl
$whatever = shift;

eval <<'EndOfEval';   $start = __LINE__;
      .
      .               # your ad here
      .
EndOfEval

# Cleanup

unlink "/tmp/myfile$$";
$@ && ($@ =~ s/\(eval\) at line (\d+)/$0 .
       " line " . ($1+$start)/e, die $@);
exit 0;
```

Note that the code supplied for an eval might not be recompiled if the text hasn't changed. On the rare occasions when you want to force a recompilation (because you want to reset a **??** operator, for instance), you could say something like this:

```
eval $prog . '#' . ++$seq;
```

exec

```
exec(LIST)
exec LIST
```

This function terminates the currently running Perl script by executing another program in place of itself. If there is more than one argument in LIST, or if LIST is an array with more than one value, the function calls C's *execvp*(3) routine with the arguments in LIST. If there is only one scalar argument, the argument is checked for shell metacharacters. If there are any, the entire argument is passed to **"/bin/sh −c"** for parsing. If there are none, the argument is split into words and passed directly to *execvp*(3) in the interests of efficiency. Ordinarily **exec** never returns—if it does return, it always returns false, and you should check **$!** to find out what went wrong. Note that **exec** (and **system**) do not flush your output buffer, so you may need to enable command buffering by setting **$|** on one or more filehandles to avoid lost output. This statement runs the echo program to print out the current argument list:

```
exec '/bin/echo', 'Your arguments are: ', @ARGV;
```

This example shows that you can **exec** a pipeline:

```
exec("sort $outfile | uniq") || die "Can't do sort/uniq: $!\n";
```

The UNIX *execv(3)* call provides the ability to tell a program the name it was invoked as. This name might have nothing to do with the name of the program you actually gave the operating system to run. By default, Perl simply replicates the first element of LIST and uses it for both purposes. If, however, you don't really want to execute the first argument of LIST, but you want to lie to the program you are executing about its own name, you can do so. Put the real name of the program you want to run into a variable and then put that variable out in front of the LIST *without* a comma, kind of like a filehandle for a **print** statement. (This always forces interpretation of the LIST as a multi-valued list, even if there is only a single scalar in the list.) Then the first element of LIST will be used only to mislead the executing program as to its name. For example:

```
$shell = '/bin/csh';
exec $shell '-sh';              # pretend it's a login shell
die "Couldn't execute csh: $!\n";
```

exit

```
exit(EXPR)
exit EXPR
```

This function evaluates EXPR and exits immediately with that value. Here's a fragment that lets a user exit the program by typing **x** or **X**:

```
$ans = <STDIN>;
exit 0 if $ans =~ /^[Xx]/;
```

If EXPR is omitted, the function exits with 0 status. You shouldn't use **exit** to abort a subroutine if there's any chance that someone might want to trap whatever error happened. Use **die** instead, which can be trapped by an **eval**.

exp

```
exp(EXPR)
exp EXPR
```

This function returns *e* to the power of EXPR. If EXPR is omitted, it gives **exp($_)**.

fcntl

```
fcntl(FILEHANDLE,FUNCTION,SCALAR)
```

This function calls UNIX's *fcntl*(2) function. (**fcntl** stands for "file control".) You'll probably have to say:

```
require "sys/fcntl.ph";
        # probably /usr/local/lib/perl/sys/fcntl.ph
```

first to get the correct function definitions. If **fcntl.ph** doesn't exist or doesn't have the correct definitions, you'll have to roll your own, based on your C header files such as *<sys/fcntl.h>*. (The Perl distribution includes a script called **h2ph** to help you do this.) SCALAR will be read and/or written depending on the FUNCTION—a pointer to the string value of SCALAR will be passed as the third argument of the actual ioctl call. (If SCALAR has no string value but does have a numeric value, that value will be passed directly rather than a pointer to the string value.)

The return value of **fcntl** (and **ioctl**) is as follows:

system call returns	Perl returns
−1	undefined value
0	string "0 but true"
anything else	that number

Thus Perl returns true on success and false on failure, yet you can still easily determine the actual value returned by the operating system:

```
($retval = fcntl(...)) || ($retval = -1);
printf "System returned %d\n", $retval;
```

For example, since Perl always sets the close-on-exec flag for file descriptors above 2, if you wanted to pass file descriptor 3 to a subprocess, you might want to clear the flag like this:

```
require "sys/fcntl.ph";
open(TTY,"+>/dev/tty") || die "Can't open /dev/tty: $!\n";
fileno(TTY) == 3 || die "Internal error: fd mixup";
fcntl(TTY, &F_SETFL, 0)
        || die "Can't clear the close-on-exec flag: $!\n";
```

Note that **fcntl** will produce a fatal error if used on a machine that doesn't implement *fcntl*(2). On machines that do implement it, you can do such things as modify the close-on-exec flags, modify the non-blocking I/O flags, emulate the *lockf*(3) function, and arrange to receive the **SIGIO** signal when I/O is pending. You might even have record-locking facilities.

fileno

```
fileno(FILEHANDLE)
fileno FILEHANDLE
```

This function returns the file descriptor for a filehandle. It's useful for construct-ing bitmaps for **select( )**, and for passing to certain obscure system calls if **sys-call( )** is implemented. It's also useful for double-checking that the **open( )** func-tion gave you the file descriptor you wanted—see the example under **fcntl( )**. If FILEHANDLE is an expression, the value is taken as the name of the filehandle.

A caution: don't count on the association of a Perl filehandle and a numeric file descriptor throughout the life of the program. If a file has been closed and reo-pened, the file descriptor may change. Filehandles **STDIN**, **STDOUT**, and **STDERR** start with file descriptors of 0, 1, and 2 (the UNIX standard convention), but even they can change if you start closing and opening them with wild aban-don. But you can't get into trouble with 0, 1, and 2 as long as you always reopen immediately after closing, since the basic rule on UNIX systems is to pick the lowest available descriptor, and that'll be the one you just closed.

flock

```
flock(FILEHANDLE,OPERATION)
```

This function calls *flock*(2) on FILEHANDLE. See manual page for *flock*(2) for definition of OPERATION. Invoking **flock** will produce a fatal error if used on a machine that doesn't implement *flock*(2). Here's a mailbox appender for some BSD-based systems:

```
$LOCK_SH = 1;
$LOCK_EX = 2;
$LOCK_NB = 4;
$LOCK_UN = 8;

sub lock {
        flock(MBOX, $LOCK_EX);
        # and, in case someone appended
        # while we were waiting...
        seek(MBOX, 0, 2);
}

sub unlock {
        flock(MBOX, $LOCK_UN);
}

open(MBOX, ">>/usr/spool/mail/$ENV{'USER'}")
        || die "Can't open mailbox: $!";

&lock();
print MBOX $msg, "\n\n";
&unlock();
```

fork

```
fork
```

This function does a **fork( )** call—see *fork*(2). The function returns the child pid to the parent process and 0 to the child process. Note that unflushed buffers remain unflushed in both processes, which means you may need to set $| on one or more filehandles to avoid duplicate output.

A nearly bulletproof way to launch a child process while checking for "cannot fork" errors would be:

```
FORK: {
        if ($pid = fork) {
                # parent here
                # child process pid is available in $pid
        } elsif (defined $pid) { # $pid is zero here if defined
                # child here
                # parent process pid is available with getppid
        } elsif ($! =~ /No more process/) {
                # EAGAIN, supposedly recoverable fork error
                sleep 5;
                redo FORK;
        } else {
                # weird fork error
                die "Can't fork: $!\n";
        }
}
```

These precautions are not necessary on operations which do an implicit **fork( )**. Be very careful to end the child code with an **exit,** or your child may inadvertently leave the conditional and start executing code intended only for the parent process.

getc

```
getc(FILEHANDLE)
getc FILEHANDLE
getc
```

This function returns the next character from the input file attached to FILEHANDLE. At EOF, it returns a null string. If FILEHANDLE is omitted, the function reads from **STDIN.** This operator is *very slow*, but occasionally useful for single character input from the keyboard.

getgrent

```
getgrent
setgrent
endgrent
```

These functions do the same thing as their like-named system library routines—see *getgrent*(3). These routines iterate through your */etc/group* file (or its moral equivalent coming from some server somewhere). The return value from **getgrent( )** is:

```
($name, $passwd, $gid, $members)
```

where **$members** is a space-separated list of the login names of the members of the group. To set up an associative array for translating group names to gids, say this:

```
while (($name, $passwd, $gid) = getgrent) {
        $gid{$name} = $gid;
}
```

getgrgid

```
getgrgid(GID)
```

This function does the same thing as *getgrgid*(3)—looks up a group file entry by group number. The return value is:

```
($name, $passwd, $gid, $members)
```

where **$members** is a space-separated list of the login names of the members of the group. If you want to do this repeatedly, consider caching the data in an associative array using **getgrent**.

getgrnam

```
getgrnam(NAME)
```

This function does the same thing as *getgrnam*(3)—looks up a group file entry by group name. The return value is:

```
($name, $passwd, $gid, $members)
```

where **$members** is a space-separated list of the login names of the members of the group. If you want to do this repeatedly, consider slurping the data into an associative array using **getgrent**.

gethostbyaddr

```
gethostbyaddr(ADDR,ADDRTYPE)
```

This function does the same thing as *gethostbyaddr*(3)—translates a network address to its corresponding names (and alternate addresses). The return value is:

```
($name, $aliases, $addrtype, $length, @addrs)
```

where **@addrs** is a list of raw addresses. In the Internet domain, each address is four bytes long, and can be unpacked by saying something like:

```
($a, $b, $c, $d) = unpack('C4', $addr[0]);
```

If you want to do this repeatedly, do **not** consider slurping the data into an associative array using **gethostent**, because you may end up interrogating half the Internet if you're running Internet nameserver software.

gethostbyname

```
gethostbyname(NAME)
```

This function does the same thing as *gethostbyname*(3)—translates a network hostname to its corresponding addresses (and other names). The return value is:

```
($name, $aliases, $addrtype, $length, @addrs)
```

where **@addrs** is a list of raw addresses. In the Internet domain, each address is four bytes long, and can be unpacked by saying something like:

```
($a, $b, $c, $d) = unpack('C4', $addr[0]);
```

If you want to do this repeatedly, do **not** consider slurping the data into an associative array using **gethostent**, because you may end up interrogating half the Internet if you are running the Internet nameserver software.

gethostent

```
gethostent
sethostent(STAYOPEN)
endhostent
```

These functions do the same thing as their like-named system library routines—see *gethostent*(3). They iterate through your */etc/hosts* file and return each entry one at a time. The return value from **gethostent**( ) is:

```
($name, $aliases, $addrtype, $length, @addrs)
```

where **@addrs** is a list of raw addresses. In the Internet domain, each address is four bytes long, and can be unpacked by saying something like:

```
($a, $b, $c, $d) = unpack('C4', $addr[0]);
```

Scripts which use these routines should not be considered portable. Machines using a nameserver will interrogate half the Internet to try to satisfy your request for all the addresses of everyone. The routines may even be unimplemented for that reason.

getlogin

```
getlogin
```

This function returns the current login from */etc/utmp*, if any. If null, use **getpwuid**. For example:

```
$login = getlogin || (getpwuid($<))[0] || "Intruder!!";
```

getnetbyaddr

```
getnetbyaddr(ADDR,ADDRTYPE)
```

This function does the same thing as *getnetbyaddr*(3)—translates a network address to the corresponding network name or names. The return value is:

```
($name, $aliases, $addrtype, $net)
```

getnetbyname

```
getnetbyname(NAME)
```

This function does the same thing as *getnetbyname*(3)—translates a network name to its corresponding network address. The return value is:

```
($name, $aliases, $addrtype, $net)
```

getnetent

```
getnetent
setnetent(STAYOPEN)
endnetent
```

These functions do the same thing as their like-named system library routines—see *getnetent*(3). They iterate through your */etc/networks* file, or moral equivalent. The return value from **getnetent( )** is:

```
($name, $aliases, $addrtype, $net)
```

getpeername

```
getpeername(SOCKET)
```

This function returns the packed sockaddr address of other end of the SOCKET connection. For example:

```
# An internet sockaddr
$sockaddr = 'S n a4 x8';
$hersockaddr = getpeername(S);
($family, $port, $heraddr) = unpack($sockaddr, $hersockaddr);
```

getpgrp

```
getpgrp(PID)
getpgrp PID
```

This function returns the current process group for the specified PID (use a PID of 0 for the current process). Invoking **getpgrp** will produce a fatal error if used on a machine that doesn't implement *getpgrp*(2). If EXPR is omitted, the function returns the process group of current process (the same as using a PID of 0).

getppid

```
getppid
```

This function returns the process-ID of the parent process. On the typical UNIX system, if your process-ID changes to 1, your parent process has died and you've been adopted by the *init* program.

getpriority

```
getpriority(WHICH,WHO)
```

This function returns the current priority for a process, a process group, or a user. (See *getpriority*(2).) Invoking **getpriority** will produce a fatal error if used on a machine that doesn't implement *getpriority*(2). For example, to get the priority of the current process, use:

```
$curprio = getpriority(0, 0);
```

getprotobyname

```
getprotobyname(NAME)
```

This function does the same thing as *getprotobyname*(3)—translates a protocol name to its corresponding number. The return value is:

```
($name, $aliases, $proto)
```

getprotobynumber

```
getprotobynumber(NUMBER)
```

This function does the same thing as *getprotobynumber*(3)—translates a protocol number to its corresponding name. The return value is:

```
($name, $aliases, $proto)
```

getprotoent

```
getprotoent
setprotoent(STAYOPEN)
endprotoent
```

These functions do the same thing as their like-named system library routines—see *getprotent*(3). The return value from **getprotoent( )** is:

```
($name, $aliases, $proto)
```

getpwent

```
getpwent
setpwent
endpwent
```

These functions do the same thing as their like-named system library routines—see *getpwent*(3). These routines iterate through your */etc/passwd* file (or its moral equivalent coming from some server somewhere). The return value from **getpwent( )** is:

```
($name,$passwd,$uid,$gid,$quota,$comment,$gcos,$dir,$shell)
```

Some machines may use the quota and comment fields for other purposes, but the other fields will always be the same. To set up an associative array for translating login names to uids, say this:

```
while (($name, $passwd, $uid) = getpwent) {
        $uid{$name} = $uid;
}
```

getpwnam

```
getpwnam(NAME)
```

This function does the same thing as *getpwnam*(3)—translates a username to the corresponding passwd file entry. The return value is:

```
($name,$passwd,$uid,$gid,$quota,$comment,$gcos,$dir,$shell)
```

If you want to do this repeatedly, consider caching the data in an associative array using **getpwent.**

getpwuid

```
getpwuid(UID)
```

This function does the same thing as *getpwuid*(3)—translates a numeric user id to the corresponding passwd file entry. The return value is:

```
($name,$passwd,$uid,$gid,$quota,$comment,$gcos,$dir,$shell)
```

If you want to do this repeatedly, consider slurping the data into an associative array using **getpwent.**

getservbyname

```
getservbyname(NAME,PROTO)
```

This function does the same thing as *getservbyname*(3)—translates a service (port) name to its corresponding port number. PROTO is a protocol name such as ´tcp´. The return value is:

```
($name, $aliases, $port, $proto)
```

getservbyport

```
getservbyport(PORT,PROTO)
```

This function does the same thing as *getservbyport*(3)—translates a service (port) number to its corresponding names. PROTO is a protocol name such as ´tcp´. The return value is:

```
($name, $aliases, $port, $proto)
```

getservent

```
getservent
setservent(STAYOPEN)
endservent
```

These functions do the same thing as their like-named system library routines—see *getservent*(3). They iterate through the */etc/services* file or its equivalent. The return value from **getservent( )** is:

```
($name, $aliases, $port, $proto)
```

getsockname

```
getsockname(SOCKET)
```

This function returns the packed sockaddr address of this end of the SOCKET connection. (And why wouldn't you know the address already? Because you might have bound an address containing wildcards to the generic socket before doing an accept. Or because you might have been passed a socket by your parent process—for example, **inetd**.)

```
# An internet sockaddr
$sockaddr = 'S n a4 x8';
$mysockaddr = getsockname(S);
($family, $port, $myaddr) = unpack($sockaddr, $mysockaddr);
```

getsockopt

```
getsockopt(SOCKET,LEVEL,OPTNAME)
```

This function returns the socket option requested, or undefined if there is an error.

gmtime

```
gmtime(EXPR)
gmtime EXPR
```

This function converts a time as returned by the time function to a 9-element array with the time correct for the Greenwich timezone (aka GMT or UTC). Typically used as follows:

```
($sec,$min,$hour,$mday,$mon,$year,$wday,$yday,$isdst) =
        gmtime(time);
```

All array elements are numeric, and come straight out of a **struct tm**. (A C programming structure—don't sweat it.) In particular this means that **$mon** has the range 0..11 and **$wday** has the range 0..6. (You can remember which ones are 0-based because those are the ones you're always using as subscripts into 0-based arrays containing month and day names.) If EXPR is omitted, it does **gmtime(time)**. For example, to print the current month in London:

```
$london_month = (Jan,Feb,Mar,Apr,May,Jun,
        Jul,Aug,Sep,Oct,Nov,Dec)[(gmtime)[4]];
```

The Perl library *timelocal.pl* contains a subroutine, **&timegm()**, that can convert in the opposite direction.

goto

```
goto LABEL
```

This function finds the statement labeled with LABEL and resumes execution there. Although it's a function, it never returns a value. Currently you may go only to statements in the main body of the program that are not nested inside a **do** {} construct. This statement is not implemented very efficiently, and is here only to make the *sed*–to–Perl translator easier. If a better way is found to make the translator work, **goto** may change or even go away. So don't use it; Perl already has many rich control constructs. Some would say too many...

grep

```
grep(EXPR,LIST)
```

This function evaluates EXPR for each element of LIST (locally setting $_ to each element) and returns the array value consisting of those elements for which the expression evaluated to true. (The operator is named after a beloved UNIX program that extracts lines out of a file that match a particular pattern.) In a scalar context, the function returns the number of times the expression was true.

Presuming @**bar** contains lines of code, this example weeds out comment lines:

```
@foo = grep(!/^#/, @bar);
```

Note that since $_ is a reference into the array value, altering $_ will modify the elements of the array. While this is useful and supported, it can occasionally cause bizarre results if the LIST is not a named array. Caveat Programmer.

hex

```
hex(EXPR)
hex EXPR
```

This function returns the decimal value of EXPR interpreted as a hex string. (To interpret strings that might start with **0** or **0x** see **oct**().) If EXPR is omitted, it interprets $_. The following code sets **$number** to 4,294,906,560:

```
$number = hex("ffff12c0");
```

To do the inverse function, use:

```
sprintf("%lx", $number);        # (That's an ell, not a one.)
```

index

```
index(STR,SUBSTR,POSITION)
index(STR,SUBSTR)
```

This function returns the position of the first occurrence of SUBSTR in STR. The POSITION, if specified, says where to start looking. Positions are based at 0, or whatever you've set the $[variable to. If the substring is not found, the function returns one less than the base, ordinarily –1. To work your way through a string, you might say:

```
$pos = $[;
while (($pos = index($string, $lookfor, $pos)) >= $[) {
    print "Found at $pos\n";
    $pos++;
}
```

int

```
int(EXPR)
int EXPR
```

This function returns the integer portion of EXPR. If EXPR is omitted, it uses $_. If you're a C programmer, you'll often forget to use **int()** in conjunction with division, which is a floating-point operation in Perl. Don't feel too bad—Larry gets burned on this one regularly.

ioctl

```
ioctl(FILEHANDLE,FUNCTION,SCALAR)
```

This function implements the *ioctl*(2) function. You'll probably have to say:

```
require "sys/ioctl.ph";
            # probably /usr/local/lib/perl/sys/ioctl.ph
```

first to get the correct function definitions. If *sys/ioctl.ph* doesn't exist or doesn't have the correct definitions you'll have to roll your own, based on your C header files such as <*sys/ioctl.h*>. (The Perl distribution includes a script called **h2ph** to help you do this.) SCALAR will be read and/or written depending on the FUNCTION—a pointer to the string value of SCALAR will be passed as the third argument of the actual ioctl call. (If SCALAR has no string value but does have a numeric value, that value will be passed directly rather than a pointer to the string value.) The **pack()** and **unpack()** functions are useful for manipulating the values of structures used by **ioctl**( ). The following example sets the erase character to DEL:

```
require 'sys/ioctl.ph';
$sgttyb_t = "ccccs";              # 4 chars and a short
if (ioctl(STDIN, &TIOCGETP, $sgttyb)) {
        @ary = unpack($sgttyb_t, $sgttyb);
        $ary[2] = 127;
        $sgttyb = pack($sgttyb_t, @ary);
        ioctl(STDIN, &TIOCSETP, $sgttyb)
                || die "Can't ioctl TIOCSETP: $!";
}
```

The return value of **ioctl** (and **fcntl**) is as follows:

system call returns	Perl returns
−1	undefined value
0	string "0 but true"
anything else	that number

Thus Perl returns true on success and false on failure, yet you can still easily determine the actual value returned by the operating system:

```
($retval = ioctl(...)) || ($retval = -1);
printf "System returned %d\n", $retval;
```

Calls to ioctl should not be considered portable. If, say, you're merely turning off echo once for the whole script, it's much more portable (and not much slower) to say:

```
system "stty -echo";
```

Just because you *can* do something in Perl doesn't mean you *ought* to. To quote the apostle Paul, "Everything is permissible—but not everything is beneficial."

join

```
join(EXPR,LIST)
```

This function joins the separate strings of LIST (which might just be an array reference) into a single string with fields separated by the value of EXPR, and returns the string. For example:

```
$_ = join(':', $login,$passwd,$uid,$gid,$gcos,$home,$shell);
```

To do the opposite, see **split**. To join things together into fixed-position fields, see **pack**.

keys

```
keys(ASSOC_ARRAY)
keys ASSOC_ARRAY
```

This function returns a normal array consisting of all the keys of the named associative array. The keys are returned in an apparently random order, but it is the same order as either the **values()** or **each()** function produces (given that the associative array has not been modified). Here is yet another way to print your environment:

```
@keys = keys %ENV;
@values = values %ENV;
while ($#keys >= 0) {
        print pop(keys), '=', pop(values), "\n";
}
```

or how about sorted by key:

```
foreach $key (sort(keys %ENV)) {
        print $key, '=', $ENV{$key}, "\n";
}
```

Note that using **keys()** on an associative array bound to a largish DBM file will produce a largish list, causing you to have a largish process. You might prefer to use the **each** function in this case, which will iterate over the array entries one-by-one without slurping them all into a single gargantuan list.

kill

```
kill(LIST)
kill LIST
```

This function sends a signal to a list of processes. The first element of the list must be the signal to send. You may use a signal name in quotes. The function returns the number of processes successfully signaled:

```
$cnt = kill 1, $child1, $child2;
kill 9, @goners;
kill 'STOP', $$;
```

If the signal is negative, the function kills process groups instead of processes. (On System V, a negative process number will also kill process groups, but that's not portable.)

length

```
length(EXPR)
length EXPR
```

This function returns the length in characters of the value of EXPR. If EXPR is omitted, the function returns length of $_, but be careful that the next thing doesn't look like the start of an EXPR, or the tokener will get confused. When in doubt, always put the parentheses.

link

```
link(OLDFILE,NEWFILE)
```

This function creates a new filename linked to the old filename. The function returns 1 for success, 0 otherwise (and puts the error code into $!). See also **symlink**() later in this chapter.

listen

```
listen(SOCKET,QUEUESIZE)
```

This function does the same thing as the **listen** system call—see *listen*(2). It tells the system that you're going to be doing accepts on this socket and that the system can queue the number of waiting connections specified by QUEUESIZE. Imagine having "call-waiting" on your phone, with up to 5 callers queued. (Gives me the willies!) The function returns true if it succeeded, false otherwise (and puts the error code into $!). See the section "Interprocess Communication" in Chapter 6.

local

```
local(LIST)
```

This function declares the listed variables to be local to the enclosing block, subroutine, or **eval**. (The **require** operator counts as an **eval** of a whole file.) All the listed elements must be legal lvalues. This operator works by saving the current values of those variables in LIST on a hidden stack and restoring them upon exiting the block, subroutine, or eval. This means that called subroutines can also reference the local variable, but not the global one (scoping is dynamic). The LIST may be assigned to if desired, which allows you to initialize your local variables. (If no initializer is given, all scalars are initialized to the null string and all arrays and associative arrays to the null array.) Commonly, this function is used to name the formal arguments to a subroutine.

Here is a routine that executes some random piece of code that depends on $i running through a range of numbers. Note that the scope of $i propagates into the **eval** code.

```
&RANGEVAL(20, 30, '$foo[$i] = $i');

sub RANGEVAL {
        local($min, $max, $thunk) = @_;
        local($result) = '';
        local($i);

        # Presumably $thunk makes reference to $i

        for ($i = $min; $i < $max; $i++) {
                $result .= eval $thunk;
        }

        $result;
}
```

This code demonstrates how to make a temporary modification to an array:

```
if ($sw eq '-v') {
        # init local array with global array
        local(@ARGV) = @ARGV;
        unshift(@ARGV, 'echo');
        system @ARGV;
}
# @ARGV restored
```

You can also temporarily modify associative arrays:

```
# temporarily add a couple entries to %digits associative array
if ($base12) {
        # (NOTE: not claiming this is efficient!)
        local(%digits) = (%digits, 't', 10, 'e', 11);
        &parse_num();
}
```

Note that **local()** is a runtime command, and so gets executed every time through a loop, using up more stack storage each time until it's all released at once when the loop is exited. Consider moving the **local()** to an enclosing block, or making it conditional.

localtime

```
localtime(EXPR)
localtime EXPR
```

This function converts a time as returned by the time function to a 9-element array with the time corrected for the local timezone. It's typically used as follows:

```
($sec,$min,$hour,$mday,$mon,$year,$wday,$yday,$isdst) =
        localtime(time);
```

All array elements are numeric, and come straight out of a **struct tm**. (That's a bit of C programming lingo—don't worry about it.) In particular this means that **$mon** has the range 0..11 and **$wday** has the range 0..6. (You can remember which ones are 0-based because those are the ones you're always using as subscripts into 0-based arrays containing month and day names.) If EXPR is omitted, it does **localtime(time)**. For example, to get the name of the current day of the week:

```
$thisday = (Sun,Mon,Tue,Wed,Thu,Fri,Sat)[(localtime)[6]];
```

The Perl library *timelocal.pl* contains a subroutine, **&timelocal()**, that can convert in the opposite direction.

log

```
log(EXPR)
log EXPR
```

This function returns logarithm (base *e*) of EXPR. If EXPR is omitted, the function returns **log($_)**.

lstat

```
lstat(FILEHANDLE)
lstat FILEHANDLE
lstat(EXPR)
```

This function does the same thing as the **stat()** function, but stats a symbolic link instead of the file the symbolic link points to. If symbolic links are unimplemented on your system, a normal stat is done.

mkdir

```
mkdir(FILENAME,MODE)
```

This function creates the directory specified by FILENAME, with permissions specified by MODE (as modified by the current umask). If it succeeds it returns 1, otherwise it returns 0 and sets **$!** (from the value of *errno*).

If the **mkdir()** routine is not built in to your C library, Perl emulates it by calling the *mkdir* program. If you are creating a long list of directories on such a system it will be more efficient to call the *mkdir* program yourself with the list of directories to avoid starting zillions of subprocesses.

msgctl

```
msgctl(ID,CMD,ARG)
```

This function calls the **msgctl( )** system call—see *msgctl*(2). If CMD is **&IPC_STAT**, then ARG must be a variable that will hold the returned **msqid_ds** structure. The return value works like **ioctl**'s: the undefined value for error, **"0 but true"** for zero, or the actual return value otherwise. On error, it puts the error code into **$!**. Before calling, you should say:

```
require "ipc.ph";
require "msg.ph";
```

This function is available only on machines supporting System V IPC.

msgget

```
msgget(KEY,FLAGS)
```

This function calls the System V IPC **msgget( )** system call—see *msgget*(2). The function returns the message queue id, or the undefined value if there is an error. On error, it puts the error code into **$!**. Before calling, you should say:

```
require "ipc.ph";
require "msg.ph";
```

This function is available only on machines supporting System V IPC.

msgrcv

```
msgrcv(ID,VAR,SIZE,TYPE,FLAGS)
```

This function calls the **msgrcv( )** system call to receive a message from message queue ID into variable VAR with a maximum message size of SIZE—see *msgrcv*(2). When a message is received, the message type will be the first thing in VAR, and the maximum length of VAR is SIZE plus the size of the message type. The function returns true if successful, or false if there is an error. On error, it puts the error code into **$!**. Before calling, you should say:

```
require "ipc.ph";
require "msg.ph";
```

This function is available only on machines supporting System V IPC.

msgsnd

```
msgsnd(ID,MSG,FLAGS)
```

This function calls the **msgsnd()** system call to send the message MSG to the message queue ID—see *msgsnd*(2). MSG must begin with the long integer message type. You can create a message like this:

```
$msg = pack("L a*", $type, $text_of_message);
```

The function returns true if successful, or false if there is an error. On error, it puts the error code into $!. Before calling, you should say:

```
require "ipc.ph";
require "msg.ph";
```

This function is available only on machines supporting System V IPC.

oct

```
oct(EXPR)
oct EXPR
```

This function returns the decimal value of EXPR interpreted as an octal string. (If EXPR happens to start off with **0x**, interprets it as a hex string instead.) The following will handle decimal, octal, and hex in the standard notation:

```
$val = oct($val) if $val =~ /^0/;
```

If EXPR is omitted, interprets $_. To do the inverse function, use:

```
sprintf("%lo", $number);
```

open

```
open(FILEHANDLE,EXPR)
open(FILEHANDLE)
open FILEHANDLE
```

This function opens the file whose filename is given by EXPR, and associates it with FILEHANDLE. FILEHANDLE may be a directly specified filehandle name, or an expression whose value will be used for the filehandle. The latter is called an indirect filehandle. Typically it is just a variable containing the name of the filehandle. (Using an indirect filehandle doesn't get you out of thinking up a name—you have make sure the expression returns the filehandle you want.) If EXPR is omitted, the scalar variable of the same name as the FILEHANDLE contains the filename. If the filename begins with "**<**" or nothing, the file is opened for input. If the filename begins with "**>**", the file is opened for output. If the filename begins with "**>>**", the file is opened for appending. (You can put a "**+**" in front of the "**>**" or "**<**" to indicate that you want both read and write access to the file.) If the filename begins with "|", the filename is interpreted as a command to which output is to be piped, and if the filename ends with a "|", the filename is interpreted as command which pipes input to us. (You may not have an open command that pipes both in and out, though it's easy to build one using the **pipe** and **fork** commands.) Any pipe command containing shell metacharacters is passed to _/bin/sh_ for execution; otherwise it is executed directly by Perl. Opening "−" opens **STDIN** and opening ">−" opens **STDOUT**. Open returns non-zero upon success, the undefined value otherwise. If the open involved a pipe, the return value happens to be the pid (process ID) of the subprocess.

Here is some code that shows the link between a filehandle and the corresponding variable:

```
$ARTICLE = 100;
open ARTICLE || die "Can´t find article $ARTICLE: $!\n";
while (<ARTICLE>) {...
```

Append to a file like this:

```
open(LOG, ´>>/usr/spool/news/twitlog´); # (log is reserved)
```

Pipe your data from a process:

```
open(ARTICLE, "caesar <$article |");   # decrypt article
```

Or pipe your data to a process:

```
open(EXTRACT, "|sort >/tmp/Tmp$$");    # $$ is our process#
```

In this next example we show one way to do recursive opens, via indirect filehandles. The files will be opened on filehandles **fh01**, **fh02**, **fh03** and so on. Because **$input** is a local variable, it is preserved through recursion, allowing us to close the correct file before we return.

```
# Process argument list of files along with any includes.

foreach $file (@ARGV) {
        &process($file, ´fh00´);
}

sub process {
        local($filename, $input) = @_;
        $input++;               # this is a string increment
        unless (open($input, $filename)) {
                print STDERR "Can´t open $filename: $!\n";
                return;
        }
```

```
while (<$input>) {        # note the use of indirection
    if (/^#include "(.*)"/) {
        &process($1, $input);
        next;
    }
    ...                   # whatever
}
}
```

You may also, in the Bourne shell tradition, specify an EXPR beginning with ">&", in which case the rest of the string is interpreted as the name of a filehandle (or file descriptor, if numeric) which is to be duped and opened. You may use & after >, >>, <, +>, +>>, and +<. The mode you specify should match the mode of the original filehandle. Here is a script that saves, redirects, and restores **STDOUT** and **STDERR**:

```
#!/usr/bin/perl
open(SAVEOUT, ">&STDOUT");
open(SAVEERR, ">&STDERR");

open(STDOUT, ">foo.out") || die "Can't redirect stdout";
open(STDERR, ">&STDOUT") || die "Can't dup stdout";

select(STDERR); $| = 1;       # make unbuffered
select(STDOUT); $| = 1;       # make unbuffered

print STDOUT "stdout 1\n";    # this works for
print STDERR "stderr 1\n";    # subprocesses too

close(STDOUT);
close(STDERR);

open(STDOUT, ">&SAVEOUT");
open(STDERR, ">&SAVEERR");

print STDOUT "stdout 2\n";
print STDERR "stderr 2\n";
```

If you open a pipe on the command "-" (that is, either "|-" or "-|"), then an implicit fork is done, and the return value of open is the pid of the child within the parent process, and 0 within the child process. (Use **defined($pid)** in either the parent or child to determine if the open was successful.) The filehandle behaves normally for the parent, but input and output to that filehandle is piped from or to the **STDOUT** or **STDIN** of the child process. In the child process the filehandle isn't opened—I/O happens from or to the new **STDOUT** or **STDIN**. Typically this is used like the normal piped open when you want to exercise more control over just how the pipe command gets executed, such as when you are running setuid, and don't want to have to scan shell commands for metacharacters. The following pairs are equivalent:

```
open(FOO, "|tr ´[a-z]´ ´[A-Z]´");
open(FOO, "|-") || exec ´tr´, ´[a-z]´, ´[A-Z]´;

open(FOO, "cat -n file|");
open(FOO, "-|") || exec ´cat´, ´-n´, ´file´;
```

Explicitly closing any piped filehandle causes the parent process to wait for the child to finish, and returns the status value in **$?**. Note that on any operation which may do a fork, unflushed buffers remain unflushed in both processes, which means you may need to set **$|** on one or more filehandles to avoid duplicate output.

Filehandles **STDIN**, **STDOUT**, and **STDERR** remain open following an exec. Other filehandles do not. (However, on systems supporting the **fcntl( )** function, you may modify the close-on-exec flag for a filehandle. See **fcntl( )** earlier in this chapter.)

The filename that is passed to open will have leading and trailing whitespace deleted. In order to open a file with arbitrary weird characters in it, it's necessary to protect any leading and trailing whitespace, like this:

```
$file =~ s#^\s#./$&#;
open(FOO, "< $file\0");
```

But we've never actually seen anyone use that in a script. . .

opendir

```
opendir(DIRHANDLE,EXPR)
```

This function opens a directory named EXPR for processing by **readdir( )**, **telldir( )**, **seekdir( )**, **rewinddir( )**, and **closedir( )**. The function returns true if successful. Directory handles have their own namespace separate from filehandles.

ord

```
ord(EXPR)
ord EXPR
```

This function returns the numeric ASCII value of the first character of EXPR. If EXPR is omitted, it uses **$_**. The return value is always unsigned. If you want a signed value, use **unpack(´c´, EXPR)**.

pack

pack(TEMPLATE,LIST)

This function takes an array or list of values and packs it into a binary structure, returning the string containing the structure. The TEMPLATE is a sequence of characters that give the order and type of values, as follows:

a   An ASCII string, will be null padded.
A   An ASCII string, will be space padded.
b   A bit string, low-to-high order (like vec()).
B   A bit string, high-to-low order.
h   A hexadecimal string, low nybble first.
H   A hexadecimal string, high nybble first.
c   A signed char value.
C   An unsigned char value.
s   A signed short value.
S   An unsigned short value.
i   A signed integer value.
I   An unsigned integer value.
l   A signed long value.
L   An unsigned long value.
n   A short in "network" order.
N   A long in "network" order.
f   A single-precision float in the native format.
d   A double-precision float in the native format.
p   A pointer to a string.
x   A null byte.
X   Back up a byte.
@   Null-fill to absolute position.
u   A uuencoded string.

Each letter may optionally be followed by a number which gives a repeat count. Together the letter and the repeat count make a field specifier. Field specifiers may be separated by whitespace, which will be ignored. With all types except **a** and **A**, the **pack** function will gobble up that many values from the LIST. Saying * for the repeat count means to use however many items are left. The **a** and **A** types gobble just one value, but pack it as a string of length *count*, padding with nulls or spaces as necessary. (When unpacking, **A** strips trailing spaces and nulls, but **a** does not.) Real numbers (floats and doubles) are in the native machine format only; due to the multiplicity of floating formats around, and the lack of a standard "network" representation, no facility for interchange has been made. This means that packed floating-point data written on one machine may not be readable on another—even if both use IEEE floating point arithmetic (as the endian-ness of the memory representation is not part of the IEEE spec). Note that

Perl uses doubles internally for all numeric calculation, and converting from double to float to double will lose precision; that is, **unpack("f", pack("f",$foo))** will not in general equal **$foo**.

This first pair of examples packs numeric values into bytes:

```
$foo = pack("cccc", 65, 66, 67, 68);      # foo eq "ABCD"
$foo = pack("c4", 65, 66, 67, 68);        # same thing
```

This does a similar thing, with a couple of nulls thrown in:

```
$foo = pack("ccxxcc", 65, 66, 67, 68);    # foo eq "AB\0\0CD"
```

Packing shorts doesn't create portable data:

```
$foo = pack("s2", 1, 2);    # "\1\0\2\0" on little-endian
                            # "\0\1\0\2" on big-endian
```

The length on an **a** field only applies to one string:

```
$foo = pack("a4", "abcd", "x", "y", "z");      # "abcd"
```

To get around that limitation, use multiple specifiers:

```
$foo = pack("aaaa", "abcd", "x", "y", "z");  # "axyz"
$foo = pack("a" x 4, "abcd", "x", "y", "z");  # "axyz"
```

The **a** format does null filling:

```
$foo = pack("a14", "abcdefg");   # "abcdefg\0\0\0\0\0\0\0"
```

This template packs a C **struct tm** record (at least on some systems):

```
$foo = pack("i9pl", gmtime, $tz, $toff);
```

The same template may generally also be used in the **unpack** function. If you want to join variable length fields with a delimiter, use the **join** function.

Note that, although all of our examples use literal strings as templates, there is no reason you couldn't pull in your templates from a disk file. You could, in fact, build an entire relational database system around this function.

pipe

```
pipe(READHANDLE,WRITEHANDLE)
```

Like the corresponding system call, this function opens a pair of connected pipes—see *pipe*(2). This call is almost always used right before a **fork**, after which the pipe's reader should close WRITEHANDLE, and the writer close READHANDLE. (Otherwise the pipe won't indicate EOF to the reader when the writer closes it.) Note that if you set up a loop of piped processes, deadlock can occur unless you are very careful. In addition, note that Perl's pipes use standard I/O buffering, so you may need to set $| on your WRITEHANDLE to flush after each command, depending on the application—see **select(FILEHANDLE)**.

pop

```
pop(ARRAY)
pop ARRAY
```

This function treats an array like a stack—it pops and returns the last value of the array, shortening the array by 1. It has the same effect as:

```
$tmp = $ARRAY[$#ARRAY--];
```

or:

```
$tmp = splice(@ ARRAY, -1, 1);
```

If there are no elements in the array, the function returns the undefined value. See also **push** and **shift**.

print

```
print(FILEHANDLE LIST)
print(LIST)
print FILEHANDLE LIST
print LIST
print
```

This function prints a string or a comma-separated list of strings. The function returns 1 if successful, 0 otherwise. FILEHANDLE may be a scalar variable name (unsubscripted), in which case the variable contains the name of the actual filehandle, thus introducing one level of indirection. (Note that if FILEHANDLE is a variable and the next token is a term, it may be misinterpreted as an operator unless you interpose a + or put parentheses around the arguments.) If FILEHAN-DLE is omitted, the function prints to the currently selected output filehandle, initially STDOUT. To set the default output filehandle to something other than **STDOUT** use the **select(FILEHANDLE)** operation.[36] If LIST is also omitted, prints $_. Note that, because **print** takes a LIST, anything in the LIST is evaluated in an array context, and any subroutine that you call will have one or more of its expressions evaluated in an array context. When you say:

```
print OUT <STDIN>;
```

it is **not** going to print out the next line from standard input, but all the rest of the lines from standard input up to end of file. Also, remembering the if-it-looks-like-a-function-it-is-a-function rule, be careful not to follow the "**print**" keyword with a left parenthesis unless you want the corresponding right parenthesis to ter-

---

[36] Thus, **STDOUT** isn't really the default filehandle for **printf()**. It's merely the default default filehandle.

minate the arguments to the **print**—interpose a **+** or put parens around all the arguments:

```
print (1+2)*3, "\n";          # wrong
print +(1+2)*3, "\n";         # ok
print ((1+2)*3, "\n");        # ok
```

printf

```
printf(FILEHANDLE FORMAT, LIST)
printf(FORMAT, LIST)
printf FILEHANDLE FORMAT, LIST
printf FORMAT, LIST
```

This function prints a formatted string to FILEHANDLE or, if omitted, the currently selected output filehandle, initially **STDOUT**. The function is exactly equivalent to:

```
print FILEHANDLE sprintf(LIST)
```

See **print** and **sprintf**. The description of **sprintf** includes the list of acceptable FORMAT specifications.

push

```
push(ARRAY,LIST)
```

This function treats ARRAY (@ is optional) as a stack, and pushes the values of LIST onto the end of ARRAY. The length of ARRAY increases by the length of LIST. This function has the same effect as:

```
foreach $value (LIST)
{
        $ARRAY[++$#ARRAY] = $value;
}
```

or:

```
splice(@ARRAY,@ARRAY,0,LIST);
```

but is more efficient (of both your time and the computer's). You can use **push** in combination with **shift** to make a fairly time-efficient shift register or queue:

```
for (;;) {
        push(@ARRAY, shift @ARRAY);
        . . .
}
```

See also **pop** and **unshift**.

rand

```
rand(EXPR)
rand EXPR
rand
```

This function returns a random fractional number between 0 and the value of EXPR. (EXPR should be positive.) If EXPR is omitted, the function returns a value between 0 and 1. See also **srand()**.

To get an integral value, combine this with **int()**, as in:

```
$roll = int(rand(6)) + 1;        # $roll is now an integer
                                 # between 1 and 6
```

read

```
read(FILEHANDLE,SCALAR,LENGTH,OFFSET)
read(FILEHANDLE,SCALAR,LENGTH)
```

This function attempts to read LENGTH bytes of data into variable SCALAR from the specified FILEHANDLE. The function returns the number of bytes actually read, 0 at end-of-file. It returns the undefined value on error. SCALAR will be grown or shrunk to the length actually read. The OFFSET, if specified, says where in the string to start reading to. For example, to copy data from filehandle **FROM** into filehandle **TO**, use something like:

```
while (read(FROM, $buf, 16384)) {
        print TO $buf;
}
```

Note that the opposite of **read** is simply a **print**, which already knows the length of the string you want to write, and can write a string of any length.

Perl's **read** function is actually implemented in terms of standard I/O's *fread()* function, so the actual *read()* system call may read more than LENGTH bytes to fill the input buffer, and *fread()* may do more than one system *read()* in order to fill the buffer. To gain greater control, specify the real system call using **sysread()**. Calls to **read()** and **sysread()** should not be intermixed unless you are into heavy wizardry (or pain).

readdir

```
readdir(DIRHANDLE)
readdir DIRHANDLE
```

In a scalar context, this function returns the next directory entry for a directory opened by **opendir()**. In an array context, it returns all the rest of the entries in the directory. If there are no more entries, the function returns an undefined value in a scalar context or a null list in an array context. For example:

```
opendir(THISDIR, ".");
@allfiles = readdir(THISDIR);
closedir(THISDIR);
print "@allfiles\n";
```

prints all the files in the current directory on one line. If you want to avoid the . and .. entries, use this instead:

```
@allfiles = grep(!/^\.\.?$/, readdir(THISDIR));
```

And to avoid all . files:

```
@allfiles = grep(!/^\./, readdir(THISDIR));
```

To get just text files, say this:

```
@textfiles = grep(-T, readdir(THISDIR));
```

readlink

```
readlink(EXPR)
readlink EXPR
```

This function returns the value of a symbolic link, if symbolic links are implemented. If not, it gives a fatal error. If there is some system error, the function returns the undefined value and puts the error code into $!. (The most common such error would be the use of **readlink** on a file that isn't a symbolic link.) If EXPR is omitted, the function uses $_.

recv

```
recv(SOCKET,SCALAR,LEN,FLAGS)
```

This function receives a message on a socket. It attempts to receive LENGTH bytes of data into variable SCALAR from the specified SOCKET filehandle. The function returns the address of the sender, or the undefined value if there's an error. SCALAR will be grown or shrunk to the length actually read. The function takes the same flags as *recv*(2). See the section "Interprocess Communication" in Chapter 6.

rename

```
rename(OLDNAME,NEWNAME)
```

This function changes the name of a file. It returns 1 for success, 0 otherwise (and puts the error code into $!). It will not work across filesystem boundaries. If there is already a file named NEWNAME, it will be destroyed.

require

```
require(EXPR)
require EXPR
require
```

This function includes and executes any Perl code found in a separate file, whose name is pointed to by EXPR. This is similar to performing an **eval** on the contents of the file, except that **require** checks to see that the library file has not been included already. It also knows how to search the include path stored in the **@INC** array (see the section "Special Variables" in Chapter 3).

If EXPR is not supplied, $_ is used. This function has semantics similar to the following subroutine:

```
sub require {
    local($filename) = @_;
    return 1 if $INC{$filename};
    local($realfilename, $result);
    ITER: {
        foreach $prefix (@INC) {
            $realfilename = "$prefix/$filename";
            if (-f $realfilename) {
                $result = do $realfilename;
                last ITER;
            }
        }
        die "Can't find $filename in \@INC";
    }
    die $@ if $@;
    die "$filename did not return true value" unless $result;
    $INC{$filename} = $realfilename;
    $result;
}
```

This operator differs from the now somewhat obsolete **do EXPR** operator in that the file will not be included again if it was done previously with either a **require** or **do EXPR** command, and any difficulties will be detected and reported as fatal errors (which may be trapped by use of **eval**). The @INC path search above, however, is actually built into the **do** operator already.

reset

```
reset(EXPR)
reset EXPR
reset
```

This function is generally used at the top of a loop or in a **continue** block at the end of a loop, to clear variables or reset **??** searches so that they work again. The expression is interpreted as a list of single characters (hyphens allowed for ranges). All variables and arrays beginning with one of those letters are reset to their pristine state. If the expression is omitted, one-match searches (**?PAT-TERN?**) are reset to match again. The function resets variables or searches for the current package only. It always returns 1.

To reset all **X** variables, say this:

```
reset ´X´;
```

To reset all lowercase variables, say this:

```
reset ´a–z´;
```

Lastly, to just reset **??** searches, say:

```
reset;
```

Note that resetting "**A–Z**" is not recommended since you'll wipe out your **ARGV, INC, ENV**, and **SIG** arrays.

The use of reset on DBM associative arrays does not change the DBM file. (It does, however, flush any entries cached by Perl, which may be useful if you are sharing the DBM file. Then again, maybe not.)

return

```
return LIST
```

This function returns from a subroutine with the value specified. (Note that a subroutine can automatically return the value of the last expression evaluated. That's the preferred method—use of an explicit **return** is a bit slower.) Use of return outside of a subroutine is verboten, and results in a fatal error.

reverse

```
reverse(LIST)
reverse LIST
```

In an array context, this function returns an array value consisting of the elements of LIST in the opposite order. This is fairly efficient because it just swaps the pointers around. The function can be used to create descending sequences:

```
for (reverse 1 .. 10) { ... }
```

It can be used to invert an associative array:

```
%barfoo = reverse %foobar;
```

In a scalar context, the function returns a string consisting of the characters of the first element of LIST in reverse character order.

A small hint: reversing an array sorted by a user-defined function can sometimes be achieved more easily by sorting in the opposite direction.

rewinddir

```
rewinddir(DIRHANDLE)
rewinddir DIRHANDLE
```

This function sets the current position to the beginning of the directory for the **readdir( )** routine on DIRHANDLE. The function may not be available on all machines that support **readdir( )**.

rindex

```
rindex(STR,SUBSTR,POSITION)
rindex(STR,SUBSTR)
```

This function works just like **index** except that it returns the position of the *last* occurrence of SUBSTR in STR (a "reverse" **index**). The function returns $[− 1 if not found. POSITION, if specified, is the rightmost position that may be returned. To work your way through a string backwards, say:

```
$pos = length($string);
while (($pos = rindex($string, $lookfor, $pos)) >= $[) {
    print "Found at $pos\n";
    $pos—;
}
```

rmdir

```
rmdir(FILENAME)
rmdir FILENAME
```

This function deletes the directory specified by FILENAME if it is empty. If it succeeds, it returns 1, otherwise it returns 0 and puts the error code into $!. If FILENAME is omitted, the function uses $_.

s

```
s/PATTERN/REPLACEMENT/[g][i][e][o]
```

This function searches a string for a pattern, and if found, replaces that pattern with the replacement text and returns the number of substitutions made. Otherwise it returns false (0). The **g** option indicates that all occurrences of the pattern are to be replaced. The **i** option indicates that matching is to be done in a case-insensitive manner. The **e** option indicates that the replacement string is to be evaluated as an expression rather than just as a double-quoted string. Additional occurrences of **e** cause additional evaluations of the resulting string.

Any non-alphanumeric delimiter may replace the slashes; if single quotes are used, no interpretation is done on the replacement string (the **e** modifier overrides this, however); if backquotes are used, the replacement string is a command to execute whose output will be used as the actual replacement text. If no string is specified via the =˜ or !˜ operator, the **$_** string is searched and modified. (The string specified with =˜ must be a scalar variable, an array element, or an assignment to one of those, that is, an lvalue.)

If the pattern contains a **$** that looks like a variable rather than an end-of-string test, the variable will be interpolated into the pattern at runtime. (You can't interpolate **$|** or **$)** into a PATTERN because they look like the end-of-string test.) If you want the pattern compiled only once, the first time the variable is interpolated, add an **o** at the end. Use this when the variable doesn't change over the life of the process. The **o** is useful only when there is a variable in the PATTERN, but doesn't hurt when included unnecessarily. See also the section "Regular Expressions" in Chapter 3.

This substitution is restricted to word matches; it would change "green" but not "wintergreen" or "greensleaves."

```
s/\bgreen\b/mauve/g;
```

Here **#** is used as an alternate delimiter to avoid unnecessary backslashing:

```
$path =˜ s#/usr/bin#/usr/local/bin#;
```

Here is a runtime pattern. The variable **$foo** may be a regular expression, since the variable is interpolated before the pattern is compiled. (The pattern is recompiled each time the statement is reached.) The variable **$bar** is re-evaluated each time a replacement is made on the string.

```
s/Login: $foo/Login: $bar/g;
```

In this example, we show how to copy a value and modify it in the same statement:

```
($foo = $bar) =˜ s/bar/foo/;
```

The **e** modifier can be used for things that are very difficult to do otherwise:

```
$_ = ´abc123xyz´;
s/\d+/$&*2/e;              # yields ´abc246xyz´
s/\d+/sprintf("%5d", $&)/e;   # yields ´abc  246xyz´
s/\w/$& x 2/eg;            # yields ´aabbcc  224466xxyyzz´
```

This next example is here to remind you that the replacement string uses **$** instead of \ to interpolate substrings.

```
s/([^ ]*) *([^ ]*)/$2 $1/;      # reverse 1st two fields
```

(See the section "Regular Expressions" in Chapter 3.)

Here's a very tiny, slightly corkbrained shell:

```
#!/usr/bin/perl
for (;;) {
        print "$_\$ ";
        last unless $_ = <STDIN>;
        s`^([^#]+)(#.*)?\n$`$1`;
}
```

The substitute takes each line and replaces it with the value of **$1** (the part before the first **#**) after processing it through backquotes (running a /*bin/sh* on it).

scalar

```
scalar(EXPR)
```

This pseudo-function may be used within a LIST to force EXPR to be evaluated in a scalar context when evaluation in an array context would produce a different result. For example:

```
local($nextvar) = scalar(<STDIN>);
```

prevents **<STDIN>** from reading all the lines from standard input before doing the assignment, since assignment to a local list is an array context. Since a **print** function is a LIST operator, you have to say:

```
print "Length is ", scalar(@ARRAY), "\n";
```

if you want the length of **@array** to be printed out.

One almost never runs into the need for the opposite operation, so there isn't one.

seek

```
seek(FILEHANDLE,POSITION,WHENCE)
```

This function randomly[37] positions the file pointer for FILEHANDLE, just like the *fseek( )* call of standard I/O. The value of WHENCE specifies what the file POSITION is relative to: **0**, the beginning of the file; **1**, the current position in the file; or **2**, the end of the file. POSITION may be negative for a WHENCE of **1** or **2**. FILEHANDLE may be an expression whose value gives the name of the filehandle. The function returns 1 upon success, 0 otherwise.

---

[37] As in "arbitrarily," not "nondeterministically!"

One interesting use for this function is to allow you to follow growing files, like this:

```
for (;;) {
    while (<LOG>) {
        ...            # Process file.
    }
    sleep 15;
    seek(LOG,0,1);     # Reset end-of-file error.
}
```

seekdir

```
seekdir(DIRHANDLE,POS)
```

This function sets the current position for the **readdir( )** routine on DIRHANDLE. POS must be a value returned by **telldir( )**. This function has the same caveats about possible directory compaction as the corresponding system library routine. The function may not be implemented everywhere that **readdir( )** is. It's certainly not implemented where **readdir( )** isn't.

select

```
select(FILEHANDLE)
select
```

```
select(RBITS,WBITS,EBITS,TIMEOUT)
```

The first form returns the currently selected filehandle, and if FILEHANDLE is supplied, sets the current default filehandle for output. This has two effects: first, a **write** or a **print** without a filehandle will default to this FILEHANDLE. Second, references to variables related to output will refer to this output filehandle. For example, if you have to set the top-of-form format for more than one output filehandle, you might do the following:

```
select(REPORT1);
$^ = 'report1_top';
select(REPORT2);
$^ = 'report2_top';
```

Library routines should generally leave the currently selected filehandle the same on exit as it was upon entry. Fortunately, FILEHANDLE may be an expression whose value gives the name of the actual filehandle. Thus, you can save and restore the currently selected filehandle:

```
local($oldfh) = select(STDERR); $| = 1; select($oldfh);
```

or (being bizarre and obscure):

```
select((select(STDERR), $| = 1)[$[])
```

This example works by building a list consisting of the returned value from **select(STDERR)** (which selects **STDERR** as a side effect) and **$| = 1** (which is always 1, but unbuffers the now-selected **STDERR** as a side effect. The first element of that list (the previously selected filehandle) is now used as an argument to the outer **select**. Bizarre, right? That's what you get for knowing just enough Lisp to be dangerous.

The second form, **select(RBITS,WBITS,EBITS,TIMEOUT)**, is totally unrelated to the first form. It calls the *select*(2) system call with the bitmasks specified, which can be constructed using **fileno( )** and **vec( )**, along these lines:

```
$rin = $win = $ein = ´´;
vec($rin, fileno(STDIN), 1) = 1;
vec($win, fileno(STDOUT), 1) = 1;
$ein = $rin | $win;
```

If you want to select on many filehandles you might wish to write a subroutine:

```
sub fhbits {
    local(@fhlist) = @_;
    local($bits);
    for (@fhlist) {
        vec($bits, fileno($_), 1) = 1;
    }
    $bits;
}
$rin = &fhbits(STDIN,TTY,SOCK);
```

The usual idiom is:

```
($nfound, $timeleft) =
        select($rout=$rin, $wout=$win, $eout=$ein, $timeout);
```

or to block until something becomes ready:

```
$nfound = select($rout=$rin, $wout=$win, $eout=$ein, undef);
```

The **$wout=$win** trick works because the value of an assignment is the left side, so **$wout** gets clobbered first by the assignment, and then by the **select()**, while **$win** remains unchanged.

Any of the bitmasks can also be **undef**. The timeout, if specified, is in seconds, which may be fractional. (A timeout of 0 effects a poll.) Note that not all implementations are capable of returning the **$timeleft**. If not, they always return **$timeleft** equal to the supplied **$timeout**.

One use for **select** is to sleep with a finer resolution than **sleep**( ) allows. To do this, specify **undef** for all the bitmasks. For example, to sleep for (at least) 4.75 seconds, use:

```
select(undef, undef, undef, 4.75);
```

semctl

```
semctl(ID,SEMNUM,CMD,ARG)
```

This function calls the System V IPC system call **semctl**( ). If CMD is **&IPC_STAT** or **&GETALL**, then ARG must be a variable which will hold the returned **semid_ds** structure or semaphore value array. The function returns like **ioctl**: the undefined value for error, **"0 but true"** for zero, or the actual return value otherwise. On error, it puts the error code into $!. Before calling, you should say:

```
require "ipc.ph";
require "sem.ph";
```

This function is available only on machines supporting System V IPC.

semget

```
semget(KEY,NSEMS,SIZE,FLAGS)
```

This function calls the system's **semget**( ) function—see *semget*(2). The function returns the semaphore id, or the undefined value if there is an error. On error, it puts the error code into $!. Before calling, you should say:

```
require "ipc.ph";
require "sem.ph";
```

This function is available only on machines supporting System V IPC.

semop

```
semop(KEY,OPSTRING)
```

This function calls the **semop**( ) system call to perform semaphore operations such as signaling and waiting—see *semop*(2). OPSTRING must be a packed array of **semop** structures. You can make each **semop** structure by saying **pack("s*", $semnum, $semop, $semflag)**. The number of semaphore operations is implied by the length of OPSTRING. The function returns true if successful, or false if there is an error. On error, it puts the error code into **$!**. Before calling, you should say:

```
require "ipc.ph";
require "sem.ph";
```

The following code waits on semaphore **$semnum** of semaphore id **$semid**:

```
$semop = pack("s*", $semnum, -1, 0);
die "Semaphore trouble: $!\n" unless semop($semid, $semop);
```

To signal the semaphore, simply replace **−1** with **1**.

This function is available only on machines supporting System V IPC.

send

```
send(SOCKET,MSG,FLAGS,TO)
send(SOCKET,MSG,FLAGS)
```

This function sends a message on a socket. It takes the same flags as the system call of the same name—see *send*(2). On unconnected sockets you must specify a destination to send TO. The function returns the number of characters sent, or the undefined value if there is an error. On error, it puts the error code into **$!**.

setpgrp

```
setpgrp(PID,PGRP)
```

This function sets the current process group (pgrp) for the specified PID (use a PID of 0 for the current process). Invoking **setpgrp** will produce a fatal error if used on a machine that doesn't implement *setpgrp*(2). Beware: some systems will ignore the arguments you provide and always do **setpgrp(0, $$)**. Fortunately, those are the arguments one usually provides.

setpriority

```
setpriority(WHICH,WHO,PRIORITY)
```

This function sets the current priority for a process, a process group, or a user. (See *setpriority*(2).) Invoking **setpriority** will produce a fatal error if used on a machine that doesn't implement *setpriority*(2). To "nice" your process down by 4 units (the same as executing **nice 4** *command*), try:

```
setpriority(0, 0, getpriority(0, 0) + 4);
```

The interpretation of a given priority may vary from operating system to operating system.

setsockopt

```
setsockopt(SOCKET,LEVEL,OPTNAME,OPTVAL)
```

This function sets the socket option requested. The function returns undefined if there is an error. OPTVAL may be specified as **undef** if you don't want to pass an argument.

shift

```
shift(ARRAY)
shift ARRAY
shift
```

This function shifts the first value of the array off and returns it, shortening the array by 1 and moving everything down. If there are no elements in the array, the function returns the undefined value. If ARRAY is omitted, it shifts the **@ARGV** array in the main program, and the **@_** array in subroutines. See also **unshift()**, **push()**, **pop()**, and **splice()**. The **shift()** and **unshift()** functions do the same thing to the left end of an array that **push()** and **pop()** do to the right end.

shmctl

```
shmctl(ID,CMD,ARG)
```

This function calls the **shmctl()** system call—see *shmctl*(2). If CMD is **&IPC_STAT**, then ARG must be a variable which will hold the returned **shmid_ds** structure. The function returns like **ioctl**: the undefined value for error, **"0 but true"** for zero, or the actual return value otherwise. On error, it puts the error code into **$!**. Before calling, you should say:

```
require "ipc.ph";
require "shm.ph";
```

This function is available only on machines supporting System V IPC.

shmget

```
shmget(KEY,SIZE,FLAGS)
```

This function calls the **shmget()** system call—see *shmget*(2). The function returns the shared memory segment id, or the undefined value if there is an error. On error, it puts the error code into **$!**. Before calling, you should say:

```
require "ipc.ph";
require "shm.ph";
```

This function is available only on machines supporting System V IPC.

shmread

```
shmread(ID,VAR,POS,SIZE)
```

This function reads from the shared memory segment ID starting at position POS for size SIZE (by attaching to it, copying out, and detaching from it). VAR must be a variable which will hold the data read. The function returns true if successful, or false if there is an error. On error, it puts the error code into $!. This function is available only on machines supporting System V IPC.

shmwrite

```
shmwrite(ID,STRING,POS,SIZE)
```

This function writes to the shared memory segment ID starting at position POS for size SIZE (by attaching to it, copying in, and detaching from it). If STRING is too long, only SIZE bytes are used; if STRING is too short, nulls are written to fill out SIZE bytes. The function returns true if successful, or false if there is an error. On error, it puts the error code into $!. This function is available only on machines supporting System V IPC.

shutdown

```
shutdown(SOCKET,HOW)
```

This function shuts down a socket connection in the manner indicated by HOW, which has the same interpretation as *shutdown*(2).

sin

```
sin(EXPR)
sin EXPR
```

Sorry, there's nothing wicked about this operator. It merely returns the sine of EXPR (expressed in radians). If EXPR is omitted, it returns sine of $_.

sleep

```
sleep(EXPR)
sleep EXPR
sleep
```

This function causes the script to sleep for EXPR seconds, or forever if no EXPR. May be interrupted by sending the process a SIGALARM. The function returns the number of seconds actually slept. On some systems, the function sleeps till the "top of the second," so, for instance, a **sleep 1** may sleep anywhere from 0 to 1 second, depending on when in the current second you started sleeping. A **sleep 2** may sleep anywhere from 1 to 2 seconds. And so on. If available, the second form of the **select()** call can give you better resolution. You may also be able to use **syscall()** to call the **itimer** routines that some UNIX systems support.

socket

```
socket(SOCKET,DOMAIN,TYPE,PROTOCOL)
```

This function opens a socket of the specified kind and attaches it to filehandle
SOCKET. DOMAIN, TYPE, and PROTOCOL are specified the same as for
select(2). You may need to run **h2ph** on *sys/socket.h* to get the proper values
handy in a Perl library file. The function returns true if successful. See the
example in the section "Interprocess Communication" in Chapter 6.

socketpair

```
socketpair(SOCKET1,SOCKET2,DOMAIN,TYPE,PROTOCOL)
```

This function creates an unnamed pair of sockets in the specified domain, of the
specified type. DOMAIN, TYPE, and PROTOCOL are specified the same as for
socketpair(2). If unimplemented, invoking this function yields a fatal error. The
function returns true if successful. This function is typically used just before a
fork. One of the resulting processes should close SOCKET1, and the other should
close SOCKET2. You can use these sockets bidirectionally, unlike the filehandles created by the **pipe**( ) function.

sort

```
sort(SUBROUTINE LIST)
sort(LIST)
sort SUBROUTINE LIST
sort LIST
```

This function sorts the LIST and returns the sorted array value. Nonexistent values of arrays are stripped out. If SUBROUTINE is omitted, it sorts in standard
string comparison order. If SUBROUTINE is specified, it gives the name of a
subroutine that returns an integer less than, equal to, or greater than 0, depending
on how the elements of the array are to be ordered. In the interests of efficiency,
the normal calling code for subroutines is bypassed, with the following effects:
the subroutine may not be a recursive subroutine, and the two elements to be
compared are passed into the subroutine not via @_ but as $a and $b (see the
examples below). The variables $a and $b are passed by reference, so don't modify them. SUBROUTINE may be a scalar variable name (unsubscripted), in
which case the value provides the name of the subroutine to use. To do an ordinary numeric sort, say this:

```
sub numerically { $a <=> $b; }
@sortedbynumber = sort numerically 53,29,11,32,7;
```

To sort an array value by some associated value, use an associative array lookup in the sort routine:

```
sub byage {
    $age{$a} <=> $age{$b};
}
@sortedclass = sort byage @class;
```

And finally, note the equivalency of the two ways to sort in reverse:

```
sub reverse { $b cmp $a; }
@harry = ('dog', 'cat', 'x', 'Cain', 'Abel');
@george = ('gone', 'chased', 'yz', 'Punished', 'Axed');
print sort @harry;
        # prints AbelCaincatdogx
print sort reverse @harry;
        # prints xdogcatCainAbel
print reverse sort @harry;
        # prints xdogcatCainAbel
print sort @george, 'to', @harry;    # Remember, it's a LIST.
        # prints AbelAxedCainPunishedcatchaseddoggonetoxyz
```

splice

```
splice(ARRAY,OFFSET,LENGTH,LIST)
splice(ARRAY,OFFSET,LENGTH)
splice(ARRAY,OFFSET)
```

This function removes the elements designated by OFFSET and LENGTH from an array, and replaces them with the elements of LIST, if any. The function returns the elements removed from the array. The array grows or shrinks as necessary. If LENGTH is omitted, the function removes everything from OFFSET onward. The following equivalencies hold (assuming $[is 0):

```
push(@a, $x, $y)     :splice(@a, $#a+1, 0, $x, $y)
pop(@a)              :splice(@a, -1)
shift(@a)            :splice(@a, 0, 1)
unshift(@a, $x, $y)  :splice(@a, 0, 0, $x, $y)
$a[$x] = $y          :splice(@a, $x, 1, $y);
```

For example, assuming array lengths are passed before arrays:

```
sub aeq {        # compare two array values
        local(@a) = splice(@_, 0, shift);
        local(@b) = splice(@_, 0, shift);
        return 0 unless @a == @b;        # same len?
        while (@a) {
            return 0 if pop(@a) ne pop(@b);
        }
        return 1;
}
if (&aeq($len, @foo[1..$len], scalar(@bar), @bar)) { ... }
```

split

```
split(/PATTERN/,EXPR,LIMIT)
split(/PATTERN/,EXPR)
split(/PATTERN/)
split
```

This function splits a string into an array of strings, and returns the array value. The PATTERN matches the delimiters that separate the desired array elements. The delimiters are not ordinarily returned. (If not in an array context, the function returns the number of fields found and splits into the @_ array. In an array context, you can force the split into @_ by using **??** as the pattern delimiters, but it still returns the array value.) If EXPR is omitted, the function splits the **$_** string. If PATTERN is also omitted, the function splits on whitespace: /[\t\n]+/. Anything matching PATTERN is taken to be a delimiter separating the fields. (Note that the delimiter may be longer than one character.) If the PATTERN doesn't match at all, it returns the original string. Strings of any length can be split:

```
@chars = split(//,$word);
@fields = split(/:/,$line);
@words = split(' ',$paragraph);
@lines = split(/^/,$buffer);
```

If LIMIT is specified, the function splits into no more than that many fields (though it may split into fewer if it runs out of delimiters). If LIMIT is unspecified, trailing null fields are stripped (which potential users of **pop**() would do well to remember).

A pattern that is capable of matching the null string (for instance, any single character modified by a * or ?) will split the value of EXPR into separate characters at each point it matches that way. (At the places it matches one or more characters, it skips the delimiter in the normal fashion.) For example:

```
print join(':', split(/ */, 'hi there'));
```

produces the output **"h:i:t:h:e:r:e"**. Note that the space disappeared because it matched normally. As a trivial case, the null pattern // simply splits into separate characters.

The LIMIT parameter can be used to split only part of a line:

```
($login, $passwd, $remainder) = split(/:/, $_, 3);
```

We encourage you to split to lists of names like this in order to make your code self-documenting. (For purposes of error checking, note that $remainder would be undefined if there were fewer than 3 fields.) When assigning to a list, if LIMIT is omitted, Perl supplies a LIMIT one larger than the number of variables in the list, to avoid unnecessary work. For the list above, LIMIT would have been 4 by default, and $remainder would have received only the third field, not all the rest of the fields. In time-critical applications it behooves you not to split into more fields than you really need.

If the PATTERN contains parentheses, additional array elements are created from each matching substring in the delimiter. The following:

```
split(/([,−])/, "1−10,20");
```

produces the array value:

```
(1, ´−´, 10, ´,´, 20)
```

The /**PATTERN**/ argument may be replaced with an expression to specify patterns that vary at runtime. (To do runtime compilation only once, use /$**variable**/o.) As a special case, specifying a space " " will split on whitespace just as **split** with no arguments does, but leading whitespace does NOT produce a null first field. Thus, **split**(´ ´) can be used to emulate *awk*'s default behavior, whereas **split**(/ /) will give you as many null initial fields as there are leading spaces.

Note that patterns containing ^ or $ may not work right unless the $* variable is set, since the value of $* tells the optimizer whether it has to deal with multiple embedded newlines or not, and it will make rash assumptions if you set $* wrong.

This example splits a a message header into $head{´Date´}, $head{´Subject´}, and so on. It uses the trick of assigning a list of pairs to an associative array, based on the fact that delimiters alternate with delimited fields. It makes use of parentheses to return the delimiters as part of the returned array value. Unfortunately this loses information for multiple lines with the same key field, such as Received-By lines. Ah, well.

```
$* = 1;
$header =~ s/\n\s+/ /g;        # Merge continuation lines.
%head = (´FRONTSTUFF´, split(/^([−\w]+):/, $header));
```

This example processes the entries in a *passwd* file. You could leave out the **chop**, in which case $**shell** would have a newline on the end of it.

```
open(PASSWD, ´/etc/passwd´);
while (<PASSWD>) {
        chop;          # remove trailing newline
        ($login, $passwd, $uid, $gid, $gcos, $home, $shell) =
                split(/:/);
        ...
}
```

The inverse of **split** is performed by **join**. To split apart a string with fixed-position fields, use **unpack**.

sprintf

```
sprintf(FORMAT,LIST)
```

This function returns a string formatted by the usual **printf** conventions. The FORMAT string contains text with embedded field specifiers into which the elements of list are substituted, one per field. Field specifiers are roughly of the form:

```
%m.nx
```

where the **m** and **n** are optional sizes whose interpretation depends on the type of field, and **x** is one of:

s	String
c	Character
d	Decimal number
ld	Long decimal number
u	Unsigned decimal number
lu	Long unsigned decimal number
x	Hexadecimal number
lx	Long hexadecimal number
o	Octal number
lo	Long octal number
e	Exponential format floating-point number
f	Fixed point format floating-point number
g	Compact format floating-point number

The various combinations are fully documented in the manual page for *printf(3)*, but we'll mention that **m** is typically the minimum length of the field (negative for left justified), and **n** is precision for exponential formats and the maximum length for other formats. Padding is typically done with spaces for strings and zeroes for number. The * character as a length specifier is not supported. However, you can easily get around this by including the length expression directly into FORMAT, as in:

```
$width = 20; $value = sin(1.0);
foreach $precision (0..($width-2)) {
        printf "%${width}.${precision}f\n", $value;
}
```

sqrt

```
sqrt(EXPR)
sqrt EXPR
```

This function returns the square root of EXPR. If EXPR is omitted, it returns square root of $_.

srand

```
srand(EXPR)
srand EXPR
```

This function sets the random number seed for the **rand** operator. If EXPR is omitted, it does **srand(time)**, which is pretty predictable, so don't use it for security-type things, such as random password generation. Try something like **srand(time|$$)** instead.

stat

```
stat(FILEHANDLE)
stat FILEHANDLE
stat(EXPR)
```

This function returns a 13-element array giving the statistics for a file, either the file opened via FILEHANDLE, or named by EXPR. Typically used as follows:

```
($dev,$ino,$mode,$nlink,$uid,$gid,$rdev,$size,
        $atime,$mtime,$ctime,$blksize,$blocks)
                = stat($filename);
```

The **$blksize** and **$blocks** are defined only on BSD-derived operating systems. The **$blocks** field (if defined) is reported in 512-byte blocks. Note that **$blocks*512** can differ greatly from **$size** for files containing unallocated blocks, or "holes," which aren't counted in **$blocks.**

If **stat** is passed the special filehandle consisting of an underline, no stat is done, but the current contents of the stat structure from the last stat or stat-based file test (the **-x** operators) are returned.

This first stats **$file** to see if it is executable. If it is, it then pulls the device number out of the existing stat structure and tests it to see if it looks like an NFS filesystem. Network File Systems tend to have negative device numbers.

```
if (-x $file && (($d) = stat(_)) && $d < 0) {
        print "$file is executable NFS file\n";
}
```

Hint: if you need only the size of the file, check out the **-s** file test operator, which returns the size in bytes directly. There are also file tests which return the ages of files in days.

study

```
study(SCALAR)
study SCALAR
study
```

This function takes extra time to study SCALAR ($_ if unspecified) in anticipation of doing many pattern matches on the string before it is next modified. This may or may not save time, depending on the nature and number of patterns you are searching on, and on the distribution of character frequencies in the string to be searched—you probably want to compare runtimes with and without it to see which runs faster. Those loops that scan for many short constant strings (including the constant parts of more complex patterns) will benefit most. If all your pattern matches are constant strings, anchored at the front, **study** won't help at all, because no scanning is done. You may have only one study active at a time—if you study a different scalar the first is "unstudied." (The way study works is this: a linked list of every character in the string to be searched is made, so we know, for example, where all the **k** characters are. From each search string, the rarest character is selected, based on some static frequency tables constructed from some C programs and English text. Only those places that contain this *rarest* character are examined.)

For example, here is a loop that inserts index-producing entries before any line containing a certain pattern:

```
while (<>) {
        study;
        print ".IX foo\n" if /\bfoo\b/;
        print ".IX bar\n" if /\bbar\b/;
        print ".IX blurfl\n" if /\bblurfl\b/;
        ...
        print;
}
```

In searching for /\bfoo\b/, only those locations in $_ that contain **f** will be looked at, because **f** is rarer than **o**. In general, this is a big win except in pathological cases. The only question is whether it saves you more time than it took to build the linked list in the first place.

Note that if you have to look for strings that you don't know till runtime, you can build an entire loop as a string and **eval** that to avoid recompiling all your patterns all the time. Together with setting $/ to input entire files as one record, this can be very fast, often faster than specialized programs like *fgrep*. The following scans a list of files (@**files**) for a list of words (@**words**), and prints out the names of those files that contain a match:

```
$search = `while (<>) { study; `;
foreach $word (@words) {
        $search .= "++\$seen{\$ARGV} if /\b$word\b/;\n";
}
$search .= "}";
@ARGV = @files;
undef $/;                 # slurp each entire file
eval $search;             # this screams
$/ = "\n";                # put back to normal input delim
foreach $file (sort keys(%seen)) {
        print $file, "\n";
}
```

substr

```
substr(EXPR,OFFSET,LENGTH)
substr(EXPR,OFFSET)
```

This function extracts a substring out of EXPR and returns it. First character is at offset 0, or whatever you've set $[to. If OFFSET is negative (and less than $[), the substring starts that far from the end of the string. If LENGTH is omitted, everything to the end of the string is returned. You can use the **substr**( ) function as an lvalue, in which case EXPR must be an lvalue. If you assign something shorter than LENGTH, the string will shrink, and if you assign something longer than LENGTH, the string will grow to accommodate it. To keep the string the same length you may need to pad or chop your value using **sprintf**( ) or the **x** operator. For example, to prepend the string "**Larry**" to the current value of $_, use:

```
substr($_, 0, 0) = "Larry";
```

To instead replace the first character of $_ with "**Moe**", use:

```
substr($_, 0, 1) = "Moe";
```

and finally, to replace the last character of $_ with "**Curly**", use:

```
substr($_, -1, 1) = "Curly";
```

These last few examples presume you haven't messed with the value of $[(an unwise presumption if you are writing a subroutine that will be used in unknown environments).

symlink

```
symlink(OLDFILE,NEWFILE)
```

This function creates a new filename symbolically linked to the old filename. The function returns 1 for success, 0 otherwise. On systems that don't support symbolic links, it produces a fatal error at run time. To check for that, use eval to trap the potential error:

```
$symlink_exists = (eval ´symlink("", "");´, $@ eq ´´);
```

See also **link**() earlier in this chapter.

syscall

```
syscall(LIST)
syscall LIST
```

This function calls the system call specified as the first element of the list, passing the remaining elements as arguments to the system call. The function produces a fatal error if the C routine *syscall*(2) is unimplemented. The arguments are interpreted as follows: if a given argument is numeric, the argument is passed as an **int** (a C integer). If not, the pointer to the string value is passed. You are responsible for making sure a string is long enough to receive any result that might be written into it. If your integer arguments are not literals and have never been interpreted in a numeric context, you may need to add 0 to them to force them to look like numbers.

This example calls the **setgroups**() system call to add to the group list of the current process. (It will only work on machines that support multiple group membership.)

```
require ´syscall.ph´;          # may need to run h2ph
syscall(&SYS_setgroups, @groups+0, pack("i*", @groups));
```

Note that some systems may require a **pack** template of "**s***" instead.

sysread

```
sysread(FILEHANDLE,SCALAR,LENGTH,OFFSET)
sysread(FILEHANDLE,SCALAR,LENGTH)
```

This function attempts to read LENGTH bytes of data into variable SCALAR from the specified FILEHANDLE using the actual **read**() system call, bypassing standard I/O. (An ordinary Perl **read** calls C's **fread**() function.) The function returns the number of bytes actually read, 0 at end-of-file; it returns the undefined value on error. SCALAR will be grown or shrunk to the length actually read. The OFFSET, if specified, says where in the string to start reading to. For an example, see **syswrite**. Calls to **read**() and **sysread**() should not be intermixed on the same filehandle unless you are into heavy wizardry (and/or pain). You should be prepared to handle the problems (like interrupted system calls) that standard I/O normally handles for you.

system

```
system(LIST)
system LIST
```

This function executes any program on the system for you. It does exactly the same thing as "**exec LIST**" except that a **fork** is done first, and the script waits for the program it's running to complete. Note that argument processing varies depending on the number of arguments, as described for **exec**. The return value is the exit status of the program as returned by the **wait()** call. To get the actual exit value divide by 256. See **exec**.

syswrite

```
syswrite(FILEHANDLE,SCALAR,LENGTH,OFFSET)
syswrite(FILEHANDLE,SCALAR,LENGTH)
```

This function attempts to write LENGTH bytes of data from variable SCALAR to the specified FILEHANDLE using the actual **write()** system call, bypassing standard I/O. (An ordinary Perl **print** calls C's **fwrite()** function.) The function returns the number of bytes actually written; or the undefined value on error. You should be prepared to handle the problems that standard I/O normally handles for you, such as partial writes. The OFFSET, if specified, says where in the string to start writing from. To copy data from filehandle **FROM** into filehandle **TO**, use something like:

```
while ($len = sysread(FROM, $buf, 16384)) {
        if (!defined $len) {
                next if $! =~ /^Interrupted/;
                die "System read error: $!\n";
        }
        $offset = 0;
        while ($len) {           # Handle partial writes.
                $written = syswrite(TO, $buf, $len, $offset);
                die "System write error: $!\n"
                        unless defined $written;
                $len -= $written;
                $offset += $written;
        };
}
```

Calls to (**print()** or **write()**) and **syswrite()** should not be intermixed on the same filehandle unless you are into heavy wizardry.

tell

```
tell(FILEHANDLE)
tell FILEHANDLE
tell
```

This function returns the current file position (in bytes) for FILEHANDLE. FILEHANDLE may be an expression whose value gives the name of the actual filehandle. If FILEHANDLE is omitted, the function returns the position of the file last read. File positions are only meaningful on regular files. Devices, pipes, and sockets have no file position.

telldir

```
telldir(DIRHANDLE)
telldir DIRHANDLE
```

This function returns the current position of the **readdir( )** routines on DIRHAN-DLE. Value may be given to **seekdir( )** to access a particular location in a directory. The function has the same caveats about possible directory compaction as the corresponding system library routine. This function may not be implemented everywhere that **readdir( )** is.

time

```
time
```

This function returns the number of non-leap seconds since January 1, 1970, UTC. The returned value is suitable for feeding to **gmtime( )** and **localtime( )**, and for comparison with file modification and access times returned by **stat( )**, and for feeding to **utime**—see the examples under **utime**.

times

```
times
```

This function returns a four-element array giving the user and system CPU times, in seconds (possibly fractional), for this process and the children of this process.

```
($user, $system, $cuser, $csystem) = times;
```

For example, to time the execution speed of a section of Perl code:

```
$start = (times)[0]; # presumes $[ = 0
...
$end = (times)[0];
printf "that took %.2f CPU seconds\n", $end - $start;
```

tr

```
tr/SEARCHLIST/REPLACEMENTLIST/[c][d][s]
y/SEARCHLIST/REPLACEMENTLIST/[c][d][s]
```

This function translates all occurrences of the characters found in the search list to the corresponding character in the replacement list. If REPLACEMENTLIST is shorter than SEARCHLIST, the last character of REPLACEMENTLIST is replicated as necessary (except with the **d** option). If REPLACEMENTLIST is null, a copy of SEARCHLIST is used (except with the **d** option). The number of characters replaced is returned. The **c** option complements the SEARCHLIST; any characters mentioned in SEARCHLIST are removed from the string **\001–\377** and the resulting string is used in place of SEARCHLIST. The **d** option deletes all characters within SEARCHLIST that are not found in REPLACEMENTLIST. The **s** option causes any substitions that would result in multiple identical REPLACEMENTLIST characters to be output consecutively to be replaced with just a single occurrence of that character. (Think of it as "squeezing" the many characters into one.) If no string is specified via the =˜ or !˜ operator, the **$_** string is translated. (The string specified with =˜ must be a scalar variable, an array element, or an assignment to one of those, that is, an lvalue.) For *sed* devotées, **y** is provided as a synonym for **tr**.

This statement canonicalizes the named scalar to lowercase:

```
$ARGV[1] =˜ y/A–Z/a–z/;
```

This one counts the stars in **$_**:

```
$cnt = tr/*/*/;
```

To translate while copying a variable, say this:

```
($HOST = $host) =˜ tr/a–z/A–Z/;
```

The complement option can be used to change all non-alphabetic characters to spaces, like this:

```
y/a–zA–Z/ /c;
```

Combined with the squeeze option, sequences of spaces turn into one space:

```
y/a–zA–Z/ /cs;
```

And this command deletes all non-alpha characters completely:

```
y/a–zA–Z//cd;
```

truncate

```
truncate(FILEHANDLE,LENGTH)
truncate(EXPR,LENGTH)
```

This function truncates the file opened on FILEHANDLE, or named by EXPR, to the specified length. The function produces a fatal error if **truncate** isn't implemented (somehow or another) on your system.

umask

```
umask(EXPR)
umask EXPR
umask
```

This function sets the umask for the process and returns the old one. (The umask tells UNIX which permission bits to disallow when creating a file.) If EXPR is omitted, the function merely returns current umask. For example, to ensure that the "other" bits are turned on, and the "user" bits are turned off, try something like:

```
umask((umask & 077) | 7);
```

undef

```
undef(EXPR)
undef EXPR
undef
```

This function undefines the value of EXPR, which must be an lvalue. Use on only a scalar value, an entire array, or a subroutine name (using the **&** prefix). Any storage associated with the object will be recovered. (The **undef** operator will probably not do what you expect on most special variables.) The function always returns the undefined value. You can omit the EXPR, in which case nothing is undefined, but you still get an undefined value that you could, for instance, return from a subroutine. Here are some uses of **undef** as a unary operator:

```
undef $foo;
undef $bar{'blurfl'};
undef @ary;
undef %assoc;
undef &mysub;
```

Without an argument, **undef** is just used for its value:

```
return (wantarray ? () : undef) if $they_blew_it;
select(undef, undef, undef, $naptime);
```

unlink

```
unlink(LIST)
unlink LIST
```

This function deletes a list of files.[38] The function returns the number of files successfully deleted. Some sample commands:

```
$cnt = unlink 'a', 'b', 'c';
unlink @goners;
unlink <*.bak>;
```

Note that **unlink** will not delete directories unless you are superuser and the –U flag is supplied to Perl. Even if these conditions are met, be warned that unlinking a directory can inflict Serious Damage on your filesystem. Use **rmdir** instead.

Here's a very simple *rm* command with very simple error checking:

```
#!/usr/bin/perl
@cannot = grep(!unlink($_), @ARGV);
die "$0: could not unlink @cannot\n" if @cannot;
```

unpack

```
unpack(TEMPLATE,EXPR)
```

This function does the reverse of **pack**: it takes a string representing a structure and expands it out into an array value, returning the array value. (In a scalar context, it can be used to unpack a single value.) The TEMPLATE has much the same format as in the **pack** function—it's a sequence of characters that give the order and type of values, as follows:

a   An ASCII string, unstripped.
A   An ASCII string, trailing nulls and spaces will be stripped.
b   A bit string, low-to-high order (like vec()).
B   A bit string, high-to-low order.
h   A hexadecimal string, low nybble first.
H   A hexadecimal string, high nybble first.
c   A signed char value.
C   An unsigned char value.
s   A signed short value.
S   An unsigned short value.
i   A signed integer value.

---

[38] Actually, under UNIX, it removes the directory entries that refer to the real files. Since a file may be referenced (linked) from more than one directory, the file isn't actually removed until the last reference to it is removed.

I   An unsigned integer value.
l   A signed long value.
L   An unsigned long value.
n   A short in "network" order.
N   A long in "network" order.
f   A single-precision float in the native format.
d   A double-precision float in the native format.
p   A pointer to a string.
x   Skip forward a byte.
X   Back up a byte.
@   Go to absolute position in string for next field.
u   Uudecode a string.

Each letter may optionally be followed by a number which gives a repeat count. Together the letter and the repeat count make a field specifier. Field specifiers may be separated by whitespace, which will be ignored. With all types except **a** and **A** the **unpack** function will gobble up that many values from the LIST. Saying * for the repeat count means to use however many items are left. Saying @* means move to the end of the string. The **a** and **A** types gobble just one value, but unpack it as a string of length *count*, stripping nulls or spaces if **A** is specified. Real numbers (floats and doubles) are in the native machine format only; due to the multiplicity of floating formats around, and the lack of a standard "network" representation, no facility for interchange has been made. This means that packed floating-point data written on one machine may not be readable on another—even if both use IEEE floating-point arithmetic (as the endian-ness of the memory representation is not part of the IEEE spec). Note that Perl uses doubles internally for all numeric calculation, and converting from double to float to double will lose precision; that is, **unpack("f",pack("f",$foo))** will not in general equal **$foo**. Here's a subroutine that does (some of) **substr**:

```
sub substr {
        local($what, $where, $howmuch) = @_;
        if ($where < 0) {
                $where = -$where;
                unpack("@* X$where a$howmuch", $what);
        }
        else {
                unpack("x$where a$howmuch", $what);
        }
}
```

and then there's:

```
sub signed_ord { unpack("c", $_[0]); }
```

Here's a complete *uudecode* program:

```
#!/usr/bin/perl
$_ = <> until ($mode,$file) = /^begin\s*(\d*)\s*(\S*)/;
open(OUT,"> $file") if $file ne "";
while (<>) {
        last if /^end/;
        next if /[a-z]/;
        next unless int(((((ord() - 32) & 077) + 2) / 3) ==
                int(length() / 4);
        print OUT unpack("u", $_);
}
chmod oct($mode), $file;
```

In addition, you may prefix a field with a % <*number*> to indicate that you want a <*number*>-bit checksum of the items instead of the items themselves. Default is a 16-bit checksum. For example, the following computes the same number as the System V **sum** program:

```
undef $/;
$checksum = unpack("%32C*", <>) % 32767;
```

unshift

```
unshift(ARRAY,LIST)
```

This function does the opposite of a **shift**. (Or the opposite of a **push**, depending on how you look at it.) It prepends list to the front of the array, and returns the number of elements in the new array:

```
unshift(ARGV, '-e', $cmd) unless $ARGV[0] =~ /^-/;
```

utime

```
utime(LIST)
utime LIST
```

This function changes the access and modification times on each file of a list of files. The first two elements of the list must be the *numerical* access and modification times, in that order. The function returns the number of files successfully changed. The inode modification time of each file is set to the current time. Here's an example of a *touch* command:

```
#!/usr/bin/perl
$now = time;
utime $now, $now, @ARGV;
```

and here's a more sophisticated *touch* command with a bit of error checking:

```
#!/usr/bin/perl
$now = time;
@cannot = grep(!utime($now, $now, $_), @ARGV);
die "$0: Could not touch @cannot.\n" if @cannot;
```

The standard *touch* actually will create missing files, something like this:

```
$now = time;
foreach $file (@ARGV) {
        utime($now, $now, $file)
                || open(TMP, ">>$file")
                || warn "Couldn't touch $file: $!\n";
}
```

values

```
values(ASSOC_ARRAY)
values ASSOC_ARRAY
```

This function returns a normal array consisting of all the values of the named associative array. The values are returned in an apparently random order, but it is the same order as either the **keys()** or **each()** function would produce on the same array. See also **keys()** and **each()**. Note that using **values** on an an associative array bound to a humongous DBM file will produce a humongous list, causing you to have a humongous process. You might prefer to use the **each()** function in this case, which will iterate over the array entries one-by-one without slurping them all into a single gargantuan list.

vec

```
vec(EXPR,OFFSET,BITS)
```

This function treats a string (the value of EXPR) as a vector of unsigned integers, and returns the value of the element specified. The function may also be assigned to, which causes the element to be modified.

The OFFSET specifies how many elements to skip over to find the one we want. BITS is the number of bits per element in the vector, so each element can contain an unsigned integer in the range 0 .. 2**BITS-1. BITS must one of **1, 2, 4, 8, 16,** or **32**. As many elements as possible are packed into each byte, and the ordering is such that **vec($vectorstring,0,1)** is guaranteed to go into the lowest bit of the first byte of the string. To find out the position of the byte in which an element is going to be put, you have to multiply the maximum OFFSET by the number of elements per byte. When BITS is 1, there are 8 elements per byte. When BITS is 2, there are 4 elements per byte. When BITS is 4, there are 2 nybbles per byte. And so on.

Regardless of whether your machine is big-endian or little-endian, **vec($foo, 0, 8)** always refers to the first byte of string **$foo**. See **select( )** for examples of bitmaps generated with **vec( )**.

Vectors created with **vec( )** can also be manipulated with the logical operators |, &, ^, and ‾ which will assume a bit vector operation is desired when the operands are strings. This interpretation is not enabled unless there is at least one **vec( )** in your program (to protect older programs).

A bit vector (BITS **== 1**) can be translated to or from a string of 1's and 0's by supplying a **b*** template to **unpack()** or **pack()**. Similarly, a vector of nybbles (BITS **== 4**) can be translated with an **h*** template.

wait

```
wait
```

This function waits for a child process to terminate and returns the pid of the deceased process, or −1 if there are no child processes. The status is returned in **$?**. If you expected a child and didn't find it, you probably had a call to **system**, a close on a pipe, or backticks between the **fork** and the **wait**. These constructs also do a wait and may have harvested your child process. Use **waitpid** to avoid this problem.

waitpid

```
waitpid(PID, FLAGS)
```

This function waits for a particular child process to terminate and returns true when the process is dead, or -1 if there are no child processes, or if the FLAGS specify non-blocking and the process isn't dead yet. The status of the dead process is returned in **$?**. To get valid flag values say this:

```
require "sys/wait.ph";
```

On systems that implement neither the *waitpid*(2) nor *wait4*(2) system call, FLAGS may be specified only as 0. In other words, you can wait for a specific PID, but you can't do it in non-blocking mode.

wantarray

```
wantarray
```

This function returns true if the context of the currently executing subroutine is looking for an array value. The function returns false if the context is looking for a scalar. Here's a typical usage:

```
return wantarray ? () : undef;
```
See also **caller**.

warn

```
warn(LIST)
warn LIST
```

This function produces a message on **STDERR** just like **die**, but doesn't exit. For example:

```
warn "Debug enabled" if $debug;
```

The **warn** operator is unrelated to the **–w** switch.

write

```
write(FILEHANDLE)
write(EXPR)
write
```

This function writes a formatted record (possibly multi-line) to the specified file, using the format associated with that file—see the section "Formats" in Chapter 3. By default, the format for a file is the one having the same name as the filehandle, but the format for the current output filehandle (see **select**) may be set explicitly by assigning the name of the format to the $˜ variable.

Top-of-form processing is handled automatically: if there is insufficient room on the current page for the formatted record, the page is advanced by writing a form feed, a special top-of-page format is used to format the new page header, and then the record is written. The number of lines remaining on the current page is in variable $–, which can be set to 0 to force a new page on the next **write.** By default the top-of-page format is the name of the filehandle with **_TOP** appended, but it may be set to the format of your choice by assigning the name to the $ˆ variable. Each filehandle maintains its own format and top-of-form format.

If FILEHANDLE is unspecified, output goes to the current default output filehandle, which starts out as **STDOUT** but may be changed by the **select** operator. If the FILEHANDLE is an EXPR, then the expression is evaluated and the resulting string is used to look up the name of the actual FILEHANDLE at runtime.

Note that **write** is *not* the opposite of **read.** Use **print** for simple string output. If you looked up this entry because you wanted to bypass standard I/O, see **syswrite( ).**

5

Common Tasks
With Perl

This chapter describes "procedures" in the form of a cookbook. In a normal cookbook, you figure out what kind of hungry you are, and you flip through the pages of the cookbook until a recipe with an appealing title strikes your fancy. The recipe contains a list of ingredients and a procedure for preparing those ingredients to produce the item named by the title. This cookbook works in a similar way, although you are less likely to gain weight.

The point of this chapter is to get you to be able to perform common (or uncommon) tasks with Perl right away, so that you can be productive and quickly begin to "think Perl" for your data transformation and system administration needs (and whatever else you find Perl useful for, such as managing a recipe file).

Each procedure consists of a title, in which we've tried to avoid using Perl-specific words (because if you knew the Perl words, you'd probably be turning directly to that section somewhere else in this book). Following the title is a description of what the procedure intends to do.

After the description comes the procedure. In general, this will simply be a section of text as an example:

```
like this
```

that you should more or less type in to your program scriptfile as is. (It may also be a Perl command-line invocation for some of the procedures.) If the example contains words in *italic*, then those words are "parameters." You don't type these words in (even if you have a fancy terminal that can do italics), but instead look at the section immediately following where each parameter is described. You must replace the italicized words with the real variable names and text strings and whatever else the recipe calls for. For example, if the procedure says:

```
unlink FILENAME unless –d FILENAME;
```

then you don't actually enter *FILENAME* into your program. Instead, you look down to the description of the *FILENAME* parameter, and replace it with something suitable. For example, in this case, *FILENAME* might have a description of "the name of the file to be destroyed, as either a string literal or an expression that evaluates to a string". If you decide that "**/etc/passwd**" fits this description for your particular needs, you'd enter:

```
unlink "/etc/passwd" unless –d "/etc/passwd";
```

into your program.

After the parameters comes the comments section. This is the place that we warn you about the procedure not working on Tuesdays for data containing the word **swine** or whatever. There might also be hints in here about ways to combine this procedure with whatever else you might already know about Perl (hopefully from having read the rest of this book).

Following the comments are a few examples to show how this procedure is used. Then, a list of titles of other similar procedures is given, in case you don't like the flavor of this particular recipe, or find that you are a few cups short of associative arrays today.

If a particular procedure begins with a call to the **local( )** function, then it is presumed that the commands are to be executed as a block (or as part of a block) within either curly braces or an **eval( )** function, so that any temporary variables created by the **local( )** function will be restored to their original state upon exiting the block.

CLOSING A PROCESS FILEHANDLE WITHOUT WAITING FOR PROCESS COMPLETION

Normally, invoking **close** on a filehandle attached to a process waits for the process to complete before finishing. With a little care, however, you can abort the process early so that the **close** will return nearly immediately.

Procedure

```
$PID = open(HANDLE, PROCESS);
   . . .
kill -9, $PID;
close(HANDLE);
```

Parameters

PROCESS A string describing the process to start. This string begins or ends with |, since the process is at one end or another of a pipe.

HANDLE The filehandle associated with the process described by *PROCESS*.

$PID A scalar variable that will hold the process ID of the process started with the **open** function.

Comments

The use of **kill −9** is specific to code running in the UNIX environment.

Examples

```
$pid = open(LAST, "last|");
while (<LAST>) {
    if (/merlyn/) {
        print;
        kill -9, $pid;
        close(LAST);
    }
}
```

This example executes the UNIX **last** command until **merlyn** is found on an output line. The line containing **merlyn** is printed, and the filehandle is then closed after aborting the process.

COMPUTING THE DIFFERENCE OF TWO ARRAYS

This procedure computes an array whose elements consist solely of elements that are present in one existing array but not another one.

Procedure
```
local(%MARK);
grep($MARK{$_}++,@ARRAY1);
@RESULT = grep(!$MARK{$_},@ARRAY2);
```

Parameters

@ARRAY1   The first array to be examined.

@ARRAY2   The second array to be examined.

%MARK   A temporary associative array name. This array will be trashed by this procedure.

@RESULT   The array to be set to the set difference between @ARRAY2 and @ARRAY1. It may be the same name as either of these arrays, in which case it will be overwritten.

Comments

%MARK is an associative array that will contain the number of times each element of @ARRAY1 occurred, although all that matters is the zero versus non-zero value. The first **grep** could be replaced by a **foreach** loop instead, if you object to using **grep** purely for its side effects.

Examples
```
@rollerskaters=('adam','dale','jodee','marji','merlyn');
@pilots=('geoff','jim','merlyn','rick');
local(%mark);
grep($mark{$_}++,@rollerskaters);
@nonskatingpilots=grep(!$mark{$_},@pilots);
print "@nonskatingpilots\n";
```

This example prints the list of names that are pilots (named in **@pilots**), but not rollerskaters (named in **@rollerskaters**).

See Also

Computing the Intersection of Two Arrays
Modifying All Elements of an Array

COMPUTING THE INTERSECTION OF TWO ARRAYS

This procedure computes an array whose elements consist solely of elements that are present in both of two existing arrays.

Procedure
```
local(%MARK);
grep($MARK{$_}++,@ARRAY1);
@RESULT = grep($MARK{$_},@ARRAY2);
```

Parameters

@ARRAY1 The first array to be examined.

@ARRAY2 The second array to be examined.

%MARK A temporary associative array name. This array will be trashed by this procedure.

@RESULT The array to be set to the intersection of *@ARRAY1* and *@ARRAY2*. It may be the same name as either of these arrays.

Comments

%MARK will have the number of times each element appears in *@ARRAY1* after the first **grep**, although all that matters is the zero versus non-zero value. The first **grep** could be replaced by a **foreach** loop instead, if you object to using **grep** purely for its side effects.

Examples
```
@rollerskaters=('adam','dale','jodee','marji','merlyn');
@pilots=('geoff','jim','merlyn','rick');
local(%mark);
grep($mark{$_}++,@rollerskaters);
@crazy=grep($mark{$_},@pilots);
print "@crazy\n";
```

This example prints the list of names that are both rollerskaters (named in **@rollerskaters**) and pilots (named in **@pilots**).

See Also

Computing the Difference of Two Arrays
Modifying All Elements of an Array

CREATING VARIABLES WITH (MOSTLY) CONSECUTIVE CONSTANT VALUES

This procedure defines a subroutine that can be used to assign consecutive increasing values (such as consecutive integers) to many variable names. These names can then be used as symbolic constants. The argument to the subroutine is split on commas and pieces are placed in the @specs array. For each piece, it is evaluated as a complete assignment if it looks like one, or else as the target of an assignment, using the incremented value from the previous assignment.

Procedure

```
sub enum {
    local($_) = @_;
    local(@specs) = split(/,/);
    local($val);
    for (@specs) {
        if (/=/) {
            $val = eval $_;
        } else {
            eval $_ . ´ = ++$val´;
        }
    }
}

&enum(<<´EOL´);
ENUMLIST
EOL
```

Parameters

ENUMLIST   A comma-separated list of scalar variables. These variables will be assigned consecutive values, starting with 1. The list can span multiple lines, but cannot contain commas except as they are used here.

A variable may optionally be followed by = expression, where expression evaluates to a value that can be autoincremented (such as an integer or a string like "aa"). The expression cannot contain a comma. This resets the value of the variable to the specified expression, and further variables in the same list will be assigned values consecutively higher from this new starting point.

Examples

```
sub enum {
    # as above
}

&enum(<<´EOL´);
    $RED, $GREEN, $BLUE,
    $CYAN=´a´, $MAGENTA, $YELLOW,
    $BLACK=—1
EOL
print "$RED $GREEN $BLUE $CYAN $MAGENTA $YELLOW $BLACK\n";
```

This example defines seven scalar variables, and prints out:

```
1 2 3 a b c —1
```

DE-HYPHENATING A FILE

This procedure joins successive input lines if the first line ends in a hyphen (removing the hyphen and the associated newline in the process). The resulting text is sent to standard output.

Procedure

```
perl —pe ´s/—\s*\n$//´ FILES
```

Parameters

FILES   One or more files. Wildcards will be interpreted by the shell. If *FILES* is empty, standard input will be used instead.

Comments

Search for /**n$**/ instead of /—\s*\n$/ in order to process backslashed line continuations.

See the section "Invocation Options" in Chapter 7 for a description of the **—p** and **—e** switches.

Examples

```
perl —pe ´s/—\n$//´ my_text >my_text.new
```

This example de-hyphenates the contents of **my_text** and places them in **my_text.new**.

See Also

Printing a File with Multiple Blank Lines Squeezed Into One

EXECUTING A BLOCK OF STATEMENTS FOR EACH USERNAME

This procedure executes a block of statements for each username in the password file (or whatever system database contains your list of user IDs). The **setpwent** and **endpwent** functions are documented under **getpwent** in Chapter 4. These routines allow you to iterate through the database of users.

Procedure

```
setpwent;
while (@user=getpwent) {
    ($name,$passwd,$uid,$gid,$quota,$comment,
        $gcos,$dir,$shell) = @user;
    BODY
}
endpwent;
```

Parameters

BODY   One or more Perl statements that will be executed repeatedly, once for each user. In these statements, **$name** is the username of the user, **$passwd** is the encrypted password field, and so on.

Comments

The users are not generated in any particular order. If you need a specific order, create an associative array with keys and values constructed from the various scalar variables assigned to in the loop.

Examples

```
setpwent;
while (@user=getpwent) {
    ($name,$passwd,$uid,$gid,$quota,$comment,
        $gcos,$dir,$shell) = @user;
    if (-e "$dir/.rnlast") {
        print "$name has used RN";
        print " recently" if -M _ < 7;
        print "\n";
    }
}
endpwent;
```

This example finds all the users on the system that have a file named **.rnlast** in their home directory. If the file exists, a message is printed that they have used *rn*. If the file has been modified in the last seven days, the word **recently** is appended to the message. (The underline in the **–M _** test refers back to the file tested by the previous **–e** test.)

EXTRACTING SELECTED COLUMNS

This procedure extracts a set of adjacent columns from one or more files (or standard input).

Procedure

```
perl —ne 'chop; print substr($_,COLUMN,WIDTH), "\n";' FILES
```

Parameters

COLUMN   The number of the leftmost column to be extracted. Columns are numbered from the left, with the leftmost column being column number zero. (Actually, we're counting how many characters to skip over.)

WIDTH   The number of adjacent columns beginning at column number *COLUMN* that will be extracted.

FILES   One or more filenames. The filenames may contain wildcard characters to be interpreted by the shell. If no files are given, standard input is examined instead.

Comments

If you need to extract several non-adjacent columns, you can substitute an **unpack** operator for the **substr** with a template describing the fields. The **—n** switch adds an implied loop—see the section "Invocation Options" in Chapter 7.

Examples

```
perl —ne 'chop; print substr($_,0,79), "\n";' .plan
```

This example prints the first 79 characters of each line of the file named **.plan** in the current directory.

```
perl —ne 'chop; print substr($_,10,5), "\n";' wide*.txt
```

This example prints the 11th through 15th characters of each line of all the files whose names begin with **wide** and end with **.txt** in the current directory.

See Also

Substituting Characters in Many Files

FINDING THE FIRST ARRAY ELEMENT FOR WHICH A CONDITION IS TRUE

This procedure scans through an array, searching for the first element that satisfies a condition, noting the array index of that element.

Procedure

```
undef $WHERE;
for ($[ .. $#ARRAY) {
    $WHERE = $_, last if CONDITION;
}
```

Parameters

@ARRAY   The name of the array. (This procedure uses the number of the last element of the array.)

CONDITION   An expression involving $ARRAY[$_] that returns true (such as a non-zero value) if that element satisfies the condition.

$WHERE   A scalar variable that will hold the index of the element that satisfies the condition. If no element satisfies the condition, the value will remain undefined (that is, **defined**($WHERE) will be false).

Comments

The .. range operator produces a list of all the subscripts of the array—see the section "Range Operator" in Chapter 3. These are temporarily assigned one-by-one to the $_ variable by the **for** loop. The $[variable is the minimum subscript for all arrays, and the $#ARRAY is the maximum subscript for that particular array. The **last** operator bombs out of the loop when the desired array element is found.

Examples

```
@a = (1..10);
undef $where;
for ($[ .. $#a) {
    $where = $_, last if ($a[$_]**2) > 32;
}
print "$where\n" if defined($where);
```

This procedure prints the index of the first element of array @a whose square is greater than 32.

See Also

Computing the Difference of Two Arrays
Computing the Intersection of Two Arrays

FINDING THE FIRST SET BIT IN A VECTOR

This procedure finds the first bit set in a vector, relying on the fact that vectors are stored as strings, eight bits to the byte. It first scans the string for a non-null byte, and then looks at each bit within that byte to find the set bit.

Procedure

```
undef $FOUND;
if ($VECTOR =~ /[^\000]/) {
    for (length($`)*8..length($`)*8+7) {
        $FOUND = $_, last if vec($VECTOR,$_,1);
    }
}
```

Parameters

$VECTOR   The scalar variable holding the vector string.

$FOUND   A scalar variable that will hold the index of the first non-zero bit in vector *$VECTOR*. If *$VECTOR* has no non-zero bits, *$FOUND* will be undefined.

Examples

```
$vector = "\000" x 256;
vec($vector,1,rand(256*8)) = 1;
undef $found;
if ($vector =~ /[^\000]/) {
    for (length($`)*8..length($`)*8+7) {
        $found = $_, last if vec($vector,$_,1);
    }
}
print "found the random bit at $found\n";
```

This example finds a random bit set within the vector.

See Also

Finding the First Array Element for Which a Condition is True

FORKING A DAEMON PROCESS

This procedure forks a process that does not become a "zombie" process. (A "zombie" process is one that still has the launcher as its parent, and requires the parent to wait for it when it exits.) This is useful when launching one or more daemon processes that are expected to take an indeterminate amount of time.

Procedure

```
unless (fork) { # this is the child
    unless (fork) { # this is the child's child
        sleep 1 until getppid == 1;
        LONGOPERATION;
        exit 0;
    }
    # first child exits quickly
    exit 0;
}
wait; # parent reaps first child quickly
```

Parameters

LONGOPERATION   One or more statements that will take an indeterminate amount of time. When the process executing *LONGO-PERATION* exits, the **init** process (PID 1) reaps it.

Comments

For a program that wants to do nothing but start a daemon, this may be sufficient:

```
fork && exit;
setpgrp(0,$$);
```

Examples

```
unless (fork) { # this is the child
    unless (fork) { # this is the child's child
        sleep 1 until getppid == 1;
        for (1..1000) {
            system "foo $_";
        }
        exit 0;
    }
    # first child exits quickly
    exit 0;
}
wait; # parent reaps first child quickly
```

This example invokes 1000 commands that look like **foo 1** to **foo 1000** from a daemon process.

INTERPRETING VARIABLE REFERENCES IN A STRING

This procedure takes an expression that evaluates to a string containing variable references, such as an expression that evaluates to:

```
hello $foo world $bar[3]!
```

and replaces each variable reference with the current contents of the variable, as if the expression were written within double quotes in the program text. (In this case, **$foo** and **$bar[3]** would be replaced with their current values.)

Procedure

```
$_ = EXPRESSION;
s/"/\\"/g;
$RESULT = eval qq/"$_"/;
```

Parameters

EXPRESSION   An expression that evaluates to the string you wish to interpret. A scalar variable is one example of this kind of string.

$RESULT   A scalar variable that will hold the result of this transformation.

Comments

Note that any double quotes in the string would confuse the **eval**, so we protect them by inserting a backslash in front. Since we're doing double the double quoting, so to speak, the outer quote uses the generalized double quote syntax, **qq//**.

You should probably not pass arbitrary user-input through such a routine, especially if you are running a setuid program, because some of the possible string substitutions that will be evaluated are of the form:

```
$ARGV[`some arbitrary shell command`]
```

or:

```
$ARGV[do {some; arbitrary; Perl; code;}]
```

which can be an easy access to execute anything the user desires.

Examples

```
while (<STDIN>) {
    # $_=... not needed because the data is already in $_
    s/"/\\"/g;
    print eval qq/"$_"/;
}
```

This example reads individual lines from standard input, and spits them out after they have been double-quote expanded.

MAKING A PASCAL-LIKE CASE STATEMENT

This procedure approximates a Pascal **case** statement using an associative array. This procedure takes advantage of the **eval** function, which can execute arbitrary code in Perl variables.

Procedure

```
sub case {
    local(*assoc,$_) = @_;
    for (split(/\n/)) {
        /^(\S+)\s+(.*)/;
        for (eval $1) {
            $assoc{$_} = $2;
        }
    }
}

&case(*VARIABLE,<<´ENDCASE´);
RANGE ACTION
RANGE ACTION
. . .
RANGE ACTION
ENDCASE

. . .

eval $VARIABLE{SELECTOR};
```

Parameters

VARIABLE The name of an associative array that will hold the code for this particular case structure. You may have an unlimited number of case structures in each program.

RANGE A single value, or a range of values, or two or more of these separated by commas. The corresponding ACTION will be executed when SELECTOR matches any one of the values within the set described by RANGE. RANGE cannot contain any whitespace. (To include whitespace, you may use \040 for the space character within a double-quoted string, for example.) Subsequent RANGE definitions override previous ones, so the most general case should be described first.

ACTION A string that will be **eval**'ed when SELECTOR matches any of the elements of RANGE (unless a later RANGE overrode an element of the current set).

SELECTOR   A scalar expression. The matching *ACTION* from the associative
array *VARIABLE* will be selected and executed.

Comments

Because the actions are replicated for each associative array element, an action
should be limited to a simple function call containing the real code for that case
element. Avoid calling **&case** unnecessarily, since it takes time to build up the
associative array.

Examples

```
sub case {
    # as above
}
&case(*foo,<<´ENDCASE´);
0..255                      print "something else\n";
ord(´a´)..ord(´z´)  print "a lowercase letter\n";
ord(´A´)..ord(´Z´)  print "an uppercase letter\n";
ord(´0´)..ord(´9´)  print "a digit\n";
ENDCASE

for (split(//,"Just another 4 perl hackers,")) {
    print "$_ is ";
    eval $foo{ord($_)};
}
```

This example shows a case structure that distinguishes three categories of characters.

MAKING YOUR PROGRAM RUN WITH SH AND CSH

This procedure enables a Perl program to run on systems that treat an initial **#** in a script as a request to run the script through *csh*.

Procedure

Put:

```
#!PERL

# Catch for sh/csh on systems without #! ability
eval '(exit $?0)' && eval 'exec PERL -S $0 ${1+"$@"}'
& eval 'exec PERL -S $0 $argv:q'
if 0;
```

at the beginning of your program.

Parameters

PERL   The full pathname of your Perl interpreter, such as */usr/bin/perl*.

Comments

This complicated-looking text will cause the proper execution of your script regardless of whether Perl, *sh*, or *csh* first gets hold of the script. It probably won't work on a non-UNIX system.

MODIFYING ALL ELEMENTS OF AN ARRAY

This procedure executes identical code on each element of an array.

Procedure

```
grep(OPERATION, @ARRAY);
```

Parameters

OPERATION An expression that examines and possibly modifies the $_ scalar variable. On each evaluation of this expression, $_ is set to the next consecutive element of *@ARRAY*. If the operation cannot easily be expressed in one expression, you can use:

```
do {
    statement_1;
    statement_2;
    ...
    statement_n;
}
```

as your expression.

@ARRAY The name of the array that you want to operate on.

Comments

As a side effect (some would say the main effect), **grep** builds an array consisting of those elements (as modified) of *@ARRAY* for which *OPERATION* returns a true value. Knowing this, you may save a small bit of time and space by ensuring that *OPERATION* always returns false.

Examples

```
grep($_ *= 2, @stats);
```

This expression doubles the values within the **@stats** array.

```
grep(($_ *= 2) && 0, @stats);
```

This expression doubles the values within the **@stats** array, ensuring that the temporary array being built by **grep** for a return value (which is later discarded) contains no elements, following the recommendation made above.

See Also

Computing the Difference of Two Arrays
Computing the Intersection of Two Arrays

PERFORMING AN OPERATION ON A SERIES OF INTEGERS

This procedure executes one or more statements for each value of a series of integers.

Procedure
```
foreach $INDEX (LOW..HIGH) {
    BODY
}
```

Parameters

$INDEX   A scalar variable. This variable will take on each successive value from *LOW* to *HIGH*. If you omit *$INDEX*, the variable **$_** is used instead.

LOW   The lower bounds of the range of integers. You may have either a literal integer, or some expression enclosed in parentheses that evaluates to an integer.

HIGH   The upper bounds of the range of integers. You may have either a literal integer, or some expression enclosed in parentheses that evaluates to an integer.

BODY   One or more Perl statements. These statements will be executed repeatedly for each different integer in the range from *LOW* to *HIGH*, with *$INDEX* set to the differing integer values.

Comments
Assigning a value to *$INDEX* will not change the number of passes—the next pass resumes with the next integer in sequence. If *HIGH* is less than *LOW*, the statements in *BODY* will be skipped. (You may use **for** in place of **foreach**, with identical results.)

Examples
```
foreach $i (1..10) {
    print "$i\n";
}
```

This example prints the integers from 1 through 10 onto **STDOUT**.

PREPENDING A LABEL TO SUCCESSIVE LINES

This procedure processes input lines, taking a label line like:

```
foo/bar:
```

and prepending the contents of that line (sans colon) to all successive lines, until the next label line comes along. (This kind of listing would be produced by a command such as *ls −1R*.)

Procedure

```
$LABEL = INITIAL;
while (<INPUT>) {
    if (/:$/) {
        $LABEL = $`;
    } else {
        print OUTPUT $LABEL, SEP, $_;
    }
}
```

Parameters

$LABEL   A scalar variable that holds the current value of the label. This variable will be trashed.

INITIAL   A string expression that gives the initial value of $LABEL.

INPUT   A filehandle from which the input lines will be read.

OUTPUT   A filehandle to which the altered lines will be written.

SEP   A separator string that separates the label from the data line.

Comments

The $` variable returns everything before the colon on the label line. See the section "Special Variables" in Chapter 3. Note that the default label is "." presuming the listing might have leading elements from the current directory before the first label.

Examples

```
$label = '.';
while (<STDIN>) {
    if (/:$/) {
        $label = $`;
    } else {
        print $label, '/', $_;
    }
}
```

This example copies standard input to standard output, as modified by the labels.
For example, the input:

```
aaa
bbb
ccc
one/hump:
ddd
eee
fff
two/hump:
ggg
hhh
iii
```

will be transformed into:

```
./aaa
./bbb
./ccc
one/hump/ddd
one/hump/eee
one/hump/fff
two/hump/ggg
two/hump/hhh
two/hump/iii
```

PRINTING LINES AFTER A DESIGNATED MATCHING LINE

This procedure prints a specified number of lines from a file that are after any line matching a specified regular expression. It counts down using the autodecrement operator.

Procedure

```
perl -ne 'print if (/REGEX/ ? ($c = LINES) : (-$c > 0))' FILES
```

Parameters

REGEX   A regular expression that is being looked for. It must match within a line, so requiring a match across line boundaries (such as with **\n**) will probably not do what you expect.

LINES   The number of lines to print for each match, beginning with and including the line that matched. If another line that matches is seen, the count restarts.

FILES   One or more filenames. Wildcard characters will be interpreted by the shell. *FILES* may be omitted, indicating that standard input is to be used instead.

Comments

Note that the outer parentheses are only necessary for clarity. Otherwise it looks as if the **if** modifier is testing the pattern directly, which it isn't. It's really testing the **$c** variable.

Examples

```
perl -ne 'print if (/caravan/ ? ($c = 5) : (-$c > 0))' book.*
```

This example prints all text lines within five lines after any line containing the word **caravan** in any file in the current directory with a name beginning with **book.**

PRINTING LINES IN REVERSE ORDER

This procedure takes one or more concatenated files (or standard input) and prints all of the lines in reverse order from end to beginning.

Procedure

```
perl -e 'print reverse <>' FILES
```

Parameters

FILES One or more filenames. If omitted, use standard input. These filenames may contain wildcard characters, which are interpreted by the shell.

Comments

The text must fit completely into memory.

Examples

```
perl -e 'print reverse <>' /etc/motd
```

This example prints the */etc/motd* file in reverse order. Not very useful, except as an example.

See Also

Reversing a Line by Characters
Reversing a Line by Words

PRINTING ONLY THE FIRST OCCURRENCE OF EACH LINE

This procedure reads standard input or a list of files and prints each line unless that line has been printed already.

Procedure

```
perl -ne 'print unless $seen{$_}++' FILES
```

Parameters

FILES   One or more filenames, separated by whitespace. If no filenames are given, the standard input is read.

Comments

Note that using this technique on a large file can use up huge amounts of memory. In such a case it might be better to use the UNIX **sort -u** command.

Using a construct like:

```
... unless $seen{SOMETHING}++;
```

is useful whenever you want to process an item only once. The first time SOME-THING is examined, the associative array value evaluates to undefined (which **unless** interprets as false), but the array value is set to 1 because of the post-increment. Thereafter, every lookup of that same SOMETHING returns a non-zero (hence true) value. When you're done, the values of the associative array record how many times you've seen each SOMETHING.

Examples

```
perl -ne 'print unless $seen{$_}++' *.list
```

This example prints only the unique lines from all the files whose names end with **.list** in the current directory.

See Also

Printing Lines After a Designated Matching Line

PRINTING A FILE WITH MULTIPLE BLANK LINES SQUEEZED INTO ONE

This procedure prints one or more files (or standard input if no files are specified), compressing multiple consecutive blank lines into one line. A non-blank line is defined as one containing at least one non-whitespace character (\S). The $s variable is used to remember if the previous line was blank.

Procedure
```
perl -ne 'print if /\S/ || !$s; $s = /^\s*$/;' FILES
```

Parameters
FILES   One or more filenames. Wildcards will be interpreted by the shell. If *FILES* is empty, standard input is processed instead.

Examples
```
man perl | perl -ne 'print if /\S/ || !$s; $s = /^\s*$/;'
```

This example takes the output of **man perl** and prints it out with extra blank lines eliminated.

See Also
Removing Pairs of Characters

PRINTING AN ENTIRE ARRAY

This procedure prints an entire array. Elements of the array are separated by an arbitrary string.

Procedure

```
print join($SEP, @ARRAY), $TERM;
```

or:

```
{
    local($,,$/) = ($SEP,$TERM);
    print @ARRAY;
}
```

Parameters

@ARRAY   The name of the array.

$SEP   The separator string. This string will be printed between each array element. To print one element per line, use "**\n**" as the string.

$TERM   The terminator string. This string will be printed at the end of the array. To print one element per line, use "**\n**" as the string.

Comments

The purpose of the **local( )** in the second method is to provide a temporary value for the **$,** and **$/** variables (which control the field and record delimiters). The previous values of those variables are restored automatically after the **{...}** block is complete. The second method is more efficient for a very long array, and is more space-conservative. The first method is generally easier to use and understand, but requires an additional copy of the data to be made.

If you just want the array elements to be space-separated, it's easiest to say something like this:

```
print "@ARRAY\n";
```

Examples

```
print join("\n",@ARGV),"\n";
```

This example prints the command line arguments of the current program.

See Also

Modifying All Elements of an Array
Processing Each Element of an Array

PRINTING THE CONTENTS OF A FILE TO STDOUT

This procedure takes a filename and prints the contents of that file to **STDOUT**.

Procedure
```
open(F,$FILENAME) || die "Cannot open $FILENAME: $!";
while (<F>) {
    print;
}
close(F);
```

Parameters

$FILENAME   A scalar variable containing the name of the file to be copied. You may replace it with a string literal (a name enclosed in single or double quotes) if you wish.

Comments

If the filehandle **F** is already in use in your program, use another filehandle name instead. This procedure destroys the current value of $_.

Examples
```
$file = "/etc/passwd";
open(F,$file) || die "Cannot open $file: $!";
while (<F>) {
    print;
}
close(F);
```

This procedure prints the contents of the */etc/passwd* file onto **STDOUT**.

PROCESSING EACH ELEMENT OF AN ARRAY

This procedure takes each element of an array, and executes one or more commands on it.

Procedure

```
foreach (@ARRAY) {
    BODY
}
```

Parameters

@ARRAY   The name of an array.

BODY   One or more Perl statements, separated by semicolons. In these statements, the variable **$_** holds the value of the element being processed.

Comments

If *BODY* executes a **next** statement, the rest of the statements are skipped, and *BODY* is restarted with the next element from the array. If *BODY* executes a **last** statement, the loop is terminated immediately. Assigning a new value to **$_** in *BODY* will result in an immediate change to the corresponding array element.

Examples

```
foreach (@ARGV) {
    last if $_ eq "—";
    print "$_ is a switch\n" if /^-/;
}
```

See Also

Printing an Entire Array
Processing an Entire Associative Array

PROCESSING STRINGS WITH ESCAPED CHARACTERS

This procedure "hides" any character preceded by a backslash so that a global operation may be performed on a string, and then "unhides" those characters.

Procedure

```
# presume string is in $_
s/\\(.)/"LEFT".ord($1)."RIGHT"/eg;
OPERATION;
s/LEFT(\d+)RIGHT/pack(C,$1)/eg;
```

Parameters

LEFT
Any character unlikely to occur in the text. A good character would be something like \376.

RIGHT
Any character unlikely to occur in the text, and distinct from *LEFT*. A good character would be something like \377.

OPERATION
Some operation that modifies $_. You must be careful not to remove parts of the *LEFT<digits>RIGHT* structures within the string, but remove them in their entirety.

Comments

This example works by replacing the escaped sequence with some encoded characters that won't match what you'd otherwise be looking for. It relies on the **ord**( ) function to turn a character value into a number, and the **pack**( ) function to turn the number back into a character.

Examples

```
s/\\(.)/"\376".ord($1)."\377"/eg;
s/foo/bar/g;
s/\376(\d+)\377/pack(C,$1)/eg;
```

This example changes all **foo**'s into **bar**'s in the string, but will not alter **..\foo..** (because the **f** character is escaped).

See Also

Processing Each Element of an Array

PROCESSING AN ENTIRE ASSOCIATIVE ARRAY

This procedure takes each element of an associative array, and executes one or more commands on it.

Procedure
```
foreach (SORT keys ARRAY) {
    BODY
}
```

Parameters

ARRAY The name of the associative array.

BODY One or more Perl statements, separated by semicolons. In these statements, the variable $_ holds the key of the element being processed. The value of the element is accessed with *$ARRAY{$_}*.

SORT Either **sort**, indicating that the elements are to be processed in the order of ascending keys, or empty, if the elements are to be processed in an unspecified order. (If the order doesn't matter, it is faster to skip the sorting.)

Comments

If *BODY* executes a **next** statement, the rest of the statements are skipped, and *BODY* is restarted with the next key from the associative array. If *BODY* executes a **last** statement, the loop is terminated immediately.

Examples
```
foreach (keys %ENV) {
    print "$_=$ENV{$_}\n";
}
```

Prints your environment variables in an unspecified order.

```
foreach (sort keys %ENV) {
    print "$_=$ENV{$_}\n";
}
```

Prints your environment variables sorted by the name of the environment variable.

See Also

Printing an Entire Array
Processing Each Element of an Array

PUTTING COMMAS INTO INTEGERS

This procedure defines and uses a subroutine to insert commas every three digits. It uses a regular expression that matches any string ending in four digits, putting the final three digits into **$2**, and the preceding string into **$1**. The **1 while** idiom is used to evaluate the substitution repeatedly, as long as it continues to succeed. The **1** itself is just a no-op expression used as a placeholder. A **0** or a " " would have worked as well.

Procedure

```
sub commas {
    local($_) = @_;
    1 while s/(.*\d)(\d\d\d)/$1,$2/;
    $_;
}
    ...
$RESULT =  &commas(EXPR);
```

Parameters

EXPR   A scalar expression giving the value into which commas are to be inserted.

$RESULT   A scalar variable that will hold *EXPR* with commas inserted.

Comments

If *EXPR* is not an integer, **&commas** may produce incorrect output, since it's assuming that **\d\d\d** will always match the next three digits to have a comma inserted in front.

Examples

```
sub commas {
    local($_) = @_;
    1 while s/(.*\d)(\d\d\d)/$1,$2/;
    $_;
}
for ($i = 1; $i <= 1e15; $i *= 7) {
    $result = &commas($i);
    print "$result\n";
}
```

This example prints powers of seven that are less than **1e15**, with commas properly inserted. See the section "Compound Statements" in Chapter 3 for an explanation of the 3-part **for** loop. See the section "Subroutines" in Chapter 3 for an explanation of how arguments are passed.

REMOVING PAIRS OF CHARACTERS

This procedure removes successive occurrences of the same character in a string.

The **tr///** function normally transliterates each character in one string into the corresponding character in another string. With no replacement string (//), the original string will simply be reproduced on output. However, the **s** option tells **tr** to squeeze multiple consecutive occurrences of any character in one. The **\0–\377** sequence defines the range of all characters.

Procedure
```
$STRING =~ tr/\0-\377//s;
```

Parameters
$STRING   The name of the scalar variable holding the string.

Comments
Without the *$STRING* =~, the transliteration will be performed on the contents of the **$_** variable.

Examples
```
while (<STDIN>) {
    tr/\0-\377//s;
    print;
}
```

This example processes all lines on standard input, removing multiple occurrences of the same character.

See Also
Printing Only the First Occurrence of Each Line
Printing a File with Multiple Blank Lines Squeezed Into One

RENAMING A FILE

This procedure renames a file.

Procedure
```
rename($OLD,$NEW) ||
    die "Could not rename $OLD to $NEW: $!";
```

Parameters

$OLD   The file's current name. You can replace this with a string literal (a string enclosed in single or double quotes).

$NEW   The file's new name. You can replace this with a string literal (a string enclosed in single or double quotes).

Comments

If the rename is unsuccessful, the program will terminate because of the **die** statement. If you want to handle the error in some other way, change the code accordingly.

Examples
```
rename("smith","smith.bak") ||
    die "Could not rename smith to smith.bak: $!";
```

This example renames the file **smith** to **smith.bak**.

```
rename($old,"$old.bak")
    || die "Could not rename $old to $old.bak: $!";
```

This example renames the file named by the current value of **$old** to the same name with **.bak** attached.

See Also

Unlinking Many Files Whose Names are Specified by Another Process

REPLACING A TARGET STRING WITH THE NAME OF THE FILE FOR MANY FILES

This procedure searches many files and, within each file, replaces any occurrence of a target string with the name of the file currently being searched. It operates in-place, not as a filter.

Procedure

```
perl —pi —e ´s/TARGET/$ARGV/g´ FILES
```

Parameters

TARGET   A target string, as a regular expression. Regular-expression meta-characters must be preceded by a backslash if you do not want them to have their special meaning.

FILES   One or more filenames. Wildcard characters will be interpreted by the shell.

Comments

Use **—i.bak** to make a backup of the modified files.

Examples

```
perl —pi —e ´s/%F%/$ARGV/g´ *.c
```

This example replaces all occurrences of **%F%** in any C source file in the current directory with the corresponding filename.

See Also

Substituting Strings in Many Files

RETURNING AN ERROR FROM A SUBROUTINE WHEN A NULL LIST MAY BE VALID

This procedure provides a method by which a subroutine, in cooperation with its callers, can return a success/fail indication along with a list that may or may not be null. The basic trick is to return an extra value on the front of the list that provides the error indication. The caller then shifts the value off the front of the list when testing the return status. If the call was successful, the remaining elements of the list are what the subroutine wanted to return.

Procedure

```
sub SUBROUTINE {
    SUBBODY;
}

{
    local(@return) = &SUBROUTINE(PARAMETERS);
    if (shift @return) {
        SUCCESS
    } else {
        FAIL
    }
}
```

Parameters

SUBROUTINE   The name of the subroutine.

SUBBODY   The body of the subroutine. Within the body, executing:

```
return 1, @somearray;
```

indicates a successful return, while:

```
return 0;
```

indicates a failing return.

PARAMETERS The actual parameters to the invocation of *SUBROUTINE*.

SUCCESS   One or more statements to be executed when this invocation of *SUBROUTINE* indicates a success. The **@return** array contains the return value.

FAIL   One or more statements to be executed when this invocation of *SUBROUTINE* indicates a failure.

Comments

If **@return** conflicts with the name of another array you need to access within the block, choose a different name.

Examples

```
sub files {
    local(*DH);
    opendir(DH, $_[0]) || return 0;
    local(@f) = sort grep(!/^\.\.?$/, readdir(DH));
    closedir(DH);
    return 1, @f;
}

{
    local(@return) = &files($ENV{HOME} || $ENV{LOGDIR});
    if (shift @return) {
        print "home files are @return\n";
    } else {
        print "cannot read home directory: $!\n";
    }
}
```

This example defines a subroutine **files** that returns a list of files in the specified directory. The files of the home directory are then grabbed and printed if successful, otherwise the error message is printed out.

REVERSING A LINE BY CHARACTERS

This procedure reverses a text string character-by-character.

Procedure

```
$NEWSTRING = reverse($OLDSTRING);
```

Parameters

$NEWSTRING   The scalar variable that will contain the string after it has been reversed. It may be the same name as *$OLDSTRING*.

$OLDSTRING   The scalar variable containing the string that is to be reversed.

Examples

```
while (<STDIN>) {
    chop;
    $new = reverse($_);
    print $new, "\n";
}
```

This example reverses each line present on standard input, placing the result on standard output.

See Also

Reversing a Line by Words
Printing Lines in Reverse Order

REVERSING A LINE BY WORDS

This procedure reverses a text string word-by-word. It illustrates the principle that operations that are difficult to perform on a scalar value may be trivial once the value is transformed in some way.

Procedure

```
$NEWSTRING = join("", reverse split(/(\S+)/, $OLDSTRING));
```

Parameters

$NEWSTRING   The scalar variable that will contain the string after it has been reversed. It may be the same name as *$OLDSTRING*.

$OLDSTRING   The scalar variable containing the string that is to be reversed.

Comments

The procedure preserves the whitespace by splitting on non-whitespace (\S+) and returning the delimiters as part of the list (by putting the pattern in parentheses). Be careful not to use this on a line with a newline at the end, or you'll end up with a newline at the beginning. If you don't care to preserve whitespace exactly, you can do an ordinary split on whitespace and join with a space. See **split** in Chapter 4, *Functions*.

Examples

```
while (<STDIN>) {
    chop;
    $new = join("", reverse split(/(\S+)/, $_));
    print $new, "\n";
}
```

This example reverses the words on each line present on standard input, placing the result on standard output.

See Also

Reversing a Line by Characters
Printing Lines in Reverse Order

SELECTING A RANDOM ELEMENT FROM AN ARRAY WITHOUT REPLACEMENT

This procedure selects a random element from an array and deletes it (so that if the procedure is repeated, each element is selected only once).

Procedure

```
$ELEMENT = splice(@ARRAY, rand @ARRAY, 1);
```

Parameters

$ELEMENT   The name of the scalar variable to contain the element.

@ARRAY   The name of the array holding all the elements. This array will be shortened by one element each time.

Comments

Since @**cards** returns the length of the array in a scalar context, **rand** @**cards** returns a random number between **0** and the number of elements in the array.

Examples

```
@cards = ('C01'..'C13','D01'..'D13','H01'..'H13','S01'..'S13');
while (@cards) {
    $card = splice(@cards, rand @cards, 1);
    print "$card ";
    print "\n" if @cards % 13 == 0;
}
```

This example deals an entire set of standard playing cards, where each card is represented by a three character string consisting of the initial letter of the suit followed by two digits for the rank of the card. The cards are printed 13 to a line (to make them come out in four even lines).

See Also

Selecting a Random Line From a File
Shuffling an Array Randomly

SELECTING A RANDOM LINE FROM A FILE

This procedure selects a line at random from a file, using just one pass over the file and without knowing in advance the number of lines. It works by calculating the probability that the current line (indicated by the $. variable) would be selected if this line were the last line in file. The first line is selected with a probability of 100%, but the second line has a 50% chance of replacing the first one, the third line a 33% chance of replacing one of the first two, and so on.

Procedure

```
perl -e 'srand;' \
     -e 'rand($.) < 1 && ($it = $_) while <>;' \
     -e 'print $it' FILE
```

Parameters

FILE   The name of the file that you wish to extract a random line from.

Comments

The command line can be put on one line instead of broken up as shown here. (We broke it in pieces just so it would fit.)

Examples

```
perl -e 'srand;' \
     -e 'rand($.) < 1 && ($it = $_) while <>;' \
     -e 'print $it' 'ypcat passwd|'
```

This example selects and prints a random line from the output of the *ypcat* command. Note the trick of passing a pipe command instead of an ordinary filename.

See Also

Selecting a Random Element From an Array Without Replacement
Shuffling an Array Randomly

SHUFFLING AN ARRAY RANDOMLY

This procedure shuffles an array uniformly.

Procedure

```
local(@TEMPARRAY);
push(@TEMPARRAY, splice(@ARRAY, rand(@ARRAY), 1))
    while @ARRAY;
@ARRAY = @TEMPARRAY;
```

Parameters

@ARRAY   The name of the array to be shuffled.

@TEMPARRAY   The name of a temporary array.

Examples

```
@numbers = 1..30;
{
    local(@temp);
    push(@temp, splice(@numbers, rand(@numbers), 1))
        while @numbers;
    @numbers = @temp;
}
print "@numbers\n";
```

This example prints the numbers from 1 to 30 in a random order.

See Also

Selecting a Random Element From an Array Without Replacement
Selecting a Random Line From a File

SORTING AN ARRAY BY NUMERIC VALUE

This procedure sorts an array using numeric comparisons, rather than by string comparisons (the default). The **sort** operator takes an optional second argument naming a subroutine to do the comparison. Typical comparison routines use the **<=>** numeric comparison operator or the **cmp** string comparison operator.

Procedure

```
sub bynumber { $a <=> $b; }

@SORTED = sort bynumber @ORIGINAL;
```

Parameters

@ORIGINAL   The name of the array variable that holds the original values.

@SORTED   The name of the array variable in which you want the sorted values stored. This may be the same as @ORIGINAL.

Comments

To sort in descending order, reverse the **$a** and **$b**. If you already have a routine **bynumber**, you should change the name of the routine defined with **sub** so that it doesn't conflict.

Examples

```
sub bynumber { $a <=> $b; }

@raw = (1,16,2,32,4,64,8);
@sorted = sort bynumber @raw;
```

This example sorts the values of **@raw** by numeric order into an array variable called **@sorted**. The values in **raw** are already in the order that the default **sort** would return (by string comparison), but the numeric sort reorders them as the consecutive powers of two (1,2,4,8,16,32,64).

See Also

Sorting an Array by a Computable Field

SORTING AN ARRAY BY A COMPUTABLE FIELD

This procedure sorts an array in an order determined by a computable field of each element of that array (such as the third colon-separated field within each array element). The computable fields are generated once and cached, so that they are not repeatedly computed during the sort.

Procedure

```
local(@KEYS);
foreach (@DATA) {
    push(@KEYS, KEYEXPR);
}
sub SORTFUNC { BYKEYEXPR; }
@SORTDATA = @DATA[sort SORTFUNC $[..$#DATA];
```

Parameters

@DATA   The array to be sorted.

@KEYS   A temporary array holding the computed values for each of the elements of *@DATA*.

KEYEXPR   Some expression that computes a key value from the current value of **$_**. For example, a possible value of *KEYEXPR* is (**split**(/:/))[**2**], which evaluates to the third colon-separated field in **$_**.

SORTFUNC   A subroutine name that does not conflict with any other subroutine names in your program.

BYKEYEXPR An expression comparing *$KEYS*[**$a**] and *$KEYS*[**$b**], returning a positive integer if the first is greater than the second, and a negative integer if the second is greater than the first. (If you want a descending sort, swap **$a** and **$b**.) For example, an ascending numeric sort could be expressed as:

*$KEYS*[$a] <=> *$KEYS*[$b];

@SORTDATA The resulting array containing the sorted data. May be the same array as *@DATA*.

Examples

```
@data = split(/\n/, `cat /etc/passwd`);
local(@datakeys);
foreach (@data) {
    push(@datakeys, (split(/:/))[2]);
}
```

```
sub bydatakeys { $datakeys[$a] <=> $datakeys[$b]; }
@sortdata = @data[sort bydatakeys $[..$#data];
print join("\n",@sortdata);
```

This example prints the */etc/passwd* file sorted by UID.

See Also

Sorting an Array by Numeric Value

SUBSTITUTING CHARACTERS IN MANY FILES

This procedure replaces all occurrences of a set of characters with corresponding characters from a new set in all the files given on the command line. This takes advantage of Perl's **–i** switch, which will do in-place edits. (Contrast this solution with one involving *sed*, in which you'd have to write a big shell wrapper to rename all the files and do the I/O redirection. In addition, *sed* doesn't allow the specification of ranges such as **A–Z**.)

Procedure

```
perl -pi.bak -e 'tr/OLDCHARS/NEWCHARS/' FILELIST
```

Parameters

OLDCHARS   The set of characters to be replaced with *NEWCHARS*. Ranges of characters may be indicated by separating the lower and upper bounds of the range with a –. The matching is case-sensitive.

NEWCHARS   The set of characters replacing *OLDCHARS*. Ranges of characters may be indicated by separating the lower and upper bounds of the range with a –.

FILELIST   One or more filenames, separated by whitespace. The names may be specified using the wildcard conventions of your shell.

Comments

The original files are saved as backup versions with a suffixed **.bak**. For example, the original file **foo** is renamed **foo.bak**, while the new modified text is placed in **foo**, with permissions and owners as close to the original **foo** as possible. If you do not want a backup file (or want a different backup suffix), change the **.bak** part of the procedure accordingly.

Examples

```
perl -pi.bak -e 'tr/A-Z/a-z/' text1 text2
```

This example changes all uppercase characters to lowercase in the files **text1** and **text2**. Note that **y** is provided as a synonym for **tr**, in deference to those who are familiar with *sed*.

```
perl -pi.bak -e 'y/a-zA-Z/n-za-mN-ZA-M/' rec.humor.21450
```

This example performs a "rot13" transformation on the contents of the file **rec.humor.21450**. (Rot13 is a trivial method of minimally encrypting the alphabetic characters in a file by switching the first half of the alphabet with the second half; many articles in a number of newsgroups on Usenet are so encrypted so that a person doesn't accidentally see something that they don't choose to see.)

See Also

Substituting Strings in Many Files

SUBSTITUTING STRINGS IN MANY FILES

This procedure replaces all occurrences of one string with another in all the files given on the command line.

Procedure

```
perl -pi.bak -e 's/OLDSTRING/NEWSTRING/g' FILELIST
```

Parameters

OLDSTRING   The string of characters to be replaced with *NEWSTRING*. If the string contains any non-alphanumeric characters, each of those characters must be preceded by a \. The matching is case-sensitive.

NEWSTRING   The string of characters replacing *OLDSTRING*. If the string contains any non-alphanumeric characters, each of those characters must be preceded by a \.

FILELIST   One or more filenames, separated by whitespace. The names may be specified using the wildcard conventions of your shell.

Comments

The original files are saved as backup versions with a suffixed **.bak**. For example, the original file **foo** is renamed **foo.bak**, while the new modified text is placed in **foo**, with permissions and owners as close to the original **foo** as possible. If you do not want a backup file (or want a different backup suffix), change the **.bak** part of the procedure accordingly.

Examples

```
perl -pi.bak e 's/randal/merlyn/g' /etc/passwd /etc/group
```

This example changes all occurrences of the string **randal** to **merlyn** in the two files */etc/passwd* and */etc/group*. Unfortunately, it also changes **crandall** to **cmerlynl**—so you've just messed up your system's files. Put a **\b** before and after *OLDSTRING* to make sure it matches only as a word.

See Also

Substituting Characters in Many Files

TABULATING THE COUNT OF SOME ITEMS

This procedure records the number of occurrences of each distinct text string within an array, and prints the result.

Procedure

```
for (@DATA) {
    $count{$_}++;
}
for (sort keys %count) {
    printf "%Ns %d\n", $_, $count{$_};
}
```

Parameters

@DATA   An array holding the values to be tabulated, one per element.

N   An integer representing the number of output columns to allocate for the values that are being tabulated.

Comments

The value of $_ is destroyed by this procedure.

Examples

```
@who = grep(s/\s.*\n?$//, `who`);
for (@who) {
    $count{$_}++;
}
for (sort keys %count) {
    printf "%16s %d\n", $_, $count{$_};
}
```

This example creates an array (**@who**) that consists of the username from each line of a *who* command. It then tabulates the number of occurrences of each username, and prints the results sorted by username.

See Also

Printing Only the First Occurrence of Each Line

TRUNCATING A FILE

This procedure truncates a file to zero length, given its name.

Procedure

If you have **truncate( )**:

```
truncate('FILE',0);
```

If you don't have **truncate( )**:

```
local(*ZERO);
open(ZERO, '> FILE') && close(ZERO);
```

Parameters

FILE   The name of the file.

Comments

The second procedure is portable to systems without the **truncate** system call, and is not significantly slower (maybe just a little more obscure), so you should use it if you are planning on having your program run as-is on many different platforms. The second procedure uses the filehandle **ZERO**. You can't localize filehandles directly, but you can localize the *name* **ZERO** by using the syntax above. This localizes everything called **ZERO**, including the filehandle.

Examples

```
truncate('logfile',0);
```

Destroys the contents of **logfile** in the current directory.

```
sub truncate {
    local(*ZERO);
    open(ZERO,"> $_[0]") && close(ZERO);
}
&truncate('logfile');
```

Does the same thing on systems without the **truncate** system call.

See Also

Unlinking Many Files Whose Names are Specified by Another Process

UNDERSTANDING VARIABLE=VALUE ON THE COMMAND LINE

This procedure takes the next consecutive parameters from the **@ARGV** array that fit the form **variable=value** and assigns the variable **$variable** the value of **value**. Note that no spaces are allowed around the equal sign.

Procedure

```
eval "\$$1=\$2" while $ARGV[0] =~ /^(\w+)=(.*)/ && shift;
```

Comments

The **\w+** will match all the alphanumeric characters before the equal sign. You may wish to limit the variables that can be set from the command line to variables beginning with a specific suffix or in a particular package. See the examples.

Examples

```
eval "\$command_$1=\$2" while
    $ARGV[0] =~ /^(\w+)=(.*)/ && shift;
```

This example sets **$command_camel** to the indicated value when **camel=***some-value* is included on the command line.

```
eval "\$commandline´$1=\$2" while
    $ARGV[0] =~ /^(\w+)=(.*)/ && shift;
```

This example sets **$commandline´camel** (that is, the **$camel** variable within the **commandline** package) to the indicated value when **camel=***some-value* is included on the command line.

UNLINKING MANY FILES WHOSE NAMES ARE SPECIFIED BY ANOTHER PROCESS

This procedure unlinks (removes) many files selected by another process that prints each filename one-by-one on its standard output.

Procedure

```
SOMECOMMAND | perl -ne 'print; chop; unlink;'
```

Parameters

SOMECOMMAND A command whose output consists of filenames specified on separate lines, such as *find*. (**chop** will remove the newline.)

Comments

You may omit the **print** statement if you do not want a running display of the filenames during the execution of the command.

Examples

```
find . -name '*~' -atime +10 -print |
    perl -ne 'print;chop;unlink;'
```

This example removes all files within the current directory (and any directories contained within the current directory recursively) that end in ˜ and have not been accessed in 10 days. Each filename is printed as the file is removed.

```
find . -name '*~' -atime +10 -print | perl -ne 'chop;unlink;'
```

This example is similar to the last one, but the filenames are not printed.

See Also

Truncating a File

UNTAINTING A VARIABLE

This procedure copies the value of a tainted variable or expression into an untainted copy. (Tainted values arise when a setuid or setgid Perl script is handling insecure user-input data.) The pattern below is specialized for untainting filenames. It will allow a variable containing only alphanumeric characters (plus dot characters) to be untainted. In particular, it disallows slashes, so that a malicious user couldn't modify *../../../etc/passwd*.

Procedure

```
$TAINTED =~ /^([\w.]*)$/;
$UNTAINTED = $1;
```

Parameters

$TAINTED   The name of the tainted scalar variable, or an expression returning a tainted scalar value.

$UNTAINTED   The scalar variable that will hold the string equal to the value of *$TAINTED* as an untainted value.

Comments

You may use other patterns if you're sure they won't allow such naughtinesses as shell metacharacters, or pathnames containing *../../../etc/passwd*. What you can allow depends on the use you'll put the variable to—variables used in **eval** operations or passed to the shell may very easily be suborned into doing things you never intended, if you untaint uncarefully.

If the value is a floating-point number, some of the least-significant digits may be changed during the number-to-string-to-number conversions. The two variables may thus no longer be equal according to = or !=.

Examples

```
$ARGV[0] = /^([\w.]*)$/;
$free = $1;
```

This example assigns the first command-line argument to the variable **$free**.

6

Real Perl Programs

Database Manipulation
Grep Programs
Programming Aids
System Administration Stuff
Filename Manipulation
Text Manipulation Tools
Processes
Interprocess Communication

Here are some sample Perl programs. There's not much to be said at this point. Simply...go thou and do likewise.[39]

Database Manipulation

There are countless ways to use Perl in database applications. Perl provides support for a number of different database styles and file formats, including **DBM** files, variable-length text records, fixed-length records, and records stored as files in a directory. Any of these can be randomly accessed.

In addition, specialized database engines can be linked into Perl to make a special version that can access commercial databases directly using, for example, SQL. See the section "Linking in C Subroutines with Perl" in Chapter 7. Or, if you prefer, you can talk to a database engine through a socket or pipe. Many of the

---

[39] Lk. 10:37.

services provided by servers running on the Internet are simply database engines. For example, the **nntp** server lets you access a database of news articles, and Sun's NIS (formerly YP) is a way of accessing **DBM** files netwide.

lastlogin—Print Out Ancient Accounts

This program illustrates the processing of both variable-length and fixed-length records. If you're a manager and have been wondering whether you need to clean out any old login accounts, you might run something like this program. It uses a report format to print out a listing resembling this:

```
Uid   Login    Full Name                     Last Login
65534 nobody   Nobody in Particular          Never
    3 bin      System Stuff                  20 Apr 1987
  187 baggins  Bilbo Baggins                 18 Aug 1987
  216 dick     Richard T. Lionhearted        28 Jul 1988
  125 charding Cyrus Harding                 21 Apr 1989
```

Note that the records are sorted into order based on date of last login. Here's the program:

```perl
#!/usr/bin/perl

    # A lastlog record format for use by pack and unpack.

$lastlog_t = "L a8 a16";        # (Your machine's may differ.)

    # Find the length of the fixed-length record.

$LEN = length(pack($lastlog_t, 0, '', ''));

    # Open the database of last logins.  Fixed length records.

open(LASTLOG, "/usr/adm/lastlog")
    || die "Can't open lastlog file: $!\n";

    # Open the database of accounts.  Variable length records.

open(PASSWD, "/etc/passwd")
    || die "Can't open passwd file: $!\n";

    # So we can look up month names later.

@month = (Jan,Feb,Mar,Apr,May,Jun,Jul,Aug,Sep,Oct,Nov,Dec);


    # Now we iterate through variable length records by using
    # the <> input symbol.  In this particular database, the
    # delimiter just happens to be \n.  How lucky can you get?

while ($varrec = <PASSWD>) {
```

```
    # And the field delimiter happens to be a colon.  Amazing!

    ($login, $pass, $uid, $gid, $gcos) = split(/:/, $varrec);

    # Extract name from gcos field portably.

    $fullname = $gcos;
    $fullname =~ s/^[^,]*-(.*)\(.*/$1/ || $fullname =~ s/,.*//;
    if ($fullname =~ /&/) {        # You don't want to know.
        $name = $login;
        substr($name,0,1) =~ tr/a-z/A-Z/;
        $fullname =~ s/&/$name/;
    }


    # Now we random access the lastlog database.  It's keyed
    # by position based on the user id we want to look up.
    # Note that we multiply by the record length, since Unix
    # always wants byte offsets.

    seek(LASTLOG, $uid * $LEN, 0);
    read(LASTLOG, $lastlog, $LEN);

    # Now that we've fetched the lastlog record, we can
    # break it out into its fields.  Note that variable-
    # length fields above are separated with the split
    # operator, while these fixed-length fields are separated
    # using unpack.

    ($time, $line, $host) = unpack($lastlog_t, $lastlog);

    # Now remember it so we can sort easily.

    push(@records, "$time:$login:$uid:$fullname");
}

    # Now sort the records, oldest first.  See the
    # "numerically" subroutine below.

@records = sort numerically @records;

foreach $record (@records) {
    ($time,$login,$uid,$fullname) = split(/:/, $record);

    # Break out the login time, stored as seconds since
    # January 1, 1970, into normal date numbers.

    if ($time) {
        ($sec,$min,$hour,$mday,$mon,$year) = localtime($time);
        $year += 1900;
        $date = "$mday $month[$mon] $year";
    }
    else {
```

```
        $date = "Never";
    }

    # Write using the format below.

    write;
}

sub numerically { $a <=> $b; }

format top =
  Uid  Login    Full Name                               Last Login

  .


format STDOUT =
@>>>>   @<<<<<<< @<<<<<<<<<<<<<<<<<<<<<<<<<<<<<<<<<<<<<< @|||||||||||
$uid,  $login,  $fullname,                              $date
  .
```

nfinger—Finger Through Mail Aliases File

Here's an illustration of the use of a **DBM** file as a database. In this case, it's the system-wide mail aliases database. This program resolves the names you give as argument by looking them up in the aliases database (recursively if necessary) in order to find their real login names on their home machines. It then passes the real names off to the *finger*(1) program. It is thus an example of a "wrapper" program. The output is the same as the normal *finger* program's output; it's the input arguments that are translated and amplified.

You'll note that, like many **DBM** files created by C programs, the **aliases** file uses keys and values with a null character appended. This isn't necessary for either **DBM** or Perl, but it does makes life easier for the C programmers. (In the short run.)

```
#!/usr/bin/perl

# Usage: finger [fingeroptions] [names]

        # Bind %ALIAS to the aliases database.

dbmopen(ALIAS,´/usr/lib/aliases´,undef)
    || die "can´t dbmopen aliases";

        # Get the host name handy.

chop($thishost = `hostname`);
```

```
        # Strip finger switches.

while ($ARGV[0] =~ /^-/) {
    push(@fingerargs, shift);
}

        # Process user names.

while ($user = shift) {
    push(@finger, &resolve($user));
}

        # Uniquify names.

@finger = grep(!$seen{$_}++, @finger);

        # And run finger.

exec 'finger', @fingerargs, @finger;

die "Couldn't run finger: $!\n";

###########################################################

sub resolve {
    local($home,$addr,$alias,@list);

    while ($addr = shift) {
      $addr =~ s/\@$thishost.*//;
        if (defined $ALIAS{$addr."\0"}) {   # In dbm file.
            chop($alias = $ALIAS{$addr."\0"});
        }
        else {
            $home = (getpwnam($addr))[7];
            if (defined($home) && -r "$home/.forward") {
                open(FORWARD,"$home/.forward");
                chop($alias = <FORWARD>);
                close FORWARD;
            }
            else {
                push(@list, $addr);          # Not aliased.
                next;
            }
        }

        $alias =~ s/"\|[^"]*",?//g;
        $alias =~ s/^\s*(.*)\s*$/$1/;
        if ($alias eq '') {                  # Oops, only pipes.
            push(@list, $addr);              # So back out alias.
            next;
        }
        $alias =~ s/([^!]*)!(.*)/$2@$1/;  # A uucp addr?
```

```
        # Now call ourselves recursively.

        push(@list,&resolve(split(/[\s,]+/,$alias)));
    }
    return @list;
}
```

flealist—Report on Status of Bugs

You've seen several kinds of databases now, but this next one is near and dear to the heart of Perl, because that's where Perl got its start. This is the kind of database consisting of multiple text files, one for each record, in which the fields are delimited by keyword lines, like a message header. The files would presumably contain information like this:

```
Subject:        Can´t stir the stir-fry in Frugal Gourmet mode
Date-Received:  4/1/99
Priority:       hi!
Assigned-To:    Chuck Huffington
Disposition:    rej 4/2/99
Reported-By:    Sharon Hopkins
Address:        153 Fishbake Lane; Santa Cruise, WA 98765-4321
Phone:          (800)555-2121 0x7ff
Description:
    This stupid program burns my dinner every time.  I´d like
    a refund, preferably in rice noodles.  I´m recommending
    this program—to my enemies!
```

This data comes out formatted like this:

```
                    Camel´s Breath Software
Contempo-Primal Spasmodulator  1   Wed Dec 12 08:28:02 PST 1990
Flea#   Date   Disposition    Subject
    Reported by                    Priority Assigned to
    Phone & Address                Description
_____

    1  4/1/99  rej 4/2/99     Can´t stir the stir-fry in Frugal
    Sharon Hopkins                 hi!      Chuck Huffington
    (800)555-2121 0x7ff        This stupid program burns my
    153 Fishbake Lane         dinner every time.  I´d like a
    Santa Cruise, WA 98765-432 refund, preferably in rice
                              noodles.  I´m recommending this
                              program—to my enemies!
_____

    Summary for Contempo-Primal Spasmodulator
        Fixed =     Rej = 1    Hi =      Med =      Lo =
```

Although the names have been changed in the interests of national security, this is very similar to some of the reports that Perl Version 1 regularly chugged out.

```
#!/usr/bin/perl

$DATA = '/data';

chop($Date = `date`);

format TOP =
                Camel's Breath Software
@<<<<<<<<<<<<<<<<<<<<<<<<<<<@|||  @>>>>>>>>>>>>>>>>>>>>>>>>>>>>
$Product,                   $%,  $Date
Flea#   Date   Disposition    Subject
    Reported by                  Priority Assigned to
    Phone & Address              Description
_____

.

format RECORD =
@>>>> @|||||||  @<<<<<<<<<<<<< @<<<<<<<<<<<<<<<<<<<<<<<<<<<<<<<<<
$Bug, $rdate, $disp,       $subject
    @<<<<<<<<<<<<<<<<<<<<<<<<<<<< @<<<<<< @<<<<<<<<<<<<<<<<<<
    $reporter,                   $prior, $assigned
~   @<<<<<<<<<<<<<<<<<<<<<<<< ^<<<<<<<<<<<<<<<<<<<<<<<<<<<<<<<
    $phone,               $description
~   @<<<<<<<<<<<<<<<<<<<<<<<< ^<<<<<<<<<<<<<<<<<<<<<<<<<<<<<<<
    shift(@addr),         $description
~   @<<<<<<<<<<<<<<<<<<<<<<<< ^<<<<<<<<<<<<<<<<<<<<<<<<<<<<<<<
    shift(@addr),         $description
~   @<<<<<<<<<<<<<<<<<<<<<<<< ^<<<<<<<<<<<<<<<<<<<<<<<<<<<<<<<
    shift(@addr),         $description
~   @<<<<<<<<<<<<<<<<<<<<<<<< ^<<<<<<<<<<<<<<<<<<<<<<<<<<<<<<<
    shift(@addr),         $description
~                         ^<<<<<<<<<<<<<<<<<<<<<<<<<<<<<<<
                          $description
~                         ^<<<<<<<<<<<<<<<<<<<<<<<<<<<<<<<
                          $description
~                         ^<<<<<<<<<<<<<<<<<<<<<<<<<<<<...
                          $description
.

# One summary record is printed for each product.

format SUMMARY =
_____

   Summary for @<<<<<<<<<<<<<<<<<<<<<<<<<<
               $Product
      Fixed = @<<<  Rej = @<<<  Hi = @<<<  Med = @<<<  Lo = @<<<
              $Xfix,     $Xrej,     $Xhigh,    $Xmed,     $Xlow
.

sub numerically { $a <=> $b; }

$^ = 'TOP';                 # Set top-of-form format.
```

```
chdir $DATA || die "Can't cd to $DATA: $!\n";


# Now we're ready to begin.  Scan our list of products.

PROD:
  foreach $Productdir (<*>) {
    reset 'X';                   # Zero out accumulators

    chdir "$DATA/$Productdir" || do {
        warn "Can't cd to $Productdir: $!\n"; next PROD; };

    if (open(NAME, '.prodname')) {
        chop($Product = <NAME>);
        close NAME;
    }
    else {
        ($Product = $Productdir) =~ tr/_/ /;
    }

    opendir(DIR, '.') || do {
        warn "Can't read $Product: $!\n"; next PROD; };

    @Buglist = sort numerically grep(/^\d+$/, readdir(DIR));
    closedir(DIR);

    $~ = 'RECORD';               # Set format for normal records.


    # Now, iterate over the bug report files.

  BUG:
    foreach $Bug (@Buglist) {
        reset 'a-z';             # Clear scratch variables.

        open(BUGFILE, $Bug) || do {
            warn "Can't open $Product/$Bug: $!\n";
            next BUG;
        };

      LINE:
        while (<BUGFILE>) {
            if    (/^Address:\s*(.*)/)
                  {@addr = split(/;\s*/, $1);}
            elsif (/^Assigned-To:\s*(.*)/)
                  {$assigned = $1;}
            elsif (/^Priority:\s*(.*)/)
                  {$prior   = $1;}
            elsif (/^Phone:\s*(.*)/)
                  {$phone   = $1;}
            elsif (/^Subject:\s*(.*)/)
                  {$subject = $1;}
            elsif (/^Reported-By:\s*(.*)/)
                  {$reporter = $1;}
```

```perl
        elsif (/^Disposition:\s*(.*)/)
            {$disp    = $1;}
        elsif (/^Date-Received:\s*(.*)/)
            {$rdate   = $1;}
        elsif (/^Description:\s*(.*)/) {
            $description = $1;

          DESCLINE:
            while (<BUGFILE>) {
                last DESCLINE if /^—/;
                $description .= $_;
            }

            # Make into one long line.

            $description =~ s/([.!?])\n\s*/$1  /g;
            $description =~ s/\n\s*/ /g;
            $description =~ s/^\s*//;
        }
    }

    # Accumulate stats about priorities and dispositions.

    if ($disp =~ /^open/i) {
        $prior =~ /^hi/  && $Xhigh++;
        $prior =~ /^med/ && $Xmed++;
        $prior =~ /^lo/  && $Xlow++;
    }
    elsif ($disp =~ /^fixed/i) {
        $Xfix++;
    }
    elsif ($disp =~ /^rej/i) {
        $Xrej++;
    }
    elsif ($disp =~ /^void/i) {
        next BUG;
    }

    write;                    # Write one record's worth.
}

$~ = 'SUMMARY';               # Select summary format.
write;                        # And write one of those.

$- = 0;                       # Force formfeed on next record.

chdir $DATA || die "Can't cd back to $DATA: $!\n";
}
```

Grep Programs

The term "grep" comes from the *ed*(1) editor, in which it stood for **g/re/p**, to globally search for lines containing a regular expression and print just those lines. A
UNIX program named *grep* was then developed which rapidly scanned multiple
files for lines matching regular expressions. As some of the limitations of the
original *grep* program became known, various variants of *grep* arose. In this fine
tradition, we present three more.

tgrep—Scans Text Files

The *tgrep* program greps only those files containing textual data. It's useful in a
directory that has mixed binary and textual files, when the filenames aren't a sufficient clue to the nature of the file. *tgrep* has one option, **–l**, which causes it to
list the files containing the pattern rather than listing the lines containing the pattern.

For maximum speed, *tgrep* uses the trick of building up the loop it's going to execute to eliminate unnecessary conditional tests and pattern recompilations.

Note that the **–B** file test following the **–d** file test doesn't use the special
stat( )-suppressing filehandle _ because **–B** isn't a **stat**( )-based file test.

```perl
#!/usr/bin/perl

# Usage: tgrep [-l] pattern [files]

# Handle
if ($ARGV[0] eq '-l') {
    shift;
    $action = <<'EOF';
            print $file,"\n";
            next FILE;
EOF
}
else {
    $action = <<'EOF';
            print $file,":\t", $_;
EOF
}

# Get pattern and protect the delimiter we'll use.

$pat = shift;
$pat =~ s/!/\\!/g;
```

```
# Generate the program.

$prog = <<EOF;
FILE: foreach \$file (\@ARGV) {
    open(FILE,\$file) || do {
        print STDERR "Can't open \$file: \$!\\n";
        next;
    };
    next if -d FILE;      # ignore directories
    next if -B FILE;      # ignore binary files
    while (<FILE>) {
        if (m!$pat!) {
            $action
        }
    }
}
EOF

# We often put in lines like this while developing scripts, so we
# can see what program the program is writing.

print $prog if $debugging;

# And finally, do it.

eval $prog;
die $@ if $@;
```

pipegrep—Scans Command Output

The **pipegrep** program greps the output of a series of commands. The difficulty with doing this using the normal *grep* program is that you lose track of which file was being processed. This program prints out the command it was executing at the time, including the filename. The command, which is a single argument, will be executed once for each file in the list. If you give the string { } anywhere in the command, the filename will be substituted at that point. Otherwise the filename will be added onto the end of the command. This program has one option, –l, which causes it to list the files containing the pattern. For example:

```
$ cd /usr/lib
$ pipegrep 'sys_nerr' nm lib*.a
```

And here's the program:

```
#!/usr/bin/perl

# Usage: pipegrep [-l] pattern command [files]

if ($ARGV[0] eq '-l') {
```

```
        shift;
        $action = <<´EOF´;
                print $file,"\n";
                next file;
EOF
    }
    else {
        $action = <<´EOF´;
                print $file,":\t", $_;
EOF
    }

    # Get pattern and protect the delimiter we´ll use.

    $pat = shift;
    $pat =~ s/!/\\!/g;

    # Get command and make sure it has a {}.

    $cmd = shift;
    $cmd .= ´ {}´ unless $cmd =~ /{}/;

    # Modify each filename into the corresponding command.

    for (@ARGV) {
        $file = $_;
        $_ = $cmd;
        s/{}/$file/;
        s/$/ |/;
    }

    # Generate the program.

    $prog = <<EOF;
file: foreach \$file (\@ARGV) {
    open(FILE,\$file) || do {
        print STDERR "Can´t open \$file: \$!\\n";
        next;
    };
    while (<FILE>) {
        if (m!$pat!) {
            $action
        }
    }
}
EOF
    print $prog if $debugging;

    # And finally, do it.

    eval $prog;
    die $@ if $@;
```

cgrep—Context Grep

The *cgrep* program greps for a pattern in the specified files, and prints out that line with several lines of surrounding context. If invoked on itself with this command:

```
cgrep eval cgrep
```

cgrep will print out two sets of lines, with the line containing "eval" in the middle of each set of lines, like this:

```
$pat =~ s#/#\\/#g;

# First line of input will be middle of array.
# In the eval below, it will be $ary[$context].

$_ = <>;
push(@ary,$_);

_____

# Now use @ary as a silo, shifting and pushing.

eval <<LOOP_END;
    while (\$ary[$context]) {
        if (\$ary[$context] =~ /$pat/) {
            print "_____\n" if \$seq++;
```

Here's the program itself:

```
#!/usr/bin/perl

# Usage: cgrep [-lines] pattern [files]

$context = 3;

# They might want more or less context.

if ($ARGV[0] =~ /^-(\d+)$/) {
    $context = $1;
    shift;
}

# Get the pattern and protect the delimiter.

$pat = shift;
$pat =~ s#/#\\/#g;

# First line of input will be middle of array.
# In the eval below, it will be $ary[$context].

$_ = <>;
```

```
    push(@ary,$_);

    # Add blank lines before, more input after first line.

    for (1 .. $context) {
        unshift(@ary,´´);
        $_ = <>;
        push(@ary,$_) if $_;
    }

    # Now use @ary as a silo, shifting and pushing.

    eval <<LOOP_END;
        while (\$ary[$context]) {
            if (\$ary[$context] =~ /$pat/) {
                print "————————\n" if \$seq++;
                print \@ary,"\n";
            }
            \$_ = <> if \$_;
            shift(\@ary);
            push(\@ary,\$_);
        }
    LOOP_END
```

Programming Aids

In this section we'll show you some programs to help you with programming.

xdump—A Mainframe-ish Hex Dump

xdump does a hex dump in the IBM mainframe tradition, with the corresponding plain text in a separate column down the right side. Running **xdump** on itself produces a listing like this:

```
00000000    23212f75 73722f62 696e2f70 65726c0a    #!/usr/bin/perl.
00000010    0a232055 73616765 3a207864 756d7020    .# Usage: xdump
00000020    5b66696c 655d0a0a 23205573 65207468    [file]..# Use th
00000030    65206669 6c652074 68657920 73706563    e file they spec
00000040    69666965 642c2069 66207370 65636966    ified, if specif
00000050    6965640a 0a6f7065 6e285354 44494e2c    ied..open(STDIN,
00000060    24415247 565b305d 29207c7c 20646965    $ARGV[0]) || die
00000070    20224361 6e277420 6f70656e 20244152    "Can't open $AR
00000080    47565b30 5d3a2024 215c6e22 0a202020    GV[0]: $!\n".
...
000002e0    0a202020 20707269 6e746620 22257325    .   printf "%s%
000002f0    73257325 73202573 25732573 25732025    s%s%s %s%s%s%s %
00000300    73257325 73257320 25732573 25732573    s%s%s%s %s%s%s%s
```

```
00000310    20202020 25735c6e 222c0a20 20202020        %s\n",.
00000320    20202040 61727261 792c2024 64617461        @array, $data
00000330    3b0a7d0a                                    ;.}.
```

The program reads from either the file specified or standard input. It uses the
read() function rather than the **<STDIN>** input symbol because we want to read
exactly 16 bytes each time. The main loop processes data four longwords at a
time for efficiency. The coda finishes things up a byte at a time so that the last
line contains spaces in all the right places.

```perl
#!/usr/bin/perl

# Usage: xdump [file]

# Use the file they specified, if specified

open(STDIN,$ARGV[0])  ||  die "Can´t open $ARGV[0]: $!\n"
    if $ARGV[0];

# Do it optimally as long as we can read 16 bytes at a time.

while (($len = read(STDIN,$data,16)) == 16) {
    @array = unpack(´N4´, $data);
    $data =~ tr/\0—\37\177—\377/./;
    printf "%8.8lx    %8.8lx %8.8lx %8.8lx %8.8lx    %s\n",
        $offset, @array, $data;
    $offset += 16;
}

# Now finish up the end a byte at a time.

if ($len) {
    @array = unpack(´C*´, $data);
    $data =~ y/\0—\37\177—\377/./;
    for (@array) {
        $_ = sprintf(´%2.2x´,$_);
    }
    push(@array, ´  ´) while $len++ < 16;
    $data =~ s/[^ —]/./g;
    printf "%8.8lx    ", $offset;
    printf "%s%s%s%s %s%s%s%s %s%s%s%s %s%s%s%s    %s\n",
        @array, $data;
}
```

fixin—Fixes Interpreter Line on Incoming Scripts

Scripts that are published on The Net[40] often begin with a **#!** (a sharp-bang, or shebang) line, which says which interpreter to use. Unfortunately, it also specifies the full pathname to the interpreter, which is inherently non-portable, since there are many different places to keep interpreter programs. The **fixin** program fixes the specified files so that the **#!** line reflects the actual location of the desired interpreter on this system. It does so by searching your current **PATH** environment variable for files matching the last component of the current **#!** line. It then changes the **#!** line to point to the located file. The files are modified in place, with a **.bak** backup. (If no files are specified, **fixin** acts as a filter.)

fixin uses only the absolute components of **PATH** in looking for interpreters. It warns you of a possible conflict if it locates more than one instance of the interpreter in your **PATH**. The –s switch makes **fixin** shut up about what it's doing.

```
#!/usr/bin/perl

# Usage: fixin [-s] [files]

# Configuration constants.

$does_shbang = 1;       # Does kernel recognize #! hack?
$verbose = 1;           # Default to verbose

# Construct list of directories to search.

@absdirs = reverse grep(m!^/!, split(/:/, $ENV{'PATH'}, 999));

# Process command-line arguments.

if ($ARGV[0] eq '-s') {
    shift;
    $verbose = 0;
}

die "Usage: fixin [-s] [files]\n" unless @ARGV || !-t;

@ARGV = '-' unless @ARGV;

# Now do each file.

FILE: foreach $filename (@ARGV) {
    open(IN, $filename) ||
        ((warn "Can't process $filename: $!\n"), next);
    $_ = <IN>;
    next FILE unless /^#!/;      # Not a shbang file.
```

---

[40] If anyone ever trademarks this term, we're all in trouble.

```
    # Now figure out the interpreter name.

    chop($cmd = $_);
    $cmd =~ s/^#! *//;
    ($cmd,$arg) = split(' ', $cmd, 2);
    $cmd =~ s!^.*/!!;

    # Now look (in reverse) for interpreter in absolute PATH.

    $found = '';
    foreach $dir (@absdirs) {
        if (-x "$dir/$cmd") {
            warn "Ignoring $found\n" if $verbose && $found;
            $found = "$dir/$cmd";
        }
    }

    # Figure out how to invoke interpreter on this machine.

    if ($found) {
        warn "Changing $filename to $found\n" if $verbose;
        if ($does_shbang) {
            $_ = "#!$found";
            $_ .= ' ' . $arg if $arg ne '';
            $_ .= "\n";
        }
        else {
            $_ = <<EOF;
:
eval 'exec $found $arg -S \$0 \${1+"\$@"}'
    if \$running_under_some_shell;
EOF
        }
    }
    else {
        warn "Can't find $cmd in PATH, $filename unchanged\n"
            if $verbose;
        next FILE;
    }

    # Make new file if necessary.

    if ($filename eq '-') {
        select(STDOUT);
    }
    else {
        rename($filename, "$filename.bak")
            || ((warn "Can't modify $filename"), next FILE);
        open(OUT,">$filename")
            || die "Can't create new $filename: $!\n";
        ($dev,$ino,$mode) = stat IN;
        $mode = 0755 unless $dev;
        chmod $mode, $filename;
```

```
        select(OUT);
    }

    # Print out the new #! line (or equivalent).

    print;

    # Copy the rest of the file.

    while (<IN>) {
        print;
    }
    close IN;
    close OUT;
}
```

retab—Shrink Indentation

Perhaps you're one of those people who likes to indent your programs on multiples of 4 columns, to prevent nested code from bunching up against the right margin. But sometimes you acquire code that contains hardware tabs, indenting by multiples of 8 columns. This bugs you. The **retab** program reads its input and shrinks all the initial whitespace down by some factor. By default it changes 8 spaces (one hardware tab) to 4 spaces, but you can give a switch to change 8 spaces to any number of spaces.

Processing happens in three stages on each line. First all initial tabs are canonicalized to the equivalent number of spaces. Then the amount of whitespace is reduced by the specified amount. Finally the whitespace is translated back to the equivalent number of tabs and spaces. This program illustrates the use of the **e** modifier on substitutions to evaluate the replacement text as an expression.

This program also makes heavy use of the string replication operator **x** to produce strings of spaces and tabs.

```
#!/usr/bin/perl

# Usage: retab [-<tabwidth>] [files]

$sw = 4;
$sw = $1, shift if $ARGV[0] =~ /^-(\d+)/;

while (<>) {
    s#^(\t+)#^ ^ x (length($1) * 8)#e;
    s#^( *)#^ ^ x (length($1) * $sw / 8)#e;
    s#^(( {8})*)#"\t" x (length($1) / 8)#e;
    print;
}
```

w4—Lists Dependencies

The **w4** program runs the C preprocessor for you on the specified files, passing along any **–D** or **–I** switches you specify. It then processes the resulting output into a list of dependencies suitable for inclusion in a **Makefile**. Unlike many **make depend** programs, this one does not attempt to modify your **Makefile**. Self-modifying code is to be avoided—instead, use a version of *make* that allows inclusion of the dependencies from a separate file. Programs that feel they must modify your **Makefile** are not good tools for your toolbox.

The dependencies produced by **w4** may be modified by using the **–d** *DIRNAME* switch, which prepends the directory name onto the front of the names of object files.

This program assumes that **cc –E** runs your C preprocessor. On some machines you might have to invoke it differently. If possible, simply modify the script to detect which kind of machine it is running on, so you can use the same script everywhere. For more on script portability, see the **wrapman** and *zap* programs later in this chapter.

```perl
#!/usr/bin/perl

# Usage: w4 [options] [files]

# Configuration parameters.

$CPP = "cc -E";
# $CPP = "cc -P";
# $CPP = "/lib/cpp";

# Process switches.

while ($ARGV[0] =~ /^-/) {
    $_ = shift;
    if (/^-D(.*)/) {
        $defines .= " -D" . ($1 ? $1 : shift);
    }
    elsif (/^-I(.*)/) {
        $includes .= " -I" . ($1 ? $1 : shift);
    }
    elsif (/^-d(.*)/) {
        $dir = ($1 ? $1 : shift);
    }
    else {
        die "Unrecognized switch: $_\n";
    }
}
```

```
# Do each file on command line.

foreach $file (@ARGV) {
    open(CPP,"$CPP $defines $includes $file|")
        || die "Can't run cpp: $!\n";

    # Scan output for line directives.

    %seen = ();
    while (<CPP>) {
        next unless /^#/;
        next unless ($filename) = /^# \d.*"(.*)"/;
        $seen{$filename}++;
    }
    close CPP;

    # Figure out the corresponding object file name.

    ($ofile = $file) =~ s/\.c$/.o/;
    $ofile =~ s#.*/##;
    $ofile = "$dir/$ofile" if $dir;

    # Print out the dependencies.

    foreach $dep (sort keys(%seen)) {
        print "$ofile: $dep\n";
    }
    print "\n";
}
```

inctree—Prints Out #include Tree for C programs

In porting large projects to new architectures, we often find that the structure of **#include** files differs greatly, and definitions are either missing or duplicated. The missing ones are easy to find by searching /usr/include with the *grep* program (or even one of the programs presented earlier in this chapter). Finding duplicate definitions can be quite difficult, however. The **inctree** program runs the C preprocessor on the specified files, passing along any **–D** or **–I** switches you specify. It then processes the output of *cpp* into a tree of who included what. Files included more than once are marked "DUPLICATE." When run on a file from the distribution of the *patch*(1) program, **inctree** prints out this:

```
patch.c
    ./INTERN.h
    ./common.h
        ./config.h
        /usr/include/stdio.h
        /usr/include/assert.h
        /usr/include/sys/types.h
```

```
        /usr/include/sys/stat.h
        /usr/include/ctype.h
        /usr/include/signal.h
./EXTERN.h
./version.h
./util.h
./pch.h
./inp.h
```

Thus you can see that **patch.c** includes (among other things) **common.h**, which in turn includes **config.h**, and some system header files.

Two additional switches may be used:

-l   Makes it list the line numbers of the include statements.

−m/pattern/ Outputs any lines containing the pattern specified, which will let you search for extra definitions of a structure, for instance. Multiple −m switches may be included. Note that you can't search for anything the C preprocessor weeds out, such as *cpp* symbols or comments. You can, however, find out where a structure is defined.

In processing these patterns, this program builds a dynamically defined subroutine that can then be called in the standard fashion. The subroutine is defined inside an **eval** statement.

Like the **w4** program above, this program assumes that **cc −E** runs your C preprocessor. We encourage you to pull configuration parameters like **$CPP** to the front of your scripts where they will be noticed by anyone who needs to modify the script.

This script works by keeping a stack of current include nesting. By examining the line number directives emitted by the C preprocessor, the script can determine whether a new filename should be pushed on the stack, or an old filename can be popped from the stack.

```perl
#!/usr/bin/perl

# Usage: inctree [options] [files]

# Configuration parameters.

$CPP = `cc -E`;
# $CPP = "cc -P";
# $CPP = "/lib/cpp";

$shiftwidth = 4;

# Process switches.

while ($ARGV[0] =~ /^-/) {
```

```perl
    $_ = shift;
    if (/^-D(.*)/) {
        $defines .= " -D" . ($1 ? $1 : shift);
    }
    elsif (/^-I(.*)/) {
        $includes .= " -I" . ($1 ? $1 : shift);
    }
    elsif (/^-m(.*)/) {
        push(@pats, $1 ? $1 : shift);
    }
    elsif (/^-l/) {
        $lines++;
    }
    else {
        die "Unrecognized switch: $_\n";
    }
}

# Build a subroutine to scan for any specified patterns.

if (@pats) {
    $sub = "sub pats {\n";
    foreach $pat (@pats) {
        $sub .= "    print '>>>>>>> ',\$_ if m$pat;\n";
    }
    $sub .= "}\n";
    eval $sub;
    ++$pats;
}

# Now process each file on the command line.

foreach $file (@ARGV) {
    open(CPP,"$CPP $defines $includes $file|")
        || die "Can't run cpp: $!\n";
    $line = 2;

    while (<CPP>) {
        ++$line;
        &pats if $pats;        # Avoid expensive call if we can.
        next unless /^#/;
        next unless /^# \d/;
        ($junk,$newline,$filename) = split;
        $filename =~ s/"//g;

        # Now figure out if it's a push, a pop, or neither.

        if ($stack[$#stack] eq $filename) {      # Same file.
            $line = $newline-1;
            next;
        }
```

```
        if ($stack[$#stack-1] eq $filename) {    # Leaving file.
            $indent -= $shiftwidth;
            $line = pop(@lines)-1;
            pop(@stack);
        }
        else {                                    # New file.
            printf "%6d  ", $line-2 if $lines;
            push(@lines,$line);
            $line = $newline;
            print "\t" x ($indent / 8), ' ' x ($indent % 8),
                $filename;
            print "  DUPLICATE" if $seen{$filename}++;
            print "\n";
            $indent += $shiftwidth;
            push(@stack,$filename);
        }
    }
    close CPP;
    $indent = 0;
    %seen = ();
    print "\n\n";
    $line = 0;
}
```

lfix—Emulates ld −L Switch

In a multiple-architecture environment, it sometimes happens that some machines
don't support the −L switch to the loader, which gives it additional directories to
search for libraries. The **lfix** program gets around this by executing an equivalent
command for you. It does this by remembering any −L switches and deleting
them from the command string, and then translating any −l switches to the actual
filename to emulate searching the library path.

This program is a good example of what we call a "wrapper"—a program that
runs before (and sometimes after) the intended program in order to transform its
arguments, environment or return value. This wrapper just transforms the input
arguments.

```
#!/usr/bin/perl

# Usage: lfix cc -L ... -l ...
#        lfix ld -L ... -l ...

while (@ARGV) {
    $_ = shift;
    if (/^-L(.*)/) {
        push(@liblist, $1);
```

```
            next;
        }

    elsif (/^-l(.*)/) {
        $libname = $1;
        foreach $dir (@liblist) {
            if (-f "$dir/lib$libname.a") {
                $_ = "$dir/lib$libname.a";
                last;
            }
            elsif (-f "$dir/llib-l$libname.ln") {
                $_ = "$dir/llib-l$libname.ln";
                last;
            }
        }
    }
    push(@newargv, $_);
}

# Now do the new command.

exec @newargv;
```

nostrict—Postprocesses lint Output to Implement /*NOSTRICT*/

Here we have an example of a wrapper that transforms the output of the *lint* command. Many versions of *lint* document a /**NOSTRICT**/ directive, which makes *lint* accept the next C statement without complaining. Few versions, if any, actually implement it. The **nostrict** wrapper runs the command supplied in the rest of the arguments on the command line, and then weeds out any *lint* complaints referring to statements preceded by the /**NOSTRICT**/ directive.

The program works by scanning any input files and building bitmaps representing which lines are parts of statements protected by /**NOSTRICT**/. The program locates these lines using the scalar .. operator. To start a line number range, it searches for /**NOSTRICT**/, and to finish the range, it searches for a semicolon followed by either the end of the line or a comment (with possible intervening whitespace).[41]

```
#!/usr/bin/perl

# Usage: nostrict lint [lint_args]
```

---

[41] This rule isn't perfect, but Lazy Programmers know that if a thing is worth doing, it's worth doing well—unless doing it well takes so long that it isn't worth doing any more. Then you just do it "good enough."

```
# Build bit vectors with 1's for protected lines.  We use vecs
# rather than normal arrays in order to save (lots of) memory.

for $arg (@ARGV) {
    next unless $arg =~ /\.[ch]$/;
    open(IN,$arg);
    while (<IN>) {
        if (m#/\*\s*NOSTRICT\s*\*/# .. m#;\s*($|/\*)#) {
            vec($ok{$arg}, $., 1) = 1;
        }
    }
    close IN;
}

# Now run the command as an input pipe.

open(LINT, "-|") || exec @ARGV;

# Note that in this loop, a "next" defaults to printing the
# line.  We null out $_ if we *don't* want to print it.

while (<LINT>) {
    $curfile = $1 if /^(\S+\.[ch])\b/;
    next unless (($file,$line) = /(\S+)\((\d+)\)/)
        || ($line) = /^\s*\((\d+)\)/;
    $file =~ s/\?$//;
    $file = $curfile unless $file;
    next unless defined $ok{$file};
    $_ = '' if vec($ok{$file}, $line, 1);

    # Some lines contain two references.

    next unless ($file,$line) = /::\s*(\S+)\((\d+)\)/;
    $file =~ s/\?$//;
    next unless defined $ok{$file};
    $_ = '' if vec($ok{$file}, $line, 1);
}
continue {
    print;
}
```

exyacc—Extracts Grammar from yacc File

Here's a program we used when we began writing the Semi-formal Grammar for this book. It's a good example of a program that slurps in an entire file and then treats $_ as an editing buffer. *exyacc* munches one or more *yacc* files and spits out just the productions (the grammar rules) to standard output, so that the action routines don't clutter up your listing. With a **–n** switch, *exyacc* numbers the productions. This can be useful for interpreting *yacc* debugging output that refers to production numbers. The program assumes that you've written rules in the standard form, with each alternative starting a new line, as in:

```
non_terminal    :        thing thing thing
                                { actions }
                |        thing
                                { actions }
                |        thing thing
                                { actions }
                ;
```

Running *exyacc* on Perl's *yacc* file with a **–n** switch produces the following listing:

```
prog     :1      lineseq
         ;

compblock:2      block CONTINUE block
         |3      block else
         ;

else     :4
         |5      ELSE block
         |6      ELSIF ´(´ expr ´)´ compblock
         ;

block    :7      ´{´ remember lineseq ´}´
         ;

. . .

aryword  :175    WORD
         |176    ARY
         ;

hshword  :177    WORD
         |178    HSH
         ;

bareword:179     WORD
```

This program uses several tricks you probably haven't seen before. It uses **index** and **rindex** to find the beginning and end of the section of interest. Whenever possible, it substitutes strings of the same length so that Perl can modify $_ in place without doing any copying. It uses a **0 while** construct to do repeated substitution passes. Some people prefer **1 while**—it makes no difference.

```
#!/usr/bin/perl

# Usage: exyacc [–n] [yaccfiles]

$num = shift if $ARGV[0] =~ /^-n/;
```

```perl
undef $/;
$* = 1;            # Treat $_ as multi—line buffer.

while (<>) {       # One file at a time because of undef above.

                   # First pull out the rules section.
                   #   (Note: Assumes no comment includes "\n%%").

    $start = index($_,"\n%%") + 1;
    $end = rindex($_,"\n%%") + 1;
    $_ = substr($_, $start, $end — $start);
    s/.*\n//;;                  # Delete the %% line.

                   # Save curly braces used as tokens.

    s/´{´/´\200´/g;             # Keep length same for inplace.
    s/´}´/´\201´/g;

                   # Strip comments.

    s#\*/#\202\202#g;           # Make terminator easy to find
    s#/\*[^\202]*\202\202##g;

                   # Strip {}´s from the inside out;
                   # several passes handle nesting.

    0 while s/{[^}{]*}//g;

                   # Restore any curly braces used as tokens.

    s/´\200´/´{´/g;
    s/´\201´/´}´/g;

                   # Eliminate unwanted blank lines.

    0 while s/^[ \t]*\n(\s)/$1/g;

                   # Number rules if desired.
                   # Assumes | always starts line.

    $seq = 0;
    s/^(\w*\s*[:|])/$1 . ++$seq/eg if $num;

                   # And there you have it...

    print;
}
```

System Administration Stuff

Perl has been particularly popular among those who must administer one or more computers. In part this is because it lets them manipulate files and processes easily, and because much of system administration involves text processing. But the biggest reason, at least among administrators of large installations, is that it's easy to write portable Perl scripts that run unmodified on multiple computer architectures. See the **fixscripts** program later on for more on portable scripts.

passwd—Password Changing Program

When a system administrator first becomes aware of the need for secure passwords, the initial urge is to write a password cracking program and see if any of the passwords in */etc/passwd* are crackable. This is lots of fun, uses up oodles of CPU time, and does very little to improve password security. To really have secure passwords, you need to disallow people from choosing bad passwords in the first place. Here is a password program that does just that. It has no rules for the formation of good passwords, only rules for bad passwords. (If you make rules for good passwords, you've made the password cracker's job much easier. If all you do is reject bad passwords, the user comes up with a private method of generating good passwords, and the cracker's job becomes much harder.)

There are hooks in this program for doing password expiration—the age of the password is mystically encoded in the salt of the encrypted password, and you can write a program that goes through the */etc/passwd* file each night and expires old accounts by changing the user's shell. If you do such a thing, it's polite to give people a warning by mail in the week before the password expires. The advantage of this method is that it works without any changes to your C library functions.

This program has the capability to search multiple dictionaries for bad passwords. At Larry's installation, they use three different dictionaries: */usr/dict/words*, */usr/dict/web2*, and a file called */usr/etc/badwords*, which contains entries like this:

```
Gandalf        Nice wizard, bad password.
Heinlein       TANSTAAFL.
Lothlorien     Yes, I want to go there too.
Popeye         Your password needs more spinach.
```

One way to choose a good password is to pick the first letter of each word of a phrase, if it's not a common phrase. To weed out common phrases, this program

also matches against a file of patterns, here called */usr/etc/badpats*. It contains
patterns, snide remarks, and comments separated by tab characters, like this:

```
^a[f4][ol],?a?[ol][f4]a All for naught.    All for one and one...
^ilbcnu                 s, ilbcnu, 2.      I´ll be seein´ you
^nitt[f4]a              Timeout.           Now is the time for...
^rd?kfomh               Password all wet.  Raindrops keep fall...
```

Here's the program. The first part collects all the necessary data and makes sure
the password file is changeable. If you're just interested in the rules, skip down to
the definition of the **&goodenough** subroutine.

```
#!/usr/local/bin/perl

# Customizable items.

$AGEWEEKS = 8;
$EXPWEEKS = 12;
$BADPATS = ´/usr/etc/badpats´;
$BADWORDS = ´/usr/etc/badwords´;

# Make a list of dictionaries to search with &look

@words = $BADWORDS;
if (-f ´/usr/dict/web2´) {
    push(@words,´/usr/dict/web2´);
}
push(@words,´/usr/dict/words´);
$fh = ´dictaa´;
foreach $dict (@words) {
    open($fh,$dict) && push(@dicts, eval "*$fh");
    $fh++;
}

# Security blankets.

$ENV{´IFS´} = ´´ if $ENV{´IFS´};
$ENV{´PATH´} = ´/bin:/usr/bin:/usr/local/bin:/usr/ucb´;
umask(022);

chdir ´/etc´ || die "Can´t find /etc.\n";
die "passwd program isn´t running setuid to root\n" if $>;

@INC = $INC[$#INC - 1];        # Use only perl library.
die "Perl library is writable by world!!!\n"
    if $< && -W $INC[0];
die "look.pl is writable by world!!!\n"
    if $< && -W "$INC[0]/look.pl";
require "look.pl";

# Uncustomizable items.
```

```perl
$| = 1;              # command buffering on STDOUT

@saltset = ('a' .. 'z', 'A' .. 'Z', '0' .. '9', '.', '/');

chop($host = `hostname`);

# Process the arguments.

$relax = shift if $ARGV[0] =~ /^-r/;
$relax = 0 if $<;                      # (superuser only)


if ($ARGV[0] =~ /^-a(.*)/) {
    $AGE = $1;
    $AGE = $AGEWEEKS + 1 if $AGE <= 0;
    $AGE = $EXPWEEKS + 1 if $AGE > $EXPWEEKS;
    shift;
}

# Whose password are we changing, anyway?

# (We use getlogin in preference to getpwuid($<)[0] in case
#  different accounts are sharing uids.)

($me) = @ARGV;
die "You can't change the password for $me.\n" if $me && $<;
$me = getlogin unless $me;
$me = (getpwuid($<))[0] unless $me;

# Trap these signals

$SIG{'INT'} = 'CLEANUP';
$SIG{'HUP'} = 'CLEANUP';
$SIG{'QUIT'} = 'CLEANUP';
$SIG{'PIPE'} = 'CLEANUP';
$SIG{'ALRM'} = 'CLEANUP';


# Check first before putting them through the wringer.  (We'll
#   check again later.)

die "/etc/passwd file busy—try again later.\n" if -f 'ptmp';

# A check to see if they have an application form on file.

open(FORMS,"forms") || die "Can't open /etc/forms";
$informs = 0;
while (<FORMS>) {
    chop;
    if ($_ eq $me) {
        $informs = 1;
        last;
    }
}
```

```perl
close(FORMS);

die <<"EOM" unless $informs;
No application on file for $me—contact system administration.
EOM

# Give them something to read so they don´t get bored.

print "\nChanging password for $me.\n";

# Get passwd entry and remember all logins

$login = ´´;
open(PASSWD,"passwd") || die "Can´t open /etc/passwd";
while (<PASSWD>) {
    /^([^:]+)/;
    if ($1 eq $me) {
        ($login,$opasswd,$uid,$gid,$ogcos,$home,$shell)
            = split(/:/);
        die "You aren´t you! ($< $uid $me $x $login)\n"
            if $< && $< != $uid;        # Just being paranoid...
        $salt = substr($opasswd,0,2);

        # Canonicalize name.

        $ogcos =~ s/,.*//;
        $mynames = $ogcos;
        $mynames =~ s/\W+/ /;
        $mynames =~ s/^ //;
        $mynames =~ s/ $//;
        $mynames =~ s/ . / /g;
        $mynames =~ s/ . / /g;
        $mynames =~ s/^. //;
        $mynames =~ s/ .$//;
        $mynames =~ s/ /|/;
        $mynames = ´^$´ if $mynames eq ´´;
    }
    ++$isalogin{$1} if length($1) >= 6;
}
close(PASSWD);
die "$me isn´t in the passwd file.\n" unless $login;


# Check for shadow password file.

if ($opasswd eq ´x´ && −f ´/etc/shadow´) {
    $shadowing = 1;
    open(SHADOW,"shadow") || die "Can´t open /etc/shadow";
    while (<SHADOW>) {
        /^([^:]+)/;
        if ($1 eq $me) {
            ($login,$opasswd) = split(/:/);
            $salt = substr($opasswd,0,2);
```

```
            last;
        }
    }
    close(SHADOW);
}

# Fetch old passwords (the encrypted version).

open(PASSHIST,"passhist");
while (<PASSHIST>) {
    /^([^:]+)/;
    if ($1 eq $me) {
        ($login,$opass,$when) = split(/:/);
        $opass{$opass} = $when;
    }
}
close PASSHIST;

# Build up a subroutine that does matching on bad passwords.
# We'll use an eval to define the subroutine.

$foo = 'sub badpats {local($_) = @_;study;';
open(BADPATS,$BADPATS);
while (<BADPATS>) {
    ($badpat,$maybe) = split(/[\n\t]+/);
    ($response = $maybe) =~ s/'/\\'/ if $maybe;
    $foo .= "return '$response' if /$badpat/;\n";
}
close BADPATS;
$foo .= 'return 0;}';
eval $foo;               # Note: this defines sub badpats


# Finally we can begin.

system 'stty', '-echo';

if ($<) {
    print "Old password: ";
    chop($pass0 = <STDIN>);
    print "\n";

    # Note: we shouldn't use die while echo is off.

    do myexit(1) unless $pass0;
    if (crypt($pass0,$salt) ne $opasswd) {
        print "Sorry.\n";
        do myexit(1);
    }
}
```

```
# Pick a password

for (;;) {
    $goodenough = 0;
    until ($goodenough) {
        print "New password: ";
        chop($pass1 = <STDIN>);
        print "\n";
        do myexit(1) unless $pass1;
        print "(Checking for lousy passwords...)\n";
        $goodenough = &goodenough($pass1);

        # If longer than 8 chars, check first 8 chars alone.

        if ($goodenough && length($pass1) > 8) {
            $pass8 = substr($pass1,0,8);
            print "(Rechecking first 8 characters...)\n";
            unless ($goodenough = &goodenough($pass8)) {
                    print <<`EOM`;
(Note that only the first 8 characters count.)
EOM
            }
        }
    };

    print "Retype new passwd: ";
    chop($pass2 = <STDIN>);
    print "\n";
  last if ($pass1 eq $pass2);
    print "Password mismatch—try again.\n";
}

system `stty`, `echo`;

# Now check again for a lock on the passwd file.

if (-f `ptmp`) {
    print "Password file busy—waiting up to 60 seconds...\n";
    for ($i = 60; $i > 0; --$i) {
        sleep(1);
        print $i,`...`;
        last unless -f `ptmp`;
    }
}
die "\n/etc/passwd file busy—try again later.\n" if -f `ptmp`;

# Create the lock using link() for atomicity

open(PTMP,">ptmptmp$$")
    || die "Can't create tmp passwd file.\n";
close PTMP;
$locked = link("ptmptmp$$",`ptmp`);
unlink "ptmptmp$$";
```

```
$locked || die "/etc/passwd file busy—try again later.\n"

open(PASSWD,"passwd") || die "Can't open passwd file.\n";
open(PTMP,">ptmp") || die "Can't copy passwd file.\n";

# Encrypt using salt that's fairly random but encodes weeks
# since 1970, mod 64.

# (We perturb the week using the first two chars of $me so
# that if everyone changes their password the same week we
# still get more than 64 possible salts.)

$now = time;
($pert1, $pert2) = unpack("C2", $me);
$week = $now / (60*60*24*7) + $pert1 + $pert2 - $AGE;
$nsalt = $saltset[$week % 64] . $saltset[$now % 64];
$cryptpass = crypt($pass1,$nsalt);

# Now build new passwd file

while (<PASSWD>) {
    chop;
    ($login,$passwd,$uid,$gid,$gcos,$home,$shell) = split(/:/);
    next if $login eq '';        # remove garbage entries

    # Disable open accounts. Login ids beginning with + are
    # NIS (aka YP) indirections and aren't a problem.

    $passwd = '*' if $passwd eq '' && $login !~ /^\+/;

    # Is this the line to change?

    if ($login eq $me) {
        if ($shadowing) {
            $passwd = 'x';
        }
        else {
            $passwd = $cryptpass;
        }

        # The following code implements a password aging scheme
        # by substituting a different shell for aged or expired
        # accounts. Ordinarily this is done by another script
        # running in the middle of the night. Unless someone
        # typed "passwd -a", this script always makes a new
        # password and unexpires the account.

        if ($shell =~ /(exp|age)\.(.*)/) {
            $shell = "/bin/$2";
        }
        if ($AGE >= $EXPWEEKS) {
            if ($shell =~ m|/bin/(.*)|) {
                $sh = $1;
```

```
                    $sh = 'csh' if $sh eq '';
                    $shell = "/usr/etc/exp.$sh";
                }
            }
            elsif ($AGE >= $AGEWEEKS) {
                if ($shell =~ m|/bin/(.*)|) {
                    $sh = $1;
                    $sh = 'csh' if $sh eq '';
                    $shell = "/usr/etc/age.$sh";
                }
            }
        }
        print PTMP "$login:$passwd:$uid:$gid:$gcos:$home:$shell\n"
            || do { unlink 'ptmp'; die "Can't write ptmp: $!"; };
}
close PASSWD;
close PTMP;

# Sanity checks.

($dev,$ino,$omode,$nlink,$uid,$gid,$rdev,$osize)
    = stat('passwd');
($dev,$ino,$nmode,$nlink,$uid,$gid,$rdev,$nsize)
    = stat('ptmp');
if ($nsize < $osize - 20 || $uid) {
    unlink 'ptmp';
    die "Can't write new passwd file! ($uid)\n";
}
chmod 0644, 'ptmp';

# Do shadow password file while we still have ptmp lock.

if ($shadowing) {
    open(SHADOW,"shadow") || die "Can't open shadow file.\n";
    umask 077;
    open(STMP,">stmp") || die "Can't copy shadow file.\n";

    # Now build new shadow file.

    while (<SHADOW>) {
        chop;
        @fields = split(/:/);
        if ($fields[0] eq $me) {
            $fields[1] = $cryptpass;
        }
        print STMP join(':',@fields), "\n";
    }
    close SHADOW;
    close STMP;
    chmod 0600, 'shadow';        # probably unnecessary
    rename('shadow','shadow.old');
    chmod 0600, 'stmp';
    rename('stmp','shadow');
```

```
    }

    # Release lock by renaming ptmp.

    rename('passwd','passwd.old');
    rename('ptmp','passwd')
        || die "Couldn't install new passwd file: $!\n";

    # Now remember the old password forever (in encrypted form).

    $now = time;
    open(PASSHIST,">>passhist") || exit 1;
    print PASSHIST "$me:$opasswd:$now\n";
    close PASSHIST;
    exit 0;

    ############################################################
    #                                                          #
    # This subroutine is the whole reason for this program.  It #
    # checks for many different kinds of bad password.  We don't #
    # tell people what kind of pattern they MUST have, because  #
    # that would reduce the search space unnecessarily.        #
    #                                                          #
    # goodenough() returns 1 if password passes muster, else 0. #
    #                                                          #
    ############################################################

    sub goodenough {
        return 1 if $relax;          # Only root can bypass this.
        $pass = shift(@_);
        $mono = $pass !~ /^.+([A-Z].*[a-z]|[a-z].*[A-Z])/;
        $mono = 0 if $pass =~ /[^a-zA-Z0-9 ]/;

        $now = time;
        ($nsec,$nmin,$nhour,$nmday,$nmon,$nyear) = localtime($now);

        # Embedded null can spoof crypt routine.

        if ($pass =~ /\0/) {
            print <<"EOM";
    Please don't use the null character in your password.
    EOM
            return 0;
        }

        # Same password they just had?

        if (crypt($pass,$salt) eq $opasswd) {
            print <<"EOM";
    Please use a different password than you just had.
    EOM
            return 0;
        }
```

```perl
    # Too much like the old password?

if ($pass0 && length($pass0) == length($pass)) {
    $diff = 0;
    for ($i = length($pass)-1; $i >= 0; --$i) {
        ++$diff
            if substr($pass,$i,1) ne substr($pass0,$i,1);
    }
    if ($diff <= 2) {
        print <<"EOM";
That's too close to your old password.  Please try again.
EOM
        return 0;
    }
}

    # Too short?  Get progressively nastier.

if (length($pass) < 6) {
    print "I SAID, " if $isaid++;
    print "Please use at least 6 characters.\n";
    print "\nIf you persist I will log you out!\n\n"
        if $isaid == 3;
    print "\nI mean it!!\n\n"
        if $isaid == 4;
    print "\nThis is your last warning!!!\n\n"
        if $isaid == 5;
    if ($isaid == 6) {
        print "\nGoodbye!\n\n";
        seek(STDIN,-100,0);  # Induce indigestion in shell.
        exit 123;
    }
    return 0;
}
$isaid = 0;

    # Is it in one of the dictionaries?

if ($pass =~ /^[a-zA-Z]/) {
    ($foo = $pass) =~ y/A-Z/a-z/;

    # First check the BADPATS file.

    if ($response = do badpats($foo)) {
        print $response, "  Please try again.\n";
        return 0;
    }

    # Truncate common suffixes before searching dict.

    $shorte = '';
    $short = $pass;
    $even =
```

```
        ($short =~ s/\d+$//)
            ? " (even with a number)"
            : "";
$short =~ s/s$//;
$short =~ s/ed$// && ($shorte = "${short}e");
$short =~ s/er$// && ($shorte = "${short}e");
$short =~ s/ly$//;
$short =~ s/ing$// && ($shorte = "${short}e");
($cshort = $short) =~ y/A-Z/a-z/;

# We'll iterate over several dictionaries.

@tmp = @dicts;
while ($dict = shift(@tmp)) {
    local(*DICT) = $dict;

    # Do the lookup (dictionary order, case folded)

    &look($dict,$short,1,1);
    while (<DICT>) {
        ($cline = $_) =~ y/A-Z/a-z/;
last if substr($cline,0,length($short)) ne $cshort;
        chop;
        ($_,$response) = split(/\t+/);
        if ($pass eq $_ ||
          ($pass eq substr($_,0,8)) ||
          ($pass =~ /^$_$/i && $mono) ||
          $shorte eq $_ ||
          ($shorte =~ /^$_$/i && $mono) ||
          $short eq $_ ||
          ($short =~ /^$_$/i && $mono)) {
            if ($response) {       # Has a snide remark.
                print $response,
                    " Please try again.\n";
            }

            elsif (/^[A-Z]/) {
                if (/a$|ie$|yn$|een$|is$/) {
                    print <<"EOM";
Don't you use HER name that way!
EOM
                }
                else {
                    print <<"EOM";
That name is$also too popular.  Please try again.
EOM
                    $also = ' also';
                }
            }
            else {
                print <<"EOM";
Please avoid words in the dictionary$even.
```

```
EOM
                        }
                        return 0;
                }
            }
        }
    }

    # Now check for two word-combinations.  This gets hairy.
    # We look up everything that starts with the same first
    # two letters as the password, and if the word matches the
    # head of the password, we save the rest of the password
    # in %others to be looked up later.  Passwords which have
    # a single char before or after a word are special-cased.

    # We take pains to disallow things like "CamelAte",
    # "CameLate" and "CamElate" but allow things like
    # "CamelatE" or "CameLAte".

    # If the password is exactly 8 characters, we also have
    # to disallow passwords that consist of a word plus the
    # BEGINNING of another word, such as "CamelFle", which
    # will warn you about "camel" and "flea".

    if ($pass =~ /^.[a-zA-Z]/) {
        %others = ();
        ($cpass = $pass) =~ y/A-Z/a-z/;
        ($oneup) = $pass =~ /.[a-z]*([A-Z][a-z]*)$/;
        $cpass =~ s/ //g;
        if ($pass !~ /.+[A-Z].*[A-Z]/) {
            $others{substr($cpass,1,999)}++
                if $pass =~ /^..[a-z]+$/;
            @tmp = @dicts;
            while ($dict = shift(@tmp)) {
                local(*DICT) = $dict;
                $two = substr($cpass,0,2);
                &look($dict,$two,1,1);
                $two++;
                word: while (<DICT>) {
                    chop;
                    s/\t.*//;
                    y/A-Z/a-z/;
                    last if $_ ge $two;
                    if (index($cpass,$_) == 0) {
                        $key = substr($cpass,length($_),999);
                        next word if $key =~ /\W/;
                        $others{$key}++ unless $oneup
                        && length($oneup) != length($key);
                    }
                }
            }
        }

        @tmp = @dicts;
```

```
            while ($dict = shift(@tmp)) {
                local(*DICT) = $dict;
                foreach $key (keys(%others)) {
                    &look($dict,$key,1,1);
                    $_ = <DICT>;
                    chop;
                    s/\t.*//;
                    if ($_ eq $key
                        || length($pass) == 8 && /^$key/) {
                        $pre = substr($cpass,0,length($cpass)
                            - length($key));
                        if (length($pre) == 1) {
                            $pre = sprintf("^%c", ord($pre)^64)
                                unless $pre =~ /[ -~]/;
                            print <<"EOM";
One char "$pre" plus a word like "$_" is too easy to guess.
EOM
                            return 0;
                        }

                        print <<"EOM";
Please avoid two-word combinations like "$pre" and "$_".
Suggestion: insert a random character in one of the words,
or misspell one of them.
EOM
                        return 0;
                    }
                    elsif (length($key) == 1
                        && $pass =~ /^.[a-z]+.$/) {
                        chop($pre = $cpass);
                        $key = sprintf("^%c", ord($key)^64)
                            unless $key =~ /[ -~]/;
                        print <<"EOM";
A word like "$pre" plus one char "$key" is too easy to guess.
EOM
                        return 0;
                    }
                }
            }
        }
    }

    # Check for naughty words.   :-)

    # (Add the traditional naughty words to the list sometime
    # when your mother isn't watching.  We didn't want to
    # print them in a family-oriented book like this one...)

    if ($pass =~ /(ibm|dec|sun|at&t|nasa)/i) {
        print qq#A common substring such as "$1" makes your#
            " password too easy to guess.\n";
        return 0;
    }
```

```perl
        # Does it look like a date?

        if ($pass =~ m!^[—\d/]*$!) {
            if ($pass =~ m!^\d{3}—\d{2}—\d{4}$! ||
                $pass =~ m!^\d\d\d\d\d\d\d\d\d$!) {
                print <<"EOM";
Please don't use a Social Security Number!
EOM
                return 0;
            }
            if ($pass =~ m!^\d*/\d*/\d*$! ||
                $pass =~ m!^\d*—\d*—\d*$! ||
                $pass =~ m!$nyear$!) {
                print "Please don't use dates.\n";
                return 0;
            }
            if ($pass =~ m!^\d\d\d—?\d\d\d\d$!) {
                print "Please don't use a phone number.\n";
                return 0;
            }
            if ($pass =~ m!^\d{6,7}$!) {
                print "Please don't use a short number.\n";
                return 0;
            }
        }

        if ($mo = ($pass =~ /^[ \d]*([a-zA-Z]{3,5})[ \d]*$/) &&
           ($mo =~ /^(jan|feb|mar(ch)?|apr(il)?|may|june?)$/i ||
            $mo =~ /^(july?|aug|sept?|oct|nov|dec)$/i) ) {
            print "Please don't use dates.\n";
            return 0;
        }

        # Login id?

        if ($pass =~ /$me/i) {
            print "Please don't use your login id.\n";
            return 0;
        }

        # My own name?

        if ($pass =~ /$mynames/i) {
            print "Please don't use part of your name.\n";
            return 0;
        }

        # My host name?

        if ($pass =~ /$host/i) {
            print "Please don't use your host name.\n";
            return 0;
        }
```

```
    # License plate number?

    if ($pass =~ /^\d?[a-zA-Z][a-zA-Z][a-zA-Z]\d\d\d$/ ||
        $pass =~ /^\d\d\d[a-zA-Z][a-zA-Z][a-zA-Z]$/) {
        print "Please don't use a license number.\n";
        return 0;
    }

    # A function key?   (This pattern checks Sun-style fn keys.)

    if ($pass =~ /^\033\[\d+/) {
        print "Please don't use a function key.\n";
        return 0;
    }

    # A sequence of closely related ASCII characters?

    @ary = unpack('C*',$pass);
    $ok = 0;
    for ($i = 0; $i < $#ary; ++$i) {
        $diff = $ary[$i+1] - $ary[$i];
        $ok = 1 if $diff > 1 || $diff < -1;
    }
    if (!$ok) {
        print "Please don't use sequences.\n";
        return 0;
    }

    # A sequence of keyboard keys?

    ($foo = $pass) =~ y/A-Z/a-z/;
    $foo =~ y/qwertyuiop[]asdfghjkl;'zxcvbnm,.//a-la-ka-j/;
    $foo =~ y/!@#\$%^&*()_+|~/abcdefghijklmn/;
    $foo =~ y/-1234567890=\\`/kabcdefghijlmn/;
    @ary = unpack('C*',$foo);
    $ok = 0;
    for ($i = 0; $i < $#ary; ++$i) {
        $diff = $ary[$i+1] - $ary[$i];
        $ok = 1 if $diff > 1 || $diff < -1;
    }
    if (!$ok) {
        print "Please don't use consecutive keys.\n";
        return 0;
    }

    # Repeated patterns: ababab, abcabc, abcdabcd

    if ( $pass =~ /^(..)\1\1/
        || $pass =~ /^(...)\1/
        || $pass =~ /^(....)\1/ ) {
        print <<"EOM";
Please don't use repeated sequences of "$1".
EOM
```

```
        return 0;
    }

    # Reversed patterns: abccba abcddcba

    if ( $pass =~ /^(.)(.)(.)\3\2\1/
       || $pass =~ /^(.)(.)(.)(.)\4\3\2\1/ ) {
        print <<"EOM";
Please don't use palindromic sequences of "$1$2$3$4".
EOM
        return 0;
    }


    # Some other login name?

    if ($isalogin{$pass}) {
        print "Please don't use somebody's login id.\n";
        return 0;
    }

    # A local host name?

    if (-f "/usr/hosts/$pass") {
        print "Please don't use a local host name.\n";
        return 0;
    }

    # Reversed login id?

    $reverse = reverse $me;
    if ($pass =~ /$reverse/i) {
        print <<"EOM";
Please don't use your login id spelled backwards.
EOM
        return 0;
    }

    # Previously used?

    foreach $old (keys(%opass)) {
        if (crypt($pass,$old) eq $old) {
            $when = $opass{$old};
            $diff = $now - $when;
            ($osec,$omin,$ohour,$omday,$omon,$oyear)
                = localtime($when);
            if ($oyear != $nyear) {
                $oyear += 1900;
                print "You had that password back in $oyear.";
            }
            elsif ($omon != $nmon) {
                $omon = (January, February, March, April, May,
                    June, July, August, September, October,
```

```
                           November, December)[$omon];
                  print "You had that password back in $omon.";
              }
              elsif ($omday != $nmday) {
                  $omday .= (0,´st´,´nd´,´rd´)[$omday%10]||´th´;
                  print "You had that password on the $omday.";
              }
              else {
                  print "You had that password earlier today.";
              }
              print "  Please pick another.\n";
              return 0;
          }
      }
      1;
}

sub CLEANUP {
    system ´stty´, ´echo´;
    print "\n\nAborted.\n";
    exit 1;
}

sub myexit {
    system ´stty´, ´echo´;
    exit shift(@_);
}
```

pchelp—Lets People Gripe About Their PC

This program interacts with a possibly naive user to allow him or her to compose
a message to send to the PC support group. The script was written by someone
Larry knows who was apparently never told to avoid the **goto** statement. Never-
theless, it's a cute way to implement a state diagram. We recommend, however,
that you avoid the **goto** statement.

```
#!/usr/bin/perl

$TEMP = "/tmp/pchelp$$";

$DEST = ´pctech@technics.pyro.edu´;

$login = $ENV{´USER´} || getlogin;
$gcos = (getpwnam($login))[6];
($name, $loc, $ext) = split(/,/, $gcos);

$EDITOR = $ENV{"VISUAL"} || $ENV{"EDITOR"} || "vi";
$PAGER = $ENV{"PAGER"} || "more";

open(FORM, ">$TEMP") || die "Can´t create temp form: $!\n";
```

```
        system ´clear´;
        chop($prompt = <<´EOP´);

What do you want to do?

        a)      PC problem report
        b)      Software order request
        c)      Hardware order request
        q)      Quit

Select an option [q]:
EOP

        print $prompt;
        ($ans = substr(<STDIN>,0,1)) =~ y/A-Z/a-z/;

        {
                goto problem    if $ans eq ´a´;
                goto software   if $ans eq ´b´;
                goto hardware   if $ans eq ´c´;
                goto end;
        }

whatnow: {

        print "\nWhat now? ";

        ($ans = substr(<STDIN>,0,1)) =~ y/A-Z/a-z;

        goto mail       if $ans eq ´s´;
        goto edit       if $ans eq ´e´;
        goto end        if $ans eq ´a´;
        goto end        if $ans eq ´q´;
        goto list       if $ans eq ´l´;
        goto help;
}


help: {
        print "Options are:\n";
        print "   abort\n";
        print "   edit\n";
        print "   list\n";
        print "   send\n";

        goto whatnow;
}

problem: {

        print FORM <<EOF;

        Name: $name
```

```
            Badge #:
           Location: $loc
              Phone: $ext
       Machine type:
            Serial #:
          Property #:

   Description of problem:

   EOF

           goto edit;

   } # end problem

   software: {

           print FORM <<EOF;

               Name: $name
              Badge #:
           Location: $loc
              Phone: $ext
       Machine type:
            Serial #:
          Property #:
           Account #:

   Software requested:


   Comments:

   EOF

           goto edit;

   } # end software

   hardware: {

           print FORM <<EOF;

               Name: $name
              Badge #:
           Location: $loc
              Phone: $ext
           Account #:
          Supervisor:

   Description of hardware desired (be specific):

   EOF
```

```
            goto edit;

} # end hardware

edit: {
            close FORM;
            print "\nInvoking editor, $EDITOR...\n";
            sleep (1);
            system $EDITOR, $TEMP;
            goto whatnow;
}


mail: {
            print "\nMailing to $DEST...\n";
            system "/bin/mail $DEST </tmp/pchelp$$";
            goto end;
}


list: {
            system $PAGER, "/tmp/pchelp$$";
            goto whatnow;
}


end: {
            unlink $TEMP;
}
```

suidscript—Puts a C Wrapper Around a Setuid or Setgid Script

A program executing with the privileges of its owner or group rather than that of the user running the program is called a **setuid** or **setgid** program. On many machines, it's a security hole to make a script setuid or setgid. The **suidscript** script creates a small C program to execute a script with setuid or setgid privileges without having to set the setuid or setgid bit on the script.

This script takes a list of directories or files that you wish to process. The names must be absolute pathnames—that is, they must start with the / character. With no arguments **suidscript** will attempt to process all the local directories for this machine. The scripts to be processed must have the setuid or setgid bit set. The **suidscript** program will delete the bits from the script and transfer them to the wrapper program.

Non-superusers may process only their own files.

```perl
#!/usr/bin/perl

# Usage: suidscript [dirlist]

# Make list of filenames to do find on.

if ($#ARGV >= 0) {
    @list = @ARGV;
    foreach $name (@ARGV) {
        die "You must use absolute pathnames.\n"
            unless $name =~ m|^/|;
    }
}
else {
    open(MT,"/etc/mount|") || die "Can't run /etc/mount: $!\n";

    while (<MT>) {
        chop;
        $_ .= <MT> if length($_) < 50;
        @ary = split;
        push(@list,$ary[2]) if ($ary[0] =~ m|^/dev|);
    }
    close MT;
    $? && die "Couldn't run mount.\n";
}

die "Can't find local filesystems" unless @list;

# Find all the set-id files.

open(FIND, "find @list -xdev -type f " .
    "\\( -perm -04000 -o -perm -02000 \\) -print|");

while (<FIND>) {
    chop;
    next unless -T;                          # Not a text file.

    # Move script out of the way.

    print "Fixing ", $_, "\n";
    ($dir,$file) = m#(.*)/(.*)#;
    chdir $dir || die "Can't chdir to $dir: $!\n";
    ($dev,$ino,$mode,$nlink,$uid,$gid) = stat($file);
    die "Can't stat $_" unless $ino;
    chmod $mode & 01777, $file;       # wipe out set[ug]id bits
    rename($file,".$file");

    # Now write the wrapper.

    open(C,">.tmp$$.c") || die "Can't write C program for $_";
    $real = "$dir/.$file";
    print C <<EOW;
```

```
main(argc,argv)
int argc;
char **argv;
{
    execv("$real",argv);
}
EOW
    close C;

    # Now compile the wrapper.

    system '/bin/cc', ".tmp$$.c", '-o', $file;
    die "Can't compile new $_" if $?;

    # Straighten out loose ends.

    chown $uid, $gid, $file;
    chmod $mode, $file;
    unlink ".tmp$$.c";
    chdir '/';
}
```

cleanup—News Expiration

If you run B news on your system, you know that it can be difficult to keep all your news spool directories trimmed down to a reasonable size, particularly if you want to expire articles at different times in different newsgroups. Here is a little script to do this efficiently. It doesn't update your active file—you'll need to run something like **expire** **−u** occasionally to do that.

This program contains an example of recursive subroutine calls. It also makes use of the directory reading routines, and does a **chdir** to each directory it visits for maximum efficiency. Note also how the newsgroup name can match more than one pattern, so that later patterns can override the default timeout supplied by a later pattern.

```
#!/usr/bin/perl

(chdir '/usr/spool/news') || die "Can't cd to /usr/spool/news";
$now = time;
$| = 1;

($dev,$ino,$mode,$nlink) = stat('.');

&dodir('.',$nlink);

exit 0;

##############################################################
```

```
sub dodir {
    local($dir,$nlink) = @_;
    local($dev,$ino,$mode,$time,$cutoff);

    $dir =~ s#^\./##;

    # Determine number of days to keep articles in group.

    $time = 14;
    $time = 3   if $dir =~ /^(junk|control)/;
    $time = 8   if $dir =~ /^talk/;
    $time = 8   if $dir =~ /^rec/;
    $time = 28  if $dir =~ /^comp/;
    $time = 10  if $dir =~ /^sci/;
    $time = 50  if $dir =~ /^comp\.sources\.(unix|misc|bugs)/;
    $time = 50  if $dir =~ /^comp\.sys\.(sun|pyramid|amiga)/;
    $time = 50  if $dir =~ /^comp\.windows\.x/;
    $time = 50  if $dir =~ /^comp\.unix\.wizards/;
    $time = 60  if $dir =~ /^comp\.lang\.perl/;
    $time = 50  if $dir =~ /^comp\.bugs/;
    $time = 50  if $dir =~ /^comp\.sources\.bugs/;
    $time = 365 if $dir =~ /^proj/;
    $cutoff = $now - $time * (60 * 60 * 24);

    # Get all the filenames in current directory handy.
    # We use readdir() instead of <*> because it doesn't start
    # a subshell and won't blow up on huge directories.

    opendir(DIR,'.') || die "Can't open $dir";
    local(@filenames) = readdir(DIR);
    closedir(DIR);

    # Separate the sheep from the goats.

    local(@subdirs);
    local(@articles);
    for (@filenames) {
        if (/^\d+$/) {
            push(@articles,$_); # Possibly a lie, but avoid stat.
        }
        else {
            push(@subdirs,$_);
        }
    }

    # Look for articles to expire.

    if ($#articles >= 0) {
        @articles = sort bynumber @articles;

        # Now the tricksy part.  Since the @articles array is
        # now in age order, we binary search for articles to
        # expire.  At the end of this loop, $min should be
```

```perl
        # first non-expiring article

        $max = $#articles;
        $min = 0;
        while ($max - $min > 0) {
            $mid = int(($max + $min) / 2);
            ($dev,$ino,$mode,$nl,$uid,$gid,$rdev,$size,$atime,
                $mtime,$ctime) = stat($articles[$mid]);
            if ($dev == 0) {
                $min = -1;
                print STDERR "$dir changed-skipping!\n";
            }
            elsif (-d _) {
                push(@subdirs, $mid);     # Oops, a directory.
                $min = -1;                # Punt this time.
            }
            elsif ($mtime >= $cutoff) { # $mid is not expiring
                $max = $mid;
            }
            else {                        # $mid is expiring
                $min = $mid + 1;
            }
        }

        # Zap any expired articles.

        if ($min > 0) {
            print "$dir: $articles[0] .. $articles[$min-1]\n";
            unlink @articles[ 0 .. $min-1 ];
        }
        else {
            print "$dir: (none)\n";
        }
    }
    if ($nlink != 2) {            # This dir has subdirectories.
        for (@subdirs) {
            next if $_ eq '.';
            next if $_ eq '..';
            $name = "$dir/$_";

            ($dev,$ino,$mode,$nlink) = stat($_);
            next unless -d _;

            chdir $_ || die "Can't cd to $name";
            &dodir($name,$nlink);
            chdir '..';
        }
    }
}

sub bynumber {
    $a <=> $b;
}
```

fixscripts—Translates Files to Know About Scripts Directory

Large installations with multiple architectures are difficult to manage. Keeping up-to-date packages compiled and installed with different compilers and different executable formats on different machines is a real headache. Even portable scripts are a bit of a pain because you have to copy them into each architecture's "bin" directory.

Recently we've discovered something that helps a lot, at least for anything that can be written as a script. You can make a single directory on a server machine and mount it everywhere using NFS (or some equivalent networked filesystem). Into that directory you put only scripts that work on every architecture. (These can be either shell scripts or Perl scripts.) Once you've added the directory to everyone's **PATH** environment variable, you never have to copy those particular files around again.

The trick, of course, is to modify everyone's "dot" files to recognize the new directory. The **fixscripts** script below looks for references to /usr/local/bin in the files specified on the command line, and fixes them to refer to the scripts directory as necessary. It would typically be run on all the "dot" files in each person's login directory. It fixes files in place, with a **.bak** backup. Note that one of the heuristics assumes that you've already moved scripts from your /usr/local/bin into your scripts directory, so that **suidscript** can decide whether to translate any direct references involving /usr/local/bin/whatever to point to the scripts directory instead.

You might be interested to know that many of the scripts in this chapter live in the /u/scripts directory at Larry's installation. This is in a top-level user filesystem, so it's mounted everywhere already. You may wish to put your scripts elsewhere, of course. That's fine, as long as you're consistent. See also the **wrapman** program to help you manage the manpages for these scripts.

Note the heavy use of the **o** modifier ("compile once") on pattern matches and substitutions, since the variables that are interpolated into patterns are all configuration constants.

```
#!/usr/bin/perl

die "Usage: fixscripts [files]\n" unless @ARGV;

# Configuration parameters.

$BIN = '/usr/local/bin';
$SCRIPTS = '/u/scripts';
$BAK = 'bak';

# Process each file.
```

```
foreach $file (@ARGV) {
    unless (-T $file) {
        warn "Can't process binary file: $file\n";
        next;
    }
    open(FILE, $file)
        || do { warn "Can't open $file: $!\n"; next; };

    # Now process the file.

    $contents = '';
    $changed = 0;
    while (<FILE>) {
        if (m#$BIN#o) {
            print STDERR "<$file:\t",$_;
            $changed++;

            if (m#:/#o) {                         # a $path
                s#$BIN#$BIN:$SCRIPTS#o;
            }
            elsif (m# /usr# && /set\s/) {         # a $PATH
                s#$BIN([^/])#$BIN $SCRIPTS$1#o;
            }
            else {

                # Try substitutions until one works.

                    s#$BIN/(\w+)#
                      -f "$SCRIPTS/$1" ?
                      "$SCRIPTS/$1" :
                      "$BIN/$1"#oeg            # a program
                ||
                    s# $BIN# $BIN $SCRIPTS#o    # $PATH?
                ||
                    s#$BIN #$BIN $SCRIPTS #o    # $PATH?
                ||
                    s#:$BIN#:$BIN:$SCRIPTS#o    # $path?
                ||
                    s#$BIN:#$BIN:$SCRIPTS:#o    # $path?
                ;
            }
            print STDERR ">$file:\t",$_;
        }
        $contents .= $_;
    }
    close FILE;

    if ($changed) {
        rename($file,"$file.$BAK") ||
                do { warn "Can't rename $file: $!\n"; next; };
        open(FILE, ">$file") ||
                do { warn "Can't make $file: $!\n"; next; };
```

```
        print FILE $contents;
        close FILE;
    }
}
```

Filename Manipulation

Directories contain filenames, and filenames are just strings. So there's no reason you can't process filenames as easily as text files.

rename—Renames Multiple Files

There are many ways of renaming multiple files under UNIX. Most of these ways are kludges. They force you to use ad hoc shell variable modifiers or multiple processes. With the **rename** script below, you can rename files according to the rule specified as the first argument. The argument is simply a Perl expression that is expected to modify the **$_** string in Perl for at least some of the filenames specified. Thus you can rename files using the very same **s///** notation you're already familiar with. If a given filename is not modified by the expression, it will not be renamed. If no filenames are given on the command line, filenames will be read via standard input.

For example, to rename all files matching ***.bak** to strip the extension, you might say:

```
rename ´s/\.bak$//´ *.bak
```

But you're not limited to simple substitutions—you have at your disposal the full expressive power of Perl. To add those extensions back on, for instance, say this:

```
rename ´$_ .= ".bak"´ *
```

or even:

```
rename ´s/$/.bak/´ *
```

To translate uppercase names to lower, you'd use:

```
rename ´tr/A-Z/a-z/´ *
```

And how about these?

```
rename ´s/foo/bar/; $_ = $was if -e´ *foo*

find . -print | rename ´s/readme/README/i´
```

```
find . —print | rename 's/$/.old/ if —M $_ > 0.5'

find . —name '*,v' —print | \
   rename 's#(.*)/#$1/RCS/#, $x{$1}++ || mkdir("$1/RCS", 0777)'
```

Note the use of the $@ variable below to propagate any syntax error back to the user.

```
#!/usr/bin/perl

# Usage: rename perlexpr [files]

($op = shift) || die "Usage: rename perlexpr [filenames]\n";
if (!@ARGV) {
    @ARGV = <STDIN>;
    chop(@ARGV);
}
for (@ARGV) {
    $was = $_;
    eval $op;
    die $@ if $@;
    rename($was,$_) unless $was eq $_;
}
```

relink—Relinks Multiple Symbolic Links

Like the **rename** program above, the **relink** program relinks the symbolic links given according to the rule specified as the first argument. The argument is a Perl expression that is expected to modify the $_ string in Perl for at least some of the names specified. For each symbolic link named on the command line, the Perl expression will be executed on the contents of the symbolic link with that name. If a given symbolic link's contents is not modified by the expression, it will not be changed. If a name given on the command line is not a symbolic link, it will be ignored. If no names are given on the command line, names will be read via standard input.

For example, to relink all symbolic links in the current directory pointing to somewhere in **X11R3** so that they point to **X11R4**, you might say:

```
relink 's/X11R3/X11R4/' *
```

To change all occurrences of links in the system from */usr/spool* to */var/spool*, you'd say:

```
find / —type l —print | relink 's#^/usr/spool#/var/spool#'
```

And here's the program:

```perl
#!/usr/bin/perl

# Usage: relink perlexpr [symlinknames]

($op = shift) || die "Usage: relink perlexpr [filenames]\n";

if (!@ARGV) {
    @ARGV = <STDIN>;
    chop(@ARGV);
}

for (@ARGV) {
    $name = $_;
    $_ = readlink($_);
    next unless defined $_;
    $was = $_;
    eval $op;
    die $@ if $@;
    if ($was ne $_) {
        unlink($name);
        symlink($_, $name);
    }
}
```

sl—Show Translation of Symbolic Link to Actual Filename

The **sl** program traverses the pathnames supplied on the command line, and for each one, tells you if it had to follow any symbolic links to find the actual filename. Symbolic links to absolute pathnames start over at the left margin. Symbolic links to relative pathnames are aligned vertically with the path element they replace. For example:

```
$ sl /usr/lib/libXw.a

/usr/lib/libXw.a:
/usr/lib/libXw.a -> /usr/lib/X11/libXw.a
/usr/lib/X11 -> /X11/lib
/X11 -> /usr/local/X11R4
/usr/local/X11R4/lib/libXw.a

$ sl /bin/rnews

/bin -> /usr/bin
/usr/bin/rnews -> /usr/lib/news/rnews
/usr/lib/news -> ../local/lib/news
    local/lib/news/rnews -> inews
                    inews
```

This program is a good example of the use of arrays to process pathnames.

```
#!/usr/bin/perl

# Usage: sl [filenames]

die "Usage: sl [filenames]\n" unless @ARGV;

# Preliminaries.

$| = 1;
chop($cwd = `pwd`) || die "Can't find current directory: $!\n"
    if @ARGV > 1;
print "\n";

# Do each name.

foreach $name (@ARGV) {
    @indent = ();
    print "$name:\n";
    @path = split(m;/;, $name);

    # Make an absolute path relative to /.

    if (@path && $path[0] eq '') {
        chdir '/';
        shift @path;
        print '/';
        $indent = 1;
    }

    # Now follow the subdirectories and links.

    while (@path) {
        $elem = shift @path;
        $new = readlink($elem);
        if (defined $new) {      # A symbolic link.
            print "$elem -> $new\n";
            $new =~ s!^\./!!;

            # Prepend symbolic link to rest of path.

            unshift(@path,split(m;/;, $new));

            # Deal with special cases.

            if (@path && $path[0] eq '') {

                # Absolute path starts over.

                chdir '/';
                shift @path;
                print '/';
```

```
              $indent = 1;
              @indents = ( );
              next;
        }


        # Back up the tree as necessary.

        while (@indents && $path[0] eq '..') {
              $indent = pop(@indents);
              chdir '..'
                  || die "\n\nCan't cd to ..: $!\n";
              shift @path;
        }

        print "\t" x ($indent / 8), ' ' x ($indent % 8);
    }
    else {                    # An ordinary directory.
        print $elem;
        push(@indents,$indent);
        $indent += length($elem) + 1;
        if (@path) {
              print '/';
              chdir $elem
                  || die "\n\nCan't cd to $elem: $!\n";
        }
    }
}
print "\n\n";
$indent = 0;
chdir $cwd || die "Can't cd back: $!\n" if $cwd ne '';
}
```

Indir—Links Identical Files Between Directories

This program is useful for saving disk space, particularly when you store multiple
version of a software package in parallel directories. It compares the files
between the two specified directories, and any file that is identical in the two
directories is turned into one file with a hard link in each directory. This program
won't run unless your operating system supports hard links like UNIX does.

Note the code that does the file comparisons. We could have simply called the
cmp(1) program, but that would entail starting up a process on nearly every file.
The code is fairly straightforward, however—we simply read a chunk from each
file until the chunks don't compare or we run out of file. We've already compared
the file sizes, so we know that when the old file peters out, the new one will, too.

```perl
#!/usr/bin/perl
#
# Usage: lndir old-dir new-dir
#
# Compare two directories, and link all identical files.

# Check args && fetch names.

(((($olddir,$newdir) = @ARGV) == 2 && -d $olddir && -d $newdir)
    || die "Usage: $0 old-dir new-dir\n";

# Get all files in the new dir.

open(FIND,"find $newdir -type f -print|");

$|=1;

FILE: while ($new = <FIND>) {
    chop $new;
    ($file = $new) =~ s#^$newdir/##o
        || die "find said $new?\n";
    $old = "$olddir/$file";

    # Get stat info for both files.

    ($ndev,$nino,$nmode,$nnlink,$nuid,$ngid,$nrdev,$nsize,
      $natime,$nmtime,$nctime,$nblksize,$nblocks)
          = stat($new);

    unless ($nino) {
        print "$new: $!\n";
        next FILE;
    }

    unless (-f _) {
        warn "$new is not a plain file\n";
        next FILE;
    }

    ($odev,$oino,$omode,$onlink,$ouid,$ogid,$ordev,$osize,
      $oatime,$omtime,$octime,$oblksize,$oblocks)
          = stat($old);

    unless ($oino) {
        next FILE;
    }

    unless (-f _) {
        warn "$old is not a plain file\n";
        next FILE;
    }
```

```
# Quick check on size and mode.

if ($nsize != $osize) {
    print "$file differs\n";
    next FILE;
}

if ($nmode != $omode) {
    print "$file mode differs\n";
    next FILE;
}

# Already linked?   (Perhaps symbolically?)
# Compare dev/inode numbers.

if ($ndev == $odev && $nino == $oino) {
    print "$file already linked\n";
    next FILE;
}

# Now compare the two files.

unless (open(NEW,"$new")) {
    print "$new: $!\n";
    next FILE;
}
unless (open(OLD,"$old")) {
    print "$old: $!\n";
    next FILE;
}
$blksize = $nblksize || 8192;
while (read(OLD,$obuf,$blksize)) {
    read(NEW,$nbuf,$blksize);
    if ($obuf ne $nbuf) {
        print "$file differs\n";
        next FILE;
    }
}

# Okay, let's link.

if (unlink($new) && link($old, $new)) {
    print "$file linked to $old\n";
    next FILE;
}

print "$file: $!\n";
}
```

Text Manipulation Tools

Perl is a natural for dealing with documentation and program text. In particular, the choice of quoting mechanisms in Perl allows you to avoid the *backslashitis* that often afflicts other languages.

wrapman—Turns a Perl Script Into Its Own Manual Page

Earlier we discussed the strategy of keeping all your portable scripts in a single directory mounted across all your architectures. This makes it easy to keep your scripts up-to-date, but it doesn't necessarily do the same for your manual pages. The difficulty is that a script doesn't have a source directory like an ordinary compiled package, so there's no obvious place to keep the master copy of the manual page. You might have a manual page for a script duplicated on this machine and that, but which copy is the most recent?

The **wrapman** program provides a way out of this dilemma. It puts magical incantations into your Perl script so that it is both a Perl script *and* its own manual page. This means that the manual page will never, ever get separated from the executable. Whenever you change the script, you can change the manpage at the same time, and know that the new documentation will be available wherever the script is.

Of course, you still have to take some action on each machine so that the *man* program can find the manual page, but once you've done it, you don't have to do it again. You can either add a symbolic link into your man directories pointing back to the executable script (see the **wrapinst** program below), or add the scripts directory to everyone's **MANPATH** environment variable (if all your various man programs support **MANPATH**—if they don't, get Tom Christiansen's *man* program written in, you guessed it, Perl, and put it into your scripts directory).

See the **wrapinst** program later on for an example of a wrapped script. Most of the scripts in this chapter (including **wrapman**) are wrapped in real life, but because of space limitations we've only wrapped the **wrapinst** script.

Including the manual page as part of the script has little influence on the script's efficiency—the Perl tokener stops reading the script as soon as it sees the __END__ token. Likewise, when processing the file as a manual page, *nroff* skips the script part rapidly because it's enclosed in "ignore" directives. The biggest problem with **wrapman** is that it doesn't write the description for you.

```
#!/usr/bin/perl

# Usage: wrapman [files]

($sec,$min,$hour,$mday,$mon,$year,$wday,$yday,$isdst)
    = localtime(time);
$month = (January,February,March,April,May,June,
    July,August,September,October,November,December)[$mon];

$user = $ENV{'USER'} || $ENV{'LOGNAME'} || (getpwuid($<))[0];
$fullname = (getpwnam($user))[6];
$fullname =~ s/.*-\s*(.*)\(.*//;
$fullname =~ s/,.*//;


substr($user,0,1) =~ tr/a-z/A-Z/;
$fullname =~ s/&/$user/;          # Propagate the & abomination.

$log = '$' . 'Log' . '$';
$header = '$' . 'Header' . '$';

foreach $file (@ARGV) {

    # Generate various strings for the manual page.

    ($prog = $file) =~ s/\.\w+$//;
    ($PROG = $prog) =~ y/a-z/A-Z/;
    $Prog = $prog; substr($Prog,0,1) =~ y/a-z/A-Z/;

    # See if we really want to wrap this file.

    open(IN,$file) || next;
    $/ = "\n";
    $line1 = <IN>;
    next unless $line1 =~ /perl/;
    $line1 .= <IN> if $line1 =~ /eval/;
    $line1 .= <IN> if $line1 =~ /argv/;
    $line2 = <IN>;
    next if $line2 eq "'di';\n";

    # Pull the old switcheroo.

    ($dev,$ino,$mode) = stat IN;
    print STDERR "Wrapping $file\n";
    rename($file,"$file.bak");
    open(OUT,">$file");
    chmod $mode, $file;

    # Spit out the new script.

    print OUT $line1;
    print OUT <<EOF;
'di';
```

```
´ig00´;
#
# $header
#
# $log
EOF

    # Copy entire script.

    undef $/;
    $_ = <IN>;
    print OUT $line2, $_;

    # Now put the transition from Perl to nroff.
    #    (We prefix the .00 below with $null in case the wrapman
    #    program is itself wrapped.)

    print OUT <<EOF;
#############################################################

    # These next few lines are legal in both Perl and nroff.

$null.00;                         # finish .ig

´di          \\" finish diversion—previous line must be blank
.nr nl 0-1   \\" fake up transition to first page again
.nr % 0         \\" start at page 1
´; __END__ ##### From here on it´s a standard manual page #####

.TH $PROG 1 "$month $mday, 19$year"
.AT 3
.SH NAME
$prog \\- whatever
.SH SYNOPSIS
.B $prog [options] [files]
.SH DESCRIPTION
.I $Prog
does whatever.
.SH ENVIRONMENT
No environment variables are used.
.SH FILES
None.
.SH AUTHOR
$fullname
.SH "SEE ALSO"

.SH DIAGNOSTICS

.SH BUGS

EOF
```

```
            close IN;
            close OUT;
        }
```

wrapinst—Installs Manual Pages Produced by Running wrapman

wrapinst attempts to make a symbolic link in /usr/man/manl (or some equivalent spot) for each specified file that happens to have been processed by **wrapman**. We present it here as it would look after itself having **wrapman** run upon it.

```
#!/usr/bin/perl
'di';
'ig00';
#
# $Header: /work/nutshell/perl/RCS/ch06,v 1.6 91/06/28 10:23:34 ellie Exp Locker: kramer $
#
# $Log:      ch06,v $
# Revision 1.6  91/06/28  10:23:34  ellie
# index stuff
#
# Revision 1.5  91/06/26  14:54:50  kramer
# fixed a pg brk and footnote numbers
#
# Revision 1.4  91/06/25  11:35:31  kramer
# did copyedits
#
# Revision 1.3  91/06/21  14:08:30  ellie
# index stuff
#
# Revision 1.2  91/06/19  15:07:21  kramer
# check in new version
#

# Usage: wrapinst [files]

        -d ($manl = '/usr/man/manl')              # (man "ell")
          || -d ($manl = '/usr/local/man/manl')   # (man "one")
          || -d ($manl = '/usr/man/manl')         # (man "one")
          || die "Can't find man directory.\n";

        chop($pwd = `pwd`);
        foreach $file (@ARGV) {
            $longfile = ($file =~ m#^/#) ? $file : "$pwd/$file";
            open(FILE,$longfile)
                || (warn("Can't open $file: $!\n"), next);
            <FILE>;
            $_ = <FILE>;
            close FILE;
            if ($_ ne "'di';\n") {
                warn "$file not its own manpage\n";
```

```
        next;
    }
    symlink($longfile, "$manl/$file.l") ||
        warn "$file: can´t make symlink: $!\n";
}
###############################################################

    # These next few lines are legal in both Perl and nroff.

.00;                # finish .ig

´di            \" finish diversion—previous line must be blank
.nr nl 0—1     \" fake up transition to first page again
.nr % 0        \" start at page 1
´; __END__ ##### From here on it´s a standard manual page #####

.TH WRAPINST 1 "December 25, 1990"
.AT 3
.SH NAME
wrapinst \— installs manual pages produced by running wrapman
.SH SYNOPSIS
.B wrapinst [files]
.SH DESCRIPTION
.I Wrapman
attempts to make a symbolic link in /usr/man/manl or some
equivalent directory for each specified file that happens
to have been processed by the wrapman program (which turns
a Perl script into its own manual page).
.SH ENVIRONMENT
No environment variables are used.
.SH FILES
None.
.SH AUTHOR
Larry Wall
.SH "SEE ALSO"
wrapman(l)
.SH DIAGNOSTICS
Complains if it can´t make the symbolic links.
.SH BUGS
It would be nice if we didn´t have to run this at all.
```

reform—Reformats Paragraphs of Text

The **reform** program reformats paragraphs in any of several ways. Input is expected to come in as paragraphs separated by blank lines. Setting $/ to ´´ tells Perl to read its input a paragraph at a time rather than a line at a time.

By specifying switches, the user may change the default margins, indents, and paragraph spacing. For example, saying:

```
reform -l10 -i5 -r75 -s0
```

will turn input block format paragraphs into indented paragraphs with a one-inch margin on 8 1/2-inch wide paper.

Ordinarily a switch parser would have separate lines to handle each different switch, but in this case all our switches are of the same general form, so we've used a single pattern, /^-(l|r|i|s)(\d+)/, to parse them all. This sets **$1** equal to one of 'l', 'r', 'i' or 's', and sets **$2** equal to the number specified after the switch. If the pattern matches, we do:

```
eval "\$$1 = \$2", next
```

which evaluates a string such as "**$s = $2**" and then bypasses the error message at the bottom of the loop by starting the next iteration of the while loop.

We've also used **eval** to generate the format that we'll use to actually do the paragraph formatting for us, since we don't know what the format will be until we've parsed the switches. (See the section "Formats" in Chapter 3 for information on formats of a more conventional nature.) This format is defined when the **eval** statement compiles the string containing the format declaration, and since the format is a declaration, it stays around after the **eval** finishes. (Note that the **eval** actually does nothing when it runs, since no statements were executed. You can use a similar trick to define subroutines at runtime.)

The string containing the format is in a special kind of quote called a "here-document." Users of shells will be familiar with the notation. The quoted string or identifier after the **<<** symbol indicates the final delimiter of the string, and the double quotes around the delimiter say that the whole text is to be treated as if it were a double-quoted string. Otherwise, our **$LEFT, $RIGHT** (and so on) variables would not be interpolated correctly. Note that we must put backslashes on the dollar signs we *don't* want interpreted. See the section "Literals and Interpreted Literals" in Chapter 3 for more on here-documents.

The final while loop does the actual work of reading in each paragraph and reformatting it. The format we're using to do filled text prefers to have a simple string of words separated by the number of spaces desired. So we have several substitution commands before the **write** statement to tweak any sequence of whitespace characters into either one or two space characters, depending on whether it looks like an ordinary space or the space at the end of a sentence.

```
#!/usr/bin/perl

Usage: reform [-lNUM] [-rNUM] [-iNUM] [-sNUM] [files]

# Set default values for left margin, right margin, indent
# and paragraph spacing.
```

```perl
$l = 0;
$r = 0;
$i = 0;
$s = 1;

# Process any switches.

while ($ARGV[0] =~ /^-/) {
    $_ = shift;
    /^-(l|r|i|s)(\d+)/ && (eval "\$$1 = \$2", next);
    die "Unrecognized switch: $_\n";
}

# Calculate format strings.

$r = $l + 65 unless $r;
$r -= $l;                         # make $r relative to $l
die "Margins too close\n" if $l + $i >= $r;

$LEFT = ' ' x $l;
$INDENT = ' ' x $i;
$RIGHT1 = '^^' . '<' x ($r - 1 - $i);
$RIGHT2 = '^^' . '<' x ($r - 1);
$SPACING = "\n" x $s;

# Define a format at run time.

$form = <<"End of Format Definition";
format STDOUT =
$LEFT$INDENT$RIGHT1
\$_
$LEFT$RIGHT2~~
\$_
$SPACING.
End of Format Definition

print $form if $debugging;
eval $form;

# Set paragraph mode on input.

$/ = '';

# For each paragraph...

while (<>) {
    s/\s+/ /g;                     # Canonicalize whitespace.
    s/ $//;                        # Trim final space.
    s/([a-z0-9][.!?][)'"]*) /$1  /g;   # Fix sentence ends.
    write;                         # Spit out new paragraph.
}
```

travesty—Writes a Parody of its Input

The **travesty** program prints out a travesty of your input text by analyzing the frequency of three-word collocations and then printing random text based on those frequencies. Word frequencies are stored in entries in the **%lookup** array. Each entry is a string composed of packed short integers, each of which in turn is the index of a word in the **@word** array.

It's difficult to appreciate until you've seen it in action. Here's a travesty of the Perl manual page:

```
A subroutine may not make much sense to you.  It's here at the
end) and does certain optimizations with the package name is
omitted, format "STDOUT" is defined. FORMLIST consists of a
loop modifier, executes the second way hides the main point
isn't whether the user typed -v or not.  References to scalar
variables, normal array values, and anything after it will not
look for a script whether the lvalue EXPR has a real value or
not. LIST operators have the newline is printed.  The special
field @* can be put anywhere a command to which output is to
include subroutines from a subroutine but rather the name of
the primary sequence of characters sent, or the right side of
the following: Semicolons are required on ifs and whiles.
Variables begin with '$', even when $* is 0.  Default is 0,
exits with 255. Equivalent examples: die "Can't open $foo: $!";
is better than verbose && print "Starting analysis" if
$verbose; is better than verbose && print "Starting analysis";
since the language has more built-in functionality, it has to
rely less upon external (and possibly untrustworthy) programs
to accomplish its purposes.
```

Right.

```perl
#!/usr/bin/perl

# Usage: travesty [files]

# First analyze the input.

while (<>) {

    # Handle article headers and ">>>" quotes.

    next if /^\./;
    next if /^From / .. /^$/;
    next if /^Path: / .. /^$/;
    s/^\W+//;

    # Do each word.

    push(@ary,split(' '));
    while ($#ary > 1) {
```

```perl
            $a = $p;
            $p = $n;
            $w = shift(@ary);
            $n = $num{$w};
            if ($n eq '') {
                push(@word,$w);
                $n = pack('S',$#word);
                $num{$w} = $n;
            }
            $lookup{$a . $p} .= $n;
        }
    }


# Now spew out the words, based on the frequencies.  If there
# is more than one possibility to choose from, choose one
# randomly.

for (;;) {
    $n = $lookup{$a . $p};
    ($foo,$n) = each(lookup) if $n eq '';        # A bootstrap.
    $n = substr($n,int(rand(length($n))) & 0177776,2);
    $a = $p;
    $p = $n;
    ($w) = unpack('S',$n);
    $w = $word[$w];


    # See if word fits on line.

    $col += length($w) + 1;
    if ($col >= 65) {
        $col = 0;
        print "\n";
    }
    else {
        print ' ';
    }
    print $w;

    # Paragraph every 10 sentences or so.

    if ($w =~ /\.$/) {
        if (rand() < .1) {
            print "\n";
            $col = 80;
        }
    }
}
```

Processes

While you're running a program, it's called a **process**. With a compiled program such as a C program, the process is executing the native machine code that the compiler translated the program into. With an interpreted program such as a Perl program, the process is executing the machine code of the Perl interpreter, a C program that just happens to be called *perl*. That program is merely reading your Perl script to decide what to do next. However, for most purposes, you can pretend that your script is being run directly.

In addition to the program it's running, a process has a number of attributes, such as a unique process number, the real and effective user and group membership, various accumulated CPU times, command-line arguments, and environment variables.

id—Print User and Group IDs of Current Shell Process

If you're at an installation with multiple architectures, you've run into the problem of commands that exist on one machine but not on another. Here's a program that falls in that category. By placing this Perl script in your scripts directory, you can have the command everywhere, and your frustration level will be reduced thereby. (In other words, this is a freely redistributable reimplementation of a semi-standard UNIX utility that not all UNIX vendors make available for their particular port.)

This *id* command prints out the ownership and group membership attributes of the currently running Perl process, but since these things are inherited from the shell that started the Perl process, the real purpose is to print out the attributes of the parent shell process.

```
#!/usr/bin/perl

# Usage: id

sub u { local($name) = getpwuid($_[0]); $name && "($name)";}
sub g { local($name) = getgrgid($_[0]); $name && "($name)";}
sub bynum { $a <=> $b; }

print "uid=$<", &u($<);
print " gid=", $(+0, &g($();
print " euid=$>", &u($>) if $> != $<;
print " egid=", $)+0, &g($)) if $) != $(;
@groups=split(´ ´, $(); shift(@groups);
@groups && print " groups=",
```

```
        join(´,´, sort bynum grep(($_ .= &g($_)) || 1, @groups));
    print "\n";
```

zap—Interactively Kill Processes Matching Pattern

The system's *ps* program can list many of the attributes of a process for you, and it's easy for Perl to use the output of *ps* for various purposes. Not only is it easy, but it's considered good form not to re-invent the wheelbarrow every time you clean up after the parade. If it's not too much hassle, you go and get the wheelbarrow out of the shed. (If it *is* too much hassle, maybe you need a new wheelbarrow after all.)

The *zap* program runs the *ps* program for you and selects those processes which match the pattern you supply. (The pattern can match anything on the line that *ps* prints out, not just the command.) It then asks you whether you want to kill each of the selected processes. Type "y" or "Y" to kill the process, anything else to leave it alone. Type "q" or "Q" to quit. The terminal is put into single-character input mode, so you don't have to type a return.

You may optionally send a different signal specified by command-line switch, in either numeric (**–1**) or string (**–HUP**) form.

```perl
#!/usr/bin/perl

# Usage: zap [—signal] pattern

# Configuration parameters.

$sig = ´TERM´;

$BSD = —f ´/vmunix´;
$pscmd = $BSD ? "ps —auxww" : "ps —ef";

open(TTYIN, "</dev/tty") || die "can´t read /dev/tty: $!";
open(TTYOUT, ">/dev/tty") || die "can´t write /dev/tty: $!";
select(TTYOUT);
$| = 1;
select(STDOUT);
$SIG{´INT´} = ´cleanup´;

if ($#ARGV >= $[ && $ARGV[0] =~ /^—/) {
    if ($ARGV[0] =~ /—(\w+)$/) {
        $sig = $1;
    } else {
        print STDERR "$0: illegal argument $ARGV[0] ignored\n";
    }
    shift;
}
```

```
if ($BSD) {
    system "stty cbreak </dev/tty >/dev/tty 2>&1";
}
else {
    system "stty", ´cbreak´,
    system "stty", ´eol´, ´^A´;
}

open(PS, "$pscmd|") || die "can´t run $pscmd: $!";
$title = <PS>;
print TTYOUT $title;

# Catch any errors with eval.  A bad pattern, for instance.

eval <<´EOF´;
while ($cand = <PS>) {
    chop($cand);
    ($user, $pid) = split(´ ´, $cand);
    next if $pid == $$;
    $found = !@ARGV;
    foreach $pat (@ARGV) {
        $found = 1 if $cand =~ $pat;
    }
    next if (!$found);
    print TTYOUT "$cand? ";
    read(TTYIN, $ans, 1);
    print TTYOUT "\n" if ($ans ne "\n");
    if ($ans =~ /^y/i) { kill $sig, $pid; }
    if ($ans =~ /^q/i) { last; }
}
EOF
&cleanup;

sub cleanup {
    if ($BSD) {
        system "stty -cbreak </dev/tty >/dev/tty 2>&1";
    }
    else {
        system "stty", ´icanon´;
        system "stty", ´eol´, ´^@´;
    }
    print "\n";
    exit;
}
```

dotime—Runs a Benchmark Program Several Times

Sometimes, when you are looking at two different ways of computing something, you need to decide between something that takes 2 milliseconds and something that takes 3 milliseconds. That may not seem like much, but when you're doing it thousands of times, it can really add up. Unfortunately, the difference in time between 2 and 3 milliseconds can be masked by things such as having fallen on just the wrong side of a clock tick when the timing was begun or ended, or having a particular page in memory as opposed to out in the swap space or on some NFS disk somewhere. So, the only *real* way to figure out if the method is longer or shorter is to run it like it will eventually be run: tens, hundreds, even thousands of times.

This program allows you to do just that. You specify a command line, and the number of times to run that command. After executing the command that many times, the average real, user, and system times are reported. It probably doesn't make any sense to do multiple runs of a command like:

```
rm foo/*
```

that change the state of the system after a run, so you do have to use your head a bit.

```perl
#!/usr/bin/perl

# Usage: dotime repeat command

die "Usage: $0 <repeat> <command>\n" if @ARGV < 2;

$repeat = shift(@ARGV);
die "invalid repeat: $repeat, stopped"
  unless (($repeat > 0) && ($repeat < 999));

# Init our accumulators.

$tt_real = $tt_user = $tt_sys = 0;
@t_real  = @t_user = @t_sys  = ();

# Now do the timing runs.

print qq/Running "@ARGV" /;
$| = 1;

for $pass (1 .. $repeat) {

    print "$pass ";

    open (TIMES, "/bin/time @ARGV 2>&1 |")
        || die ("Can't run /bin/time @ARGV: $!\n");
```

```perl
        while (<TIMES>) {
            if (/^real\s+(\d+\.\d+)\n/) {
                push (@t_real, $1);          # AT&T style
                $tt_real += $1;
            }
            elsif (/^user\s+(\d+\.\d+)/) {
                push (@t_user, $1);
                $tt_user += $1;
            }
            elsif (/^sys\s+(\d+\.\d+)/) {
                push (@t_sys , $1);
                $tt_sys += $1;
            }
            elsif (/^\s*(\S+) real\s*(\S+) user\s*(\S+) sys/) {
                push (@t_real , $1);         # BSD style
                $tt_real += $1;
                push (@t_user , $2);
                $tt_user += $2;
                push (@t_sys , $3);
                $tt_sys += $3;
            }
        }
        close (TIMES);
}

print " done\n\n";

# Build a dynamic format.

$fields = '@>>>>>' x $repeat;
$values = ',shift @_' x $repeat;

$form = <<EOFORM;
format STDOUT =
\@<<<\@>>>>>$fields
\$arg,\$avg $values
.
EOFORM

print $form if $debugging;
eval $form;

sub write {
    $avg = shift;
    write;
}

# So write the report already.

&write('Avg', 1 .. $repeat);

&write(split(' ', '———' x ($repeat+1)));
```

```
for $arg ("real","user","sys ") {
    &write(sprintf("%6.1f", eval "\$tt_$arg/$repeat"),
        eval "\@t_$arg");
}
```

START—Start Application Daemon Processes

Some applications require that developers and users be able to start and kill daemons that run as root. This script is a wrapper to take care of many of the house-
keeping chores associated with starting such daemons. It runs setuid to root, so
the individual daemon programs don't have to. It checks to make sure a particular daemon isn't already running. You can disable the starting of a daemon by
creating appropriate flag files. **START** sets up logging to a standard location, and
resets the process group so the daemon is protected from signals. All these things
could be done by the daemons themselves, but it's convenient to have the code in
one place if you're starting multiple daemons.

Some things a daemon simply can't do for itself, such as capture the return value
of the process (the status) if it dies. **START** captures the status value and logs it.
Unlike the way shells handle status values, the status value used by Perl distinguishes normal exit status from signal and core dump information. If the daemon
performed a core dump, **START** will rename the core dump to a unique name
based on the current time, so that multiple core dumps in the same directory don't
wipe out previous core dumps. If the daemon was particularly important, **START**
can broadcast a message to everyone on the machine that the daemon crashed. To
stop your daemons on purpose, see the following program, which is called
KILL.[42]

This particular version of **START** is set up to start the daemons for three subsystems, named "abc," "def," and "xyz." Note that the name of the daemon may
actually differ from the subsystem name. If no subsystem is specified to **START**,
it starts the daemons for all subsystems. All the daemons are stored in a directory
called */appl/bin*, which could be mounted across the network, and all the logging
and (potential) core dumping happen in a directory called */local/tmp*, which
should *not* be mounted across the network.

```
#!/usr/bin/perl

$> && die "Not running as root\n";

@INC = $INC[$#INC - 1]; # Use only the perl library.
```

---

[42] You'll note that names **START** and **KILL** were chosen to be easy to type with one hand while the
other holds down the shift key!

```perl
die "Perl library is writable by world!!!\n"
    if $< && -W $INC[0];
die "getopts.pl is writable by world!!!\n"
    if $< && -W "$INC[0]/getopts.pl";
require "getopts.pl";
&Getopts('cst');

$wall = !$opt_s;

$_ = "$0 @ARGV";         # To allow "ln START STARTxyz"

$ENV{'IFS'} = '' if $ENV{'IFS'};            # plug sh security hole
$ENV{'PATH'} = '/appl/bin:/bin:/usr/bin:/usr/local/bin';

# Which daemon to start?

if (/abc/) {
    $sys = 'abc';
    $task = 'abcdaemon';
    if (-f '/local/tmp/NO_ABC') {
        die "Can't start abcdaemon while NO_ABC exists\n";
    }
}

elsif (/def/) {
    $sys = 'def';
    $task = 'def';
    if (-f '/local/tmp/NO_DEF') {
        die "Can't start def while NO_DEF exists\n";
    }
}
elsif (/xyz/) {
    $sys = 'xyz';
    $task = 'xyzzy';    # Forks plugh and plover.
    if (-f '/local/tmp/NO_XYZ') {
        die "Can't start lm while NO_XYZ exists\n";
    }
}
elsif (/appl/ || !@ARGV) {
    system $0, 'abc';
    system $0, 'def';
    system $0, 'xyz';
    exit 0;
}
else {
    die "Usage: START subsystem\n";
}

# Get info for logging.

chop($whoami = `who am i`);
$whoami =~ s/[ \t]+/ /g;
```

```perl
chop($tty = `tty`);
$tty = `` if $tty !~ m|/dev/|;

# Set real uid to effective uid so core dumps will happen.

$< = $>;

# Move to directory for core dumps.

chdir `/local/tmp` || die "Can´t chdir to /local/tmp";

# See if they should have run KILL.

chop($oldpid = `/bin/cat .pid$sys 2>&1`);
if ($oldpid > 0 && kill 0, $oldpid) {
    die "$sys appears to be running already!\n"
        if `/bin/ps -p$oldpid` =~ /START/;
}

print "Any core dump of $task will be put into /local/tmp.\n";

# Redirect output to log file.

open(STDERR,">/local/tmp/${sys}_err_log")
    || (print STDOUT "Can´t open log file\n");
open(STDOUT,">&STDERR");

# Log the startup.

chop($date = `date`);
$date =~ s/ [A-Z][DS]T 19[89][0-9]//;
open(KILLLOG,">>/local/tmp/${sys}_kill_log");
print KILLLOG $date, ` `, $whoami, " $sys started\n";
close(KILLLOG);
if ($tty) {
    open(KILLLOG,">$tty");
    print KILLLOG $date, ` `, $whoami, " $sys started\n";
    close(KILLLOG);
}

if ($pid = fork) {           # Run the rest in background.
    open(PID,">.pid$sys");   # Remember pid for quick check above
    print PID "$pid\n";      # (pid of START, not of $task).
    close(PID);
    sleep(3);                # Give each daemon a chance to start
    exit 0;
}
defined $pid || die "Can´t fork: $!\n";

$SIG{'TERM'} = 'IGNORE';

setpgrp(0,$$);  # Prevent kills from infecting other daemons.
```

```
        # Finally, run the poor daemon and collect its status.

        if ($opt_t) {
            $st = (system "/usr/bin/trace /appl/bin/$task");
        }
        else {
            $st = (system "/appl/bin/$task");
        }


        # Now get info necessary for logging.

        chop($date = `date`);
        $date =~ s/ [A-Z][DS]T 19[89][0-9]//;

        # Rename any core dump to a unique name.

        if ($st & 128) {
            $tm = join(´´,unpack("x8 a2 x a2 x a2", $date));
            $tm =~ s/ /0/g;
            rename("/local/tmp/core", "/local/tmp/core.$sys$tm");
        }

        sleep(2);

        # Log it everywhere that makes sense.

        $entry = "$date $whoami $sys exit " . ($st >> 8) . ", sig " .
            ($st & 127) . ($st & 128 ? ", core dump\n" : "\n");
        open(KILLLOG,">>/local/tmp/${sys}_kill_log");
        print KILLLOG $entry;
        close(KILLLOG);


        close(STDERR);
        close(STDOUT);
        open(STDOUT,">&STDIN");
        open(ERR,"/local/tmp/${sys}_err_log");
        open(CONSOLE,"/dev/console") if $opt_c;
        $tty = ´´ unless -t;
        while (<ERR>) {
            if ($_ eq $last) {
                $repeat = 1;
                while (<ERR>) {
                    if ($_ eq $last) {
                        ++$repeat;
                    }
                    else {
                        $last = "Last message repeated $repeat time" .
                            ($repeat == 1 ? "" : "s") . ".\n";
                        print CONSOLE $last if $opt_c;
                        print STDOUT $last if $tty;
                    }
                }
```

```
        }
        print CONSOLE $_ if $opt_c;
        print STDOUT $_ if $tty;
        $last = $_;
}

if ($wall) {
        open(KILLLOG,"| wall"); # Might as well share the good news
        print KILLLOG $entry;
        close(KILLLOG);
}

unlink "/local/tmp/.pid$sys";
```

KILL—Stop Application Daemons

This program undoes what **START** does. You may kill off a particular subsystem's daemon, or all of them. If you choose to kill off all daemons, any program executing out of */appl/bin* will be killed. **KILL** also attempts to clear out all shared memory, semaphores, and message queues. Note that when you kill a specific subsystem, you may actually be killing several processes.

```
#!/usr/bin/perl

$BSD = -f '/vmunix';

$_ = $0;
if ($_ =~ /KILL$/) {
    if ($#ARGV >= 0) {
        $_ .= ' ' . shift;
    }
    else {
        $_ .= ' appl';
    }
}

$ENV{'IFS'} = '' if $ENV{'IFS'};            # plug sh security hole
$applbin = '/appl/bin';
$ENV{'PATH'} = "$applbin:/bin:/usr/bin:/usr/local/bin";

if (/xyz/) {
    do killsys('xyz');
}
elsif (/def/) {
    do killsys('def');
}
elsif (/abc/) {
    do killsys('abc');
}
elsif (/appl/) {
```

```
    @ARGV = ();
    do killsys('xyz');
    do killsys('def');
    do killsys('abc');
    do killipc();
    do killall();
    sleep 1;                      # give them a chance to die
    if (&count_attached()) {
        sleep 5;                  # give them a longer chance
        if (&count_attached()) {
            die <<CURTAINS;
WARNING: I can't find all the processes with shared memory.
CURTAINS
        }
    }
}
else {
    die "Usage: KILL subsystem [pids]";
}
exit 0;

sub killsys {
    $sys = shift(@_);
    if ($sys =~ /xyz/) {
        $pat1 = ' xyzzy$| plugh$| plover$';
        $pat2 = 'xyzzy|plugh';
    }
    elsif ($sys =~ /def/) {
        $pat1 = ' def$| [a-zA-Z].def$';
        $pat2 = 'def';
    }
    elsif ($sys =~ /abc/) {
        $pat1 = ' abcdaemon$';
        $pat2 = 'abc';
    }
    else {
        die "Internal error, stopped";
    }

# If no pids specified, make up our own list

    if ($#ARGV < 0) {
        if ($BSD) {
            open(PS, '/bin/ps axc|') || warn "Can't run ps\n";
        }
        else {
            open(PS, '/bin/ps -ef|') || warn "Can't run ps\n";
        }

        while (<PS>) {
            if ($BSD) {
                $pid = $_ + 0;
            }
```

```
            else {
                $pid = substr($_,9,6) + 0;
                $COMMAND = index($_,"COMMAND") if $COMMAND < 1;
                $_ = substr($_,$COMMAND);
                @ary = split;
                $_ = shift(@ary);
                s|.*/||;
                $_ = ´ ´ . $_;
            }
            push(ARGV,$pid) if $_ =~ $pat1;
        }
        warn "No $sys processes found.\n" unless @ARGV;
        close(PS);
        $checking = 0;
    }
    else {
        $checking++;     # we´ll need to check propriety
    }

    # now get info necessary for logging

    chop($date = `date`);
    $date =~ s/ [A-Z][DS]T 19[89][0-9]//;
    chop($whoami = `who am i`);
    $whoami =~ s/[ \t]+/ /g;
    $whoami =~ s/^[a-z]*!//;

    while ($pid = shift) {
        open(KILLLOG,">>/local/tmp/${sys}_kill_log");
        if ($checking && `/bin/ps -p$pid` !~ $pat2) {
            print KILLLOG $date, ´ ´, $whoami,
                " not allowed to kill ",$pid,"\n";
            print "$pid is not a $sys process!\n";
        }
        else {
            print KILLLOG $date, ´ ´, $whoami,
                ´ killed ´,$pid,"\n";
            $pid =~ /(.*)/;
            $pid = $1;
            kill 15, $pid;    # Give ´em a shot across the bow.
            sleep(5);         # I hope this is long enough...
            kill 9, $pid;     # Deep six ´em.
        }
        close(KILLLOG);
    }
}

sub killipc {
    @goners = ();
    open(IPCS,"ipcs -a |") || warn "Can´t run ipcs\n";
    while (<IPCS>) {
        $LSPID = index($_,´LSPID´) unless $LSPID > 0;
        $LRPID = index($_,´LRPID´) unless $LRPID > 0;
```

```
        $CPID = index($_,' CPID') unless $CPID > 0;
        $LPID = index($_,' LPID') unless $LPID > 0;
        $SEGSZ = index($_,'SEGSZ') unless $SEGSZ > 0;
        if (/^q/) {
            if ($LSPID > 0) {
                $pid = substr($_,$LSPID,6) + 0;
                $pid =~ /^(\d+)$/;       # Untaint $pid.
                $pid = $1;
                push(@goners,$pid) if $pid > 1;
            }
            if ($LRPID > 0) {
                $pid = substr($_,$LSPID,6) + 0;
                $pid =~ /^(\d+)$/;       # Untaint $pid.
                $pid = $1;
                push(@goners,$pid) if $pid > 1;
            }
        }

        elsif (/^m/) {
            next if substr($_,$SEGSZ,6) == 4096;
            if ($CPID > 0) {
                $pid = substr($_,$CPID,6) + 0;
                $pid =~ /^(\d+)$/;       # Untaint $pid.
                $pid = $1;
                push(@goners,$pid) if $pid > 1;
            }
            if ($LPID > 0) {
                $pid = substr($_,$LPID,6) + 0;
                $pid =~ /^(\d+)$/;       # Untaint $pid.
                $pid = $1;
                push(@goners,$pid) if $pid > 1;
            }
        }
    }
    close(IPCS);

    kill 9, @goners;
}


sub killall {
    @goners = ();
    if ($BSD) {
        open(PS, '/bin/ps axww|') || warn "Can't run ps\n";
    }
    else {
        open(PS, '/bin/ps -ef|') || warn "Can't run ps\n";
    }
    $head = <PS>;
    $COMMAND = index($head,"COMMAND") if $COMMAND <= 0;
    while (<PS>) {
        if ($BSD) {
            $pid = $_ + 0;
```

```perl
        }
        else {
            $pid = substr($_,9,6) + 0;
        }
        $cmd = substr($_,$COMMAND);
        @ary = split(´ ´,$cmd);
        $_ = shift(@ary);
        s|.*/||;
        if (/^(perl|csh|sh|\[.*\])$/) { # Ignore 1st argument?
            $_ = shift(@ary);
            s|.*/||;
        }

        $prog = $_;
        if (! -f "$applbin/$prog" && $cmd =~ /\((\w+)\)/) {
            $prog = $1;
        }
        if ($prog eq ´START´
          || $prog eq ´.START´
          || $prog eq ´wall´
          || ($prog =~ /KILL$/ && $pid != $$)) {
            push(@finally,"$pid $prog");
            next;
        }
        next if $prog =~ /KILL$/;
        if (-f "$applbin/$prog") {
            $pid =~ /(.*)/;
            $pid = $1;
            push(goners,$pid);
            print "Killing $prog, pid $pid\n";
        }
    }
    close(PS);

    kill 15,@goners;
    sleep(5);
    kill 9,@goners;

    if ($#finally >= 0) {
        sleep(6);
        for (@finally) {
            ($pid,$prog) = split;
            $pid =~ /(\d+)/;
            $pid = $1;
            print "Killing $prog, pid $pid\n" if kill 9,$pid;
        }
    }
}

sub count_attached {
    $attached = 0;
    open(IPCS,"ipcs -a |") || warn "Can´t run ipcs\n";
    $ipcrm = ´´;
```

```
        while (<IPCS>) {
            $SEGSZ = index($_,'SEGSZ') unless $SEGSZ > 0;
            $NATTCH = index($_,'NATTCH') unless $NATTCH > 0;
            $killnum = $1 if /^[msq]\s*(\d+)/;
            if (/^m/) {
                next if substr($_,$SEGSZ,6) == 4096;
                $ipcrm .= " -m $killnum";
                $attached += substr($_,$NATTCH,6) if $NATTCH > 0;
            }
            elsif (/^s/) {
                $ipcrm .= " -s $killnum";
            }
            elsif (/^q/) {
                $ipcrm .= " -q $killnum";
            }
        }
        close(IPCS);
        if ($ipcrm) {
            $ipcrm =~ /(.*)/;
            $ipcrm = $1;
            print "ipcrm$ipcrm\n";
            system "ipcrm$ipcrm";
        }
        $attached;
    }
```

Interprocess Communication

The Interprocess Communication (IPC) facilities of Perl are built on the Berkeley socket mechanism. If you don't have sockets, you can ignore this section. The calls have the same names as the corresponding system calls, but the arguments tend to differ, for two reasons. First, Perl filehandles work differently than C file descriptors. Second, Perl already knows the length of its strings, so you don't need to pass that information.

client—A Simple Sample Client

Here is a small TCP/IP client that connects to a server and then lets you type lines to the server. It displays any lines the server sends back. This client uses one of the common tricks of handling two-way socket conversations—it forks a child process to read from the socket while it writes to the socket.

```perl
#!/usr/bin/perl

($them,$port) = @ARGV;
$port = 2345 unless $port;
$them = `localhost` unless $them;

$AF_INET = 2;
$SOCK_STREAM = 1;

$SIG{`INT`} = `dokill`;
sub dokill {
    kill 9,$child if $child;
}


$sockaddr = `S n a4 x8`;

chop($hostname = `hostname`);

($name,$aliases,$proto) = getprotobyname(`tcp`);
($name,$aliases,$port) = getservbyname($port,`tcp`)
    unless $port =~ /^\d+$/;;
($name,$aliases,$type,$len,$thisaddr) =
        gethostbyname($hostname);
($name,$aliases,$type,$len,$thataddr) = gethostbyname($them);

$this = pack($sockaddr, $AF_INET, 0, $thisaddr);
$that = pack($sockaddr, $AF_INET, $port, $thataddr);

# Make the socket filehandle.

if (socket(S, $AF_INET, $SOCK_STREAM, $proto)) {
    print "socket ok\n";
}
else {
    die $!;
}


# Give the socket an address.

if (bind(S, $this)) {
    print "bind ok\n";
}
else {
    die $!;
}


# Call up the server.

if (connect(S,$that)) {
    print "connect ok\n";
}
else {
```

```
        die $!;
    }

    # Set socket to be command buffered.

    select(S); $| = 1; select(STDOUT);

    # Avoid deadlock by forking.

    if($child = fork) {
        while (<STDIN>) {
            print S;
        }
        sleep 3;
        do dokill();
    }
    else {
        while(<S>) {
            print;
        }
    }
```

server—A Simple Sample Server

Here's a server to go with the client above. Note how concisely the **socket**, **bind**, **listen**, and **accept** calls can be written. If you're not familiar with the way servers work, the general idea is that the first socket you open isn't a real socket, but a generic socket that gets instantiated every time a connection comes in and is accepted. That's why the **accept** call has two socket filehandles—one for the fake socket, and one for the new real socket. After a server gets a real socket, it typically forks off a child process to do the dirty work with that connection, while it goes back and listens for more connections on the fake socket. Note that the child simply exits when it is done with the connection it is handling. Otherwise, you'd suddenly have two processes waiting for connections, and then four, and then eight ...

```
#!/usr/bin/perl

($port) = @ARGV;
$port = 2345 unless $port;

$AF_INET = 2;
$SOCK_STREAM = 1;

$sockaddr = 'S n a4 x8';

($name, $aliases, $proto) = getprotobyname('tcp');
if ($port !~ /^\d+$/) {
```

```
        ($name, $aliases, $port) = getservbyport($port, ´tcp´);
}

print "Port = $port\n";

$this = pack($sockaddr, $AF_INET, $port, "\0\0\0\0");

select(NS); $| = 1; select(stdout);

socket(S, $AF_INET, $SOCK_STREAM, $proto) || die "socket: $!";
bind(S,$this) || die "bind: $!";
listen(S,5) || die "connect: $!";

select(S); $| = 1; select(stdout);

for($con = 1; ; $con++) {
    printf("Listening for connection %d....\n",$con);
    ($addr = accept(NS,S)) || die $!;

    if (($child = fork()) == 0) {
        print "accept ok\n";

        ($af,$port,$inetaddr) = unpack($sockaddr,$addr);
        @inetaddr = unpack(´C4´,$inetaddr);
        print "$con: $af $port @inetaddr\n";

        while (<NS>) {
            print "$con: $_";
        }
        close(NS);
        exit;
    }
    close(NS);
}
```

receptionist—An Internet Daemon Handler

Here is a special kind of server that doesn't do any real work itself but merely answers the phone for others, so to speak. It is, in fact, a simpleminded clone of the program **inetd** (Internet daemon) that runs on many UNIX machines. The purpose of such a program is reduce the number of daemon processes you need to keep around. When the receptionist finds out that there is an incoming connection or datagram, it starts up the correct daemon process, which handles the request and then dies. This version of the receptionist handles TCP and UDP sockets (but not RPC). It lets you specify services either by name or by port number, so you can run this program even if you're not the superuser. If you are the superuser, you may specify which user ID to run the program under.

Like a real receptionist, you have to tell this one which phone lines (ports) to
monitor. This is specified in the configuration file. Here's a sample:

```
#service type   protocol wait-st uid      server-prog    arguments
4444     stream tcp      nowait  grady    /bin/cat       cat
4455     stream tcp      nowait  lwall    /usr/bin/perl  Perl
comsat   dgram  udp      wait    root     /tmp/comsat.pl comsat
```

Note that you can't start up a named service like **comsat** if the **inetd** on your system already is doing that. Also note that the **Perl** line above is a potential security hole—anyone could run any perl script as the user specified by **uid**. The
wait status indicates whether the receptionist should wait till the current daemon
dies before starting another, or start as many of them as it likes in parallel.

```perl
#!/usr/bin/perl

# Usage:
#       receptionist [-d] [conf file]
#       -d: debug
#       conf file: configuration file
#                  (default file is /etc/recept.conf)

require 'sys/socket.ph';
require 'sys/errno.ph';
require 'sys/wait.ph';
require 'getopts.pl';

$SIG{'CHLD'} = 'reapchild';
$WNOHANG = defined &WNOHANG ? &WNOHANG : 1;

$sockaddr = 'S n a4 x8';
$fileDescs = '';
do Getopts('d');
$debug = $opt_d;

($conf) = @ARGV;
$conf = "/etc/recept.conf" unless $conf;

        # Read the entries from the configuration file.

open(CONF, "<$conf") || die "open: $conf: $!";
while (<CONF>) {
    next if (/^#/ || /^$/);
    ($service, $sockettype, $proto,
            $waitstatus, $uid, $server, @commandlist) = split;
    $tmp = (getpwnam($uid))[2];
    $uid = $tmp if defined $tmp;
    $service .= "/$proto";
    push (@services, $service);
    $sockettype{$service} = $sockettype;
    $proto{$service} = $proto;
    $waitstatus{$service} = $waitstatus;
```

```perl
        $uid{$service} = $uid;
        $server{$service} = $server;
        $commandlist[0] = $server unless @commandlist;
        $command{$service} = "@commandlist";
}
close(CONF);

        # Begin each service in the conf file.

foreach $service (@services) {
    &addBits(&startService($service));
}

        # Main loop (never exits)

$| = 1;
for (;;) {
    print "fileDescs:  ", &printVec($fileDescs), "\n"
        if $debug;
    $nfound = select($rout = $fileDescs, undef, undef, undef);
    if ($nfound == -1) {
        if ($! == &EINTR) {
            next;
        }
        else {
            die "select: $!";
        }
    }

    print "rout:  ", &printVec($rout), ", " if $debug;
    foreach $service (@services) {
        if (vec($rout, $fileno{$service}, 1)) {
            print "$service ready\n" if $debug;
            &spawn($service);
        }
    }
}
die "Shouldn't ever get here!!!  Stopped";

        # Start an individual service.

sub startService {
    local($serviceName) = @_;

    print "starting service $serviceName...\n" if ($debug);

    $protoName = $proto{$serviceName};
    local($serv) = split(m#/#, $serviceName);
    (($pname, $paliases, $proto) = getprotobyname($protoName))
        || die "Couldn't get proto by name $protoName: $!";
```

347

```
            if ($serviceName =~ /\d+/) {
                $port = $serviceName;
            }
            else {
                print "Getting service from ($serv, $proto)\n"
                    if $debug;
                (($name, $aliases, $port)
                    = getservbyname($serv, $protoName))
                  || die "Couldn't get by name $serviceName: $!";
            }

            if ($sockettype{$serviceName} eq "stream") {
                $socktype = &SOCK_STREAM;
            }
            elsif ($sockettype{$serviceName} eq "dgram") {
                $socktype = &SOCK_DGRAM;
            }
            else {
                $socktype = -1;
            }


            $name = pack($sockaddr, &AF_INET, $port, "\0\0\0\0");
            socket($service, &PF_INET, $socktype, $proto) ||
                    die "socket ($serviceName): $!";
            print "binding to port $port.\n" if $debug;
            bind($service, $name) || die "bind($serviceName): $!";
            if ($socktype == &SOCK_STREAM) {
                listen($service, 10) || die "listen($serviceName): $!";
            }
            $fileno{$service} = fileno($service);
}


        # Utility functions to deal with select() bits.

sub addBits {
    local($fd) = @_;
    vec($fileDescs, $fd, 1) = 1;
}

sub delBits {
    local($fd) = @_;
    vec($fileDescs, $fd, 1) = 0;
}


        # Start a new server.

sub spawn {
    local($service) = @_;
    local($stream) = ($sockettype{$service} eq "stream");
    local($fd);

    # Only datagram sockets can be 'wait'.
```

```
local($wait)
    = ($waitstatus{$service} eq "wait" && (! $stream));

if ($wait) {
    $fd = $service;
}
else {
    accept($fd, $service) || die "accept: $!";
}

print "Running: ", $command{$service}, "\n";
for (;;) {
    $pid = fork;
    last if defined $pid;
    sleep 5;
}
if (! $pid) {
    select($fd);
    $| = 1;

    $inputStr = "<&" . fileno($fd);
    $outputStr = ">&" . fileno($fd);

    close(STDIN);
    open(STDIN, $inputStr) || die "open STDIN: $!";

    close(STDOUT);
    open(STDOUT, $outputStr) || die "open STDOUT: $!";

    # Die can't print an error, since STDERR is closed.

    close(STDERR);
    open(STDERR, $outputStr) || die;

    # Change uid, even on machines that only do setuid().

    $uid = $uid{$service};
    ($<, $>) = ($uid,$uid) unless $>;

    # Insulate against any signals coming from above.

    setpgrp(0,$$);

    # Exec the daemon, lying to it about its name.
    #  (Is it wrong to lie to a daemon?  Beats me.)

    $realname = $server{$service};
    exec $realname split(' ', $command{$service});
    exit 255;
}
else {
    if ($wait) {
```

```
                   $serviceof{$pid} = $service;
                   &delBits($fileno{$service});
               }
               else {
                   close($fd);
               }
            }
        }


            # When a child dies, if it's a "wait" server, put the
            # file descriptor for the child back in select mask.

    sub reapchild {
        while (1) {
            print "Reaping child\n";
            $pid = waitpid(-1,$WNOHANG);
            last if ($pid < 1);
            $service = $serviceof{$pid};
            last unless $service;
            print "$service restored\n" if $debug;
            &addBits($fileno{$service});
        }
    }


            # Debugging subroutine.

    sub printVec {
        local($v) = @_;
        local($i, $result);

        for ($i = (8*length($v)) - 1; $i >= 0; $i--) {
            $result .= (vec($v, $i, 1)) ? "1" : "0";
        }
        $result;
    }
```

7

Other Oddments

Invocation Options
Debugging
Common Goofs for Novices
Efficiency
Setuid Scripts
Distribution and Installation
Perl Poetry
History Made Practical

In this chapter we try to nail down all those loose flounders, so expect things to be even less coherent than they are here.

This section describes the command-line switches (also called options) that may be used when invoking Perl on a UNIX-like system. Other systems have different ways of passing arguments to a program, so your kilometerage may vary. Some MS-DOS machines require all quoting to be done with double quotes, for instance.

Any option that doesn't take an argument may be combined with the following option. This is particularly useful when invoking a script using the #! construct which only allows one argument. For example:

```
#!/usr/bin/perl -spi.bak      # same as -s -p -i.bak
...
```

One additional note about **#!** lines: If Perl sees that you've got a **#!** line but that it doesn't refer to the *perl* interpreter, it will execute the interpreter it finds on the **#!** line for you. In the cases where you don't want this to happen, merely mention *perl* in a comment, like this:

```
#!/usr/local/bin/weirdname —switches  # perl
```

−0 *digits*

Specifies the input record separator ($/) as an octal number. If there are no digits, the null character is the separator. Other switches may precede or follow the digits. For example, if you have a version of *find* which can print filenames terminated by the null character, you can say this:

```
find . —name ´*.bak´ —print0 | perl —n0e unlink
```

The special value **00** will cause Perl to slurp files in paragraph mode. The value **0777** will cause Perl to slurp files whole since there is no legal character with that value.

−a

Turns on autosplit mode when used with a **−n** or **−p**. Performs an implicit **split** on whitespace as the first thing inside the implicit **while** loop produced by the **−n** or **−p**. The fields produced are put into an array called **@F**:

```
perl —ane ´print pop(@F), "\n";´
```

which is equivalent to:

```
while (<>) {
      @F = split(´ ´);
      print pop(@F), "\n";
}
```

The **@F** array is otherwise a perfectly normal array.

−c

Checks the syntax of the script, and then exits without executing it. (If the script is OK, prints **syntax OK**.) Obviously, any other switches that have effects at runtime will not have those effects.

−d

Runs the script under the Perl debugger. See the section "Debugging" in this chapter for more information.

−D *number*

Sets debugging flags. (This only works if debugging is compiled into your Perl executable. If you are installing Perl and want to enable this feature, give a **−DDEBUGGING** switch when Configure asks for *cc* flags. See the README file in the distribution kit for more on installation.) To watch how Perl executes your script, use **−D14**. Another nice value is **−D1024**, which lists your compiled syntax tree (and works well with –c). And **–D512** displays compiled regular expressions. Here's the whole list:

Value	Meaning
1	Tokenizing and Parsing
2	Command Linkage
4	Label Stack Processing
8	Trace Execution
16	Operator Node Construction
32	String/Numeric Conversions
64	Print Preprocessor Command for –P
128	Memory Allocation
256	Format Processing
512	Regular Expression Parsing
1024	Syntax Tree Dump
2048	Tainting Checks
4096	Memory Leaks (with –DLEAKTEST)
8192	Hash Dump—Usurps values()

–e *commandline*

May be used to enter one line of script. Multiple **–e** commands may be given to build up a multi-line script. If **–e** is given, Perl will not look for a script filename in the argument list.

–i *extension*

Specifies that files processed by the **<>** construct are to be edited in-place. It does this by renaming the input file, opening the output file by the same name, and selecting that output file as the default for **print** statements. The extension, if supplied, is added to the name of the old file to make a backup copy. If no extension is supplied, no backup is made, and the file is modified in place. This switch is often used in conjunction with the **–p** and **–n** switches, which supply an implicit loop that reads **<>**. Saying:

```
perl –p –i.bak –e "s/foo/bar/;" ...
```

is the same as using the script:

```
#!/usr/bin/perl –pi.bak
s/foo/bar/;
```

which is equivalent to:

```
#!/usr/bin/perl
while (<>) {
        if ($ARGV ne $oldargv) {
        rename($ARGV, $ARGV . `.bak`);
        open(ARGVOUT, ">$ARGV");
```

```
            select(ARGVOUT);
            $oldargv = $ARGV;
        }
        s/foo/bar/;
    }
    continue {
        print;# this prints to original filename
    }
    select(STDOUT);
```

except that the **–i** form doesn't need to compare **$ARGV** to **$oldargv** to know when the filename has changed. It does, however, use **ARGVOUT** for the selected filehandle. Note that **STDOUT** is restored as the default output filehandle after the loop.

You can use **eof** to locate the end of each input file, in case you want to append to each file, or reset line numbering. For example, to start the line numbers over, add:

```
    close(ARGV) if eof;
```

to the body of your loop.

–I *directory*

> May be used in conjunction with **–P** to tell the C preprocessor where to look for include files. By default */usr/local/lib/perl* (or whatever Perl library directory was selected with Configure) and the current directory are searched when looking for include files of the form:

```
    #include <somefilename>
```

> Any directories you specify with this switch are searched before the default locations.

> As with C, include files of the form:

```
    #include "somefilename"
```

> are **not** searched for along this directory list, but must exist exactly where specified.

> The same directories are put into the **@INC** array for searching by the **require** function.

–l *digits*

> Enables automatic line-ending processing. This has two effects: first, it automatically chops the line terminator when used with **–n** or **–p**, and second, it assigns $\ to have the value of *digits* (interpreted as an octal number) so that any print statements will have that line terminator added back

on. If no *digits* are specified, sets $\backslash$ to the current value of $/. For instance, to trim lines to 80 columns:

```
perl -lpe 'substr($_, 80) = ""'
```

Note that the assignment $\backslash = $/ is done when the switch is processed, so the input record separator can be different than the output record separator if the **-l** switch is followed by a **-0** switch:

```
gnufind / -print0 | perl -ln0e 'print "found $_" if -p'
```

This sets $\backslash$ to newline and then sets $/ to the null character.

-n   Causes Perl to assume the following loop around your script, which makes it iterate over filename arguments somewhat like "**sed -n**" or *awk*:

```
while (<>) {
        ...# your script goes here
}
```

Note that the lines are **not** printed by default. See **-p** to have lines printed. Here is an efficient way to delete all files older than a week:

```
find . -mtime +7 -print | perl -ne 'chop;unlink;'
```

This is faster than using the **-exec** switch of *find* because you don't have to start a process on every filename found.

-p   Causes Perl to assume the following loop around your script, which makes it iterate over filename arguments somewhat like *sed*:

```
while (<>) {
        ...# your script goes here
} continue {
        print;
}
```

Note that the lines are printed automatically. To suppress printing use the **-n** switch instead. A **-p** overrides a **-n** switch.

-P   Causes your script to be run through the C preprocessor before compilation by Perl. Since both comments and *cpp* directives begin with the **#** character, you should avoid starting comments with any words recognized by the C preprocessor such as **if**, **else**, or **define**. A common trick (used in the library routines from the Perl distribution, for example) is to begin the lines with **;#** rather than **#**, which is legal syntax for Perl and is clearly **not** a preprocessor directive.

−s   Enables some rudimentary switch parsing for switches on the command line after the script name but before any filename arguments (or before a −−). Any switch found there is removed from **@ARGV** and sets the same-named scalar variable in the Perl script to a value of 1, unless the switch is followed by an equals sign and a value, in which case the variable is set to that value. The following script prints **"true"** if and only if the script is invoked with a **−xyz** switch.

```
#!/usr/bin/perl -s
if ($xyz) { print "true\n"; }
```

−S   Makes Perl use the **PATH** environment variable to search for the script (unless the name of the script starts with a slash). Typically this is used to emulate **#!** startup on machines that don't support **#!**, in the following manner:

```
#!/usr/bin/perl
eval "exec /usr/bin/perl -S $0 $*"
        if $running_under_some_shell;
```

The system ignores the first line and feeds the script to */bin/sh*, which proceeds to try to execute the Perl script as a shell script. The shell executes the second line as a normal shell command, and thus starts up the Perl interpreter. On some systems **$0** doesn't always contain the full pathname, so the **−S** tells Perl to search for the script in your **PATH** directories if necessary. After Perl locates the script, it parses the lines and ignores them because the variable **$running_under_some_shell** is never true.

A better construct than **$*** would be **${1+"$@"}**, which handles embedded spaces and such in the filenames, but doesn't work if the script is being interpreted by *csh*. In order to start up *sh* rather than *csh*, some systems may have to replace the **#!** line with a line containing just a colon, which will be politely ignored by Perl. Other systems can't control that, and need a totally devious construct that will work under any of *csh*, *sh*, or Perl. If you are so blessed, either get a new system, or put this at the front of your Perl script:

```
eval ´(exit $?0)´ && eval ´exec /usr/bin/perl -S $0 ${1+"$@"}´
& eval ´exec /usr/bin/perl -S $0 $argv:q´
        if 0;
```

Yes, it's ugly, but so are the systems that work[43] this way.

---

[43] We use the term advisedly.

−u   Causes Perl to dump core after compiling your script. You can then take this core dump and turn it into an executable file by using the **undump** program (not supplied, and may not even be available for a particular port of Perl). This speeds startup at the expense of some disk space. (Which you can minimize by stripping the executable — still, a **"hello world"** executable comes out to about 200K on a Vax. It will be larger on other machines, especially on RISC architectures.) If you are going to run your executable as a set-id program then you should probably compile it using **taintperl** rather than normal Perl (see Setuid Scripts later in this chapter). If you want to execute a portion of your script before dumping, use the **dump** operator instead.

−U   Allows Perl to do unsafe operations. Currently the only "unsafe" operation is the unlinking of directories while running as superuser.

−v   Prints the version and patchlevel of your Perl executable, along with some information about Perl's distribution policy.

−w   Prints warnings about identifiers that are mentioned only once, and scalar variables that are used before being set. Also warns about redefined subroutines, and references to undefined filehandles or filehandles opened readonly that you are attempting to write on. Also warns you if you use == on values that don't look like numbers, and if your subroutines recurse more than 100 deep. Doesn't warn you if your code could be written better, or will run forever without terminating, or doesn't function according to the description in the comments or the manpage.

−x   Tells Perl that the script is embedded in a message. Leading garbage will be discarded until the first line that starts with **#!** and contains the string **"perl"**. Any meaningful switches on that line will be applied (but only one group of switches, as with normal **#!** processing). The **−x** switch controls the disposal of only the leading garbage. The script must be terminated with **__END__** (or the single ASCII characters \004 [control-D] or \032 [control-Z]) if there is trailing garbage to be ignored (the script can process any or all of the trailing garbage via **<DATA>** if desired).

Debugging

If you invoke Perl with a **−d** switch, your script will be run under a debugging monitor. It will ordinarily halt before the first executable statement and ask you for a debugging command. The prompt will display the current package, function, file and line number, as well as the current line itself. There are commands to set and delete breakpoints, to turn tracing on and off, to step through your program and to print out items of interest.

Here are the standard debugging commands:

h   Prints out a help message.

T   Stack trace. Lines starting with $ = indicate the listed function is being called in a scalar context, while a @ = indicates the function is being called in an array context.

s   Single step. Executes until it reaches the beginning of another statement.

n   Next. Executes over subroutine calls, until it reaches the beginning of the next statement.

r   Return from the current subroutine. Executes statements until it has finished the current subroutine.

c *line*   Continue. Sets a one-time breakpoint at *line*, and executes until the next breakpoint is reached. If *line* is omitted, merely continues until the next breakpoint is reached.

<CR>   Repeat last s or n.

l *min+incr*   List *incr*+1 lines starting at *min*. If *min* is omitted, starts where last listing left off. If *incr* is omitted, previous value of *incr* is used.

l *min–max*   List lines in the indicated range.

l *line*   List just the indicated line.

l   List next window.

f *filename*   Switch to the named file and begin listing it. You need only mention enough of the name to make it unique among the files that have been visited by Perl.

–   List previous window.

w *line*   List window around line.

l *subname*   List subroutine. If it's a long subroutine it just lists the beginning. Use l to list more.

/pattern/	Regular-expression-search forward for *pattern*; the final / is optional.
?pattern?	Regular-expression-search backward for *pattern*; the final **?** is optional.
L	List lines that have breakpoints or actions.
S	List the names of all subroutines. Each name is prefixed with the package the subroutine is declared in.
t	Toggle trace mode on or off.
b *line condition*	Set a breakpoint. If *line* is omitted, sets a breakpoint on the line that is about to be executed. If a condition is specified, it is evaluated each time the statement is reached and a breakpoint is taken only if the condition is true. Breakpoints may only be set on lines that begin an executable statement.
b *subname condition*	
	Set breakpoint at first executable line of subroutine.
d *line*	Delete breakpoint. If *line* is omitted, deletes the breakpoint on the line that is about to be executed.
D	Delete all breakpoints.
a *line command*	Set an action for *line*. An action is a Perl command that happens each time a particular line is encountered. A multi-line command may be entered by backslashing the newlines.
A	Delete all line actions.
< *command*	Set an action to happen before every debugger prompt. A multi-line command may be entered by backslashing the newlines.
> *command*	Set an action to happen after the prompt when you've just given a command to return to executing the script. A multi-line command may be entered by backslashing the newlines.
V *package vars*	List specified variables in *package*. If *vars* is omitted, all variables are listed. Default is the *current* package (usually **main**).
X *vars*	Same as **V** command but assumes current package (usually **main**).

! *number*	Redo a debugging command. If *number* is omitted, redoes the previous command.
! *–number*	Redo the command that was that many commands ago.
H *–number*	Display last *number* commands. Only commands longer than one character are listed. If *number* is omitted, lists them all.
q or ^D	Quit.
command	Execute command as a Perl statement. A missing semicolon will be supplied.
p *expr*	Same as **print DB´OUT** *expr*. The **DB´OUT** filehandle is opened to **/dev/tty**, regardless of where **STDOUT** may be redirected to.
= *alias value*	Set an alias, or list current aliases if *alias* and *value* are omitted.

If you want to modify the debugger, copy the Perl library's **perldb.pl** file to a different name (either in the library or in your own private directory), and modify it as necessary. Then set your **PERLDB** environment variable to a Perl command that will read the file, such as:

```
require ´myperldb.pl´;
```

This could be used to implement a form of profiling, for instance. You can also do some customization with the standard debugger by setting up a **.perldb** file in your home directory which contains initialization code. For instance, you could make aliases like these:

```
$DB´alias{´len´} = ´s/^len(.*)/p length($1)/´;
$DB´alias{´stop´} = ´s/^stop (at|in)/b/´;
$DB´alias{´.´} =
   ´s/^\./p "\$DB\´sub(\$DB\´line):\t",\$DB\´line[\$DB\´line]/´;
```

When processing commands, the debugger looks up the first word of the command in the %**DB´alias** array, and if an entry is found, its value is expected to be a substitution command that is to be applied to the current command.

Common Goofs for Novices

- Not running with the **−w** switch to catch obvious typographical errors.

- Putting a comma after the filehandle in a **print** statement.

  Although it looks extremely regular and pretty to put:

  ```
  print STDOUT, "hello", " ", "world!\n";# wrong
  ```

  this is nonetheless **wrong**, because of that first comma. What you want instead is:

  ```
  print STDOUT "hello", " ", "world!\n";# right
  ```

  which is much more correct (although for this example, doing it in one string would probably be more likely). The syntax is this way so that you can say:

  ```
  print $filehandle "hello", " ", "world!\n";
  ```

  where **$filehandle** is a scalar holding the name of a filehandle at runtime, distinct from:

  ```
  print $notafilehandle, "hello", " ", "world!\n";
  ```

  where **$notafilehandle** is simply a string that is added to the list of things to be printed.

- Using == instead of **eq** and != instead of **ne**.

  The == and != are *numeric* tests. The other two are *string* tests. The strings "**123**" and "**123.00**" are equal numerically, but not equal as strings. And all non-numeric strings are equal to zero. You probably want string comparison operators nearly always unless you are dealing with numbers.

- Leaving **$** off the front of the variable on the left side of an assignment.

  A sign of too much shell or *awk* programming, which hopefully Perl will cure you of. The assignment statement is not:

  ```
  camel=´dromedary´  # wrong
  ```

  but rather:

  ```
  $camel=´dromedary´;   # right
  ```

• Forgetting the **&** on a subroutine call.

A sign of too much C programming (poor lost soul). The proper Perl subroutine invocation looks like:

```
$back = &hump($one,$two);
```

or:

```
$back = do hump($one,$two);
```

but never:

```
$back = hump($one,$two);
```

(unless you have extended the Perl syntax to recognize your **hump** operator).

• Leaving $ off of the loop variable of **foreach**.

A sign of too much C shell programming (oxymoronic, isn't it?). Although the C shell likes:

```
foreach hump (one two)
stuff_it $hump
end
```

you will need to say the same thing in Perl as:

```
foreach $hump ('one','two') {
    &stuff_it($hump);
}
```

• Using **else if** or **elif** instead of elsif.

Syntax like:

```
if (expression) {
   block;
} else if (another_expression) {
   another_block;
}
```

is illegal. The **else** part is always a block, and a naked **if** is not a block. That's what you get when you expect Perl to be exactly the same as C. What you want instead is:

```
if (expression) {
   block;
} elsif (another_expression) {
   another_block;
}
```

Note that **elif** is **file** spelled backwards. Only Algol-ers would want a keyword that was the same as another word spelled backwards.

- Forgetting the trailing semicolon.

  Obviously you've done too much *awk* hacking recently. Every statement in Perl is terminated by a semicolon.

- Forgetting that BLOCK requires curly braces.

  Naked statements are not BLOCKs. If you are creating a control structure, like a **while** loop or an **if** statement (which requires a BLOCK or two), you *must* use curly braces for each BLOCK.

- Not saving **$1..$9** across regular expressions.

  Remember that every new **m/atch/** or **s/ubsti/tute/** will set (or clear, or mangle) your **$1** through **$9** variables, as well as $\`, $´, and $&. One way to save them right away is to evaluate the match within an array context, as in:

  ```
  ($one,$two) = /(\w+) (\w+)/;
  ```

  which doesn't even bother stuffing them into **$1** just so that you can pull it out later.

- Not realizing that a **local( )** also changes the variable name within other subroutines called within the scope of the local.

  It's easy to forget that **local** is a runtime statement, because there's no equivalent in C.

- Losing track of curly pairings.

  A good text editor will help you find the pairs. Get one.

- Using loop control statements in **do—{ }—while**.

  Although the curly braces in this control structure look suspiciously like part of a BLOCK, they aren't.

- Forgetting the **$** or **@** on the front of variables.

- Not chopping the output of `` `command` ``.

  Another sign of too much shell programming. The shell (both Bourne and C flavors) trim the trailing newline for you. In Perl, you'll have to do it explicitly, as in:

  ```
  chop($thishost = `hostname`);
  ```

- Saying @foo[1] when you mean $foo[1].

  The @foo[1] reference is an array **slice**, and means an array consisting of the single element $foo[1]. Sometimes, this doesn't make any difference, as in:

  ```
  print "the answer is @foo[1]\n";
  ```

  but it makes a big difference for things like:

  ```
  @foo[1] = <STDIN>;
  ```

  which will slurp up all the rest of **STDIN**, and assign the *first* line to $foo[1]. Probably not what you intended. Get into the habit of thinking "$ means a single value, while @ means a list of values," and you'll do OK.

- Forgetting to select the right filehandle before setting $^, $~, or $|.

  These variables depend on the currently selected filehandle, as determined by **select(FILEHANDLE)**. The initial filehandle so selected is **STDOUT**. You must use some combination of **select** and assignment to set these for the others. For example, to set the buffering for pipes returned by **pipe(R,W)**, use something like:

  ```
  $oldhandle = select(R);
  $| = 1;
  select(W);
  $| = 1;
  select($oldhandle);
  ```

  (It is bad programming practice to presume that **STDOUT** is the default selection. Someday, you'll appreciate us having told you that.)

Efficiency

While most of the work of programming may be simply getting a program working properly, you may find yourself wanting more bang for the buck out of your Perl program. Perl's rich set of operators, datatypes, and control constructs are not necessarily intuitive when it comes to speed and space optimization. Many trade-offs were made during Perl's design, and such decisions are buried in the guts of the code. In general, the shorter and simpler your code is, the faster it runs, but there are exceptions. This section attempts to help you make it work "just a wee bit better."

You'll note sometimes that optimizing for time may cost you in space or programmer efficiency (indicated by conflicting hints below). Them's the breaks. If programming was easy, they wouldn't need something as complicated as a human being to do it, now would they?

Time Efficiency

- Avoid **getc** for anything but single character terminal I/O.

- Avoid subscripting when **foreach** or array operators will do.

  Subscripting involves floating-point operations and conversion from floating point to integer, and there's often a better way to do it. Consider using **foreach**, **shift**, and **slice** operations.

- Avoid **goto.**

  It scans the program from the top for the indicated label.

- Avoid **printf** if **print** will work.

  Quite apart from the extra overhead of **printf**, some implementations have field length limitations that **print** gets around.

- Avoid $&, $`, and $´.

  Any occurrence in your program causes all matches to save the searched string for possible future reference. However, once you've blown it, it doesn't hurt to have more of them.

- Avoid **eval** and its equivalents.

  Any **eval** forces all special variables to be initialized, including $&. But this is a one-time overhead, so more instances of **eval** don't cost you more (apart from the intrinsic overhead of recompiling the evaluated code).

- Avoid **eval** inside a loop.

  Put the loop into the **eval** instead, to avoid redundant recompilations of the code.

- Avoid runtime-compiled patterns.

  Use the /**pattern**/**o** (once only) pattern modifier to avoid pattern recompilation when the pattern doesn't change over the life of the process. For patterns that change occasionally, you can use the fact that a null pattern refers back to the previous pattern, like this:

```
/$currentpattern/;# Dummy match.
while (<>) {
    print if //;
}
```

You can also use the **eval** function—see the section "Grep Programs" in Chapter 6.

- Multiple simple statements are often faster than corresponding expressions or patterns.

  This is because the optimizer likes to hoist certain simple operations up into the tightest part of the interpreter loop, and a complicated expression or pattern defeats this.

- Reject common cases early with **next if**.

  As with multiple simple statements, the optimizer likes this. And it just makes sense to avoid unnecessary work. You can typically discard comment lines and blank lines even before you do a split or chop:

```
while (<>) {
    next if /^#/;
    next if /^$/;
    chop;
    @piggies = split(/,/);
    ...
}
```

- Avoid subroutine calls in tight loops, especially with lengthy parameters.

- Use **readdir** rather than **<*>**.

  To get all the files within a directory, say something like:

```
opendir(DIR,".");
@files = sort grep(!/^\./, readdir(DIR));
closedir(DIR);
```

- Avoid frequent **substr** on long strings.

- Use **pack** and **unpack** instead of multiple **substr** invocations.

- Use **substr** as an lvalue rather than concatenating substrings.

For example, to replace the fourth through sixth characters of **$foo** with the contents of the variable **$bar**, don't do:

```
$foo = substr($foo,0,3) . $bar . substr($foo,6);
```

Instead, simply identify the part of the string to be replaced, and assign into it, as in:

```
substr($foo,3,3) = $bar;
```

- Use s/// rather than concatenating substrings.

- Use modifiers and equivalent **&&** and **||**, instead of full-blown conditionals.

  Statement modifiers avoid the overhead of entering and leaving a BLOCK, and can often be more readable. The logical operators are translated internally to the equivalent statement modifiers whenever possible.

- Use **$foo = $a || $b || $c.**

  This is much faster (and shorter to say) than:

```
if ($a) {
    $foo = $a;
} elsif ($b) {
    $foo = $b;
} elsif ($c) {
    $foo = $c;
}
```

- Use associative arrays instead of linear searches.

  For example, instead of searching through **@keywords** to see if **$_** is a keyword, construct an associative array with:

```
undef %keywords;
for (@keywords) {
    $keywords{$_}++;
}
```

  Then, you can quickly tell if **$_** is a keyword by testing **$keyword{$_}** for a non-zero value.

- Group similar cases to help the switch optimizer.

  When testing a string for various prefixes, put together all the /^a/ patterns, all the /^b/ patterns, and so on. The switch optimizer will build a branch directly to the first case that can possibly match.

- Don't test things you know won't match (use **next** or **elsif** to avoid falling through).

- Avoid unnecessary system calls.

  For example, don't call *time* when a cached value of **$now** would do. Use the special _ filehandle to avoid unnecessary *stat*(2) calls.

- Use special operators like **study**, vector ops, **unpack** ´u´ and **unpack** ´%´ formats.

- Beware of the tail wagging the dog.

  (<STDIN>)[0], **0 .. 2000000** and similar misstatements can cause Perl to go through much unnecessary work. In accord with UNIX philosophy, Perl gives you enough rope to hang yourself.

- Avoid regular expressions with many globs, or big **{m,n}** numbers on parenthesized expressions.

  Such patterns can result in exponentially slow backtracking behavior unless the globs usually match.

- Try to maximize length of any non-optional literal strings in regular expressions.

  The optimizer looks for these and hands them off to a Boyer-Moore search, which benefits from longer strings. Compile your pattern with the **–D512** debugging switch to see what Perl thinks the longest literal string is.

- Factor operations out of loops.

  The Perl optimizer does not attempt to remove invariant code from loops. It expects you to exercise some sense.

- Slinging strings can be faster than slinging arrays.

- Slinging arrays can be faster than slinging strings.

  It all depends on whether you're going to reuse the strings or arrays, and on which operations you're going to perform—heavy modification of each element implies that arrays will be better, and occasional modification of some elements implies that strings will be better. But you just have to try it and see.

- Use **??** search and **reset** where appropriate.

- Package variables can be faster than **local( )** variables, especially for scratch arrays.

- Sorting on a manufactured key array may be faster than using fancy sort subroutine.

  See the section "Sorting an Array by a Computable Field" in Chapter 5.

- **tr/abc/ /d** is faster than **s/[abc]/ /**.

- Prefer **print** with a comma separator to a series of concatenated strings.

  For example:

  ```
  print $fullname{$name} . " has a new home directory " .
      $home{$name} . "\n";
  ```

  has to glue together the two associative arrays and the two fixed strings before passing them to the low-level print routines, whereas:

  ```
  print $fullname{$name}, " has a new home directory ",
      $home{$name}, "\n";
  ```

  doesn't.

- Prefer **join("", ...)** to a series of concatenated strings.

  Multiple . concatenations cause strings to be copied back and forth multiple times. The **join** operator avoids this.

- **split** on a fixed string is generally faster than **split** on a pattern.

  That is, use **split(/ /,...)** rather than **split(/ +/,...)** if you know there will only be one space. However, the patterns /\s+/, /^/ and // are specially optimized.

- Pre-extending an array or string can save some time.

  As strings and arrays grow, Perl extends them by allocating a new copy with some room for growth and copying in the old value. Pre-extending a string with the **x** operator or an array by setting **$#array** can prevent this occasional overhead.

- Don't **undef** long strings and arrays if they'll be reused for the same purpose.

  This helps prevent reallocation copying when the string must be re-extended.

- Prefer **"\0" x 8192** over **unpack("x8192",( ))**.

- **system("mkdir...")** may be faster on multiple directories if *mkdir* isn't a system call.

- Avoid using **eof** if return values will already indicate it.

- Cache entries from passwd and group (and so on) that are apt to be reused.

  For example, to cache the return value from **gethostbyaddr** when you are converting numeric addresses (like **137.102.1.58**) to names (like **r.iWarp.intel.com**), you can use something like:

  ```
  sub numtoname {
      local($_) = @_;
      unless (defined $numtoname{$_}) {
          local(@a) = gethostbyaddr(pack('C4', split(/\./)),2);
          $numtoname{$_} = @a > 0 ? $a[0] : $_;
      }
      $numtoname{$_};
  }
  ```

- Worry about starting subprocesses, but only if they're frequent.

  A single *pwd*, *hostname*, or *find* process isn't going to hurt you—after all, a shell starts subprocesses all day long. We do encourage the toolbox approach, believe it or not.

- Keep track of your working directory yourself rather than calling **pwd** repeatedly.

  (A package is provided in the standard library for this. See **pwd.pl** in Appendix B.)

- Avoid shell metacharacters in commands—**exec** lists where appropriate.

- Set the sticky bit on the Perl interpreter on machines without demand paging.

- Using defaults *doesn't* make your program faster (much).

Space Efficiency

- Use **vec** for compact integer array storage.

- Prefer numeric values over string values—they require no additional space over that allocated for the scalar header structure.

- Use **substr** to store constant length strings in a longer string.

- Use **__END__** and the **<DATA>** filehandle to avoid storing program data as both a string and an array.

- Prefer **each** to **keys** where order doesn't matter.

- Delete or **undef** globals that are no longer in use.

- Use **dbm** to store associative arrays.

- Use temp files to store array values.

- Use pipes to offload processing to other UNIX tools.

- Avoid array operations and slurps.

- Avoid using **tr**///, each of which must store a translation table of 256 short integers (not characters, since we have to remember which characters are to be deleted).

- Don't unroll your loops or inline your subroutines.

Programmer Efficiency

- Use defaults.

- Use funky shortcut command-line switches like **–a, –n, –p, –s, –i**.

- Use **for** to mean **foreach**.

- Sling UNIX commands around with backticks.

- Use **<*>** and such.

- Use runtime-compiled patterns.

- Use patterns with lots of *****, **+** and **{ }**.

- Sling whole arrays and slurp entire files.

- Use **getc**.

- Use **$&, $`** and **$´**.

- Don't check error values on **open**—**<HANDLE>** and **print HANDLE** will simply no-op.

- Don't **close** your files—they'll be closed on the next **open**.

- Pass subroutine arguments as globals.

- Don't name your subroutine parameters.

  You can access them directly as $_[expr].

- Use whatever you think of first.

Maintainer Efficiency

- Don't use defaults.
- Use **foreach** to mean **foreach**.
- Use meaningful loop labels with **next** and **last**.
- Use meaningful variable names.
- Use meaningful subroutine names.
- Put the important thing first on the line using **&&**, **||**, modifiers.
- Close your files when you're done with them.
- Use packages to hide your implementation details.
- Pass arguments as subroutine parameters.
- Name your subroutine parameters using **local**.
- Parenthesize for clarity.
- Put in lots of (useful) comments.
- Write the script as its own manpage.

  See **wrapman** in Chapter 6 for a way to do this automagically.

Porter Efficiency

- Wave a handsome tip under his nose.
- Avoid functions that aren't implemented everywhere.

  You can use **eval** tests to see what's available.

- Don't expect native float and double to **pack** and **unpack** on foreign machines.

- Use network byte order when sending binary data over the network.

- Don't send binary data over the network.

- Check **$]** to see if the current version supports all the features you use.

- Put the **eval exec** hack in even if you don't use it.

- Put the **#!/usr/bin/perl** line in even if you don't use it.

- Test for variants of UNIX commands.

  Some *find*s can't handle **–xdev**, for example.

- Avoid variant UNIX commands if you can do it internally.

- Use the C preprocessor to find out what kind of machine you're running on.

- Put all your scripts into a single NFS filesystem that's mounted everywhere.

User Efficiency

- Avoid forcing prompt order—pop them into their favorite editor with a form.

- Put up something for them to read while you continue doing work.

- Give the option of helpful messages at every prompt.

- Give a helpful usage message if they don't give correct input.

- Display the default action at every prompt, and maybe a few alternatives.

- Choose defaults for beginners. Allow experts to change the defaults.

- Use single character input where it makes sense.

- Pattern the interaction after other things the user is familiar with.

- Make error messages clear about what needs fixing. Include all pertinent information such as filename and *errno*, like this:

```
open(FILE, $file) || die "Can't open $file for reading: $!\n";
```

- Use **fork && exit** to detach when the rest of the script is batch processing.

- Allow arguments to come either from the command line or via **STDIN**.

- ·Use text-oriented network protocols.

- Don't put arbitrary limitations into your program.

- Prefer variable length fields over fixed length.

- Be vicariously lazy.

Setuid Scripts

Perl is designed to make it easy to write secure setuid and setgid scripts. Unlike shells, which are based on multiple substitution passes on each line of the script, Perl uses a more conventional evaluation scheme with fewer hidden "gotchas." Additionally, since the language has more built-in functionality, it has to rely less upon external (and possibly untrustworthy) programs to accomplish its purposes.

In an unpatched 4.2bsd or 4.3bsd kernel, setuid scripts are intrinsically insecure due to a race condition, but it's possible to patch your kernel so that the setuid (and setgid) permission bits are ignored on scripts (that is, on anything that selects an interpreter via the **#!** mechanism). Future versions of UNIX will get around this problem in a different way (by passing to the interpreter an already opened file descriptor instead of the filename of the script, which is subject to spoofing).

Meanwhile, if you disable setuid scripts in the kernel, Perl can emulate the setuid and setgid mechanism when it notices the otherwise useless setuid/gid bits on Perl scripts. Perl does this by running a special version of Perl for you that is setuid to root, called **suidperl** (which should never be run explicitly). If the kernel feature isn't disabled, Perl will complain loudly that your setuid script is insecure. You'll need to either disable the kernel setuid script feature, or put a C wrapper around the script (see the **suidscript** program in Chapter 6).

When Perl is executing a setuid script, it takes special precautions to prevent you from falling into any obvious traps. (In some ways, a Perl script is more secure than the corresponding C program.) What it does is run a special version of Perl called **taintperl** (unless it's already running **suidperl**, which does everything **taintperl** does), which behaves as follows. Any command line argument, environment variable, or input to **taintperl** is marked as "tainted," and may not be used, directly or indirectly, in any command that invokes a subshell, or in any command that modifies files, directories, or processes. Nor may it be used in an

eval—allowing someone to submit arbitrary Perl code to be run with your privileges is not the epitome of security. Any variable that is set within an expression
that has previously referenced a tainted value also becomes tainted (even if it is
logically impossible for the tainted value to influence the variable). The following sequence illustrates this:

```
$foo = shift;             # $foo is tainted
$bar = $foo,´bar´;        # $bar is also tainted
$xxx = <>;                # Tainted
$path = $ENV{´PATH´};     # Tainted, but see below
$abc = ´abc´;             # Not tainted

system "echo $foo";       # Insecure
system "/bin/echo", $foo; # Secure (doesn´t use sh)
system "echo $bar";       # Insecure
system "echo $abc";       # Insecure until PATH set

$ENV{´PATH´} = ´/bin:/usr/bin´;
$ENV{´IFS´} = ´´ if $ENV{´IFS´} ne ´´;

$path = $ENV{´PATH´};     # Not tainted
system "echo $abc";       # Is secure now!

open(FOO,"$foo");         # OK
open(FOO,">$foo");        # Not OK

open(FOO,"echo $foo|");   # Not OK, but...
open(FOO,"-|") || exec ´echo´, $foo;   # OK

$zzz = ´echo $foo´;       # Insecure, zzz tainted

unlink $abc,$foo;         # Insecure
umask $foo;               # Insecure
eval $foo;                # Very insecure

exec "echo $foo";         # Insecure
exec "echo", $foo;        # Secure (doesn´t use sh)
exec "sh", ´-c´, $foo;    # Considered secure, alas
```

The taintedness is associated with each scalar value, so some elements of an array
can be tainted while others aren't.

If you try to do something insecure, you will get a fatal error saying something
like "Insecure dependency" or "Insecure PATH." Note that you can still write an
insecure system call or **exec**, but only by explicitly doing something like the last

example above. You can also bypass the tainting mechanism by referencing sub-patterns—Perl presumes that if you reference a substring using **$1**, **$2**, and so on, you knew what you were doing when you wrote the pattern:

```
$ARGV[0] =~ /^-P(\w+)$/;
$printer = $1;                 # Not tainted
```

This is fairly secure since **\w+** doesn't match shell metacharacters. *Note* however that use of **.+** would have been insecure, but Perl doesn't check for that, so you must be careful with your patterns. This is the ONLY mechanism for untainting user-supplied filenames if you want to do file operations on them (unless you make **$>** equal to **$<**).

It's also possible to get into trouble with other operations that don't care whether they use tainted values. Make judicious use of the file tests in dealing with any user-supplied filenames. When possible, do opens and such after setting **$> = $<**.[44] Perl doesn't prevent you from opening tainted filenames for reading, so be careful what you print out. The tainting mechanism is intended to prevent stupid mistakes, not to remove the need for thought.

Scripts running setuid would do well to execute the following lines before doing anything else, just to keep any subshells honest:

```
$ENV{'PATH'} = '/bin:/usr/bin';    # or whatever you need
$ENV{'SHELL'} = '/bin/sh' if $ENV{'SHELL'} ne '';
$ENV{'IFS'} = '' if $ENV{'IFS'} ne '';
```

If you want to perform taint checks on a script that isn't currently running setuid or setgid, you can run **taintperl** directly, or mention it on the **#!** line. This is advisable when developing a script that will be used later as a setuid script. It's also necessary when running a script that will be made setuid after using the **dump** operator or the **-u** switch.

Distribution and Installation

Specific installation instructions come in the **README** file of the Perl distribution kit. In general, you'll get the Perl kit either as a tar file or as a set of shar (shell archive) scripts. You then unpack these as appropriate, read the **README** file and run a massive shell script called **Configure**, which tries to figure out everything about your system. After this is done, you do a series of "makes" to

---

[44] Systems that support the *setreuid(2)* system call (or equivalent) can temporarily swap real and effective uids by saying (**$<,$>**) = (**$>,$<**); both before and after the desired security checks.

find header file dependencies, to compile Perl (and *a2p*), to run regression tests and to install Perl in your system directories.

It's possible you'll get a copy of Perl that is already compiled. You'll have to make sure you get *suidperl*, *taintperl*, *a2p* and *s2p* as well, and the Perl library routines (see Appendix B). Install these files in the directories that your version was compiled for. Note: binary distributions of Perl are made available because they're handy, not because you are restricted from getting the source and compiling it yourself. The people who give you the binary distribution ought to provide you with some form of access to the source, if only a pointer to where *they* got the source from. See the **Copying** file in the distribution for more information.

Translation from Awk and Sed

Along with the Perl distribution come three translators: *a2p*, which translates *awk* scripts to Perl, *s2p*, which translates *sed* scripts to Perl, and *find2perl*, which translates *find*(1) commands to Perl. These translators don't necessarily produce idiomatic Perl, but you can use the output as a starting place. The translators can also help you see how the features of the other language map into those of Perl.

The *a2p* translator is written in C, so it is compiled and installed automatically along with Perl. The *s2p* and *find2perl* translators are themselves written in Perl, so no further compilation is necessary. They are installed automatically when Perl is installed.

a2p and *s2p* are both invoked as ordinary filter programs, and have some switches that modify the translation process. (For example, *a2p* lets you specify the names of the fields you want each record to be split into.) The syntax and switches for these programs are documented fully in their respective manual pages, so we won't go into them here. The *a2p* manual page in particular will tell you some ways to make your translated script more idiomatic.

The *find2perl* translator is used just like the *find*(1) command, but instead of doing the find, it spits out a Perl script that can be fed directly to the Perl interpreter to do the find. Or, you can modify it to do something perhaps that *find* can't do. Apart from that, you might use *find2perl* because it supports almost all the common *find* options (and some uncommon ones), including **–fstype**, **–print0**, **–ctime**, **–prune**, **–xdev**, **–depth**, **–ls**, **–cpio**, **–ncpio**, **–tar** and **–eval**.

Examples

The Perl source distribution comes with some sample scripts in the the **eg/** subdirectory. Feel free to browse among them and use them. They are not installed automatically, however, so you'll need to copy them to the appropriate directory, and possibly fix the **#!** line to point to the right interpreter (see the **fixin** script in Chapter 6 for a way to do this easily).

The files in the *t/* and *lib/* subdirectories, though incredibly arcane in spots, can also serve as examples.

The examples in this book are also available for anonymous FTP from **uunet.uu.net**.

Patches

Since Perl is constantly being improved (and broken), Larry frequently posts patches to the Usenet newsgroup **comp.lang.perl**. Subscribe to this newsgroup if possible. Your distribution is likely to have had most of the patches applied already—check the **patchlevel.h** file to see the current patchlevel of your distribution. If you find you are missing any intermediate patches, look in one of the newer patches for instructions on getting older patches.

Bug reports may be posted to **comp.lang.perl** or sent directly to Larry at the address **lwall@netlabs.com**.

Patches are sent out with complete instructions on how to apply them. You'll want to have the *patch* program handy. (This program was written in self-defense by Larry when he couldn't persuade people to apply by hand all his *rn* patches in order, resulting in cascading chaotic catastrophes around the world.) The *patch* program is available from most of the places that Perl itself is available from.

Linking in C Subroutines with Perl

It is possible to link in C subroutines with Perl to make a special version of the interpreter. When Perl is compiled in the source distribution directory, a special version called **uperl.o** is made that has a single unresolved global, a call to the subroutine **userinit( )**. You can link this object file, supplying your own version of **userinit( )**. This routine is then expected to call the initialization routines of any packages that you want to link in with Perl. This mechanism currently supports only static linking of C subroutines. It is designed, however, with the idea of providing dynamic linking someday, at least on those architectures which support it.

In order to link in a set of C routines such as a library, you have to provide a set of "glue" routines that translate Perl subroutine calls to the corresponding C subroutine calls, handling all the type conversion in both directions. A set of glue routines consists of an initialization function called from **userinit( )**, a function that can call any of the C subroutines supported by the glue routines, and a pair of functions that can read and write any magical variables supported by the package. The initialization function adds symbols to the Perl symbol table that refer back to the other glue routines, along with an index to be passed to the routine when it is called so that it knows which C subroutine or variable is being referenced.

The exact details of this are still subject to revision, so look for additional documentation in the **README** file of the **usub/** subdirectory of the Perl distribution directory. You'll also find there a sample set of glue routines that link in the BSD curses library. The glue routines are in the **usub/curses.mus** file, which is preprocessed into **usub/curses.c** by the **mus** program. The **mus** format lets you specify in a simple table format the translation of arguments from Perl's internal form to the form required by C. It's not 100% effective but it beats a kick in the head. The cases it doesn't cover can be generated by analogy with some of the routines in the **do*.c** files in the Perl distribution.

There is also a **man2mus** program that attempts to translate the specifications found in typical manual pages into **.mus** format entries. Like **mus** itself, **man2mus** is not 100% effective, but can save you a lot of time producing the initial boilerplate.

Perl Poetry

The following forgery appeared on Usenet on April Fool's Day, 1990. It is presented here without comment, merely to show how disgusting the metaphors of a typical programming language really are:

```
Article 970 of comp.lang.perl:
Path: jpl-devvax!jpl-dexxav!lwall
From: lwall@jpl-dexxav.JPL.NASA.GOV (Larry Wall)
Newsgroups: news.groups,rec.arts.poems,comp.lang.perl
Subject: CALL FOR DISCUSSION: comp.lang.perl.poems
Message-ID: <0401@jpl-devvax.JPL.NASA.GOV>
Date: 1 Apr 90 00:00:00 GMT
Reply-To: lwall@jpl-devvax.JPL.NASA.GOV (Larry Wall)
Organization: Jet Prepulsion Laboratory, Pasadena, CA
Lines: 61


It has come to my attention that there is a crying need for a
place for people to express both their emotional and technical
natures simultaneously.  Several people have sent me some items
```

which don´t fit into any newsgroup. Perhaps it´s because I
recently posted to both comp.lang.perl and to rec.arts.poems,
but people seem to be writing poems in Perl, and they´re
asking me where they should post them. Here is a sampling:

From a graduate student (in finals week), the following haiku:

> study, write, study,
> do review (each word) if time.
> close book. sleep? what´s that?

And someone writing from Fort Lauderdale writes:

> sleep, close together,
> sort of sin each spring & wait;
> 50% die

A person who wishes to remain anonymous wrote the following
example of "Black Perl". (The Pearl poet would have been
shocked, no doubt.)

```
BEFOREHAND: close door, each window & exit;  wait until time.
    open spellbook, study, read (scan, select, tell us);
write it, print the hex while each watches,
    reverse its length, write again;
      kill spiders, pop them, chop, split, kill them.
        unlink arms, shift, wait & listen (listening, wait),
sort the flock (then, warn the "goats" & kill the "sheep");
    kill them, dump qualms, shift moralities,
      values aside, each one;
          die sheep! die to reverse the system
             you accept (reject, respect);
next step,
    kill the next sacrifice, each sacrifice,
      wait, redo ritual until "all the spirits are pleased";
    do it ("as they say").
do it(*everyone***must***participate***in***forbidden**s*e*x*).
return last victim; package body;
    exit crypt (time, times & "half a time") & close it,
      select (quickly) & warn your next victim;
AFTERWORDS: tell nobody.
    wait, wait until time;
      wait until next year, next decade;
          sleep, sleep, die yourself,
             die at last
```

I tried that, and it actually parses in Perl. It doesn´t
appear to do anything useful, however. I think I´m glad,
actually...

I hereby propose the creation of comp.lang.perl.poems as a
place for such items, so we don´t clutter the perl or poems
newsgroups with things that may be of interest to neither.

```
Or, alternately, we should create rec.arts.poems.perl for
items such as those above which merely parse, and don't do
anything useful. (There is precedent in rec.arts.poems,
after all.) Then also create comp.lang.perl.poems for poems
that actually do something, such as this haiku of my own:

print STDOUT q
Just another Perl hacker,
unless $spring

Larry Wall
lwall@jpl-devvax.jpl.nasa.gov
```

Well, so much for anything resembling literary value.

History Made Practical

In order to understand why Perl is defined the way it is (or isn't), one must first understand why Perl even exists. So, let's drag out the old, dusty, history book. . .

Way back in 1986, Larry was a systems programmer on a project that was developing multi-level-secure wide-area networks. He was in charge of an installation consisting of three Vaxen and three Suns on the West Coast, connected over an encrypted, 1200-baud serial line to a similar configuration on the East Coast. Since Larry's primary job was support (he wasn't a programmer on the project, just the system guru), he was able to exploit his three virtues (laziness, impatience, and hubris) to develop and enhance all sorts of useful tools—such as *rn*, **patch** and **warp**.[45]

One day, after Larry had just finished ripping *rn* to shreds, leaving it in pieces on the floor of his directory, the great Manager came to him and said, "Larry, we need a configuration management and control system for all 6 Vaxen and all 6 Suns. We need it in a month. Go to it!"

So, Larry, never being one to shirk work, asked himself what was the best way to have a bi-coastal CM system, without writing it from scratch, that would allow viewing of problem reports on both coasts, with approvals and control. The answer came to him in one word: B-news.

---

[45] It was about this time that Larry coined the phrase "feeping creaturism" in a desperate attempt to justify on the basis of biological necessity his overwhelming urge to add "just one more feature." After all, if Life is Simply Too Complicated, why not programs too? Especially programs like *rn* that really ought to be treated as advanced Artificial Intelligence projects so that they can read your news for you. Of course, some people say that the **patch** program is already *too* smart.

Larry went off and installed news on these machines, and added two control commands: an "append" command to append to an existing article, and a "synchronize" command to keep the article numbers the same on both coasts. CM would be done using RCS, and approvals and submissions would be done using news and *rn*. Fine so far.

Then the great Manager asked him to produce reports. News was maintained in separate files on a master machine, with lots of cross references between files. Larry's first thought was "Let's use *awk*." Unfortunately, *awk* couldn't handle opening and closing of multiple files based on information in the files. Larry didn't want to have to code a special-purpose tool. As a result, a new language was born.

It wasn't originally called Perl. Larry bandied about a number of names with his officemates and cohorts (Dan Faigin and Mark Biggar, his brother-in-law, who also helped greatly with the initial design). Larry actually considered every 3 or 4 letter word in the dictionary. One of the earliest names was "Gloria," after his sweetheart (and wife). He soon decided that it would cause too much domestic confusion. The name then became "Pearl," which mutated into our present day "Perl," partly because Larry saw a reference to a graphics language called "pearl," but mostly because he's too lazy to type 5 letters all the time. And, of course, so that Perl could be used as a 4 letter word. (You'll note, however, the vestiges of the former spelling in the acronym's gloss: "Practical Extraction **And** Report Language.")

This early Perl lacked many of the features of today's Perl. Pattern matching and filehandles were there, scalars were there, and formats were there, but there were very few functions, no associative arrays, and only a crippled implementation of regular expressions, borrowed from *rn*. The manual page was only 15 pages long. But Perl was faster than *sed* and *awk*, and began to be used on other applications on the project.

But Larry was needed elsewhere. Another great Manager came over one day and said "Larry, support R&D." And Larry said, okay. He took Perl with him, and discovered that it was turning into a good tool for system administration. He borrowed Henry Spencer's beautiful regular expression package and butchered it into something Henry would prefer not to think about during dinner. Then Larry added most of the goodies he wanted, and a few goodies other people wanted. He released it on the network. The rest, as they say, is history.[46]

---

[46] And this, so to speak, is a footnote to history. When Perl was started, *rn* had just been ripped to pieces in anticipation of a major rewrite. Since he started work on Perl, Larry hasn't touched *rn*. It is still in pieces. Larry is talking about rewriting it in Perl.

A

Semi-formal Description

We're using a modified form of BNF to describe the syntax of Perl:

UPPERCASE_WORD	A non-terminal
NAME ::= whatever	May be composed of
whatever | whatever	Alternation
(* whatever *)	Occurs 0 or more times, usually done { x }
(+ whatever +)	Occurs 1 or more times, usually done x { x }
(? whatever ?)	Occurs 0 or 1 time, usually done [x]
someNAME...sameNAME	Strings or delimiters that must match

Also note that (in this grammar, at least):

(* operand operator *) operand	Implies left associativity
operand (* operator operand *)	Implies right associativity

In addition, the following describe literal chunks of your Perl script:

`!#$@`	Literal text without the single quotes
lowercaseword	A literal keyword
[charlist]	A single character in the set of characters

[^charlist]	A single character *not* in the set of characters
\\	A literal backslash
\nnn	A character represented by octal value
\n	A newline

Note that the grammar below is not identical to the *yacc* grammar that Perl actually uses. The *yacc* grammar is much more ambiguous, relying on both operator precedence and semantic filtration to produce an effect much like the grammar below. We believe this grammar will be more useful to you as a description, but if you want to know how it really works, look at the file **perl.y** in the Perl distribution directory.

```
PROGRAM         ::=    (* ITEM *)

ITEM            ::=    DECLARATION
                  |    (? LABEL ?) STATEMENT

STATEMENT       ::=    CONDITIONAL
                  |    LOOP
                  |    `;`
                  |    SIDE_EFFECT `;`

CONDITIONAL     ::=    if `(` EXPR `)` BLOCK (? ELSE ?)
                  |    unless `(` EXPR `)` BLOCK (? ELSE ?)
                  |    if BLOCK BLOCK (? ELSE ?)
                  |    unless BLOCK BLOCK (? ELSE ?)

LOOP            ::=    while `(` (? OPTEXPR ?) `)`
                            BLOCK (? CONT ?)
                  |    until `(` EXPR `)` BLOCK (? CONT ?)
                  |    while BLOCK BLOCK (? CONT ?)
                  |    until BLOCK BLOCK (? CONT ?)
                  |    FOR SCALAR `(` LIST `)`
                            BLOCK (? CONT ?)
                  |    FOR `(` LIST `)` BLOCK (? CONT ?)
                  |    FOR `(` (? SIDE_EFFECT ?) `;`
                            (? EXPR ?) `;`
                            (? SIDE_EFFECT ?) `)` BLOCK
                  |    BLOCK (? CONT ?)

FOR             ::=    for | foreach

CONT            ::=    continue BLOCK

ELSE            ::=    (* ELSIF *) else BLOCK

ELSIF           ::=    elsif `(` EXPR `)` BLOCK

BLOCK           ::=    `{` PROGRAM `}`

LABEL           ::=    WORD `:`
```

```
DECLARATION      ::=    FORMAT
                 |      SUBROUTINE
                 |      PACKAGE
```

Within a format, newlines are allowed only where explicitly mentioned.

```
FORMAT           ::=    format WORD `=` `\n`
                            (* FORM_LINE *) `.`
                 |      format `=` `\n` (* FORM_LINE *) `.`

FORM_LINE        ::=    `#` COMMENT_LINE `\n`
                 |      TEXT_LINE `\n`
                 |      PICTURE_LINE `\n` LIST `\n`

PICTURE_LINE     ::=    (+ (* NON_FIELDCHAR *) FIELD +)
                            (* NON_FIELDCHAR *)

FIELD            ::=    FIELDCHAR (? JUSTCHARS ?)

FIELDCHAR        ::=    [@^]

JUSTCHARS        ::=    LEFTJUSTS | CENTERS | RIGHTJUSTS
                 |      NUMERIC | `*`

LEFTJUSTS        ::=    (+ `<` +)

CENTERS          ::=    (+ `|` +)

RIGHTJUSTS       ::=    (+ `>` +)

NUMERIC          ::=    (+ `#` +) (? `.` (* `#` *) ?)
                 |      `.` (+ `#` +)

NON_FIELDCHAR    ::=    [^@^]

COMMENT_LINE     ::=    TEXT

TEXT_LINE        ::=    TEXT

SUBROUTINE       ::=    sub WORD BLOCK

PACKAGE          ::=    package WORD `;`

SIDE_EFFECT      ::=    EXPR
                 |      EXPR MOD_OP EXPR

MOD_OP           ::=    if | unless | while | until
```

Note that LIST and EXPR are syntactically the same. We distinguish between them only to document whether the operator in question supplies an array context or a scalar context. The comma in EXPR is like the C comma operator; the comma in LIST is not.

```
LIST            ::=    (* SIMPLE `,` *) SIMPLE

EXPR            ::=    (* SIMPLE `,` *) SIMPLE

SIMPLE          ::=    ASSIGNMENT
                  |    CONDEXPR

ASSIGNMENT      ::=    LVALUE `=` SIMPLE
                  |    LVALUE ASSIGN_OP `=` SIMPLE

ASSIGN_OP       ::=    `**` | `*` | `/` | `%` | `x`
                  |    `+` | `_` | `.` | `<<` | `>>`
                  |    `&` | `^` | `|`

LVALUE          ::=    VARIABLE
                  |    `(` ASSIGNMENT `)`
                  |    local `(` LVALUELIST `)`
                  |    `(` LVALUELIST `,` `)`
                  |    `(` LVALUELIST `)`

LVALUELIST      ::=    (* LVALUE `,` *) LVALUE

CONDEXPR        ::=    (* RANGE `?` RANGE `:` *) RANGE

RANGE           ::=    OR `..` OR
                  |    OR

OR              ::=    (* AND `||` *) AND

AND             ::=    (* BITOR `&&` *) BITOR

BITOR           ::=    (* BITAND BITOR_OP *) BITAND

BITOR_OP        ::=    `|` | `^`

BITAND          ::=    (* EQUALITY `&` *) EQUALITY

EQUALITY        ::=    RELATIONAL EQ_OP RELATIONAL
                  |    RELATIONAL

EQ_OP           ::=    `==` | `!=` | `<=>` | eq | ne | cmp

RELATIONAL      ::=    UNIFUNC REL_OP UNIFUNC
                  |    UNIFUNC

REL_OP          ::=    `<` | `<=` | `>` | `>=`
                  |    lt | le | gt | ge

UNIFUNC         ::=    STRICT_UNIFUNC
                  |    FILETEST

STRICT_UNIFUNC  ::=    UNARY_FUNC FILETEST
                  |    UNARY_FUNC
```

```
UNARY_FUNC        ::=    alarm | caller | chdir | cos | chroot
                  |      exit | eval | exp | getpgrp
                  |      getprotobyname | gethostbyname
                  |      getnetbyname | gmtime | hex | int
                  |      length | localtime | log | ord | oct
                  |      require | reset | rand | rmdir
                  |      readlink | scalar | sin | sleep
                  |      sqrt | srand | umask

FILETEST          ::=    STRICT_FILETEST
                  |      BITSHIFT

STRICT_FILETEST   ::=    FILETEST_OP (? BITSHIFT | WORD ?)

FILETEST_OP       ::=    `-´ [rwxoRWXOezsfdlpSugkbctTBMAC]

BITSHIFT          ::=    (* TERM `<<´ *) TERM

TERM              ::=    (* FACTOR ADD_OP *) FACTOR

ADD_OP            ::=    `+´ | `-´ | `.´

FACTOR            ::=    (* MATCH MUL_OP *) MATCH

MUL_OP            ::=    `*´ | `/´ | `%´ | `x´

MATCH             ::=    (* MATCH MATCH_OP *) UNARY

MATCH_OP          ::=    `=~´ | `!~´

UNARY             ::=    STRICT_UNARY
                  |      POW

STRICT_UNARY      ::=    UNI_OP UNITHING

UNI_OP            ::=    `!´ | `-´ | `+´ | `~´

POW               ::=    CREMENT (* `**´ CREMENT *)

CREMENT           ::=    LVALUE UPDOWN_OP
                  |      UPDOWN_OP LVALUE
                  |      THING

UPDOWN_OP         ::=    `++´ | `--´

UNITHING          ::=    STRICT_FILETEST
                  |      STRICT_UNIFUNC
                  |      STRICT_UNARY
                  |      CREMENT

THING             ::=    LIST_CONS
                  |      VARIABLE
                  |      LITERAL
```

```
                  |        PATTERN
                  |        SUBST
                  |        TRANSLATION
                  |        DO
                  |        LOOP_EXIT
                  |        FILE_OPERATION
                  |        ARRAY_OPERATION
                  |        LIST_OPERATION
                  |        FUNCTION
                  |        WORD

LIST_CONS     ::=          local `(´ LIST `)´
                  |        `(´ LIST `,´ `)´
                  |        `(´ OPTLIST `)´

OPTLIST       ::=          (? LIST ?)

VARIABLE      ::=          INTERPVAR
                  |        NON_INTERPVAR

INTERPVAR     ::=          SCALAR
                  |        SCALAR `[´ EXPR `]´
                  |        SCALAR `{´ LIST `}´
                  |        `$´ `{´ WORD `[´ EXPR `]´ `}´
                  |        ARRAY
                  |        ARRAY `[´ LIST `]´
                  |        ARRAY `{´ LIST `}´
                  |        `$#´ WORD

NON_INTERPVAR ::=          ASSOC
                  |        `*´ WORD

LITERAL       ::=          STRING | NUMBER

STRING        ::=          `\´´ SINGLESTUFF `\´´
                  |        `"´ DOUBLESTUFF `"´
                  |        ``´ DOUBLESTUFF ``´
                  |        `<´ DOUBLESTUFF `>´
                  |        `<<\´´ someTEXT `\´´ SINGLESTUFF
                                 LINEBREAK sameTEXT `\n´
                  |        `<<"´ someTEXT `"´ DOUBLESTUFF
                                 LINEBREAK sameTEXT `\n´
                  |        `<<`´ someTEXT ``´ DOUBLESTUFF
                                 LINEBREAK sameTEXT `\n´
                  |        `q´ someDELIM SINGLESTUFF sameDELIM
                  |        `qq´ someDELIM DOUBLESTUFF sameDELIM
                  |        `qx´ someDELIM DOUBLESTUFF sameDELIM
                  |        `__FILE__´

PATTERN       ::=          `/´ DOUBLESTUFF `/´ MATCHOPTIONS
                  |        `m´ someDELIM DOUBLESTUFF sameDELIM
                                 MATCHOPTIONS
```

```
MATCH_OPTIONS    ::=    (* [io] *)

SUBST            ::=    `s´ someDELIM DOUBLESTUFF sameDELIM
                             DOUBLESTUFF sameDELIM
                             SUBSTOPTIONS

SUBST_OPTIONS    ::=    (* [egio] *)

TRANSLATION      ::=    TR someDELIM DOUBLESTUFF sameDELIM
                             DOUBLESTUFF sameDELIM
                             TRANSOPTIONS

TRANS_OPTIONS    ::=    (* [cds] *)

TR               ::=    y | tr

DO               ::=    do UNITHING
                   |    do BLOCK
                   |    do WORDSCALAR `(´ OPTLIST `)´
                   |    `&´ WORDSCALAR `(´ OPTLIST `)´
                   |    `&´ WORDSCALAR

LOOP_EXIT        ::=    TRANSFER_OP (? WORD ?)

TRANSFER_OP      ::=    next | last | redo | goto | dump
```

Names containing numbers refer to the number of allowable arguments. If there are two numbers, the first indicates how many of the arguments are filehandles.

```
FILE_OPERATION   ::=    select
                   |    select `(´ FILEHANDLE `)´
                   |    select `(´ SIMPLE `,´ SIMPLE `,´
                                   SIMPLE `,´ SIMPLE `)´
                   |    open WORD
                   |    open `(´ WORD `)´
                   |    open `(´ FILEHANDLE `,´ EXPR `)´
                   |    FL_OP `(´ FILEHANDLE `)´
                   |    FL_OP WORDSCALAR
                   |    FL_OP `(´ `)´
                   |    FL_OP
                   |    FL2_OP `(´ FILEHANDLE `,´ EXPR `)´
                   |    FL3_OP `(´ FILEHANDLE `,´ SIMPLE `,´
                                   LIST `)´
                   |    FL22_OP `(´ FILEHANDLE `,´
                                   FILEHANDLE `)´
                   |    FL4_OP `(´ FILEHANDLE `,´ SIMPLE `,´
                                   SIMPLE `,´ LIST `)´
                   |    FL25_OP `(´ FILEHANDLE `,´
                                   FILEHANDLE `,´ SIMPLE `,´
                                   SIMPLE `,´ EXPR `)´

FL_OP            ::=    binmode | close | closedir | eof
                   |    fileno | getc | getpeername
```

```
                    |       getsockname | lstat | readdir
                    |       rewinddir | stat | tell | telldir
                    |       write

FL2_OP          ::=         bind | connect | flock | listen
                    |       opendir | seekdir | shutdown | truncate

FL22_OP         ::=         accept | pipe

FL3_OP          ::=         fcntl | getsockopt | ioctl | read
                    |       seek | send | sysread | syswrite

FL4_OP          ::=         recv | setsocktopt | socket

FL25_OP         ::=         socketpair

ARRAY_OPERATION ::=         SPLICE_OP `(´ ARRAYNAME `,´ LIST `)´
                    |       pop ARRAYNAME
                    |       pop `(´ ARRAYNAME `)´
                    |       shift ARRAYNAME
                    |       shift `(´ ARRAYNAME `)´
                    |       shift
                    |       split `(´ SIMPLE `,´ SIMPLE `,´
                                    SIMPLE `)´
                    |       split `(´ SIMPLE `,´ SIMPLE `)´
                    |       split `(´ SIMPLE `)´
                    |       split
                    |       delete SCALAR `{´ LIST `}´
                    |       `(´ LIST `)´ `[´ EXPR `]´

SPLICE_OP       ::=         push | splice | unshift

FUNCTION        ::=         FLIST_OP `(´ LIST `)´
                    |       FLIST2_OP `(´ SIMPLE `,´ LIST `)´
                    |       LVAL_OP (? LVALUE ?)
                    |       FUNC0_OP (? `(´ `)´ ?)
                    |       FUNC1_OP `(´ (? EXPR ?) `)´
                    |       FUNC2_OP `(´ SIMPLE `,´ EXPR `)´
                    |       FUNC2OR3_OP `(´ SIMPLE `,´ EXPR `)´
                    |       FUNC2OR3_OP `(´ SIMPLE `,´ SIMPLE `,´
                                    EXPR `)´
                    |       FUNC3_OP `(´ SIMPLE `,´ SIMPLE `,´
                                    EXPR `)´
                    |       FUNC4_OP `(´ SIMPLE `,´ SIMPLE `,´
                                    SIMPLE `,´ EXPR `)´
                    |       FUNC5_OP `(´ SIMPLE `,´ SIMPLE `,´
                                    SIMPLE `,´ SIMPLE `,´ EXPR `)´
                    |       ASSOCFUNC_OP ASSOCNAME
                    |       ASSOCFUNC_OP `(´ ASSOCNAME `)´
                    |       ASSOCFUNC3_OP `(´ ASSOCNAME `,´
                                    SIMPLE `,´ EXPR `)´
```

```
FLIST_OP          ::=    sprintf
                  |      LIST_OP

FLIST2_OP         ::=    grep | join | pack

LVAL_OP           ::=    chop | defined | study | undef

FUNC0_OP          ::=    endhostent | endnetent | endservent
                  |      endprotoent | endpwent | endgrent
                  |      fork | getgrent | gethostent | getlogin
                  |      getnetent | getppid | getprotoent
                  |      getpwent | getservent | setgrent
                  |      setpwent | time | times | wait
                  |      wantarray

FUNC1_OP          ::=    getgrgid | getgrnam | getprotobynumber
                  |      getpwnam | getpwuid | sethostent
                  |      setnetent | setprotoent | setservent

FUNC2_OP          ::=    atan2 | crypt | gethostbyaddr
                  |      getnetbyaddr | getpriority
                  |      getservbyname | getservbyport
                  |      index | link | mkdir | msgget
                  |      rename | semop | setpgrp
                  |      symlink | unpack | waitpid

FUNC2OR3_OP       ::=    index | rindex | substr

FUNC3_OP          ::=    msgctl | msgsnd | semget |
                  |      setpriority | shmctl | shmget | vec

FUNC4_OP          ::=    semctl | shmread | shmwrite

FUNC5_OP          ::=    msgrcv

ASSOCFUNC_OP      ::=    dbmclose | each | keys | values

ASSOCFUNC3_OP     ::=    dbmopen

LIST_OPERATION    ::=    LIST_OP
                  |      LIST_OP LIST
                  |      LIST_OP WORD
                  |      LIST_OP WORDSCALAR LIST

LIST_OP           ::=    chmod | chown | die | exec | kill
                  |      print | printf | return | reverse
                  |      sort | system | syscall | unlink
                  |      utime | warn

WORDSCALAR        ::=    WORD | SCALAR

SCALAR            ::=    `$´ WORD
                  |      `$´ `{´ WORD `}´
```

```
                 |        `$´ NON_ALPHANUM
                 |        `$´ `^´ [@—\177]

FILEHANDLE      ::=      WORD | SIMPLE

ARRAYNAME       ::=      WORD | ARRAY

ARRAY           ::=      `@´ WORD

ASSOCNAME       ::=      WORD | ASSOC

ASSOC           ::=      `%´ WORD

NUMBER          ::=      DECIMAL
                 |       OCTAL
                 |       HEXADECIMAL
                 |       `__LINE__´

DECIMAL         ::=      MANTISSA (? EXP ?)

MANTISSA        ::=      [1—9] (* DIGIT *) (? `.´ (* DIGIT *) ?)
                 |       `.´ (+ DIGIT +)

EXP             ::=      [eE] (? [+—] ?) (+ DIGIT +)

WORD            ::=      LETTER (* ALPHANUM *)

ALPHANUM        ::=      LETTER | DIGIT

NON_ALPHANUM    ::=      [^A—Za—z_0—9]

LETTER          ::=      [A—Za—z_]

DIGIT           ::=      [0—9]

OCTAL           ::=      `0´ (* OCTDIGIT *)

OCTDIGIT        ::=      [0—7]

HEXADECIMAL     ::=      `0x´ (+ HEXDIGIT +)

HEXDIGIT        ::=      [0—9a—fA—F]
```

The ´ in [] below represents DELIM from the enclosing construct.

```
SINGLESTUFF     ::=      (* [^´\\] | `\\´ [´\\] *)
```

The " in [] below represents DELIM from the enclosing construct.

```
DOUBLESTUFF      ::=      (*      [^"\\$@]
                         |       `\\´ [0—7][0—7][0—7]
                         |       `\\´ [0—7][0—7]
                         |       `\\´ [^0—7]
                         |       INTERPVAR
                         *)

TEXT             ::=      (* CHAR *)

DELIM            ::=      [^A—Za—z_0—9]

CHAR             ::=      [\000—\377]

LINEBREAK        previous character must be a `\n´
```

The Perl Library

abbrev.pl
bigint.pl
bigfloat.pl
bigrat.pl
cacheout.pl
complete.pl
ctime.pl
dumpvar.pl
find.pl
finddepth.pl
flush.pl
getopt.pl
getopts.pl
importenv.pl
look.pl
perldb.pl
pwd.pl
shellwords.pl
stat.pl
syslog.pl
termcap.pl
timelocal.pl
validate.pl

Perl comes with a number of stock Perl subroutines and packages. These subroutines (if installed properly) are located in a directory along the **@INC** path. To use the routines from, say, the file **abbrev.pl**, put the following at the beginning of your program:

```
require ´abbrev.pl´;
```

This works because all the library routines described in this section end with the line:

```
1;
```

which causes the **require** to succeed if the include file is found and executes properly. If you add routines to the standard include directory, you must return non-zero from your include file, or **require** will fail. We expect many more such files to be added to the standard Perl library, so look in the Perl manpage for updates.

The Perl library may also contain files that have been translated from your C header files. Such files have an extension of ".ph". You system administrator creates them by running a program called **h2ph**. The .ph files are not complete translations—they are good enough for deriving certain defined constants, but other values may require tweaking. In particular, some of the definitions require that you define the sizes of certain C types in the **%sizeof** array. (You may need to write a little C program to do this. There are some tools in the Perl distribution's **h2pl/** subdirectory to help with this.) In order to emulate the semantics of C preprocessor macros, macros are translated not to variable definitions but to subroutine definitions. For efficiency you may wish to evaluate these subroutines just once at the front of your program, like this:

```
require "sys/fcntl.ph";
$F_SETFL = &F_SETFL;
defined $F_SETFL || die "Definition of F_SETFL screwed up";
```

abbrev.pl

Usage:

```
require "abbrev.pl";

%abdul = ();
&abbrev(*abdul,LIST);
...
$long = $abdul{$short};
```

Defines an associative array to have all possible mappings from unique abbreviations into their full names. For example, a program containing:

```
require ´abbrev.pl´;
%abdul = ();
&abbrev(*abdul,´he´,´help´,´hi´,´bye´,´wally´,´world´);
```

sets up the **abdul** associative array as follows:

Key	Value
b	bye
by	bye
bye	bye
he	he
hel	help
help	help
hi	hi
wa	wally
wal	wally
wall	wally
wally	wally
wo	world
wor	world
worl	world
world	world

Note that **h** does not appear, because it would be ambiguous; but **he** appears even though it is also a prefix of **help**.

You would then use the **abdul** associative array to look up potentially abbreviated words, as in:

```
while (<>) {
        chop;
        $long = $abdul{$_};
        print "$long\n" if length($long);
}
```

bigint.pl

Usage:

```
require "bigint.pl";

$BINT = &bneg($BINT);                        # negation
$BINT = &babs($BINT);                        # absolute value
$CODE = &bcmp($BINT, $BINT);                 # comparison, like <=>
$BINT = &badd($BINT, $BINT);                 # addition
$BINT = &bsub($BINT, $BINT);                 # subtraction
$BINT = &bmul($BINT, $BINT);                 # multiplication
($BINT,$BINT) = &bdiv($BINT, $BINT);         # division (quotient, rem)
$BINT = &bdiv($BINT, $BINT);                 # division (just quotient)
$BINT = &bmod($BINT, $BINT);                 # modulus
$BINT = &bgcd($BINT, $BINT);                 # greatest common divisor
$BINT = &bnorm($BINT);                       # normalization
```

The **bigint** package provides arbitrary-sized integer arithmetic. Input values may be of the form:

```
/^\s*[+-]?[\d\s]+$/
```

For example:

```
"+0"
123454321
"   -109 098 187 536 016 109 234 568 020 987 101 944 682 712"
```

are all legal, while:

```
1.23
"123e6"
```

are not. Note also that on most machines, numbers containing more than about 15 digits must have quotes around them, since that is how much a floating-point number can hold.

Output values always consist of a sign following by a sequence of digits, except for the value **NaN**, which indicates either erroneous input or division by zero. (Note that this is not quite IEEE usage, which returns an infinite value on overflow.)

bigfloat.pl

Usage:

```
require "bigfloat.pl";

$FNUM = &fneg($FNUM);               # negation
$FNUM = &fabs($FNUM);               # absolute value
$CODE = &fcmp($FNUM, $FNUM);        # comparison, like <=>
$FNUM = &fadd($FNUM, $FNUM);        # addition
$FNUM = &fsub($FNUM, $FNUM);        # subtraction
$FNUM = &fmul($FNUM, $FNUM);        # multiplication
$FNUM = &fdiv($FNUM, $FNUM);        # division
$FNUM = &fdiv($FNUM, $FNUM, $SCALE); # division to SCALE places
$FNUM = &fround($FNUM, $SCALE);     # round to SCALE digits
$FNUM = &ffround($FNUM, $SCALE);    # round to SCALEth place
$FNUM = &fnorm($FNUM);              # normalization
$FNUM = &fsqrt($FNUM);              # square root,
$FNUM = &fsqrt($FNUM, $SCALE);      # square root, SCALE places
```

The **bigfloat** package provides arbitrary-sized floating-point arithmetic. Input values may be of the form:

```
/^[+-]?\d*(\.\d*)?([Ee][+-]?\d+)?$/
```

with the proviso that there must be at least one digit in the mantissa. Whitespace is allowed anywhere, but is stripped out. Output values always match:

```
/^[+-]\d+E[+-]\d+$/
```

except for the value: **NaN**, which indicates either erroneous input, division by zero, or taking the square root of a negative number.

Two package variables control rounding and default scale, and start out as:

```
$bigfloat'rnd_mode = 'even';
$bigfloat'div_scale = 40;
```

The rounding modes are **even, odd, +inf, –inf, zero,** and **trunc**. In the absence of an explicit scale argument, division is computed to at least **$div_scale** digits, but possibly more if the size of the numbers justifies it. Similarly for square roots.

The **bigfloat** package makes use of the **bigint** package.

bigrat.pl

Usage:

```
require "bigrat.pl";

$RAT = &rneg($RAT);                  # negation
$RAT = &rabs($RAT);                  # absolute value
$CODE = &rcmp($RAT, $RAT);           # comparison, like <=>
$RAT = &radd($RAT, $RAT);            # addition
$RAT = &rsub($RAT, $RAT);            # subtraction
$RAT = &rmul($RAT, $RAT);            # multiplication
$RAT = &rdiv($RAT, $RAT);            # division
($RAT,$RAT) = &rmod($RAT);      # modulus (int, frac parts)
$RAT = &rnorm($RAT);                 # normalization
$RAT = &rsqrt($RAT, $CYCLES);        # square root
```

The **bigrat** package provides arbitrary-sized rational arithmetic. Input values may be of the form:

```
/^[+—]?\d+(/[+—]?\d+)?$/
```

Whitespace is allowed anywhere, but is stripped out. Essentially, an input value can look like either a valid **bigint** value, or the concatenation of two **bigint** values with a slash between them.

Output values always match:

```
/^[+—]\d+/\d+$/
```

except for the value **NaN**, which indicates either erroneous input, division by zero, or taking the square root of a negative number.

The **bigrat** package makes use of the **bigint** package.

cacheout.pl

Usage:

```
require "cacheout.pl";

while (<>) {
    $filename = (split(/:/,$_))[3];      # Or whatever.
    if ($filename ne $lastfilename) {
        &cacheout($filename);
        $lastfilename = $filename;
    }
```

```
    print $filename $_;
}
```

The **cacheout** routine is a substitute for the **open( )** function that allows you to have more output files than your system allows. You might want this when splitting a big file into smaller files according to some key, when the values of that key are intermixed with each other in an unpredictable fashion. (A simple example would be if you wanted to split your /etc/passwd file into separate files by the GID field, but maintain the current ordering of records.) The **cacheout** routine, when called, simply guarantees that the filename passed to it is opened for output. It may never have been opened before, in which case it is opened with a **>** mode. If it has been opened before but has been closed since, it is reopened with a **>>** mode. If it is already opened, it is merely marked as having been referenced recently.

When **cacheout** determines that too many files will soon be open, it closes some of the least-recently-used files to make room for the new filehandle. You'll note that the filehandle used for each file is simply the filename itself, which is why the **print** function above simply uses **$filename** as an indirect filehandle.

complete.pl

Usage:

```
require "complete.pl";

$input = &Complete('prompt_string', @completion_list);
```

Works like an Emacs or tcsh completion to the terminal. The **prompt_string** is displayed, and the user is asked for one of many values given in the completion list. For example, to get a filename for an output file in the current directory (which may not necessarily exist), try the following:

```
open(THISDIR,".");
@files = grep(-f $_ && -w _, readdir(THISDIR));
close(THISDIR);
$input = &Complete("output file? ", @files);
```

(The first few lines create an array **@files** that contains all writable files in the current directory.)

Completion is done by typing the **TAB** key. A ^D will list the available options remaining. The routine has a hardcoded kill character (^U) and a pair of hardcoded erase characters (^H and **DEL**). It puts the user's /dev/tty into raw mode. It should probably also pass the array by reference. If you don't like the way it works, copy it and modify it.

ctime.pl

Usage:

```
require "ctime.pl";

$Date = &ctime(time);
```

Works like the UNIX C library **ctime** routine to create a human-readable date from a timestamp. For example:

```
require 'ctime.pl';
print &ctime(time),"\n";
```

works just like the standard **date** command.

dumpvar.pl

Usage:

```
require "dumpvar.pl";

&dumpvar($package[,@vars]);
```

Displays the contents of the indicated package on the currently selected output. Variable names can be restricted to the listed variables:

```
&dumpvar('main', 'foo', 'bar', '@', '_');

foreach $package (grep(/^_\w+$/, keys(%_main))) {
    print "\nPACKAGE = $package\n";
    &dumpvar(substr($package,1)) unless $package eq "_dumpvar";
}
```

find.pl

Usage:

```
require "find.pl";

&find("/foo", "/bar");

sub wanted { ... }
```

These routines are primarily for the support of the *find2perl* translator. The **&find()** routine traverses each listed directory just as the *find*(1) program does. For each file found, the **&wanted** subroutine will be called to perform any desired conditionals and actions. Within the subroutine, **$dir** contains the current directory name, and **$_** the current filename within that directory. You are also supplied the variable **$name**, which contains "$dir/$_". You are *cd*'ed to **$dir** when the function is called. The function may set **$prune** to prune the search tree at that point.

The best way to find out how to use these routines is to run a find command through *find2perl* and see what it spits out. Saying:

```
find2perl / —name '.nfs*' —mtime +7 \
    —exec rm —f '{}' \; —o —fstype nfs —prune
```

makes it spit out this:

```
require "find.pl";

&find('/');

sub wanted {
    /^\.nfs.*$/ &&
    (($dev,$ino,$mode,$nlink,$uid,$gid) = lstat($_)) &&
    int(—M _) > 7 &&
    (unlink($_) && 1)
    ||
    ($nlink || (($dev,$ino,$mode,$nlink,$uid,$gid) = lstat($_))) &&
    $dev < 0 &&
    ($prune = 1);
}
```

You could then take this and modify it to do something that find can't do.

finddepth.pl

Usage:

```
require "finddepth.pl";

&finddepth("/foo", "/bar");

sub wanted { ... }
```

These routines work just like those in *find.pl*, except that they implement a depth-first search, listing the directories on the way back up instead of the way down. The *find2perl* program uses this package when you use the **—depth** switch, or some option that implies depth-first searching such as **—cpio** or **—ncpio**.

flush.pl

Usage:

```
require "flush.pl";

&flush(FILEHANDLE)
&printflush(FILEHANDLE, "prompt: ")
```

The **flush** routine flushes the named filehandle—any output pending on that filehandle is moved from Perl's process dataspace into system space (although the system can be lazy in getting it to its destination).

The **printflush** routine prints the text specified by the arguments after the first argument on the filehandle specified by the first argument. It then flushes that filehandle.

Note that you might need to prefix the filehandle with its package name if the package the filehandle was created in is different from the package the flush routines were **require**-d from.

getopt.pl

Usage:

```
require "getopt.pl";

&Getopt('oDI');  # -o, -D & -I take arg.
        # Sets opt_* as a side effect.
```

Process single-character switches with switch clustering. Pass one argument which is a string containing all switches that take an argument. For each switch found, sets $opt_x (where x is the switch name) to the value of the argument, or 1 if no argument. Switches which take an argument don't care whether there is a space between the switch and the argument.

Compare this to **getopts.pl**.

getopts.pl

Usage:

```
require "getopts.pl";

&Getopts('a:bc');   # -a takes arg. -b & -c not.
           # Sets opt_* as a side effect.
```

Process single-character switches with switch clustering. Pass one argument
which is a string containing all allowed switches. If an argument character is followed by a colon, the argument takes the following argument as the value of that
argument. For each switch found, sets $opt_x (where x is the switch name) to the
value of the argument, or 1 if no argument. Switches which take an argument
don't care whether there is a space between the switch and the argument. Thus
such a switch must be the final switch in its cluster.

Compare this to **getopt.pl**.

importenv.pl

Usage:

```
require "importenv.pl";

# nothing else (all the action is done by the require).
```

Creates Perl scalar variables that are equal to the corresponding environment
variables (where possible). Note that these variables are "read-only"; although
changing the value of such a variable is allowed, that change will not be reflected
in the corresponding environment variable.

For example:

```
require "importenv.pl";
$USER = $LOGNAME unless $USER;
print "Home directory for $USER is $HOME\n";
```

look.pl

Usage:

```
require "look.pl";

&look(*FILEHANDLE,$key,$dict,$fold)
```

Sets file position of FILEHANDLE to be the first line greater than or equal to **$key** using a binary search. The filehandle must be opened onto a sorted text file such as */usr/dict/words*. If **$dict** is non-zero, dictionary order is used. (Only letters, digits, and whitespace characters are used in comparisons.) If **$dict** is zero, all characters participate in comparisons. If **$fold** is non-zero, uppercase is folded to lowercase during comparisons. (Searching */usr/dict/words* requires both flags to be non-zero.)

Returns the file position of the line found.

To find all words in */usr/dict/words* beginning with "camel" (including such gems as *camellia* and *Camelot*), say this:

```
require "look.pl";
open(DICT,"/usr/dict/words") || die "Illiterate computer";
&look(*DICT, "camel", 1, 1);
while (<DICT>) {
    last unless /^camel/i;
    print;
}
```

perldb.pl

Used internally for the **−d** command-line option. Normally you wouldn't invoke this directly.

pwd.pl

Usage:

```
require "pwd.pl";

&initpwd;
...
&chdir($newdir);
```

Tracks the current working directory so that the **PWD** environment variable is more or less correct (although these routines can still be fooled by symlinks).

shellwords.pl

Usage:

```
require "shellwords.pl";

@words = &shellwords($line);
```

or:

```
@words = &shellwords(@lines);
```

or:

```
@words = &shellwords;     # Defaults to $_ (and clobbers it).
```

This routine splits a line (or array of lines) into words in the same way that a shell would. Leading whitespace is discarded, and the words are split apart on any non-quoted whitespace. You may quote with single quotes, double quotes, and backslashes. The following line would be split into four words:

```
first_word "second word" third\ word '"last word"'
```

and the four words would be:

```
first_word
second word
third word
"last word"
```

stat.pl

Usage:

```
require "stat.pl";

@ary = stat('foo');
$st_dev = @ary[$ST_DEV];
# or
&Stat('foo');
print "$st_dev\n";
```

Simply **require**-ing this file sets the 13 scalar variables beginning with **ST_** to be correct for indexing into an array returned from a **stat** or **lstat** function.

For convenience, **&Stat** assigns the 13-element array into 13 scalar variables beginning with **st_**.

syslog.pl

Usage:

```
require "syslog.pl";

&openlog($program,'cons,pid','user');
&syslog('info',"The camel's nose is in the tent");
&syslog('mail|warning','My watch reads %d', time);
&closelog();
&syslog('debug',
    'This is a test of the emerging broadcast system');
&openlog("$program $$",'ndelay','user');
&syslog('notice',"warp: somebody's playing during work time");
syswrite(STDOUT,$pig,length($pig)) ||
    &syslog('info','problem was %m');  # %m == $!
```

These routines provide logging functions on machines that support the *syslogd*(8) program. There are identical to the corresponding *syslog*(3) functions, except that the flags are passed in as lowercase strings, without the **LOG_** prefix.

termcap.pl

Usage:

```
require "sys/ioctl.ph";        # (or equivalent)

ioctl(TTY,&TIOCGETP,$params);
($ispeed,$ospeed) = unpack(´cc´,$params);

require "termcap.pl";

&Tgetent($ENV{´TERM´}); # sets $TC{´cm´}, etc.
&Tputs(&Tgoto($TC{´cm´},$col,$row), 0, ´FILEHANDLE´);
&Tputs($TC{´dl´},$affcnt,´FILEHANDLE´);
```

These routines are similar to the C library termcap routines. See the C library description for details.

timelocal.pl

Usage:

```
require "timelocal.pl";

$time = &timelocal(@timearray);
$time = &timegm(@timearray);
```

These functions are the inverse of **localtime( )** and **gmtime( )** built-in operators. They take an array value broken out into seconds, minutes, and so on, and encode it into seconds since 1970.

validate.pl

Usage:

```
require "validate.pl";

$warnings += &validate(´
/vmunix                 -e || die
/boot                   -e || die
/bin                    cd
    csh                 -ex
    csh                 !-ug
```

```
    sh              -ex
    sh              !-ug
  /usr              -d || warn "What happened to $file?\n"
  ');
```

The validate routine takes a single multi-line string consisting of lines containing a filename plus a file test to try on it. (The file test may also be a *cd*, causing subsequent relative filenames to be interpreted relative to that directory.) After the file test you may put || **die** to make it a fatal error if the file test fails. The default is || **warn**. The sense of the file test may be reversed by putting ! in front of the −. If you do a cd and then list some relative filenames, you may want to indent them slightly for readability. If you supply your own **die** or **warn** message, you can use **$file** to interpolate the filename.

File tests may be bunched: **−rwx** tests for all of **−r**, **−w** and **−x**. Only the first failed test of the bunch will produce a warning—the rest of the tests on the line are skipped. The routine returns the number of warnings issued.

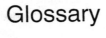

Glossary

Actual Arguments

The scalar values that you supply to a subroutine when you call it. When you call **&piglatin(´bingo´)**, the string ´**bingo**´ is the actual argument. See also *Argument* and *Formal Arguments*. Note: be very careful in choosing your terms for actual arguments—they sometimes turn violent.

Address

See *Address Operator* or *Network Address*.

Address Operator

Directory assistance at the Post Office. Or, a language construct for manipulating the actual location of an object in your computer's memory. There are no such operators in Perl, since it handles all that for you automatically. You just tell Perl that you want a new array element with such-and-such a key, and Perl will worry about creating, moving, and destroying the object for you.

Alternatives

A list of possible choices from which you may select only one, as in "Would you like door A, B, or C?" Alternatives in regular expressions (and in the Formal Grammar) are separated with a vertical bar: |. Alternatives in normal Perl expressions are separated with a double vertical bar: ||.

Architecture

The kind of computer you're working on, where one "kind" of computer means all those computers that can run the same binary program. Since Perl programs aren't binary programs, a Perl program is much less sensitive to the architecture it's running on than programs in other languages such as C. See also *Operating System*.

Argument

What you have with someone who prefers a different architecture. Or, a piece of data supplied as input to a program, subroutine, or function when it is invoked to tell it what it's supposed to do. Also called a "parameter."

ARGV

What you say to the dentist when the Novocaine isn't working. Or, the name of the array containing the argument "vector" from the command line. If you use the <> construct, **ARGV** is both the name of the filehandle used to traverse the arguments, and of the scalar containing the name of the current input file.

Arithmetic Operator

A symbol that tells Perl to do arithmetic, such as + or **. See also *Operator*.

Array

A named list of values, each of which has a unique key to identify it. In a normal array, the key is numeric (an integer, in fact). In an associative array, the key is a string. In a solar array, the key is efficiency.

Array Context

When an expression is expected by its surroundings (the code calling it) to return a list of values rather than a single value. Functions whose syntax contains the non-terminal LIST supply array contexts to any expressions used as part of the LIST. See also *Context*.

Array Literal

Strictly, a comma-separated, parenthesized LIST of scalar literals. Used loosely to refer to any parenthesized LIST even if it contains variables or expressions.

Array Value

An unnamed list of scalar values that may be passed around within a program and passed to any function that provides an array context.

Array Variable

A named list that may be processed by functions such as **shift** and **splice** that require an array name as the first argument.

ASCII

Used roughly to mean the American Standard Code for Information Interchange (a 7-bit character set), and any international extensions based on it.

Assignment

A statement whose mission is to change the value of a variable, should it choose to accept it.

Assignment Operator

A kind of assignment statement that changes the value of a variable relative to its old value. For example, **$a += 2** adds 2 to **$a**.

Associative Array

A named list of key-value pairs, arranged such that you can easily use any key to find its associated value; a binary relation, to database users. This Glossary is like an associative array, where the word to be defined is the key, and the definition is the value.

Associativity

Whether, when you have "A operator B operator C," and the two operators are of the same precedence, you do the left operator first or the right operator first. Operators like **+** are left associative, while operators like ****** are right associative. See the section "Operator Precedence" in Chapter 3 for a precise (and concise) list of associativity. Not related to associative arrays, except by association.

Autoincrement

See "dealer prep." Or, to add one to something automatically. Usually used with the **++** operator.

Autosplit

Another name for "Midnight Auto Supply." Or, to split a string automatically on whitespace, such as the **-a** switch does in order to emulate *awk*.

awk

Descriptive editing term—short for "awkward." Also coincidentally refers to a venerable text processing language from which Perl stol—er, uh, derived some of its ideas.

BASIC/PLUS

Another ancient language (reminiscent of Indo-European) from which Perl derived exactly one idea. Well, OK, maybe two...[47]

Big-Endian

From Swift, someone who eats eggs big end first. Also used of computers that store the most significant byte of a word at a lower byte address than the least significant byte. Often considered superior to little-endian machines. See also *Little-Endian*.

Binary

Having to do with numbers represented in base 2. That means there's basically 2 numbers, 0 and 1. Some people think in binary, as shown by the kinds of questions they ask: "Should we all use Perl or shell?" Also used to describe a non-text file, presumably because it makes full use of all the binary bits in its bytes.

Bit

A very small piece of litter. Also a number in the range 0 to 1, inclusive.

Bit Shift

The movement of bits left or right in a computer word, which has the effect of multiplying or dividing by a power of 2.

Block

A mental construct, most prevalent when writing up glossary entries. Similarly, what a process does when it has to wait for something: *"My process blocked waiting for the disk."* As an unrelated noun, it refers to a large chunk of data, of a size that the operating system likes to deal with (normally a power of two such as 512 or 8192). Typically refers to a chunk of data that's coming from or going to a disk file.

BLOCK

A syntactic construct consisting of a sequence of Perl statements bounded by curly braces. The **if** and **while** statements are defined in terms of BLOCKs. Sometimes we also say "block" to mean a sequence of statements that act like a BLOCK, such as within an **eval**, even though they aren't bounded by curly braces.

Block Buffering

A method of making input and output efficient by doing it a block at a time. By default, Perl does block buffering to disk files. See *Buffer* and *Command Buffering*.

---

[47] BASIC/PLUS is a registered trademark of Digital Equipment Corporation. And the answers are: statement modifiers and maybe formats.

Boolean Context

A special kind of scalar context (see *Scalar Context*) in which the program is expecting to decide whether the scalar value returned by an expression is true or false. See *Context*.

Breakpoint

A spot in a tennis game where, if you get another point, your opponent will break his racket. Also, a spot in your program where you've told the debugger to stop execution so you can poke around and see if anything is wrong yet.

BSD

A psychoactive drug, popular in the 80's, probably developed at U. C. Berkeley or thereabouts. Similar in many ways to the prescription-only medication called "System V," but infinitely more useful. (Or, at least, more fun.) The full chemical name is "Berkeley Standard Distribution."

Buffer

A temporary holding location, like a large kitchen trash can. If it's block-buffered, you carry it out whenever the can fills. If it's line-buffered, you carry it out whenever the trash starts to smell. If it's command-buffered, you carry it out whenever your spouse tells you to. If your output is unbuffered, you carry every piece of trash out separately.

Byte

A piece of data worth 8 bits in most places.

C

A language beloved by many for its inside-out type definitions, inscrutable precedence rules, and heavy overloading of the subroutine call mechanism. (Well, actually, people first switched to C because they found lower case easier to read than upper.) The current Perl interpreter is written in C, so it's not surprising that Perl borrowed a few ideas from it. Almost forgivable, in fact.

C Preprocessor

The typical C compiler's first pass, which processes lines beginning with # for conditional compilation and macro definition, and does various manipulations of the program text based on the current definitions.

Call By Reference

Throwing encyclopedias at your kids until they come to dinner. (See also *Call By Value*). Also, an argument-passing mechanism in which the formal arguments refer directly to the actual arguments, and the subroutine can change the actual arguments by changing the formal arguments.

Call By Value

Throwing money at your kids until they come to dinner. (See also *Call By Reference*). Also, an argument-passing mechanism in which the formal arguments refer to a copy of the actual arguments, and the subroutine cannot change the actual arguments by changing the formal arguments.

Character

A small pattern of bits (usually 7, 8, or 16) that is the machine's representation of a unit of orthography. Americans typically confuse characters with bytes. So does Perl.

Character Class

A school where combinations of bits (usually 8 at a time) learn to form shapes on a screen. Also, a square-bracketed list of characters used in a regular expression to indicate that any character of the set may occur at this point.

Client

In networking, a process that initiates contact with a server process in order to exchange data with it and perhaps get some satisfaction. See *Server*.

Collating Sequence

The order that characters sort into. This is used by string comparison routines to decide where in this Glossary to put "Collating Sequence."

Command

In shell programming, the syntactic combination of a program name with its arguments. More loosely, anything you type to a shell (a command interpreter) that starts it doing something. In Perl programming, a "statement," which might start with a label, and typically ends with a semicolon.

Command Buffering

An option in Perl that lets you store up the output of each Perl command and then flush it out as a single request to the operating system. It's enabled by setting the $| variable to a non-zero value. It's used when you don't want data sitting around not going where it's supposed to, which may happen because the default on a file or pipe is to use block buffering. See also *Buffering*.

Command Line Arguments

The values you supply along with a program name when you tell a shell (a command interpreter) to execute a command. These values are passed to a Perl script through @ARGV.

Command Name

The name of the program currently executing, as typed on the command line. In C the command name is passed to the program as the first command-line argument. In Perl, it comes in separately as **$0**.

Comment

A remark that doesn't affect the meaning of the program. In Perl, a comment is introduced by a **#** character and continues to the end of the line.

Compile Time

The time when Perl is trying to make sense of your program, as opposed to when it thinks it knows what your program means and is merely trying to do what it says to do. See also *Runtime*.

Compiler

Strictly speaking, a program that munches up another program and spits out yet another file containing the program in a more executable form, typically containing native machine instructions. Perl is not a compiler by this definition, but it does contain a kind of compiler that takes a program and turns it into a more executable form (syntax trees) within the Perl process itself, which the Perl interpreter then interprets. See *Interpreter*.

Concatenation

The process of gluing one cat's nose to another cat's tail. Also, a similar operation on two strings.

Conditional

Something "iffy."

Connection

In telephony, the temporary electrical circuit between the caller's and the callee's phone. In networking, the same kind of temporary circuit between a client and a server.

Construct

A piece of syntax made up of littler pieces.

Context

The surroundings, the environment—just what you think it means. Within Perl, it means what kind of data the surrounding code is expecting a particular expression (subroutine, function, operator, variable, or literal) to return. The two primary contexts are "Array Context" and "Scalar Context." Scalar context is sometimes subdivided into "Boolean Context," "Numeric Context," and "String Context."

Continuation

The treatment of more than one physical line as a single logical line. Makefile lines are continued by putting a backslash before the newline. Internet message headers are continued by putting a space or tab *after* the newline. Perl lines in general do not need any form of continuation mark, because whitespace (including newline) is gleefully ignored. Usually.

Core Dump

The corpse of a process, left in its working directory.

Curly Braces

Larry and Moe. Or { }.

Current Package

Which package the current statement is compiled in. Scan backwards in the text of your program till you find a package declaration at the same block level, or in an enclosing block at that block's block level. That's your current package name.

Current Working Directory

See Working Directory.

Currently Selected Output Channel

The last filehandle mentioned by **select(FILEHANDLE)**, or **STDOUT** if none has been selected.

Dangling Statement

A fashion point being made through the use of inadequately attached articles of clothing or jewelry. Or, a bare, single statement, without any curly braces, hanging off an **if** or **while** conditional. C allows them. Perl doesn't.

Data Reduction

The process of extracting only the most interesting tidbits because the boss can't read fast enough.

Data Structure

How your various pieces of data relate to each other, and what shape they make when you put them all together, as in a rectangular table, or a triangular-shaped tree.

Data Type

A data type consists of a set of possible values, together with all the operations that know how to deal with those values. For example, a numeric data type has a certain set of numbers that you can work with, and it has various mathematical operations you can do on the numbers that would make little sense on, say, a string such as "**Kilroy**". Strings have their own operations, such as concatenation. Compound types made of a number of smaller pieces generally have operations to compose and decompose them, and perhaps to rearrange them.

Dataflow

What your program looks like from the perspective of a particular piece of data from the time it enters your program to the time it leaves or is combined with some other data to make new data.

DBM

Stands for "Data Base Management" routines, a particular set of UNIX routines which emulate an associative array using a pair of disk files. The routines use a dynamic hashing scheme to locate any entry with only two disk accesses. DBM files allow a Perl script to keep a persistent associative-array object across multiple invocations. See the **dbmopen( )** function in Chapter 4.

Declaration

An assertion you make that something exists and perhaps what it's like, without any commitment as to how or where you'll use it. A declaration is like the part of your recipe that says, "2 cups flour, 1 large egg, 4 or 5 tadpoles..." See *Statement* for its opposite.

Decrement

A coarse euphemism for subtracting one from something.

Default

The value or object which is chosen automatically if you don't supply one. Or if you don't supply the next loan payment.

Defined

Having a meaning. Perl thinks that some of the things people try to do are devoid of meaning; in particular, making use of variables that have never been given a value, and performing certain operations on data that isn't there. For example, if you try to read data past the end of a file, Perl will hand you back an undefined value. See also *False*.

Delimiter

Some character or string that "limits" the size of an arbitrarily-sized textual object. Some novelists should learn to use them.

Device

Removing a vice (also known as "installing a virtue"). Also, a whiz-bang hardware gizmo (like a disk or tape drive) attached to your computer that the operating system tries to make look like a file (or a bunch of files), and sometimes succeeds. Under UNIX, these fake files tend to live in the /**dev** directory.

Directory

A place where you find files, and perhaps other directories. Some operating systems call these "folders," "drawers," or "catalogs."

Directory Handle

A name that represents a particular instance of opening a directory to read it, until you close it.

Dump

A Perl statement that is one of the many ways to get a Perl program to produce a core file. Most of the other ones are undocumented.

Eclectic

Derived from many sources. Some would say *too* many.

Element

A basic building block. In the context of an array, one of the items that make up the array.

Endian

See *Little-Endian* or *Big-Endian*, but not both.

Environment

The collective set of environment variables your process inherits from its parent.

Environment Variable

A mechanism by which some high level agent such as a user can pass its preferences down to child processes, grandchild processes, great-grandchild processes, and so on. Each environment variable is a key-value pair, like one element of an associative array.

EOF

End of File. Sometimes used metaphorically as the trailing delimiter of a here-is file (see *Here-is File*).

errno

The error number returned by a UNIX system call when it fails. Perl refers to it by the name **$!**.

Exception Handling

How you handle it when Perl takes exception to something you said to do. The exception handling mechanism in Perl is the **eval** statement.

Executable

A file that is specially marked to tell the operating system that it's okay to run this file as a program.

Execute

> To run a program.

Execute Bit

> The special mark that tells the operating system it can run this program. There are actually three execute bits under UNIX, and which bit gets used depends on whether you own the file singularly, collectively, or not at all.

Exit Status

> See *Status*.

Exponent

> The part of a floating-point number that says where to put the decimal point in the other part. See *Mantissa*.

Expression

> Anything you can legally say in a spot where a value is required. Typically composed of literals, variables, operators, functions, and subroutine calls.

False

> In Perl, any value that looks like "" or "**0**" when evaluated in a string context. Since undefined values evaluate to "", all undefined values are false, but not all false values are undefined.

Fatal Error

> An error that causes termination of the process after printing a nasty message on your standard error stream. However, normally fatal errors that happen inside an **eval** are not fatal to the whole program, but just to that particular **eval**, and the nasty message then shows up in the $@ variable. You can cause a fatal error with the **die** operator.

Field

> A single piece of numeric or string data that is part of a longer string, record, or line. Variable-width fields are usually separated by delimiters (so use **split**), while fixed-width fields are usually at fixed positions (so use **unpack**).

File

> A named collection of data, usually stored on a disk in a directory. Roughly like a document, if you're into office metaphors. In some operating systems like UNIX, you can actually give a file more than one name.

File Descriptor

The little number the operating system uses to keep track of which opened file you're talking about. Perl hides the file descriptor inside a standard I/O stream, and then attaches the stream to a filehandle, so don't worry about it unless you're the worrying type.

File Test Operator

A built-in Perl operator that you use to determine if something is true about a file, such as whether you could open it if you tried.

Filehandle

What you pick up a file with. Or, a name (unrelated to the real name of a file) that represents a particular instance of opening a file until you close it. Thus if you're going to open and close several different files in succession, it's possible to open each of them with the same filehandle, so you don't have to write out separate code to process each file. It's like the game show host calling someone "Contestant #1" so that he doesn't have to remember too many names from day to day.

Filename

The name for a file that is stored in a directory, and that is used in an **open** statement to tell the operating system exactly which file you want to open.

Filesystem

A set of directories and files residing on a partition of the disk. You can move a file around from directory to directory within a filesystem without actually moving the file itself.

Floating Point

A method of storing numbers in "scientific notation," such that the precision of the number is independent of its magnitude (the decimal point "floats"). Perl does all of its numeric work with floating-point numbers.

Flush

Turning bright red when asked if you could do something crafty "in something other than Perl this time, please." Also, the act of emptying a buffer, often before it's really full. See *Buffer*.

Fork

To create a child process identical to the parent process, at least until it gets ideas of its own.

Formal Arguments

A difference of opinion handled by attorneys. Or, the generic names a subroutine knows its arguments by. In many languages, formal arguments are always given individual names, but in Perl they are passed via arrays. The formal arguments to a Perl program are **$ARGV[0]**, **$ARGV[1]**, and so on. Similarly, the formal arguments to a Perl subroutine are **$_[0]**, **$_[1]**, and so on. You may give the arguments individual names by assigning to a **local( )** list. See the **local( )** function in Chapter 4.

Format

A specification of how many spaces and digits and things to put somewhere so that whatever you're printing comes out nice and pretty.

Freely Available

Means you don't have to pay money to get it, although you can if you like (hint).

Freely Redistributable

Means you're not in trouble if you give a bootleg copy of it to your friends (hint).

Function

Mathematically, a mapping of each set of input values to a particular output value. In computers, refers to a subroutine or operation which returns a value. It may or may not have input values.

GID

Group ID. Always refers to the numeric group ID which the operating system uses to identify you and members of your group, never to the alphanumeric group ID which you *think* the system uses.

Glob

Strictly, the shell's ***** character, which will match a "glob" of characters when you're trying to generate a list of filenames. Loosely, the act of using globs and similar symbols to do pattern matching.

Global

Something you can see from anywhere, usually used of variables and subroutines that are visible everywhere in your program. In Perl, only certain special variables are truly global—most variables (and all subroutines) are local to the current package (module). See *Local* and *Package*.

Group

A set of users that you're a member of. You can give certain file access permissions to other members of your group.

Hash Table

Long narrow pieces of furniture on which finely chopped meat-and-potatoes are served. Also, a method of implementing associative arrays efficiently that Perl happens to use, but that you don't have to know anything about. Be thankful.

Header File

A file containing certain required definitions that you must include "ahead" of the rest of your program to do certain obscure operations. A C header file has a **.h** extension. A Perl header file has a **.ph** extension. See the **require** operator in Chapter 4.

Here-is File

So called because of a similar construct in shells which pretends that the lines following the command are a separate file to be fed to the command, up to some trailing delimiter string. In Perl, however, it's just a fancy form of quoting. Also called a "Here Document."

Hexadecimal

A number in base 16. The digits for 10 through 15 are customarily represented by the letters **a** through **f**. Hexadecimal constants in Perl start with **0x**.

Home Directory

The directory you are placed into when you log in. On a UNIX system, the name is often placed into **$ENV{´HOME´}** or **$ENV{´LOGDIR´}** by the login program, but you can also find it with **(getpwuid($<))[7]**.

Host

What a parasite lives in or on. Your programs have this relationship to the computer.

Hubris

Excessive pride, the sort of thing Zeus zaps you for. Also the quality that makes you write (and maintain) programs that other people won't want to say bad things about. Hence, the third great virtue of a programmer. See also *Laziness* and *Impatience*.

Identifier

A legally formed name for most anything in which a computer program might be interested. Many languages (including Perl) allow identifiers that start with a letter and contain letters and digits. Perl also counts the underline character as a valid letter.

Impatience

The anger you feel when the computer is being lazy. This makes you write programs that don't just react to your needs, but actually anticipate them. Or at least that pretend to. Hence, the second great virtue of a programmer. See also *Laziness* and *Hubris*.

Increment
>Used of bad weather. Also, to add one to.

Indexing
>Formerly, the act of looking up a key in an index (like the phone book), but now merely the act of using any kind of key or position to find the corresponding value, even if no index is involved. Things have degenerated to the point that Perl's **index** function merely locates the position (index) of one string in another. See *Key*.

Indirection
>When Randal says, "I don't know the answer... go ask Larry." Similarly, if something in a program isn't the answer, but indicates where the answer is, that's indirection.

Integer
>A number with no fractional part; a whole number.

Interpolation
>The insertion of one piece of text somewhere in the middle of another piece of text. Allegedly practiced by Gnostics and programmers.

Interpreter
>Strictly speaking, a program that reads a program and does what it says directly without turning the program into a different form first, which is what compilers do. Perl is not an interpreter by this definition, because it contains a kind of compiler that takes a program and turns it into a more executable form (syntax trees) within the perl process itself, which the Perl runtime system then interprets. See *Compiler* and *Runtime*.

Invocation
>The act of calling up a program, subroutine, spirit, or function to do what it's supposed to do.

IPC
>Short for Inter-Process Communication. Sometimes a process just needs to talk to some other process.

Iteration
>Doing something again and again and again and again and again and... For a complete example, see *Iteration*.

Iterator
>A special programming gizmo that keeps track for you of where you are in something that you're trying to iterate over. The **foreach** loop in Perl contains an iterator.

Key

A special kind of data, such as your Social Security number, that can be used to locate other data. See also *Value*. In fact, when you look up "Value" in this Glossary, you're using the word "Value" as a key, not the value. And that's something of value. Believe it or not.

Keyword

A word with a specific, built-in meaning to a compiler, such as **if** or **delete**. In many languages (not Perl) it's illegal to use keywords to name anything else. Also called a reserved word.

Label

A kind of key you can give to a statement so that you can talk about that statement elsewhere in the program.

Laziness

The quality that makes you go to great effort to reduce overall energy expenditure. It makes you write labor-saving programs that other people will find useful, and document what you wrote so you don't have to answer so many questions about it. Hence, the first great virtue of a programmer. Also hence, this book. See also *Impatience* and *Hubris*.

Left Shift

A bit shift (see *Bit Shift*) which multiplies the number by some power of 2. Also, what you drive with in England.

Library

A collection of procedures, like recipes, often burned.

Line

In UNIX, a sequence of zero or more non-newline characters terminated with a newline (line feed) character.

Line Buffered

Said of a standard I/O output stream that flushes its buffer after every newline. Many standard I/O libraries automatically set up line buffering on output that is going to the terminal.

Line Number

The number of lines read prior to this one, plus 1. Perl keeps a separate line number for each script or input file it opens. The current script line number is represented by **__LINE__**. The current input line number (for the file that was most recently read from via <>) is represented by $.. Many error messages report both values, if available.

Link

In UNIX, a name in a directory, representing a file. A given file can have multiple links to it. It's like having the same phone number listed in the phone directory under different names.

List

An ordered set of values with a beginning and an end. Or, an attribute of a leaning ship, decreasing in value, at the beginning of its end.

LIST

A syntactic construct representing a comma-separated list of expressions, evaluated to produce an array value. Each expression in a LIST is evaluated in an array context. See also *Context* and *Array Context*.

List Context

See *Array Context*.

List Operator

Generally, an operator that does something with a list of values, such as *join* or *grep*. More specifically, those operators (such as **print**, **unlink**, and **system**) that do not require parentheses around their argument list.

Literal

Often means "figurative," as in "I'm literally scared to death." More literally, a symbol in a programming language like a number or string that gives you an actual value instead of merely representing possible values.

Little-Endian

From Swift, someone who eats eggs little end first. Also used of computers that store the least significant byte of a word at a lower byte address than the most significant byte. Often considered superior to big-endian machines. See also *Big-Endian*.

Local

Something that doesn't mean the same thing everywhere. A variable in Perl can be localized inside a block or a package. See *Global* and *Package*.

Logical Operator

Symbols representing the concepts "and," "or," and "not."

Loop

A syntactic construct that can make things happen more than once. See *Loop*.

Loop Control Statement

Any statement within the body of a loop that can make a loop stop looping or skip an iteration.

Loop Label

The nutritional information on the side of the popular (at Randal's house) cereal box. Or, a kind of key or name attached to a loop so that loop control statements can talk about which loop they want to control.

Lvalue

Term used by language-lawyers for a thing you can assign a new value to, such as a variable or an element of an array. The "L" is short for "left," as in the left side of an assignment statement, a typical place for lvalues.

Magical Increment

An increment operator that knows how to add 1 to alphanumeric strings as well as to numbers.

Magical Variables

Special variables that have side effects when you access them or assign to them. For example, in Perl, changing elements of the %ENV array also changes the corresponding environment variables that subprocesses will use. Reading the $! variable gives you the current UNIX error number or message.

Manpage

A "page" from the UNIX manuals, typically accessed online via the *man(1)* command. A manpage contains a SYNOPSIS, a DESCRIPTION, a list of BUGS, and so on, and is typically longer than a page. There are manpages documenting commands, system calls, library functions, devices, protocols, files, and such.

Mantissa

The part of a floating-point number that gives the digits of the number without saying where the decimal point really belongs. See *Exponent*.

Matching

See *Pattern Matching*.

Metacharacter

A character that is **not** supposed to be treated normally. Which characters are to be treated specially varies greatly from context to context. The shell has certain metacharacters, double-quoted Perl strings have other metacharacters, and patterns have all the double-quote metacharacters plus some extra ones. In addition, people sometimes use this term to describe characters that have the eighth bit set.

Minimalism

The belief that "small is beautiful." Paradoxically, however, if you say something in a small language, it turns out big, and if you say it in a big language, it turns out small. Go figure.

Mode

Ordinarily means ice cream. However, in the context of the **stat**() system call, refers to the word holding the permissions and the type of the file. What that has to do with ice cream is beyond me. (For that matter, which of the values returned by the **stat** call are actually statistics?)

Modifier

A conditional or loop that isn't very important, so you put it after the statement instead of before, if you know what I mean.

Modulus

A divisor, when you're interested in the remainder instead of the quotient. Don't tell any mathematicians that, or they'll start complaining about negative numbers and such.

Multi-dimensional Array

An array with multiple subscripts that must all match to find the element you're interested in. Perl does them using associative arrays.

Name

What you call something, Silly!

Namespace

The little blank on the "Pay to the order of..." part of your checks. See *Freely Available*. Also, a method of classifying names so that names in one namespace don't have to worry about whether that name has been used in some other namespace. See *Package*.

Network

A bunch of machines you can't get to talk to each other till the night before someone sets a worm or virus loose.

Network Address

The most important attribute of a socket, like your telephone's telephone number.

Newline

A single character that represents the end of a line, with the ASCII value of 012 octal under UNIX, and represented by **\n** in Perl strings. For certain physical devices like terminals, this gets translated to a line feed and a carriage return. It's just an accident that a newline and a line feed happen to have the same code—they could have been different and still worked right.

Null Character

A character with the ASCII value of 0. It's used by C and some UNIX system calls to terminate strings, but Perl allows strings to contain a null.

Null List

A list value with 0 elements, represented in Perl by ().

Null String

A string containing 0 characters, not to be confused with a string containing a null character, which has a positive length.

Numeric Context

The situation in which an expression is expected by its surroundings (the code calling it) to return a number. See also *Context* and *String Context*.

Nybble

Half a byte, equivalent to one hexadecimal digit.

Octal

A number in base 8. Only the digits 0 through 7 are allowed. Octal constants in Perl start with **0**.

Offset

When counting over to a position in a string or array, how many things you have to skip over to get where you are going. Thus, the minimum offset is 0, not 1, because you don't skip anything to get to the first item.

Operand

You, after you dial zero on your phone. Or, an expression that gives a value that an operator operates on. See also *Precedence*.

Operating System

Nonexistent, unless the meaning of "operating" is used rather loosely. Or, in the strict sense, a special program that runs on the bare machine and hides the gory details of managing processes and devices. It is usually used in a looser sense to indicate a particular culture of programming. The loose sense can be used at varying levels of specificity. At one extreme, you might say that all versions of UNIX and UNIX-lookalikes are the same operating system (upsetting many people, especially some lawyers). At the other extreme, this particular version of this particular vendor's operating system is different than any other version of this or any other vendor's operating system. Perl is much more portable across operating systems than many other languages. See also *Architecture*.

Operator

A function, generally one that is built into a language, often with a special syntax or symbol. A given operator may have specific expectations about what types of data you give as its arguments (operands) and what type of data you want back from it.

Owner

The one user (apart from the superuser) that has absolute control over a file. A file also has a group of users that may exercise joint ownership if the real owner permits them. See *Permission Flags*.

Package

A quantity of code that values its privacy, and tries to keep other code from trespassing by fencing all of its private belongings (variables and subroutines) into its own area. A variable or subroutine mentioned in the package belongs only to that package, even if there's another variable or subroutine with an identical name in some other package.

Package Local

A variable or subroutine belonging to a package and not visible to anyone else. At least, not without peeking. See *Namespace*.

Parameter

What you get when you cross a paramedic and meter maid. See also *Argument*, which is what you get when you just cross a meter maid.

Parsing

The subtle but sometimes brutal art of attempting to turn your possibly malformed program into a hopefully valid syntax tree. (If it doesn't work, you probably just end up with a useless piece of a dead tree.)

PATH

The list of directories the system looks in to find the program you want to execute. It's stored as one of your environment variables, accessible in Perl as $ENV{'PATH'}.

Pathname

A fully qualified filename such as */usr/bin/perl*.

Pathological

Diseased. As in certain imprecations involving camels.

Pattern Matching

Taking a pattern, expressed as a regular expression, and trying the pattern various ways on a string to see if there's any way to make it fit. Often used to pick interesting tidbits out of a file. See *Regular Expression*.

Permission Flags

What the owner of a file sets or unsets in order to allow or disallow access to other people. These flags are part of the "mode" word returned by the **stat** operator when you ask about a file.

Pipe

A direct connection that carries the output of one process to the input of another without the necessity of an intermediate temporary file. Once the pipe is set up, the two processes in question can just read and write as if they were talking to a normal file.

Pipeline

A series of processes all in a row, linked by pipes, where each passes its output to the next.

Pointer

A variable in a language like C that contains the exact memory location of some other item. Perl handles pointers internally so you don't have to worry about them. Instead, you just use symbolic pointers in the form of keys and subscripts.

Port

The left side of a ship. See *List*. Also, the part of the address of a TCP or UDP socket that directs packets to the correct process after finding the right machine, something like the phone extension number you give when you reach the company operator.

Precedence

The rules of conduct that, in the absence of other guidance, determine what should happen first. For example, in the absence of parentheses, you always do multiplication before addition.

Preprocessing

What some other helper process did to transform the incoming data into a form more suitable for the current process. Often done with an incoming pipe. See also *C Preprocessor*.

Process

An instance of a running program. Under multi-tasking systems like UNIX, two or more separate processes could be running the same program independently at the same time—in fact, the fork function is designed to bring about this happy state of affairs. Under other operating systems processes are sometimes called "tasks" or "jobs."

Procedure

Usually, a subroutine. Unless you're a doctor.

Protocol

In networking, an agreed-upon way of sending messages back and forth so that neither correspondent will get too confused.

Pseudo Literal

An operator that looks something like a literal, such as the output-grabbing operator, `command`.

Pseudo Terminal

A thing that looks like an ordinary terminal to the computer, but instead of being attached to a real terminal, is really attached to another computer program, which is doing the pseudo-typing.

Public Domain

Something not owned by anybody. Perl is copyrighted, and is thus **not** in the public domain—it's just freely available and freely redistributable (q.v.).

Readable

With regard to files, one that has the proper permission bit set to let you access the file.

With regard to computer programs, one that's well enough written that someone can come back later and have a chance of figuring out what it's trying to do. Who knows, you might even have to come back and figure out your own program.

Record

A set of related data values in a file or stream, often associated with a unique key field. In UNIX, often commensurate with a line, or a blank line delimited set of lines. Each line of the */etc/passwd* file is a record, keyed on login name, containing information about that user.

Recursion

The art of defining something (at least partly) in terms of itself, which is a naughty no-no in dictionaries. This is similar in many ways to "recursion," although the differences are subtle.

Regular Expression

A single object with variable interpretations, like an elephant. To a computer scientist, a grammar for a little language in which some strings are legal and others aren't. To normal people, a pattern that you can use to find what you're looking for when it varies from case to case. Example of a regular expression:

```
/Oh s.*t./
```

This will match strings like "**Oh say can you see by the dawn's early light,**" and "**Oh sit!.**"

Regular File

A file that's not a directory, a device, a named pipe or socket, or a symbolic link. Most files are regular, unlike gasoline. Perl uses **–f** to identify regular files.

Relation

Jargon used by relational database folks to mean a file—albeit a particular sort of file, tabular in form, in which all the tuples (records) are of the same kind, each containing the same domains (keys) and ranges (fields). The UNIX */etc/passwd* file is a relation keyed on login name. It's called a relation because it relates keys and fields in much the same way as an associative array associates keys and values.

Relational Operator

Your sister-in-law, who works for the phone company. Or, an operator that says whether a particular ordering relationship is true about a pair of operands. Perl has both numeric and string relational operators.

Reserved Words

A word with a specific, built-in meaning to a compiler, such as **if** or **delete**. In many languages (not Perl) it's illegal to use reserved words to name anything else. (Which is why they're reserved, after all.) In Perl, you just can't use them to name labels or filehandles. Also called a keyword.

Return Value

The value produced by a subroutine or expression when evaluated. In Perl, a return value may be either a list or a scalar. The subroutine call **&piglatin('bingo')** returns the value **'ingobay'**.

Right Shift

A bit shift (see *Bit Shift*) that divides the number by some power of 2. In politics, the application of this operator to the number of liberals.

Runtime

The time when Perl is actually doing what your script says to do, as opposed to the earlier period of time when it was trying to figure out whether what you said made any sense whatsoever. See also *Compile Time.*

Runtime Pattern

Six A.M. on weekdays, 7:30 A.M. on Saturday, and not at all on Sunday. Or, a pattern that contains one or more variables to be interpolated before parsing the pattern as a regular expression, and hence cannot be analyzed at compile time, but must be re-analyzed each time the pattern match operator is evaluated. Runtime patterns are useful but expensive. [I have friends like that—Randal.]

Rvalue

A value that you might find on the right side of an assignment statement. See *lvalue.* Not to be confused with R-value, a measure of the insulative value of your skull.

Scalar

A simple value, such as a number or string. Or, someone who simply climbs mountains.

Scalar Context

A competition to see who can climb the mountain the hardest way. Also, the situation in which an expression is expected by its surroundings (the code calling it) to return a single value rather than a list of values. See also *Context* and *Array Context.*

A scalar context sometimes imposes additional constraints on the return value—see *String Context* and *Numeric Context.* Sometimes we talk about a "boolean context" inside conditionals, but this imposes no additional constraints, since any scalar value, whether numeric or string, is already true or false.

Scalar Literal

A very small mountain climber. Or, a number or quoted string—an actual value in the text of your program, as opposed to a variable.

Scalar Value

How important something is to a mountain climber. (The scalar value of a big-screen TV is nearly zero.) In Perl, a value that happens to be a scalar as opposed to a list.

Scalar Variable

An unreliable mountain climber. Or, a variable that holds a single value, prefixed with $ in Perl.

Scope

How far away you can see a variable from, using one. In Perl, the scope (visibility) of local variables is dynamic, meaning that any subroutine that is called by the block can see the variables that are local to the block. In other languages having static scope, the variables would not be visible.

Script

A text file that is a program intended to be executed directly rather than compiled to another form of file before execution.

sed

A venerable stream editor from which Perl derives some of its ideas.

Semi-formal

When the girls get to dress up and the boys don't have to.

Server

In networking, a process that either advertises a service or just hangs around at a known location and waits for clients who need service to get in touch with it.

Service

Something you do for someone else to make them happy, like give them the time of day (or of their life). On some UNIX machines, well-known services are listed by the **getservent** function.

SetGID

Same as SetUID, only having to do with giving away group privileges.

SetUID

Said of a program that runs with the privileges of its owner rather than the privileges of the person running it, which is the usual case. Also describes the bit in the mode word that implements the feature. This bit must be explicitly set by the owner to implement this feature, and the program must be carefully written not to give away more privileges than it ought.

Shell

A command-line interpreter. The program that interactively gives you a prompt, accepts one or more lines of input and executes the programs you mentioned, feeding each of them their proper arguments and input data. Shells can also execute scripts containing such commands. Under the

UNIX operating system, typical shells are the Bourne shell (*/bin/sh*), the C shell (*/bin/csh*), and the Korn shell (*/bin/ksh*). Perl is not strictly a shell because it's not interactive (although Perl programs can be interactive).

Side Effects

Something extra that happens when you evaluate an expression or run in air that's too cold, or if you're a computer, too hot.

Signal Handler

A subroutine that, instead of being content to be called in the normal fashion, sits around waiting for a bolt out of the blue before it will deign to execute. Under UNIX, bolts out of the blue are called signals, and you send them with a **kill** command, though it doesn't always have that effect.

Slice

A tasty beverage allegedly consumed by hookers before they make their rounds, or when they return to the clubhouse. Or, if you prefer, a selection of fine array elements from our list.

Socket

An endpoint for network communication between two processes that works much like a telephone. The most important thing about a socket is its address (like a phone number). Different kinds of sockets have different kinds of addresses—some look like filenames, and some don't.

Standard Error

The default output stream for making nasty remarks that don't belong in standard output. Represented within a Perl program by the filehandle **STDERR**. You can use this stream explicitly, but the operators **die** and **warn** write to your standard error stream automatically.

Standard I/O

A standard C library for doing buffered input and output to the operating system. (The "standard" of standard I/O is only marginally related to the "standard" of standard input and output.) In general, Perl relies on whatever implementation of standard I/O a given operating system supplies, so the buffering characteristics of a Perl program on one machine may not exactly match those on another machine. Normally this only influences efficiency, not semantics. If your standard I/O package is doing block buffering and you want it to flush the buffer more often, you can do so by setting the $| variable.

Standard Input

The default input stream for your program, which if possible shouldn't care where the data is coming from. Represented within a Perl program by the filehandle **STDIN**.

Standard Output

The default output stream for your program, which if possible shouldn't care where the data is going. Represented within a Perl program by the filehandle **STDOUT**.

Stat Structure

A special internal buffer in which Perl keeps the information about the last file you requested information on.

Statement

A command to the computer about what to do next, like a step in a recipe: *"Add marmalade to batter and mix until mixed."* Not to be confused with a "declaration," which doesn't tell the computer to do anything, but just to learn something. See *Declaration*.

Status

The value returned to the parent process when one of its child processes dies. Eight bits of it are the last request of child (if it had a chance to make one) and eight more bits say whether foul play was involved in the death. Perl keeps the status in the **$?** variable.

STDERR

See *Standard Error*.

STDIN

See *Standard Input*.

STDIO

See *Standard I/O*.

STDOUT

See *Standard Output*.

String

A sequence of characters such as "**He said !@#*&%@#*?\n.**" A string does not have to be entirely printable.

String Context

A competition involving cat's cradles and bikinis. (See *Concatenation*.) Also, the situation in which an expression is expected by its surroundings (the code calling it) to return a string. See also *Context* and *Numeric Context*.

struct

C keyword introducing a structure definition or name.

Structure

See *Data Structure*.

Subroutine

Normal behavior at periscope depth. Or, a named piece of program that can be invoked from elsewhere in the program in order to accomplish some sub-goal of the program. A subroutine is often parameterized to accomplish different but related things depending on its input arguments. If the subroutine returns a value, it is also called a function.

Subscript

A value that indicates the position of a particular array element in an array.

Substitution

Replacing one thing with another. Such as replacing the money in your pocket with some ice cream from the vending machine, represented in Perl as **s/money/ice_cream/**. If you instead write this as **s/money/ice_cream/g**, you will need to buy larger clothes the next time you go shopping, and possibly get a better paying job. Your pocket will get pretty messy, too.

Substring

A portion of a string, starting at a certain character position, and proceeding for a certain number of characters.

Superuser

The person whom the operating system will let do almost anything, typically your system administrator or someone pretending to be your system administrator. On UNIX systems, the **root** user.

Switch

The options you give on a command line to influence the way your program works. In UNIX, these are introduced with a minus sign.

Switch Clustering

The combining of multiple command line switches –a –b –c into one switch –abc. In Perl, any switch with an additional argument must be the last switch in a cluster.

Switch Statement

A program construct that lets you evaluate an expression and then, based on the value of the expression, do a multi-way branch to the appropriate piece of code for that value. Also called a "case structure," named after the similar Pascal construct.

Symbol Table

Where a compiler remembers symbols. A program like Perl must somehow remember all the names of all the variables, filehandles, and subroutines you've used. It does this by placing the names in a symbol table. There is a separate symbol table for each package, to give each package its own namespace. See *Namespace*.

Symbolic Debugger

A program that lets you step through the execution of your program, stopping or printing things out here and there to see if anything has gone wrong, and if so, what. The "symbolic" part just means that you can talk to the debugger using the same symbols in which your program is written.

Symbolic Link

An alternate filename that points to the real name. Whenever the operating system is trying to parse a pathname containing a symbolic link, it merely substitutes in the real name and continues parsing.

Syntax

From Greek, "with-arrangement." How things (particularly symbols) are put together with each other.

Syntax Tree

An internal representation of your program wherein lower level constructs dangle off the higher level constructs enclosing them.

System Call

A subroutine call directly to the operating system. Many of the important subroutines and functions you use aren't direct system calls, but built up in one or more layers above the system call level. In general, Perl users don't need to worry about the distinction.

Tainted

Said of data that might be derived from the grubby hands of a user, and thus unsafe for a secure program to rely on.

taintperl

BASIC, Fortran, or C. Also, a special version of the Perl interpreter that does tainting checks for setuid and setgid programs. See *SetUID*.

TCP

Short for Transmission Control Protocol. A protocol wrapped around the Internet Protocol to make an unreliable packet transmission mechanism appear to the application program to be a reliable stream of bytes. (Well, most of the time.)

Text

Normally, a string or file containing primarily printable characters. The word has been usurped in some UNIX circles to mean the portion of your process that contains machine code to be executed.

Tokenizing

Splitting up a program text into its separate words and symbols, each of which is called a token.

Toolbox Approach

The notion that, with a complete set of simple tools that work well together, you can build almost anything you want. Which is fine if you're assembling a tricycle, but if you're building a defranishizing comboflux, you really want your own machine shop to build special tools in. Perl is sort of a machine shop.

True

See *False*. (And hold it up to a mirror for the secret message.)

Tuple

In the lingo of relational databases, a record or line containing fields. See *Relation*.

Type Casting

A variant of flyfishing in which used font cartridges are attached to the line as bait. Also used of people who do this too often on TV. Also used of programmers who convert data from one type to another in C programs too often. This never happens to Perl programmers.

Type

See *Data Type*.

UID

User ID. Always refers to the numeric user ID which the operating system uses to identify you, never to the alphanumeric login ID which you *think* the system uses.

Unary Operator

An operator with only one operand, like – or *chdir*. Unary operators are usually prefix operators, that is, they precede their operand. The ++ and −− operators can be either prefix or postfix. (Of course, that *does* change their meaning.)

Undefined

Nobody has ever given this a reasonable definition. See also *Defined*.

UNIX

A very large and constantly evolving language with several alternate and largely incompatible syntaxes (syntacies?), in which anyone can define anything any way they choose, and usually do. Speakers of this language think it's easy to learn because it's so easily twisted to one's own ends, but dialectical differences make tribal intercommunication nearly impossible, and travelers are often reduced to a pidgin-like subset of the language. To be universally understood, a UNIX shell programmer must spend years of study in the art. Many have abandoned this discipline and now communicate via an Esperanto-like language called Perl.

In ancient times UNIX was also used to refer to some code that a couple of people at Bell Labs wrote to make use of a PDP7 computer that wasn't doing much of anything else at the time.

Value

This is hard to define. It's something like real data—the actual numbers and strings that wander around in your program. But we don't really need to define it. If you didn't know a value when you see it, you wouldn't have this book.

Variable

A named storage location that can hold any of various values, as your program sees fit.

Vector

Mathematical jargon for a list of scalar values. Strictly speaking, the term implies that the values are coordinates in an n-dimensional space, but who speaks strictly?

Warning

A message printed to the **STDERR** stream to the effect that something might be wrong but it isn't worth blowing up over. See the **warn** operator in Chapter 4.

Whitespace

A character that moves your cursor around but doesn't otherwise put anything on your screen. Typically refers to any of: space, tab, newline (line feed), carriage return, form feed, or vertical tab.

Word

In normal "computerese," the piece of data of the size most efficiently dealt with by your computer, typically 32 bits or so, give or take a few powers of two. In Perl, it more often refers to an alphanumeric identifier, or to a string of non-whitespace characters bounded by whitespace or line boundaries.

Working Directory

Your current directory, from which relative pathnames are interpreted by the operating system. The operating system knows your current directory because you told it with a *chdir*, or because you started out the same place your parent process was when you were born.

Wrapper

A program that runs some other program for you, modifying some of its input or output to better suit your purposes. More generally, just about anything that wraps things up. And that just about wraps things up.

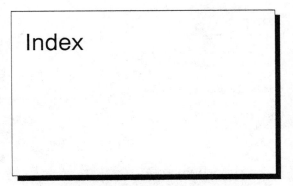

Index

The first part of this index lists symbols beginning with non-alphabetic characters. Since the sort order of these characters isn't ingrained in us the way the alphabet is, it is summarized below, from left to right:

! " # $ % & ´ ( ) * + , − . / : ; < = > ? @ [\ ] ^ _ ` { | } ˜

For symbols consisting of a special character followed by an alphabetic (like **@ARGV** or **-w**), look under the alphabetic character.

!, 11
  as negating operator, 82
!=, 6, 9
  as relational operator, 88
  compared to ne, 361
!˜, and effects on tr///, 194
  and s///, 175
  as pattern binding operator, 82,
    125
#!, 5
  and command-line options, 36

as initial characters of script, and
    command-line switches, 351
  as interpreter specification, 274
#, as comment character, and C
    preprocessor, 355
  in format fields, 107
  in formats, 43
$, and formats, 107
  as initial character of a name, 4,
    14
  and $*, 39, 105

command substitution, 24
command-line arguments, 35,
    117, 351
    and #!, 36
    and @ARGV, 117
    processing, 404-405
command-line processing, 256,
    277
commas, as operators, 93
    in integers, 237
    in print(), changing, 113
    optional at end of list, 74
comments, 2
comparison operators, 9, 88
comp.lang.perl, xvi
complement operator, 82
completing reads, 401
concatenation, with . operator, 83
conditional operator, 91
Configure script, 376
connect(), 133, 344
context, array, 18, 66
    Boolean, 66
    scalar, 18, 66
continue, within compound state-
    ments, 95
control D, in source file, 71
control Z, in source file, 71
conventions, xix
converting sed and awk, xiii
core, creating (intentionally) with
    −u command-line option, 357
core dumps, with dump, 139
cos(), defined, 133
counting, 254
cpio(1), emulation, 377, 403
CPU time, with times(), 193
CRLF on IBM machines, 128
crypt(), 134
curly braces, as compound state-
    ment delimiter, 94
curly brackets, 9, 30
    and globbing, 78
    as delimiters, 70
    in regular expressions, 103
    to delimit variable names, 24

to remove interpolation ambigu-
    ity, 72
current time, with time(), 193
customizing, with C subroutines,
    378

D

d, as option to tr///, 194
−D, and displaying the syntax tree,
    98
    as command-line option,
        defined, 352
$^D, as a special variable, 116
−d, as command-line option, 352
    as file test operator, 85
    example of, 269
daemons, creating, 216
    managing, 333
DATA, and efficiency, 370
    as a filehandle, 71
    as a special filehandle, 117
data, in tabular form, processing,
    41
data types, 65
databases, manipulating, 259
date(1), emulating, 402
DBM files, and associative arrays,
    134
    and delete(), 136
    and keys(), 157
    and readonly access, 135
    and reset(), 173
    and values(), 199
    lack of locking for, 135
    processing, 262
dbmclose(), 134
dbmopen(), 134
    example of, 263
debugging, xiii
    and −w command-line option,
        357
    control via $^P, 116
    with the debugger, 357
debugging flags, access via $^D,
    116
    on command line, 353

R

−R, as file test operator, 85
−r, 11
  as file test operator, 85
raising exceptions, with die, 137
rand(), 11, 20, 246
  defined, 170
  example of, 327
random numbers, with rand(), 170
random-access files, 46
range generation, 20
range operator, 89
rational numbers, manipulating, 400
raw mode, on terminal, setting, 401
read(), 170
  and sysread(), 170
  example of, 46, 261
read(2), via sysread(), 191
readdir(), 170
  and efficiency, 366
  contrasted with <*>, 78
  examples of, 57
reading directories, and readdir(), 170
readlink(), 171
  example of, 314
read/write access, in open(), 163
real gid, and $(, 116
real uid, and $<, 115
record locking, and fcntl(), 144
record separator, $/, 113
records, processing fixed-length,, 260
  processing variable-length, 260
recursion, 53
recursive descent parsing, 58
recursive subroutines, 307
recv(), 171
redo, within compound statements, 95
regular expressions, 103
  and $*, 114
  and //, 125

  and interpolation ambiguity, 72
relational operators, 88
relative files, 46
removing directories, with rmdir(), 174
rename(), 171, 239
  example of, 306, 312
renaming files, 171, 312
repeated patterns, 301
repetition of strings, 83
replication of strings, 83
reports, formatting, 41
require(), 172
  and @INC, 118
  and package declarations, 63
  and the standard library, 396
  compared with do, 139, 172
  examples of, 346
reserved words, and variable names, 68
reset(), 172
  and ??, 127
  and DBM caches, 135
  and efficiency, 368
  and erasing an associative array, 137
  and write(), 109
  example of, 266
return(), 99, 173
  and subroutines, 53
return value, 53
reverse(), 22, 243
  defined, 173
reversing, 20
rewinddir(), 174
right-justification, in printf(), 40
right-shift, with >> operator, 84
rindex(), 174
  example of, 285
rmdir(), defined, 174
rn(1), and history, 378, 381
rollerskating, 206
rot13, as an encryption method, 252
RPG II, 10
runaway string, as error message, 69

About the Authors

Randal L. Schwartz is an eclectic tradesman and entrepreneur, making his living through software design, technical writing, system administration, security consultation, and video production. He is known internationally for his prolific, humorous, and occasionally incorrect spatterings on Usenet—especially his "Just another Perl hacker" signoffs in comp.lang.perl.

Randal honed his many crafts through seven years of employment at Tektronix, ServioLogic and Sequent. For the past five years, he has owned and operated Stonehenge Consulting Services in his home town of Portland, Oregon.

Larry Wall is a programmer at JPL; in his copious free time :-), he has authored some of the most popular free programs available for UNIX, including the rn news reader, the ubiquitous patch program, and the Perl programming language. He's also known for metaconfig, a program which writes Configure scripts, and for the warp space-war game, the first version of which was written in BASIC/PLUS at Seattle Pacific University. By training Larry is actually a linguist, having wandered about both U.C. Berkeley and UCLA as a grad student. (Oddly enough, while at Berkeley, he had nothing to do with the UNIX development going on there.)

He also spent time at Unisys, playing with everything from discrete event simulators to software development methodologies. It was there, while trying to glue together a bicoastal configuration management system over a 1200 baud encrypted link using a hacked over version of Netnews, that Perl was born.

Colophon

Our look is the result of reader comments, our own experimentation, and distribution channels. Distinctive covers complement our distinctive approach to technical topics, breathing personality and life into potentially dry subjects. UNIX and its attendant programs can be unruly beasts. Nutshell Handbooks help you tame them.

The animal featured on the cover of *Programming Perl* is a camel, a one-humped dromedary. A hoofed mammal, relative of the llama and alpaca, camels first appeared 38 million years ago and once populated all large land masses but Australia. For some unknown reason, they died off in all but the Middle East, Central Asia, India, and North Africa, and now only two species remain, the one-humped dromedary and the two-humped bactrian. The dromedary is the larger and stronger of the two, standing seven feet tall at the top of its hump and able to carry an average load of 400 pounds. With only the weight of one rider, a dromedary can move at ten mph all day. Loaded down in caravan, they will move 30 miles per day.

Edie Freedman designed this cover and the entire UNIX bestiary that appears on other Nutshell Handbooks. The beasts themselves are adapted from 19th-century engravings from the Dover Pictorial Archive.

The text of this book is set in Times Roman; headings are Helvetica; examples are Courier. Text was prepared using SortQuad's sqtroff text formatter. Figures are produced with a Macintosh. Printing is done on a Tegra Varityper 5000.

USING

UNIX AND X

Books from O'Reilly & Associates, Inc.

FALL/WINTER 1994-95

–Basics–

Our UNIX in a Nutshell *guides are the most comprehensive quick reference on the market—a must for
every* UNIX *user. No matter what system you use,
we've got a version to cover your needs.*

UNIX in a Nutshell: System V Edition

By Daniel Gilly & the staff of O'Reilly & Associates
2nd Edition June 1992
444 pages, ISBN 1-56592-001-5

You may have seen UNIX
quick-reference guides, but
you've never seen anything
like *UNIX in a Nutshell*. Not
a scaled-down quick reference
of common commands, *UNIX
in a Nutshell* is a complete
reference containing all commands and options, along with
generous descriptions and examples that put the
commands in context. For all but the thorniest
UNIX problems, this one reference should be all
the documentation you need. Covers System V,
Releases 3 and 4, and Solaris 2.0.

"This book is the perfect desktop reference...
The authors have presented a clear and concisely
written book which would make an excellent
addition to any UNIX user's library."
—*SysAdmin*

SCO UNIX in a Nutshell

By Ellie Cutler & the staff of O'Reilly & Associates
1st Edition February 1994
590 pages, ISBN 1-56592-037-6

The desktop reference to
SCO UNIX and Open Desktop®,
this version of *UNIX in a
Nutshell* shows you what's
under the hood of your SCO
system. It isn't a scaled-down
quick reference of common
commands, but a complete
reference containing all user,
programming, administration,
and networking commands.

Contents include:

- All commands and options
- Shell syntax for the Bourne, Korn, C, and
  SCO shells
- Pattern matching, with *vi, ex, sed*, and
  *aw*k commands
- Compiler and debugging commands for
  software development
- Networking with email, TCP/IP, NFS, and UUCP
- System administration commands and
  the SCO sysadmsh shell

This edition of *UNIX in a Nutshell* is the most
comprehensive SCO quick reference on the market,
a must for any SCO user. You'll want to keep
SCO UNIX in a Nutshell close by as you use your
computer: it'll become a handy, indispensible
reference for working with your SCO system.

Learning the UNIX Operating System

By Grace Todino, John Strang & Jerry Peek
3rd Edition August 1993
108 pages, ISBN 1-56592-060-0

If you are new to UNIX, this concise introduction will tell you just what you need to get started and no more. Why wade through a 600 page book when you can begin working productively in a matter of minutes? It's an ideal primer for Mac and PC users of the Internet who need to know a little bit about UNIX on the systems they visit.

Topics covered include:

- Logging in and logging out
- Window systems (especially X/Motif)
- Managing UNIX files and directories
- Sending and receiving mail
- Redirecting input/output
- Pipes and filters
- Background processing
- Basic network commandsThis book is the most effective introduction to UNIX in print.

This book is the most effective introduction to UNIX in print. The third edition has been updated and expanded to provide increased coverage of window systems and networking. It's a handy book for someone just starting with UNIX, as well as someone who encounters a UNIX system as a visitor via remote login over the Internet.

"Once you've established a connection with the network, there's often a secondary obstacle to surmount.... *Learning the UNIX Operating System* helps you figure out what to do next by presenting in a nutshell the basics of how to deal with the 'U-word.' Obviously a 92-page book isn't going to make you an instant UNIX guru, but it does an excellent job of introducing basic operations in a concise nontechnical way, including how to navigate through the file system, send and receive E-mail and—most importantly—get to the online help...."
—Michael L. Porter, Associate Editor,
Personal Engineering & Instrumentation News

Learning the vi Editor

By Linda Lamb
5th Edition October 1990
192 pages, ISBN 0-937175-67-6

A complete guide to text editing with *vi*, the editor available on nearly every UNIX system. Early chapters cover the basics; later chapters explain more advanced editing tools, such as *ex* commands and global search and replacement.

"For those who are looking for an introductory book to give to new staff members who have no acquaintance with either screen editing or with UNIX screen editing, this is it: a book on *vi* that is neither designed for the UNIX in-crowd, nor so imbecilic that one is ashamed to use it."
—*;login*

Learning the Korn Shell

By Bill Rosenblatt
1st Edition June 1993
363 pages, ISBN 1-56592-054-6

A thorough introduction to the Korn shell, both as a user interface and as a programming language. This book provides a clear explanation of the Korn shell's features, including *ksh* string operations, co-processes, signals and signal handling, and command-line interpretation. *Learning the Korn Shell* also includes real-life programming examples and a Korn shell debugger (*kshdb*).

"Readers still bending back the pages of Korn-shell manuals will find relief in...*Learning the Korn Shell*...a gentle introduction to the shell. Rather than focusing on syntax issues, the book quickly takes on the task of solving day-to-day problems with Korn-shell scripts. Application scripts are also shown and explained in detail. In fact, the book even presents a script debugger written for *ksh*. This is a good book for improving your knowledge of the shell."
—*Unix Review*

MH & xmh: E-mail for Users & Programmers

By Jerry Peek
2nd Edition September 1992
728 pages, ISBN 1-56592-027-9

Customizing your email environment can save time and make communicating more enjoyable. *MH & xmh: E-Mail for Users & Programmers* explains how to use, customize, and program with the MH electronic mail commands available on virtually any UNIX system. The handbook also covers *xmh*, an X Window System client that runs MH programs.

The second edition added a chapter on *mhook*, sections explaining under-appreciated small commands and features, and more examples showing how to use MH to handle common situations.

"The MH bible is irrefutably Jerry Peek's *MH & xmh: E-mail for Users & Programmers*. This book covers just about everything that is known about MH and *xmh* (the X Windows front end to MH), presented in a clear and easy-to-read format. I strongly recommend that anybody serious about MH get a copy."
—James Hamilton, *UnixWorld*

Learning the GNU Emacs

By Debra Cameron & Bill Rosenblatt
1st Edition October 1991
442 pages, ISBN 0-937175-84-6

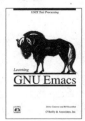

An introduction to the GNU Emacs editor, one of the most widely used and powerful editors available under UNIX. Provides a solid introduction to basic editing, a look at several important editing modes (special Emacs features for editing specific types of documents), and a brief introduction to customization and Emacs LISP programming. The book is aimed at new Emacs users, whether or not they are programmers.

"Authors Debra Cameron and Bill Rosenblatt do a particularly admirable job presenting the extensive functionality of GNU Emacs in well-organized, easily digested chapters.... Despite its title, *Learning GNU Emacs* could easily serve as a reference for the experienced Emacs user."
—Linda Branagan, Convex Computer Corporation

The USENET Handbook

By Mark Harrison
1st Edition Winter 1994-95 (est.)
250 pages (est.), ISBN 1-56592-101-1

The USENET Handbook describes how to get the most out of the USENET news network, a worldwide network of cooperating computer sites that exchange public user messages known as "articles" or "postings." These postings are an electric mix of questions, commentary, hints, and ideas of all kinds, expressing the views of the thousands of participants at these sites.

Tutorials show you how to read news using the most popular newsreaders—*tin* and Trumpet for Windows and *nn*, *emacs* and *gnus* for UNIX. It also explains how to post articles to the Net.

The book discusses things you can do to increase your productivity by using the resources mentioned on USENET, such as anonymous FTP (file transfer protocol), mail servers, FAQs, and mailing lists. It covers network etiquette, processing encoded and compressed files (i.e., software, pictures, etc.), and lots of historical information.

Using UUCP and Usenet

By Grace Todino & Dale Dougherty
1st Edition February 1986 (latest update October 1991)
210 pages, ISBN 0-937175-10-2

Shows users how to communicate with both UNIX and non-UNIX systems using UUCP and *cu* or *tip* and how to read news and post articles. This handbook assumes that UUCP is already running at your site.

"Are you having trouble with UUCP? Have you torn out your hair trying to set the Dialers file? *Managing UUCP and Usenet* and *Using UUCP and Usenet* will give you the information you need to become an accomplished Net user. The companion book is *!%@:: A Directory of Electronic Mail Addressing & Networks*, a compendium of world networks and how to address and read them. All of these books are well written, and I urge you to take a look at them."
—*Root Journal*

X User Tools

By Linda Mui & Valerie Quercia
1st Edition October 1994 (est.)
750 pages (est.) (CD-ROM included)
ISBN 1-56592-019-8

 X User Tools provides for
X users what *UNIX Power
Tools* provides for UNIX
users: hundreds of tips,
tricks, scripts, techniques,
and programs—plus
a CD-ROM—to make
the X Windowing
System more enjoy-
able, more powerful,
and easier to use.

This browser's book emphasizes useful programs,
culled from the network and contributed by X
programmers worldwide. Programs range from
fun (games, screensavers, and a variety of online
clocks) to business tools (calendar, memo, and
mailer programs) to graphics (programs for
drawing, displaying, and converting images).
You'll also find a number of tips and techniques
for configuring both individual and systemwide
environments, as well as a glossary of common
X and UNIX terms.

The browser style of organization—pioneered
by *UNIX Power Tools*—encourages readers to
leaf through the book at will, focusing on what
appeals at the time. Each article stands on its
own, many containing cross-references to related
articles. Before you know it, you'll have covered
the entire book, simply by scanning what's of
interest and following cross-references to more
detailed information.

The enclosed CD-ROM contains source files for
all and binary files for some of the programs—
for a number of platforms, including Sun 4,
Solaris, HP 700, Alpha/OSF, and AIX. Note that
the CD-ROM contains software for both emacs
and tcl/tk.

Volume 3: X Window System User's Guide

Standard Edition
By Valerie Quercia & Tim O'Reilly
4th Edition May 1993
836 pages, ISBN 1-56592-014-7

 The *X Window System User's
Guide* orients the new user
to window system concepts
and provides detailed tutorials
for many client programs,
including the *xterm* terminal
emulator and window man-
agers. Building on this basic
knowledge, later chapters
explain how to customize the X environment and
provide sample configurations. The *Standard
Edition* uses the *twm* manager in most examples
and illustrations. Revised for X11 Release 5. This
popular manual is available in two editions, one
for users of the MIT software, and one for users
of Motif. (see below).

"For the novice, this is the best introduction to
X available. It will also be a convenient reference
for experienced users and X applications
developers."—*Computing Reviews*

Volume 3M: X Window System User's Guide

Motif Edition
By Valerie Quercia & Tim O'Reilly
2nd Edition January 1993
956 pages, ISBN 1-56592-015-5

This alternative edition of the *User's Guide* highlights the Motif window manager for users of the
Motif graphical user interface. Revised for Motif 1.2
and X11 Release 5.

Material covered in this second edition includes:

- Overview of the X Color Management System (Xcms)
- Creating your own Xcms color database
- Tutorials for two "color editors": *xcoloredit* and *xtici*
- Using the X font server
- Tutorial for *editres*, a resource editor
- Extensive coverage of the new implementations
  of *bitmap* and *xmag*
- Overview of internationalization features
- Features common to Motif 1.2 applications:
  tear-off menus and drag-and-drop

–Advanced–

UNIX Power Tools

By Jerry Peek, Mike Loukides, Tim O'Reilly, et al.
1st Edition March 1993
1162 pages (includes CD-ROM)
Random House ISBN 0-679-79073-X

Ideal for UNIX users who hunger for technical—yet accessible—information, *UNIX Power Tools* consists of tips, tricks, concepts, and freeware (CD-ROM included). It also covers add-on utilities and how to take advantage of clever features in the most popular UNIX utilities.

This is a browser's book... like a magazine that you don't read from start to finish, but leaf through repeatedly until you realize that you've read it all. You'll find articles abstracted from O'Reilly Nutshell Handbooks®, new information that highlights program "tricks" and "gotchas," tips posted to the Net over the years, and other accumulated wisdom. The goal of *UNIX Power Tools* is to help you think creatively about UNIX and get you to the point where you can analyze your own problems. Your own solutions won't be far behind.

The CD-ROM includes all of the scripts and aliases from the book, plus *perl*, GNU *emacs*, *pbmplus* (manipulation utilities), *ispell*, screen, the *sc* spreadsheet, and about 60 other freeware programs. In addition to the source code, all the software is precompiled for Sun3, Sun4, DECstation, IBM RS/6000, HP 9000 (700 series), SCO Xenix, and SCO UNIX. (SCO UNIX binaries will likely also run on other Intel UNIX platforms, including Univel's new UNIXware.)

"Chockful of ideas on how to get the most from UNIX, this book is aimed at those who want to improve their proficiency with this versatile operating system. Best of all, you don't have to be a computer scientist to understand it. If you use UNIX, this book belongs on your desk."
—Book Reviews, *Compuserve Magazine*

"*Unix Power Tools* is an encyclopedic work that belongs next to every serious UNIX user's terminal. If you're already a UNIX wizard, keep this book tucked under your desk for late-night reference when solving those difficult problems."
—Raymond GA Côté, *Byte*

Making TEX Work

By Norman Walsh
1st Edition April 1994
522 pages, ISBN 1-56592-051-1

TeX is a powerful tool for creating professional-quality typeset text and is unsurpassed at typesetting mathematical equations, scientific text, and multiple languages. Many books describe how you use TeX to construct sentences, paragraphs, and chapters. Until now, no book has described all the software that actually lets you build, run, and use TeX to best advantage on your platform. Because creating a TeX document requires the use of many tools, this lack of information is a serious problem for TeX users.

Making TEX Work guides you through the maze of tools available in the TeX system. Beyond the core TeX program there are myriad drivers, macro packages, previewers, printing programs, online documentation facilities, graphics programs, and much more. This book describes them all.

The Frame Handbook

By Linda Branagan & Mike Sierra
1st Edition October 1994 (est.)
500 pages (est.), ISBN 1-56592-009-0

A thorough, single-volume guide to using the UNIX version of FrameMaker 4.0, a sophisticated document production system. This book is for everyone who creates technical manuals and reports, from technical writers and editors who will become power users to administrative assistants and engineers. The book contains a thorough introduction to Frame and covers creating document templates, assembling books, and Frame tips and tricks. It begins by discussing the basic features of any text-formatting system: how it handles text and text-based tools (like spell-checking). It quickly gets into areas that benefit from a sophisticated tool like Frame: cross-references and footnotes; styles, master pages, and templates; tables and graphics; tables of contents and indexes; and, for those interested in online access, hypertext. Once you've finished this book, you'll be able to use Frame to create and produce a book or even a series of books.

Exploring Expect

By Don Libes
1st Edition Winter 1994-95 (est.)
500 pages (est.), ISBN 1-56592-090-2

Written by the author of Expect, this is the first book to explain how this new part of the UNIX toolbox can be used to automate *telnet*, *ftp*, *passwd*, *rlogin*, and hundreds of other interactive applications. Based on *Tcl* (Tool Control Language), Expect lets you automate interactive applications that have previously been extremely difficult to handle with any scripting language.

The book briefly describes *Tcl* and how Expect relates to it. It then describes the *Tcl* language, using a combination of reference material and specific, useful examples of its features. It shows how to use Expect in background, in multiple processes, and with standard languages and tools like C, C++, and *Tk*, the X-based extension to *Tcl*. The strength in the book is in its scripts, conveniently listed in a separate index.

sed & awk

By Dale Dougherty
1st Edition November 1990
414 pages, ISBN 0-937175-59-5

For people who create and modify text files, *sed* and *awk* are power tools for editing. Most of the things that you can do with these programs can be done interactively with a text editor; however, using *sed* and *awk* can save many hours of repetitive work in achieving the same result.

"*sed & awk* is a must for UNIX system programmers and administrators, and even general UNIX readers will benefit. I have over a hundred UNIX and C books in my personal library at home, but only a dozen are duplicated on the shelf where I work. This one just became number twelve."
—*Root Journal*

Learning Perl

By Randal L. Schwartz, Foreword by Larry Wall
1st Edition November 1993
274 pages, ISBN 1-56592-042-2

Learning Perl is ideal for system administrators, programmers, and anyone else wanting a down-to-earth introduction to this useful language. Written by a Perl trainer, its aim is to make a competent, hands-on Perl programmer out of the reader as quickly as possible. The book takes a tutorial approach and includes hundreds of short code examples, along with some lengthy ones. The relatively inexperienced programmer will find *Learning Perl* easily accessible. Each chapter of the book includes practical programming exercises. Solutions are presented for all exercises.

For a comprehensive and detailed guide to advanced programming with Perl, read O'Reilly's companion book, *Programming perl*.

"All-in-all, *Learning Perl* is a fine introductory text that can dramatically ease moving into the world of *perl*. It fills a niche previously filled only by tutorials taught by a small number of *perl* experts.... The UNIX community too often lacks the kind of tutorial that this book offers."
—Rob Kolstad, ;login:

Programming perl

By Larry Wall & Randal L. Schwartz
1st Edition January 1991
482 pages, ISBN 0-937175-64-1

This is the authoritative guide to the hottest new UNIX utility in years, co-authored by its creator, Larry Wall. Perl is a language for easily manipulating text, files, and processes. Perl provides a more concise and readable way to do many jobs that were formerly accomplished (with difficulty) by programming in the C language or one of the shells. *Programming perl* covers Perl syntax, functions, debugging, efficiency, the Perl library, and more, including real-world Perl programs dealing with such issues as system administration and text manipulation. Also includes a pull-out quick-reference card (designed and created by Johan Vromans).

O'Reilly & Associates—
GLOBAL NETWORK NAVIGATOR

The Global Network Navigator (GNN)™ is a unique kind of information service that makes the Internet easy and enjoyable to use. We organize access to the vast information resources of the Internet so that you can find what you want. We also help you understand the Internet and the many ways you can explore it.

In GNN you'll find:

Navigating the Net with GNN

 The *Whole Internet Catalog* contains a descriptive listing of the most useful Net resources and services with live links to those resources.

 The *GNN Business Pages* are where you'll learn about companies who have established a presence on the Internet and use its worldwide reach to help educate consumers.

 The *Internet Help Desk* helps folks who are new to the Net orient themselves and gets them started on the road to Internet exploration.

News

 NetNews is a weekly publication that reports on the news of the Internet, with weekly feature articles that focus on Internet trends and special events. The Sports, Weather, and Comix Pages round out the news.

Special Interest Publications

 Whether you're planning a trip or are just interested in reading about the journeys of others, you'll find that the *Travelers' Center* contains a rich collection of feature articles and ongoing columns about travel. In the *Travelers' Center*, you can link to many helpful and informative travel-related Internet resources.

 The *Personal Finance Center* is the place to go for information about money management and investment on the Internet. Whether you're an old pro at playing the market or are thinking about investing for the first time, you'll read articles and discover Internet resources that will help you to think of the Internet as a personal finance information tool.

All in all, GNN helps you get more value for the time you spend on the Internet.

 The Best of the Web

GNN received "Honorable Mention" for **"Best Overall Site," "Best Entertainment Service,"** and **"Most Important Service Concept."**

The *GNN NetNews* received "Honorable Mention" for **"Best Document Design."**

Subscribe Today

GNN is available over the Internet as a subscription service. To get complete information about subscribing to GNN, send email to **info@gnn.com**. If you have access to a World Wide Web browser such as Mosaic or Lynx, you can use the following URL to register online: http://gnn.com/

If you use a browser that does not support online forms, you can retrieve an email version of the registration form automatically by sending email to **form@gnn.com**. Fill this form out and send it back to us by email, and we will confirm your registration.

O'Reilly on the Net—
ONLINE PROGRAM GUIDE

O'Reilly & Associates offers extensive information through our online resources. If you've got Internet access, we invite you to come and explore our little neck-of-the-woods.

Online Resource Center

Most comprehensive among our online offerings is the O'Reilly Resource Center. Here, you'll find detailed information and descriptions on all O'Reilly products: titles, prices, tables of contents, indexes, author bios, CD-ROM directory listings, reviews...you can even view images of the products themselves. We also supply helpful ordering information: how to contact us, how to order online, distributors and bookstores around the world, discounts, upgrades, etc. In addition, we provide informative literature in the field, featuring articles, interviews, bibliogrphies, and columns that help you stay informed and abreast.

 The Best of the Web

The *O'Reilly Resource Center* was voted "**Best Commercial Site**" by users participating in "Best of the Web '94."

To access ORA's Online Resource Center:

Point your Web browser (e.g., `mosaic` or `lynx`) to:
`http://gnn.com/ora/`

For the plaintext version, `telnet` or `gopher` to:
`gopher.ora.com`

(telnetters login: `gopher`)

FTP

The example files and programs in many of our books are available electronically via FTP.

To obtain example files and programs from O'Reilly texts:

`ftp` to:

`ftp.uu.net`

`cd published/oreilly`

or

`ftp.ora.com`

Ora-news

An easy way to stay informed of the latest projects and products from O'Reilly & Associates is to subscribe to "ora-news," our electronic news service. Subscribers receive email as soon as the information breaks.

To subscribe to "ora-news":

Send email to:
listproc@online.ora.com

and put the following information on the first line of your message (not in "Subject"):
subscribe ora-news "your name" **of** "your company"

For example:
subscribe ora-news Jim Dandy of Mighty Fine Enterprises

Email

Many other helpful customer services are provided via email. Here's a few of the most popular and useful.

Useful email addresses

nuts@ora.com
> For general questions and information.

bookquestions@ora.com
> For technical questions, or corrections, concerning book contents.

order@ora.com
> To order books online and for ordering questions.

catalog@ora.com
> To receive a free copy of our magazine/catalog, "ora.com" (please include a snailmail address).

Snailmail and phones

O'Reilly & Associates, Inc.
103A Morris Street, Sebastopol, CA 95472
Inquiries: **707-829-0515, 800-998-9938**
Credit card orders: **800-889-8969**
FAX: **707-829-0104**

O'Reilly & Associates—
LISTING OF TITLES

INTERNET

!%@:: A Directory of Electronic Mail
    Addressing & Networks
Connecting to the Internet:
    An O'Reilly Buyer's Guide
Internet In A Box
MH & xmh: E-mail for Users & Programmers
The Mosaic Handbook for Microsoft Windows
The Mosaic Handbook for the Macintosh
The Mosaic Handbook for the
    X Window System
Smileys
The Whole Internet User's Guide & Catalog

SYSTEM ADMINISTRATION

Computer Security Basics
DNS and BIND
Essential System Administration
Linux Network Administrator's Guide
    (Fall 94 est.)
Managing Internet Information Services
    (Fall 94 est.)
Managing NFS and NIS
Managing UUCP and Usenet
sendmail
Practical UNIX Security
PGP: Pretty Good Privacy (Winter 94/95 est.)
System Performance Tuning
TCP/IP Network Administration
termcap & terminfo
X Window System Administrator's Guide:
    Volume 8
X Window System, R6, Companion CD
    (Fall 94 est.)

USING UNIX AND X

BASICS

Learning GNU Emacs
Learning the Korn Shell
Learning the UNIX Operating System
Learning the vi Editor
SCO UNIX in a Nutshell
The USENET Handbook (Winter 94/95 est.)
Using UUCP and Usenet
UNIX in a Nutshell: System V Edition
The X Window System in a Nutshell
X Window System User's Guide: Volume 3
X Window System User's Guide, Motif Ed.:
    Volume 3M
X User Tools (10/94 est.)

ADVANCED

Exploring Expect (Winter 94/95 est.)
The Frame Handbook (10/94 est.)
Making TeX Work
Learning Perl
Programming perl
sed & awk
UNIX Power Tools (with CD-ROM)

PROGRAMMING UNIX, C, AND MULTI-PLATFORM

FORTRAN/SCIENTIFIC COMPUTING

High Performance Computing
Migrating to Fortran 90
UNIX for FORTRAN Programmers

C PROGRAMMING LIBRARIES

Practical C Programming
POSIX Programmer's Guide
POSIX.4: Programming for the Real World
    (Fall 94 est.)
Programming with curses
Understanding and Using COFF
Using C on the UNIX System

C PROGRAMMING TOOLS

Checking C Programs with lint
lex & yacc
Managing Projects with make
Power Programming with RPC
Software Portability with imake

MULTI-PLATFORM PROGRAMMING

Encyclopedia of Graphics File Formats
Distributing Applications Across DCE and
    Windows NT
Guide to Writing DCE Applications
Multi-Platform Code Management
Understanding DCE
Understanding Japanese Information
    Processing
ORACLE Performance Tuning

BERKELEY 4.4 SOFTWARE DISTRIBUTION

4.4BSD System Manager's Manual
4.4BSD User's Reference Manual
4.4BSD User's Supplementary Documents
4.4BSD Programmer's Reference Manual
4.4BSD Programmer's Supplementary
    Documents
4.4BSD-Lite CD Companion
4.4BSD-Lite CD Companion:
    International Version

X PROGRAMMING

Motif Programming Manual: Volume 6A
Motif Reference Manual: Volume 6B
Motif Tools
PEXlib Programming Manual
PEXlib Reference Manual
PHIGS Programming Manual
    (soft or hard cover)
PHIGS Reference Manual
Programmer's Supplement for R6
    (Winter 94/95 est.)
Xlib Programming Manual: Volume 1
Xlib Reference Manual: Volume 2
X Protocol Reference Manual, R5: Vol. 0
X Protocol Reference Manual, R6: Vol. 0
    (11/94 est.)
X Toolkit Intrinsics Programming Manual:
    Volume 4
X Toolkit Intrinsics Programming Manual,
    Motif Edition: Volume 4M
X Toolkit Intrinsics Reference Manual: Vol.5
XView Programming Manual: Volume 7A
XView Reference Manual: Volume 7B

THE X RESOURCE

A QUARTERLY WORKING JOURNAL FOR X PROGRAMMERS

The X Resource: Issues 0 through 12
    (Issue 12 available 10/94)

BUSINESS/CAREER

Building a Successful Software Business
Love Your Job!

TRAVEL

Travelers' Tales Thailand
Travelers' Tales Mexico
Travelers' Tales India (Winter 94/95 est.)

AUDIOTAPES

INTERNET TALK RADIO'S "GEEK OF THE WEEK" INTERVIEWS

The Future of the Internet Protocol, 4 hrs.
Global Network Operations, 2 hours
Mobile IP Networking, 1 hour
Networked Information and
    Online Libraries, 1 hour
Security and Networks, 1 hour
European Networking, 1 hour

NOTABLE SPEECHES OF THE INFORMATION AGE

John Perry Barlow, 1.5 hours

O'Reilly & Associates—
INTERNATIONAL DISTRIBUTORS

Customers outside North America can now order O'Reilly & Associates books through the following distributors. They offer our international customers faster order processing, more bookstores, increased representation at tradeshows worldwide, and the high quality, responsive service our customers have come to expect.

EUROPE, MIDDLE EAST, AND AFRICA
(except Germany, Switzerland, and Austria)

INQUIRIES
International Thomson Publishing Europe
Berkshire House
168-173 High Holborn
London WC1V 7AA
United Kingdom
Telephone: 44-71-497-1422
Fax: 44-71-497-1426
Email: ora.orders@itpuk.co.uk

ORDERS
International Thomson Publishing Services, Ltd.
Cheriton House, North Way
Andover, Hampshire SP10 5BE
United Kingdom
Telephone: 44-264-342-832 (UK orders)
Telephone: 44-264-342-806 (outside UK)
Fax: 44-264-364418 (UK orders)
Fax: 44-264-342761 (outside UK)

GERMANY, SWITZERLAND, AND AUSTRIA
International Thomson Publishing GmbH
O'Reilly-International Thomson Verlag
Attn: Mr. G. Miske
Königswinterer Strasse 418
53227 Bonn
Germany
Telephone: 49-228-970240
Fax: 49-228-441342
Email: gerd@orade.ora.com

ASIA
(except Japan)

INQUIRIES
International Thomson Publishing Asia
221 Henderson Road
#05 10 Henderson Building
Singapore 0315
Telephone: 65-272-6496
Fax: 65-272-6498

ORDERS
Telephone: 65-268-7867
Fax: 65-268-6727

AUSTRALIA
WoodsLane Pty. Ltd.
Unit 8, 101 Darley Street (P.O. Box 935)
Mona Vale NSW 2103
Australia
Telephone: 61-2-979-5944
Fax: 61-2-997-3348
Email: woods@tmx.mhs.oz.au

NEW ZEALAND
WoodsLane New Zealand Ltd.
21 Cooks Street (P.O. Box 575)
Wanganui, New Zealand
Telephone: 64-6-347-6543
Fax: 64-6-345-4840
Email: woods@tmx.mhs.oz.au

THE AMERICAS, JAPAN, AND OCEANIA
O'Reilly & Associates, Inc.
103A Morris Street
Sebastopol, CA 95472 U.S.A.
Telephone: 707-829-0515
Telephone: 800-998-9938 (U.S. & Canada)
Fax: 707-829-0104
Email: order@ora.com

TO ORDER: **800-889-8969** *(CREDIT CARD ORDERS ONLY);* **ORDER@ORA.COM**

Here's a page we encourage readers to tear out...

O'REILLY WOULD LIKE TO HEAR FROM YOU

Please send me the following:

❏ *ora.com*
O'Reilly's magazine/catalog, containing behind-the-scenes articles and interviews on the technology we write about, and a complete listing of O'Reilly books and products.

❏ *Global Network Navigator*™
Information and subscription.

Please print legibly

Which book did this card come from?

_____

Where did you buy this book?
     ❏ Bookstore   ❏ Direct from O'Reilly
     ❏ Bundled with hardware/software   ❏ Class/seminar

Your job description: ❏ SysAdmin   ❏ Programmer

     ❏ Other _____

What computer system do you use?   ❏ UNIX
     ❏ MAC   ❏ DOS(PC)   ❏ Other _____

Name	Company/Organization Name
Address	
City State	Zip/Postal Code Country
Telephone	Internet or other email address (specify network)

Nineteenth century wood engraving
of the horned owl from the O'Reilly
& Associates Nutshell Handbook®
Learning the UNIX Operating System

O'Reilly & Associates, Inc., 103A Morris Street, Sebastopol, CA 95472-9902

BUSINESS REPLY MAIL
FIRST CLASS MAIL   PERMIT NO. 80   SEBASTOPOL, CA

Postage will be paid by addressee

O'Reilly & Associates, Inc.
103A Morris Street
Sebastopol, CA 95472-9902